HISTORY IS LIVED BEFORE IT IS WRITTEN

The Autobiography of
Leroy Wilson, Jr., Esq.

ISBN: 979-8-9938249-0-1

First Edition Printed in USA

I dedicate this book to my parents and paternal grandmother; without whose love and guidance I might have wound up as another statistic. They are Mary Louise Wilson and Leroy Wilson, Sr., and Pauline Shepherd, his mother. I also dedicate it to my late wife Jane Beaver Wilson, and my ex-wife Maleta Luna-Rosa Mogwe, each of whom enriched my life immeasurably with their love and wisdom.

They foretold the teachings of Dr. Benjamin E. Mays:

"It is not a disgrace to reach for the stars, but it is a disgrace to have no stars to reach for. Not failure, but low aim is sin," and

"Whatever you do, strive to do it so well that no man dead and no man yet to be born could do it any better."

Dr. Benjamin Elijah Mays, President of Morehouse College.

Dr. Benjamin Elijah Mays, with Alumnus Jose Ananias

The title of this book is suggested by a column that Ralph McGill wrote in 1962 titled "A Door Begins to Open," about new opportunities for black college graduates. McGill was a distinguished journalist for the Atlanta Journal and Constitution. I graduated from Morehouse in 1962. McGill mentioned me and the other graduates for whom the door began to open.

Acknowledgements

I wrote this book without the assistance of a professional editor, so any and all typographical errors are mine alone, although I tried to be as accurate as I could be.

I also had no professional publishing house either. What I did have were news articles, documents, and photos that I had collected over the years. Undoubtedly, I was spurred on by the memory of my father pulling from his wallet a copy of a news article that he had kept when I was a sophomore at Morehouse in order to persuade the bank officer to give him a loan to help me.

I thank Linda Engram of Elly Virtually, LLC for her inestimable assistance of shepherding this book from draft to polished published product.

Over a lifetime of 86 years, there are so many people to thank - and I thank them all. Some of them are the next-door Wilson family in West Savannah, headed by Mr. Joe and Ms. Annie, who were like a surrogate set of parents to our family; Mr. Carmichael, our cubmaster and scoutmaster, who taught us all many delightful things that were outside what we learned in our immediate environments; all of my teachers and professors from elementary school through two graduate schools in the United States; my professors and staff during my one-year Morehouse Merrill travel and study grant which enabled me to travel throughout Europe and study at the University of Vienna and the Institute of European Studies facilities in Vienna. Charles Merrill, Jr., the visionary Chairman of Morehouse's Board of Trustees, made this possible.

Esther Hardin, my 10th grade English teacher was one of those who lit the path for me to follow by telling me that I wasn't applying myself hard enough.

I thank Captain Frank Bynes Sr., one of the owners of Bynes-Royall Funeral Home, who extended a loan to my father to help me continue my studies at Morehouse.

I also thank Pickett & Hatcher Educational Fund, Inc. a nonprofit student loan foundation established in 1938 through the will of Claud Adkins Hatcher of Columbus, Georgia for the loans they extended to me while I was a student at Morehouse.

At my graduation from Alfred E. Beach High School in 1957, Principal Otha L. Douglass gave me a $100.00 scholarship award from Alpha Kappa Psi fraternity which instilled in me the ethos of giving forward.

In addition to the many photos I had taken, I must thank my sister Gloria Edwards for saving and forwarding other photos and articles to me, including the City of Savannah, Georgia Proclamation of "Original Nine Day," issued on 08 May 1997 by Floyd Adams, the first black Mayor of Savannah. My brother Louis provided useful information on our Handy and Jenkins family ancestry, and the Jenkins Orphanage Band, in and around Olar and Charleston, South Carolina.

My professors at Morehouse exposed me to worlds that I almost found impossible to believe. Doctors McBay and Huggins, Mr. McCray, "Pop" Dansby and Ms. Walton led this charge into chemistry and mathematics. Dr. Lonnie Cross (Abdulalim A. Shabazz), a pure mathematician, taught me advanced calculus. However, one of the greatest life foundations he gave me was the advice to always stay calmly in my own skin and not be concerned or rattled by what others thought.

Given the events in the civil rights movement that we traversed during this period, the advice and the many sermons of Dr. Benjamin E. Mays, and the lectures of Dean Brailsford Brazeal, and others, taught us at Chapel, gave me great confidence in graduate school and in corporate America when oftentimes, I was the only black person in the room. I did not feel self-conscious.

George Pimental, who was my research advisor in graduate school chemistry at Berkeley was a source of great support when neither of us understood the severity of my emotional turmoil at the time. Professors Herb Strauss, Andrew Streitweiser, Leo Brewer, William Jolley and Nobel Laureates Emilio Segrè(1959) and Dudley Herschbach (1986) rounded out my experience in the field of advanced chemistry, mathematics and physics.

At Berkeley Law (then Boalt Hall), I didn't feel a personal connection with any of my professors except Jesse Choper. However, they were all great teachers. I think the reason was that he was pretty close to our own ages, had clerked for Chief Justice Earl Warren who presided over some of the most important constitutional law cases, and Jesse was teaching some of those cases. These were personal to me because, as a black person, I was interested in learning how we achieved certain rights and what that meant.

Rev. Ray S. Blake was also helpful to me in providing support when I needed it in the early days in appreciation for my services in creatively negotiating a mortgage loan that enabled his small church of about 100- seat capacity to acquire one of 2500 - seat capacity.

I did not write these pages alone. I wrote them in spaces held together by others here in Botswana over the years — for the last 3 years, by Kim Hall, my personal assistant, who insured that I had clean clothes, which doctors rendered the best medical care, who knew where to shop for groceries, bottled water, eat out, and who drove me to places that I could not drive at night, and rewarded me with good conversations, much of which reflected her experiences as an American living here in Botswana for the past 30 years and interacting with all sorts of people who came to live, work, teach or pass through here.

Meanwhile, the housing staff kept things in order while I wrestled with history and hope in writing this book. History, to faithfully recite the highlights of where my life had taken me; hope that I could write an account that people would enjoy reading.

Facilities Manager Gorata Ditsilepele, Masego Keatholetswe, Annah Jorisi, Bangani Mondlani, Boago Kabomo, Elvis Baaitsi Lebopo, and Chris, the gardener, diligently maintained the living conditions for me to think clearly. Their care allowed me to reflect, to write, and to honor the stories that demanded telling. I thank them not only for their work, but for their role in this narrative.

I must also thank Professor (ret.) Monageng Mogalakwe for introducing me to Mma Orefitlhetse C. Masire (and former Botswana Defense Forces Commander, General Tebogo Masire)who made this comfortable apartment available to me after months of looking for a suitable place to re-settle in Gaborone, Botswana. Their fully-furnished 6-unit Phatuma Self-Catering apartment flats and the beautiful garden out front were ideal for me to rest, reflect and to write.

Lastly, this book is a tribute to the Original Nine Black police officers of Savannah, Georgia — my father among them — whose courage reshaped a city and whose legacy I continue to benefit from, to document and to discharge the duty of carrying on in their spirit.

Table of Contents

Introduction

One day I looked out my kitchen window onto the field 2 stories below. I saw a chicken pecking at the ground, where Botswana's red clay was visible through the rough grass. Then there were four hens and a rooster. It took me back to my childhood, in Savannah, Georgia, where seeing chickens pecking the red clay ground was commonplace. This was not the case after I left home in 1957. It was rare for me to see a chicken pecking the ground, wherever I went in the world.

From time to time, as I related various events to friends, they would say: "You ought to write a book."

And so, this is my story; the story of an African American boy who shared the experiences of living in and visiting many places in the United States and the world at large where he was not supposed to be. I tell you how I traveled the path from Savannah to Gaborone, Botswana, having visited some 30+ countries and many of the states in the United States.

I share this story for the benefit of my family and future generations of young people who dare to think that they may achieve and aspire to what might seem like the impossible dream. To give back some of that which was given to me.

The Beginnings – West Savannah, Georgia

Looking back on it, I have had a blessed life, and now it is time to tell my story, on behalf of all those who had faith in me and on behalf of all those who thought I had a story to tell. I have stood on the edge of history many times; in many places. I hope others might gain from the various lessons I learned as I traveled along the many personal and professional pathways of my life.

West Savannah, where I grew up, was sort of a magical place for me. My love of learning and reading happened at an early age.

My father and mother read the morning and afternoon local daily newspapers. Several houses owned a set of encyclopedias. To save money my mother and Ms. Hattie shared the newspapers and magazines. Ms. Hattie was our next-door neighbor.

Mama at her 80th birthday celebration, with Ms. Hattie standing on the right and her daughter Pat on the left (1999).

Mama and her children at her 80th Birthday Celebration
(Gloria, Vernon, Me, Louis, Donald and Mary Deloris)(1999)

Mama and her grandchildren at her 80th birthday celebration (Joseph, Darren, Christopher, Susan, Andrea, Monica, Angelyne, Jason, and Dina. (Tonja , Lisa, Victor, Louis Jr, Travis and Jesse do not appear in this photo)(1999)

Mama and her great grandchildren at her 80th birthday celebration (Left to right back row: Kyle, Kendra, Tamala, William, Latara, Danielle, Tiffani and that's Cameron in her arms front row: Devin, Keyionna, Elise and Joshua (1999)

Mama going shopping

The newspapers and magazines that I read took me to distant places, at home and overseas. Along with my parents, and siblings, I always looked forward to reading the local black newspapers – The Herald[1] and the Savannah Tribune.[2] We also enjoyed reading The Afro-American from Baltimore, Chicago Defender, and the Pittsburgh Courier newspapers, and the Readers Digest..

The black magazines we read were Ebony, the Black World, and Jet. There was a saying "If you didn't read it in Jet, it didn't happen."

These newspapers and magazines fueled my imagination into thinking that one day, I could visit some of the places and meet some of the people I read about.

For my first schooling, I walked down the street to West Savannah Elementary School. Somehow, it fell to Mr. Joe, who lived next door, to take us children, along with his grandchildren, to First Bryan Baptist Church, located in Yamacraw Village. I never thought that our schools were inferior to any others. The white people had their schools, and we had ours. We had never visited the white schools, so we had no basis for comparisons.

---

1 *The Savannah Herald*, founded in 1945, has been Savannah's leading African American newspaper for over seven decades. Established after the second World War, the paper quickly grew during the height of the Civil Rights Movement, the Savannah Herald has a proud history of advocating for the rights and advancement of the city's Black community. The paper was founded by a group of prominent African American businessmen and community leaders who recognized the need for a strong, independent Black voice in Savannah's media landscape. From its inception, the Herald has provided exceptional journalism that informs, empowers and uplifts its readers. https://savannahherald.com/about-us/ (Accessed 15 January 2025)

2 The *Savannah Tribune*, a weekly newspaper covering news and issues related to **Savannah**'s African American community, was founded in 1875. Except for two hiatuses, from 1878 to 1886, and from 1960 to 1973, the paper has operated continuously. As of 2008 the *Tribune* circulated to approximately 10,000 readers under the direction of Shirley B. James, the paper's owner, publisher, and editor. Sverdlik, Alan. "Savannah Tribune." New Georgia Encyclopedia, last modified Mar 20, 2021. https://www.georgiaencyclopedia.org/articles/arts-culture/savannah-tribune/ (Accessed 15 January 2025)

There was one white family that lived around the corner from us, but I do not remember having any interactions with them.

Except for one family where the children lived with their grandmother, I think all the families in my neighborhood were 2-parent families. Even so, their mother lived around the corner. No one treated them any differently because their father was not in the house. I don't remember ever meeting him.

All the fathers worked; some of the mothers worked, generally when their children were older, and the children worked when they became of age. Savanah, being a major shipping port, longshoremen jobs paid well and were highly desirable.

As far as I know, all these families owned their residences, following centuries old practices of black people owning property in Savannah and elsewhere[3].

This was normal for us.

There was little to no crime in the area. Bobby Greene, however, was constantly getting into trouble. Bobby and his sisters were being raised by a single mother, Ms. Virginia. Whatever his faults, Bobby was a delightful fellow and always a pleasure to be around. At that point, we did not make the connection between poverty and petty crimes. I never did find out how Bobby cracked one of his upper front teeth. I was always curious about that.

There was a rumor that Johnnie Mae, one of our neighbors, smoked marijuana, but I never witnessed it. That was the extent of any drug activity I heard about.

No professionals, such as doctors, or lawyers lived in West Savannah. Indeed, I knew of only fewer than five black doctors and dentists in Savannah as a whole. They were doctors Henry Collier (who lived in a white neighborhood on Victory Drive), Dr. McAdew, Dr. Cooper.

---

[3] Whittington B. Johnson, *Black Savannah 1788-1864* (Fayetteville: The University of Arkansas Press, Appendix G, 1996); Loren Schweninger, *Black Property Owners in the South, 1790-1915* (Urbana and Chicago, University of Illinois Press, pages 69-70, 80, 1990)

The one black lawyer, in town, was Eugene Gadsen, who later became a judge.

There were few black businesspeople. Floyd Adams, who published The Savannah Herald weekly newspaper, was one. He and his family lived on Newell Street, in the only 2-story house in the neighborhood, until many years later when we were startled to see another 2-story structure being erected down the street from us. Robert Wright's family owned that structure. I think there was a small convenience store on the ground floor.

Floyd Adams's nickname was "Pressboy." I started working for him as a newspaper boy when the Herald was selling for $0.08 a copy. Some years later, when I was traveling on a Morehouse Merrill Travel Study Grant in Europe, I wrote a weekly column for The Savannah Herald titled "Impressions of Europe" that I mailed to him as soon as I wrote them. There were no email and fax machines in those days.

Floyd's son, Floyd Adams, Jr., would become Savannah's first black Mayor, in 1995.

I traveled from New York to Savannah for his inauguration.

There were only a few small black businesses, Mr. Freeman's barber shop, Mr. Walter Dukes shoe shop, and Mac Willie's little store on Lathrop Avenue, where he sold seafood and roasted oysters on the weekend. One dreaded task for us children was we had to gut and scale the fish that our father would invariably buy on Saturdays – whiting, croaker, and mullet; sometimes catfish. There were also a few beauty parlors, but most hair dressing was done in the homes. All of us learned how to plait and braid hair.

Then someone opened a dry cleaner at the corner of Newell Street and Augusta Avenue, which was succeeded by a barbeque joint.

However, reviewing these references in footnote 3, discloses that the occupations for black people in Savannah did not change much from the 1790 – 1915, and 1837 to the time I was growing up in the 1940s and 50s.

I was born in a little bedroom downstairs in my paternal grandmother's house at 304 West Taylor Street in Savannah, Georgia. The date was 16 June 1939. Savannah was segregated by race at the time, but somehow my parents, teachers and the adults I interacted with never allowed me and my siblings to feel inferior to anyone. So, you might say I had a solid psychological foundation from which to observe the absurdities of the acts and actors who maintained the segregated system. With scholarships and fellowships, I would grow up to leave that system and attend some of the finest colleges and universities on the planet.

In 1969, I was admitted to practice law at the bar of the State of New York, one of the most demanding and prominent bars in the United States. Along the way, I will have had the opportunity to visit some 30 - odd different countries, and through marriage and a twist of fate, I would wind up living in Botswana, located in the southern part of Africa. I had always envisaged spending part of my life in Africa; while writing the later stages of this book, I visited Ethiopia, but that comes later.

Leroy at 2, 20, and 35

Leroy at 86

My Ancestors

My paternal great grandfather was Handy Shepherd (b. 1846 d. 1900), and my paternal great grandmother was Emma Lawton (b. 1847 d.1900). They were married in 1865.[4]

They had nine children, with my grandmother, Pauline Hill (Shepard, Wilson) being the only girl. She would eventually find her way to Savannah, Georgia to live with her older brother, John. I am not sure if I ever met John, but I did meet another of her brothers, "Uncle" Joe. I heard that he came from an exotic place in Brooklyn, New York, called Brownsville. I visited Brownsville many years after I moved away from Savannah. My son Christopher accompanied me to meet this collection of our relatives.

[4] Planters of the Seed from Madegascar [sic] at 16, by Louis Edgar Wilson, Sr.

My paternal grandmother, Pauline Shepherd, a/k/a Pauline Hill in whose house I was born.

My youngest brother, Louis Edgar Wilson, Sr., tells the story of how Uncle Joe and Aunt Mamie blasted our cousin Reverend Daniel Joseph Jenkins out of jail, with dynamite, to escape a lynching that Olar', South

Carolina's Mayor Chitty had planned so that he could monopolize Daniel's knowledge of wood and take over his business.[5]

He also documents that Jenkins Orphanage was founded by our extended cousin, Reverend Daniel Joseph Jenkins on December 16, 1891[6].

The 1910 census records show that my grandmother, Pauline, married Willie Dyches in 1905. They became the parents of two sons, my father Leroy (b. 2008, d. 1994), and my uncle Booker T. (b. 2006, d.________). In 1910, they lived in Georges Creek, Barnwell, S.C.

The 1900 Census Records also tell us that my grandfather, Willie, 14 years old at the time, was adopted by the family of Robert Wood and Genia Wood. That record also tells us that Mory Dyches also lived

[5] Id. at 14 -19.
[6] Id. at 19.

in that household. I have not been able to find the records for Mory. I understand that Mory could be a boy or girl's name.

As far as I know, I have never met my grandfather, Willie Dyches. One of my siblings thought that the photo of the man in the hat on grandmama's mantlepiece is that of my grandfather, but I don't know.[7]

Grandmama was one of the calm voices of reason in my family. Not only did she have a home remedy for everything, from using sassafras tea, to rubbing the oil from cans of sardines to cure the mumps, to placing a copper penny on my forehead with a small piece of brown paper bag to stop nosebleeds. I never followed up to see how they worked scientifically, but they did work. Many years later, I read an article in Men's Health magazine about the healing properties of elemental copper used at the Copper Hospital in Chile.

She also cooked on an iron stove that used wood to cook the food. One of her specialties was sweet potato poon. It was nice and sweet, and she always used a one-pound block of butter with copious amounts of sugar. The stove was equipped with a warmer, a little compartment above the cooking panel of the stove, which kept food warm. I always eagerly waited to lick the spoon and wipe my finger around her mixing bowl to eat the tasty residue when she made sweet potato poon and cakes.

She had this habit of dipping snuff and putting it inside her bottom lip, which always fascinated me, though not to the point where I wanted to try it.

She also was an avid drinker of Dr. Pepper sodas; I never acquired the taste.

I always loved to visit her, so I could sleep in a bed by myself, and listen to the traffic passing by in the street below. One night, we had a mini-Earthquake in Savannah. It was powerful enough to wake me up.

---

[7] There is a Dyches Realty and Construction Company in Savannah, Georgia. I hope to follow up with them to see if they have any information on him.

It scared me to death because everything was shaking, and I couldn't stand up.

Tragically, she lost her life when she was forced to jump out of the second story window because a fire had burned up the stairs leading downstairs to the only exit. As far as I was able to determine, the fire was started downstairs by a mentally ill boarder that Grandmama had taken in.

The Savannah Morning News reported that when she jumped, grandmama landed on a pile of junked cars, auto parts and discarded appliances.[8] There was a neighbor, Mrs. Mary Ann Davis, 45, who jumped and did not land on a pile of junk. She survived.

The newspaper described the house as being in a section labeled deplorable by Mayor John Rousakis. I think we did not know the meaning of that term when I was growing up. It was a happy place for us; same as it was for many other children in the world who were happy with whatever they had.

From the Staff Photographer Paul Reichert's photo of the house and junk pile that I read, it was an ugly scene.

The newspaper described grandmama as being a "self-proclaimed minister who frequently held ceremonies attempting to contact the spirit world in her home."

The interesting thing about this quote is that millions of people in the United States also try to contact the spirit world, many trying to connect with a man called Jesus.

Mrs. Willie Dean Frazier and Jimmy Bennett from the Economic Opportunity Administration protested to the Mayor's Special Assistant Al Henderson about the urgent need to do something about the area.

The house has been torn down and replaced with a modern structure. I don't know when that happened.

---

[8] The Savannah Morning News, [1969/1970]

The article quotes Daddy as saying before the fire Daddy had tried to have grandmama come live with us, but she refused.

At the time, I was married and living in New York. I was looking forward to introducing her to her great grandson Jason, who had recently been born.

My friend Edwin was working at the Savannah fire department at the time when I requested a copy of the fire report. The department chief would not release it for some reason. Edwin told him I was an attorney admitted in New York. He asked for my bar number, but I did not know what he was talking about. In any case, the Chief would not release it. I later learned years later that the NYS Office of Court Administration does assign an attorney number to us.

The Formative Years

When I was a little boy growing up in West Savannah, Georgia, part of my day would be consumed laying on the sidewalk in front of our modest 3-bedroom house.

This is the house I grew up in at 1011 Richards Street in West Savannah Georgia.

I used to watch the clouds roll by and I could imagine riding them to the California. I had read about. That was my fondest wish - to see

California. Somehow, I had come to believe that the streets there were paved with gold and milk and honey dripped from trees.

Ironically, before I ever got to see California, I would visit many countries in Europe.

My interest in traveling would extend to other countries. By now, I have visited over 30 countries and have lived in two – Vienna, Austria and Lobatse and Gaborone Botswana.

Along the way, another of my professional dreams came true. Nano Matlala, a prominent South African lawyer, asked me to assist his South African law firm as an external consultant in the Chambers of Lembede, Tambo and Pitje. These chambers were formally launched on September 15th, 2015, in Tshwane (Pretoria) South Africa.

This is how it all started. One dream. One sidewalk. Now, having lived in California for 6 years and some 30 to 35 countries later, I have lived many parts of my dream.

I am now retired in Botswana at age 86. I feel extremely comfortable here, as it reminds me a lot of Savannah.

My birth certificate says that I was born in Savannah Georgia, of parents Mary L. Frazier (maiden name) and Leroy Wilson. It tells me that my mother was a native of Liberty County, Georgia and my father was a native of South Carolina. I later learned that my father was born in and spent his early years in Olar, S.C. The attending physician who brought me into the world at my grandmother's house at 304 West Taylor Street, Savannah, GA., was Dr. Simon Fennimore Frazier. I was the first born.

My mother Mary Louise Wilson and father Leroy Wilson, Sr.

I don't know if Mama and Dr. Frazier were related or not. Her maiden name was Mary Louise Frazier. She and he had been born in Liberty County, GA. I do remember meeting him when I was a little boy.

Given the absurd issue of the place of President Obama's birth and the inane comments about releasing the original birth certificate, I point out the following text on my certificate "In accordance with the law, the originals of all birth certificates issued since April, 1919, are filed in the Bureau of Vital Statistics of the State of Georgia State Board of Health, Atlanta, Georgia, and duplicates thereof in the Savannah Health Department." My certificate is dated 7/25/39 and duly notes that I am a member of the colored race.

The certificate notes that my father was a waiter and that my mother was a domestic worker at the date of my birth.

Mama

My mother, Mary Louise Wilson was born November 23, 1919, in Dorchester, Georgia. She was the only child of Viola Frazier and Russell Harris. Russell was a white man. Both had preceded her in death. My brother Louis has had some interaction with the white side of the family. Given the history of Russell I take my hat off to Louis, as I have had no desire to meet with them.

On December 1, 1992, my mother gave me a small glance at her early life's history.

Mama had gone to the 10th grade and daddy had gone through the 3rd grade. Both could read and write. Both Mama and Daddy were avid readers of the local newspapers, Jet, the Black World, and Ebony magazines, the Pittsburgh Courier, the Afro-American out of Baltimore, and the Chicago Defender. These newspapers carried national and international news about black people. I also read the local black newspapers, The Herald and the Savannah Tribune, and any other source that carried news about black people. Rarely did the general circulation local papers carry news about black people.

Mama attended the sixth grade at the Maple Street School, Cuyler Junior High School from 7th through 9th grade and then Beach Cuyler High School up to 1/2 year in the 10th grade.

Reverend John Quincy Adams taught her English at Cuyler. He pastored Mount Zion Baptist Church at 1008 Martin Luther King Jr Blvd (West Broad Street)[9] (and Waldburg Street?). When I attended Cuyler or Beach, Reverend Adams was still teaching, although I do not remember if I ever took any courses from him.

After 1/2 year in the 10th grade, Mama had to leave school. Her aunt Mamie, with whom she lived, told Mama she had to go to work. Aunt Mamie mainly took in washing and ironing. She had had a job in a factory before they moved out of Frogtown[10] in 1929. Sometime after

[9]The name at the time we were growing up.
[10] A part of Savannah close to the Savannah River.

that they moved to West Taylor Street. Viola, my mother's mother, and therefore my maternal grandmother, died in December of 1928.

Aunt Mamie, mama's mother, Grandma Viola, and Uncle Briggs all lived in Frogtown. Frogtown was a part of Savannah settled by freed slaves after the Civil War.

Mama did not go to school every day because she had to stay home to help her Aunt Mamie wash and iron clothes.

In her neighborhood, there was a little white girl that wanted Mama to play with her. She carried on so when Mama was absent her parents paid Mama to play with the little girl to keep her company . When Mama was 13 or 14 years old, the girl's parents took Mama with the family but made her sleep on the porch outside . They fed her very well. The little white girl next door took a job, and she had lots of clothes versus Mama's skimpy collection.

After junior high school Mama ran away to stay in Charleston with her Uncle Sam Frazier. Maybe this was because Mamie made her work and took all her money and would not let her go anywhere. Mama stayed in Charleston from September to December of 1935. At that time, she would have been about 17 years old. She returned to Savannah .

In Charleston she washed dishes in a restaurant and the cook would camouflage the food, put pork chops under greens or roast beef on the side and give it to Mama to eat. Mamie wanted Mama to help her wash and iron clothes, but in Charleston, Mama made $3 or $4 a week; she owned a suit and bought shoes on layaway. She used to give her family $1 and keep the rest of the money for herself . Sometimes people from the cigar factory will come into the restaurant and eat. Mama would take dishes off the tables, and she also used to slice the bread .

When Mama returned to Savannah she worked at a little restaurant at the corner of Saint Julian and Drake Streets. She had gotten her first job when she was 12 to 14 years old, washing floors for $0.50 on weekends.

After Mama returned to Savannah, Aunt Mamie was not going to let Mama go back to school. School cost $1.35. Mama was not sure if this was a reason but thought that maybe Aunt Mamie wanted to keep her out of school to pick up washing and ironing clothes and deliver them to their owners.

Nevertheless, after Christmas 1935 vacation Aunt Mamie would not let Mama return to school . Some children did not want to go to school. There was a big dropout rate, as some children worked after school, some with jobs where their parents worked.

Mama washed clothes until 1937 when she married daddy, Leroy Wilson Senior . She worked for a little while after that. Mama and Daddy had rooms on Duffy St from October 1937 until after Christmas. Then they had a room on East Broad Street and finally an apartment at 1306 Price St upstairs. At that time people could not afford to rent a whole house.

Then Mr. Sam Frazier, Mama's Charleston uncle, died. Daddy's mother, Grandma Pauline, wanted them to move back with her. They did so, and I was born at 304 W Taylor Street, Savannah GA . Dr. Simon F. Frazier also delivered all my siblings except Louis, the youngest. Louis was born in the hospital in February 1952. Mama had changed doctors by then. She kept being sick because she was anemic. The new doctor had taken some blood tests and found that she was anemic.

My parents met when my mother came to live across the street from my paternal grandmother and my father on West Taylor St. in Savannah GA.

In July of 1940, Mama and Daddy moved into Fellwood Homes. Daddy had gotten a job maintaining property at Fellwood, but then he returned to work as a waiter at Morrison's cafeteria. When they got married though, Daddy was working at the DeSoto hotel, then the Plaza then back to the DeSoto. He worked at Morrisons Cafeteria two or three times in 1948.

Mama had a soft spoken, lovely southern accent. She had a way of calming all situations and assuring us that everything was going to be alright. She was known for her charming smile and quick sense of humor.

Mama was also very frugal, clipping coupons, knowing where food was on sale, and how to select fresh ingredients. She always knew how to solve our problems.

When I was being considered for a Danforth Scholarship, I remember the interviewer telling me how he was moved when I wrote about how my mother always saw to it that we ate breakfast before going to school, regardless of how cold the kitchen was, and how she would cook breakfast in a cold kitchen in her cloth well-worn bathrobe.

She was employed first by Dr. Harry E. Rollings, and later by the Atlanta Life Insurance Company (formerly Guaranty Life Insurance Company). She also worked at Nicholson's Pharmacy on Bay Street near Fellwood Homes. I enjoyed visiting her at the pharmacy because I loved the 16 cents milkshakes she used to make.

Mama was an active member of St. Paul CME Church where she served on the Missionary Society. She was active in our community, serving at the Moses Jackson Golden Age Center, the West Savannah Community Organization, and the Savannah Chapter 159 of the Order of the Eastern Star.

Daddy

On November 30th, 1992 , I was able to get Daddy to give me a few sketches of his life. When he was 8 years old, he delivered milk in Louisville GA (Jefferson County). This is near Manor, where Grandmama had taken them to live after leaving Olar, South Carolina. Daddy worked for a man named Willis, who had a milk delivery route. Willis and his brother-in-law owned or operated a grocery store. Willis' brother-in-law was named Nesbitt Baker. One of Daddy's jobs was to clean up the store. He wanted to go to school but he couldn't because he had to work.

At the same time, Uncle Booker T. , daddy's brother, was working on odd jobs.

Grandmama was not working at that time. She was married a man named Doc Wilson, a preacher in Louisville. He had no church, but he preached everywhere. Daddy thought he was an exceptionally good preacher. Doc Wilson had had four children with his first wife, Louise. She passed away leaving Henry, Harvey, Nellie, and Rosa. By 1992, all four of these children were dead. Rosa had one child who was named Louise, and Nellie had no children.

At some point, Grandmama, Daddy and Uncle Booker T. lived in a small town known as Manor Georgia, near Waycross. Manor was a small settlement; there was no stop light and only three houses. However, there was a turpentine still in Manor. Doc Wilson taught daddy and Uncle Booker T how to dip turpentine from the gum that ran from trees. The trees would be cut in a certain way, and the gum ran into a cup which they later poured into a gum bucket; they dumped the contents of the gum bucket into a barrel. At the end of the day a man picked up the barrel and carried it to the still where it was distilled and made into turpentine. It was a nasty job because they had to work in the woods and in the water that was full of moccasin snakes and alligators. At the end of the first payday Uncle Booker T and Daddy left the turpentine job.

In about 1930, Grandmama eventually brought Daddy and Uncle Booker T. to Savannah. When he was away, Daddy wrote her a letter once a week and sent her some money.

Bertha Rickenbacker (our cousin) told Grandmama that she had a friend who lived in Jacksonville who told her that jobs might be available for Booker T and Daddy. The family moved to Savannah, but then Daddy and Uncle Booker T moved to Jacksonville. Bertha had contacted them. At that time, they were about 19 and 22 years old, respectively. They could not go to school because they had to work, and Daddy got a job in a cafeteria washing dishes and pots. Then he left Jacksonville and moved to Miami leaving Uncle Booker T. in

Jacksonville. He lived in a room and worked in a cafeteria waiting table for about two or three years.

As far as Daddy could recall he came to Savannah after living in Miami. Times were very, very hard. After Daddy returned to Savannah, he got a job at a restaurant on West Broad Street at B & B restaurant. After that he went downtown to work at the Plaza hotel.

He became a member of St. Paul's C.M.E. Church.

During one of the summers after I had received a fellowship to study overseas, I worked with daddy as a waiter at Morrisons Cafeteria located 15 Bull St, in Savannah. Many days, I would walk or run to work, on Lathrop Avenue to Bay Street, across the viaduct, past Yamacraw Village, continuing along Bay Street until I came to Bull. Morrison's was on Bull Street, about 1 block south of Bay Street and City Hall.

The "dressing room" for waiters left a lot to be desired.

One special gift stands out for me. Mr. Moore, the white manager of the restaurant, was a low-key individual who did not talk much. One day he learned from Daddy that I had been awarded a Morehouse Merrill Fellowship to study overseas. He called me over, congratulated me, and gave me a lemon meringue pie, which happened to be my favorite pie. I will never forget his kind gesture.

After I had worked my first day, daddy asked me how are you doing? I complained to him that my feet were hurting, to which he responded that his feet were still hurting after 30 years or something to that effect. After that I never complained about my feet hurting again.

One of the most gratifying experiences when I was working at Union Carbide was to turn my legal training as a lawyer to benefit my parents. Morrison's operated mainly in the Southern states. From a modest beginning in 1920 in Mobile, Alabama with one restaurant, Morrison's would expand to a chain of 151 cafeterias operating in13 states.[11]

---

[11] Encyclopediaofalabama.org (accessed 02 April 2025)

At the Savannah location, the waiters were all black, as were the chef and kitchen workers. White women operated the cash register, and the managers were all white. I think some of the servers on the food line were white.

As the time approached for daddy to retire, I learned that Morrison's provided retirement benefits to its white employees, but not to its black employees.

At the time, the United States Supreme Court had come down with a decision which suggested that I might be able to get a pension for my father using the securities laws. I also thought we might have a claim to challenge Morrison's deductibility of its contributions to its pension plans.

I drafted a complaint, and Morey McDaniel, Union Carbide's securities lawyer, and Jerry Robinson, one of its tax lawyers, agreed to review the draft complaint to advise me on whether I had stated colorable claims.

They thought that I did. I finalized the complaint and sent it to Morrison's lawyers in Alabama for their review, and to give them notice that if they did not grant retirement benefits to my father and the other black employees, I would file the lawsuit contained in the complaint.

To my delightful surprise, Morrison's agreed to give retirement benefits to all its black employees throughout their chain. Daddy's would last for at least 10 years after he retired. I do not recall what the term was for all the employees. I do not know if the plan was amended or continued when Piccadilly, Inc., acquired Morrison's in April 1996.

The negotiations with Morrison's lawyers were pleasant and civil.

My training as a lawyer resulted in a tangible benefit for my parents. This recalled the saying "give a man a fish and you feed him for a day. Teach him how to fish and you feed him for a lifetime.[12]"

---

[12] Most Credible Origin: Anne Isabella Thackeray Ritchie (1885)

The "Original Nine Black Savannah Police Officers"

On May 3, 1947, Daddy and eight black men became police officers in Savannah. They were the first black police officers in Savannah since reconstruction.[13] Arguably, they were the first black police officers in the South since Reconstruction.[14]They are known as the "Original Nine." To begin the process, Savannah recruited some 60 candidates. Given the state of segregation at the time, they were limited to arresting black people only.

This was to be Savannah's experiment with beginning to breakdown racial barriers.

The Atlanta Daily World (black newspaper) sent a reporter to cover the introduction of the black policemen to the public; both the Atlanta Journal and the Atlanta Constitution printed editorials praised "Savannah's Experiment "Common Sense Law and Order." Atlanta officials came to Savannah for a first-hand look at the black policeman in Savannah before hiring their own.[15]

---

[13] However, the Savannah Police Department's history of this event said that Richmond and Norfolk VA, Knoxville TN, Durham and Charlotte NC, Charleston SC, Little Rock AR, Jacksonville, Tampa , and Miami FL had black policemen at the time. This history is reported in a Savannah Police Department document "A Forty-Seven Year Legacy." This was incorporated and reprinted in my father's homegoing Services program, courtesy of my sister, Gloria Edwards.

[14] Id.

[15] Id.

Daddy is second from the left.

Daddy would later resign because the police department would allow white officers certain privileges that it did not allow black officers.

While working as a police officer, Daddy also worked part time at the DeSoto hotel. After leaving the police force, he went to work at the DeSoto hotel.

Over time, this pioneering experiment would open opportunities for black Savannahians in other areas of life. Hence their legendary title "The Original Nine,"

The story of the Original Nine is told in the Savannah Police Department's document "A Forty-Seven Year Legacy."[16]"They are: Alexander Grant, Jr., John A. White, Howard J Davis, Milton Hall, James

[16] In the private collection of my sister Gloria Wilson Edwards. Gloria obtained the document from the City of Savannah and included it in my father's Funeral Services program. The funeral was held on May 7, 1994.

Neely, William N Malone, Leroy Wilson, Stephney Houston, and Frank Mullino.

A photo of them also appears in the Ralph Mark Gilbert Civil Rights Museum on Martin Luther King Blvd., Savannah, Georgia.

On the 8th day of May 1997, Floyd Adams Jr., the first black Mayor of Savannah, GA and one of our neighbors growing up, issued a proclamation designating May 1, 1997 "Original Nine Day."

The purpose of the proclamation was to recite what happened in the 50 years from the time nine men became the first black police officers in Savannah GA since Reconstruction to that date.

Following are some of the pertinent recitals in the proclamation:

Whereas: Fifty years ago, sixteen men forged ahead with the need for political and social change in Savannah and trained in secret for three months, without pay, to become the first black police officers in the state of Georgia; and

Whereas: Of these sixteen, nine were hired on May 1, 1947, and were sworn in at City Hall by Mayor John Kennedy; and

Whereas: Their names were James Nealy, John A. White, William N. Malone, Milton Hall, Leroy Wilson, Howard Davis, Alexander Grant Jr., Stepney Houston, and Frank Mullino; William Day replaced Alexander Grant Jr.; henceforth this group became known as the "Original Nine;" and

Whereas: These men had to forfeit, at times, their personal and professional values under often demeaning conditions: patrol cars that would not run an entire eight- hour shift, inaccessibility to facilities, segregation from their white colleagues, lack of authority to arrest white people breaking the law, limited boundaries to their beat, and were denied the right to wear their uniforms when riding public buses; and

Whereas: Because the Original Nine black Savannah Police officers endured hard times and good times and served with pride and dignity, currently two black police officers have attained the rank of major, three are captains, six are lieutenants and twenty are sergeants; and

Whereas: The black officers who have since climbed up in the ranks did so on the shoulders of the Original Nine; and

Whereas: The hiring of the Original Nine black police officers is as significant to the Savannah community as Jackie Robinson breaking the color barrier in major league baseball.

That is the effect that these appointments had on the black community.

When Daddy died, I thought it was a singular honor that the police department honored Daddy with a full-blown funeral cortege from our residence in West Savannah to the cemetery. There was a police motorcycle escort all the way, with the police stopping traffic on all the cross streets along the way. Ironically, when we turned onto the street leading to the gravesite, the name of the street was Wilson Blvd (no relation to Daddy, as far as I know).

My parents, paternal grandmother, and brother Vernon are buried in Lincoln cemetery, probably one of the world's most secure cemeteries, as it is contained entirely within the grounds of Hunter Air Force base in Savannah, Georgia.

Both of my parents instilled in us the importance of getting an education. One of my father's favorite tactics was to tell us that we did not want to wind up working on the chain gang. We often saw them working in the hot, unforgiving Savannah sun. I wanted no part of that.

The Family Move West Taylor St., Fellwood, and Richards St

In June/July 1940, we moved away from grandmama's house located at 304 West Taylor Street in the city into Fellwood Homes, a housing project in West Savannah. If there was any criminal activity there, I never witnessed any. The situation has changed in later years.

My memories of Fellwood are all pleasant ones. It was also in Fellwood that I saw snow for the first time, in 1944. What a treat, although, as I remember, there wasn't a lot of it. I remember fondly the little wagon that my parents bought for me and how I used to ride it throughout Fellwood.

From one family photograph taken in Fellwood, I can be seen holding a large racing car; I have no independent memory of it, but I know it must have been important to me.

The family in Fellwood Homes about 1943 before Vernon was born.

The house on Taylor Street was demolished some time ago and there is now no trace of it. I used to always enjoy going to visit my grandmother at that house. I loved spending the night on the second floor, above the room where I was born. Perhaps that is why I enjoyed it so much. The house was constructed of wood and was 2 stories. For some reason, going up and down the rickety stairs fascinated me. This was something I could not do in our one floor house on Richards Street.

There was an adjoining house next door to grandmama's house, with a partition that separated the front porch between the two houses. I somehow remember my first cousin Laura Mae, Uncle Booker T.'s daughter, pulling me through a hole in the partition. It was a lot of fun.

On one occasion, when I was about 12 years old, I rode my bicycle from our house in West Savannah to my grandmother's house on West Taylor St. I don't think I realized the risk that I had undertaken at the time.

But that was not the only one. When they were constructing the Eugene Talmadge Bridge over the Savannah River, we used to ride our bicycles down the steep incline that curved at the bottom.

One of our most dangerous stunts was riding our bicycles down the incline of the bridge and then round the curve so that the pedals scraped against the concrete which caused sparks to fly. Accomplishing that feat showed that you were a certified bicycle rider. What an extremely dangerous thing to have done!

After we moved into our house at 1011 Richards Street in 1945, we were eventually a family of six, our parents, sisters Gloria and Mary Deloris, me and brothers Donald, Vernon and Louis. My parents slept in the front bedroom; Vernon and I shared one of the beds in back bedrooms and Gloria and "Lolie" slept in the other. Our brothers Donald and Louis would come later.

Me and my siblings Standing L-R Mary Deloris, Me, Gloria; seated Donald, Vernon) at 1011 Richards Street, before Louis was born

Of course we did all the things children did. We played hopscotch, pick up sticks, jackstones, marbles, jump rope, and made sling shots. As we grew older, we also shot BB guns. To this day, I feel guilty for shooting birds.

All of my siblings had some level of college experience, but Deloris went on to earn two bachelor's degrees from Savannah State University and University of Maryland, and a master's degree from Johns Hopkins University.

Gloria became the first black person from West Savannah to be elected to the Chatham County Board of Education. Her children are Susan, Jody, Darren and Angelique.

My sister Lolie was the head high school majorette at one point; you should have seen her strut with pride which carried over for all the majorettes and band members. Many years after I graduated, Edwin and I watched a parade on MLK Boulevard prior to a Savannah State football game. The same sense of pride had been passed down through the generations.

Lolie had two children, Victor and Lisa, five grandsons Devin, Damein, Cameron, Julian, and Jay'Den; three granddaughters, Tiffani, Amber, and Ondreia; four great granddaughters, Marlie, Rylie, Jace, and Azori.

She served for 15 years as a Forensic Histopathologist in Office of District of Columbia Medical examiner. She was forced to retire because of a serious burn to her hand after hot paraffin wax spilled onto her hands. She then embarked upon a new career.

She capped off her working career as a 34-year Special Educator in the Charles County Public Schools.

In 2022, Vernon left our lives all too soon. Bubby, we called him.

I also saw my brother Louis play a football game at Groves High School. He made a long run down the field, but I don't remember if he scored a touchdown. I was enormously proud of him.

Louis had the distinction of being the only one in his class at Savanah State to solve a difficult economics problem. He is a realtor in Savannah

Each of my brothers served honorably in the armed services of our country.

When it came time for me, I was a student in Berkeley, California when I received a notice on Tuesday telling me to report to the Savannah draft board on the preceding Saturday. This was impossible, and after I explained my status, I was allowed to transfer my registration to Berkeley. I did not hear from them again.

The living room kitchen/dining room, bathroom and laundry room and the pantry completed the other rooms in the house. We had a small front yard and slightly larger backyard. There was an orange tree in the front yard which bore sweet oranges like clockwork. There was a chinaberry tree, a fig tree, a banana tree and a pomegranate tree in the backyard. At one point the orange tree produced so many sweet oranges that a photo made the local paper, which showed how Daddy had to prop up the branches because of the large crop of oranges.

This was to be contrasted to Lobatse, Botswana, where I lived for many years after I retired. In Lobatse the baboons regularly helped themselves to our orange tree in the back; many times before they were ripe.

In Savannah, our floors along the passageway from the front of the house to the back, was covered with linoleum with wood in the uncovered spaces running along the sides. There was a long linoleum covering then the length of the hallway, ran from the front door to the kitchen. On either side the linoleum did not completely cover the word. I think I found it therapeutic to scrub the wood clean. We all chipped in to do various chores around the house.

I think most of the floors were also covered with linoleum.

Although we had a bathroom, during the wintertime when it was cold, we bathed in a #2 or #3 tub in the living room where there was some heat. I have forgotten what the source of the heat was, but I do remember that it was replaced at some point with natural gas heaters. That was a big deal. Somehow, we always seemed to be moving with the times.

Our street was not paved, which was a very sore point with my father. His reasoning was that since the streets in the white areas of Savannah were paved, ours should be as well. I am not sure I was entirely in favor of paving the street, since I didn't know how my Popsicle sticks would negotiate the rivulets of water on a paved street in the same ways as they had moved in the little gulleys created in the dirt road when it rained.

This is where my ships of popsicle sticks navigated. The ants that populated the front yard were my people. They built their little villages in the garden.

We lived next door to another family of Wilsons - no relation. Mr. Joe was the family patriarch; Mrs. Annie was his matriarch. They had a daughter and a son - Ms. Hattie Howard, and Bubba, Joseph Jr.; Ms. Hattie had two sons - Willie Howard Jr. ("Jr.") and Charles Howard. Charles was Charlesetta's twin. Dee Dee (for Delores) was the oldest, then Jr., then Dot (for Dorothy), Ann was in there somewhere.

We also called Junior "Rev." Not only was Jr. closely attached to First Bryan Baptist Church in Savannah, but he was also attached to Community Protestant Church in Bronx, New York pastored by Rev. Dr. Calvin E. Owens.

When Junior passed away on April 4, 2022, I was temporarily residing in Pooler, Ga., adjacent to Savannah, while I rode out the Covid-19 restrictions and vaccination periods. Rev. Owens came down for the funeral on April 8. My sister Gloria made a few remarks at the funeral about Junior. He was always dependable and spoke with wisdom on many occasions.

When I was living and practicing law in New York, I represented Rev. Owens's church in a civil matter in federal court in New York concerning the right to acquire a former bingo hall to use as a church. That is how I learned that Jr. had become a deacon in that church. It was good to see Rev. Owens again at Junior's funeral after so many years.

Bubba was not living next door when we moved into 1011 Richards Street. He was a sailor in the Navy. When he finally got out, I think he was the first serviceman that I had ever met. I was in awe of him as I watched him build his own house from scratch, next to Mr. Joe and Mrs. Annie's.

Mr. Joe was the only one in the neighborhood who owned a car, as I remember. He seemed to take great joy in giving us kids a ride. I think it was a Nash. This was a church-going neighborhood. Mr. Joe always gave us a big treat when he announced that on any given Sunday we would be going to church at "5 Mile Bend." I don't remember where this was exactly, but it seems that we went around the traffic circle (or roundabouts as my Botswana - oriented friends would say).

The religious services were great, but for us children, the big events were the whole afternoon eating - all kinds of delicious food– fried chicken, fried fish , biscuits, collard greens, macaroni and cheese, cornbread, corn on the cob, sweet potato pie, cakes, lemonade, and soft drinks. During those days, we didn't know it was called soul food. It was delicious and there were a lot of very excellent cooks.

Also, on Saturdays, daddy would go around the corner on Lathrop Avenue to "Mac Willie's" shop and buy some whiting or croaker or mullet fish for us to gut and scale. On Saturday afternoons, Mac Willie would boil freshly caught crabs and shrimp. He would roast oysters in the shell on a piece of corrugated tin. Savannah is a seaport city, so we always had an abundance of seafood.

Summertime was a time of new experiences. We used to go to one or more of the various farms owned by some grownup person. I learned how to pick cotton - not too much, but enough to earn a few pennies. One of those farms grew some outstanding pears, whose sweet taste I have never found again in a pear, searching in vain throughout the places that I visit.

Another lovely activity was called vacation bible school. I loved the lemonade and sandwiches, and I learned something about religion in the process. These were usually held at churches. I remember First African Baptist Church pastored by Rev. Ralph Mark Gilbert, as being one of the venues. Reverend Dr. Ralph Mark Gilbert, the 13th pastor of the First African Baptist Church and the "Modern father of Savannah's Civil Rights Movement."[17]

W. W. Law was president of the local chapter of the National Association for the Advancement of Colored People (NAACP) and founder of the Civil Rights Museum and the Black Heritage Festival. The Museum is named for its mentor, Ralph Mark Gilbert Civil Rights Museum.[18]

W.W. Law was the longest serving President of the Savannah Chapter of the NAACP. Although he was highly active in civil rights issues, his job was protected at the U.S. Post Office, because he was a federal employee.

Daddy was President of a group that focused on voting rights with the motto " A voteless people is a hopeless people." Hence, we were keenly tuned into voting rights from an early age.

Even though Savannah society was segregated, we acted as if we were equal to everyone else. I dutifully wrote letters to the editor about various subjects. I do not recall if any were ever responded to or even

---

[17] The History of Savannah's Civil Rights Movement | Ralph Mark Gilbert Civil Rights Museum (rmgcivilrightsmuseum.com) (Accessed 12 October 2024)

[18] Id.

printed. I believed in freedom of speech and the various issues that daddy was writing about, and the NAACP was advocating. I remember writing about the various governors, and the racist practices of Lester "Axe Handle" Maddox in Atlanta who promised to beat any black person who sought to eat in his restaurant. We thought these people were simply insane because their racism made no sense to us.

In the present day, Donald J. Trump, who has been elected for a non-contiguous second term, beginning January 20, 2025, has endorsed Plan 2025 prepared by the conservative Heritage Foundation. Under Plan 2025 supported by his MAGA Republicans and acquiesced to by the remnants of the Republican Party.[19] If it were up to President Trump, no current black federal civil servant would enjoy the job protection that W.W. Law and all the black federal employees enjoyed up to this point.

I have concluded that the word "conservative" means stopping and turning back humane human progress and freedom for the masses, with reservations and privileges to societal control by a few white male oligarchs.

---

[19] It's essentially a 900-page "wish list" for an ultra-conservative social vision. https://www.bbc.com/news/articles/c977njnvq2do?form=MG0AV3 (Accessed 12 October 2024)

West Savannah Elementary School

As a little 6-year-old boy, I was happy to learn that I was going to be going to school! There was no question that I would be going to school; I was simply happy I was going. The thought of having my own pencils, paper to write with, and learning to read and write excited me immensely. The school was right down the street from where we lived on Richards Street. The schoolhouse was made of wood. In winter we were warmed by a pot-bellied wood and coal burning stove.

The school has since been replaced by a modern brick building.

Like neighborhoods everywhere, there were a few bullies. There was one, whose name I will not repeat, that I had the pleasure of beating the stuffing out of.

I distinctly remember the pall that fell over the neighborhood when Franklin Delano Roosevelt died in 1945. Also, the end of the war was cause for high and loud celebrations. As a little boy, I didn't understand what was going on, but I knew that these were two major events.

In those days, the schools were all segregated. This was so in all the schools I attended, until I got to Morehouse College. We had a few white students there. Our Morehouse professors were of mixed racial and ethnic groups. Throughout all of this, I don't ever remember feeling an inferiority complex. Throughout my years of education, our teachers and professors cared about us.

Some decades later, my friend Joseph Rivers asked me to meet with him at the Savannah airport before I was about to fly off from Savannah to someplace. I agreed. Usually, Joe, along with John Finney and I would normally meet for tea or coffee or a meal when I visited Savannah. Although we were classmates at Beach High, we became much closer in our later years. I was intrigued by him wanting to meet as I was about to leave town. There was a sound of urgency in his voice.

L-R Joe Murray Rivers, Me, and John Finney at the Inaugural Reception for Floyd Adams, Jr., newly elected first black Mayor of Savannah, GA (1996).

Joe was highly active in the Savannah civil rights movement, as attested by a bronzed replica of the shoes he wore as he marched through Savannah. I was thrilled that the transportation hub in Savannah had been named after Joe. "Opened on Oct. 7, 2013, the Joe Murray Rivers, Jr. Intermodal Transit Center is the culmination of a transportation dream more than 15 years in the making. It was named for Joe Murray Rivers, Jr., a staunch transit advocate, former Chatham County commissioner, CAT board member, and interim executive director at CAT".[20] Joe gave me a personal tour of the facility. I could not have been prouder of him. I had the joy of him showing me his bronzed shoes that are on display in the center.

When I met Joe at the airport, he showed me an astonishing photo. The photo showed me, and a collection of other black elementary school students from all over Savannah. The astonishing thing about the photo is that someone had collected this little group of these students from all over the city who would later go on to have stellar academic and career success. I had wanted to see that photograph again to identify these students, but Joseph passed away on April 2, 2023, before I was able to see it again. What this meant to me was that the

---

[20] https://www.catchacat.org/about-cat/intermodal-transit-facility/ (Accessed 19 December 2023)

teachers had identified those of us across the city who showed academic promise.

There is no telling how long Joe had had this photo.

Another enlightening fact is that Joe told me that he had attended elementary school on St. Helena Island. By this time, I had become enamored by the history of black people in South Carolina, having visited my father's birthplace in 2009, and the Penn Center. My wife Maleta and I also visited the Boone Plantation.[21]

John, Finney, on the other hand, had made a name for himself as a champion of poor people. He created several initiatives in Savannah regarding health care, housing, recycling and teaching communities about natural gas deregulation.

On September 24, 2020, the Savannah Morning News reported that John Finney, longtime executive director at the Equal Opportunity Authority for Savannah-Chatham County Area Inc., died on Tuesday, Sept. 22. He was 81.

---

[21] My brother Louis E. Wilson, Sr., has written extensively about the Boone Plantation in his book *Planters of the Seed from Madegascar*

Cuyler Jr High School

We lived in West Savannah. The schools in Savannah "in town" were thought to be better, so we planned to enroll me at Cuyler. You see, you had to live "in town" to go to Cuyler.

Fortunately, my grandmother lived on West Taylor Street, in town, so we used her address so that I could enroll. If any of the administrators ever found out, I never knew it.

I think I must have attended from 1951-1954.

When I visited the school in 2015, I read a plaque that had been placed just next to the entrance which read " Cuyler Street School, Designed by Henrik Wallin 1913 – First Public School Built for Negroes in Savannah."

It was at Cuyler that I met my lifelong best friend, Edwin Curtis Brown. Edwin died on Friday, September 14, 2018. Though residing in Botswana at the time of his death, I was in Savanah at the time of the funeral and was fortunate enough to make a few remarks at Edwin's funeral.

Edwin lived on 44th street "in town" in a 2-storey house. I think Edwin was the only friend that I had who lived in a 2-storey house.

Edwin was scheduled to have an operation in Savannah on June 18, 2009, so he could not make my 70th birthday anniversary celebration, which was scheduled for June 20th at the Fair Deal Cafe in White Plains, New York. He sent a glowing tribute, part of which read as follows:

"In our early days as young men, I got to know Leroy's mother and father, even though we lived a good ways apart. Leroy's mother always took the time (when she saw me) to ask if everything was okay and kept tabs on us about the girls and other things; she was a very sweet lady. Leroy's father was just as kind; he gave Leroy and I driving lessons in a big black fluid drive Dodge. He even secured us a job shining shoes at Lamas Brother's Cleaners and Newsstand."

For a grown man with a family, the minimum wage was one dollar an hour ($40 a week plus overtime); Leroy and I were paid $10 for 10 hours on Saturday and $5 for 5 hour [sic] on Sunday. This is where Mr. Wilson was smart, he knew the tips were good and we made between $25-$30 in tips plus our $15, so we earned $40-$45 for the weekend. [22]

Although we both would make the track team, Edwin was the star. He ran so fast that we called him "Smokey." At one time, Edwin held the Georgia state record for running the fastest 100-yard dash (before they switched to meters) *Edwin and me as I was on a stopover in Atlanta when he was living there*

[22] From Edwin's letter tribute that was read at my 70th birthday celebration.

Me, Alex (Edwin's Daughter) and Edwin in Kissimmee, Florida

Alfred E. Beach High School

In 1867, the American Missionary Association (A.M.A.) and the Freedmen's Bureau established the Beach Institute with funds donated by Alfred Ely Beach, editor of Scientific American. The school was privately funded as a manual training school to provide support for newly freed African Americans. By 1874, the Institute was appropriated by the Savannah-Chatham Board of Education for the purpose of providing free education to Savannah's African American citizenry. Although the Beach Institute closed its doors in 1915, it was reopened as an African American cultural center and is currently operated by the King-Tisdell Cottage Foundation.[23]

The Beach name survives in the name of Alfred E. Beach High School.[24]

I was excited about going to high school. And just as we had done when I attended Cuyler Junior High school, we used my grandmother's address W Taylor St, so that I could go to A.E. Beach High School in town.

Beach High School covered grades 10-12.

I used to walk to the corner of West Lathrop and Augusta Avenue to catch the bus to go to school. When we arrived at West Broad Street and Henry Streets, there was a small corner store that sold Krispy Crème donuts. They cost ten cents each at the time. They were super delicious. A little over 60 years later, Airlink served Krispy Crème

---

[23] https://en.wikipedia.org/wiki/Beach_High_School (Accessed 22 December 2023)

[24] Id.

donuts as a snack on one of its flights I took in southern Africa-Botswana or South Africa. I was pleasantly surprised.

On a visit to my son Christopher in Washington, D.C. in the summer of 2022, I mentioned this to him, and he told me that there was a Krispy Crème donut shop in D.C. on the way to my sister's house in Maryland. I had asked her if I could bring anything to supplement her sumptuous dinner. She wanted these donuts. I obliged by bringing a dozen varieties to her. I will never forget those collard greens and turkey wings she served, along with red rice, one of my favorites.

10th Grade

All my teachers were great and instilled in us a desire to learn. Of course, my father had reinforced this from an early age, telling us that we did not want to grow up to dig ditches, especially in the hot sun. In those days, chain gangs of prisoners dug ditches and worked in the blazing hot sun. My mother echoed his admonition.

I do not remember who all my homeroom teachers were, from 10th and 11th grade; Mr. Lester B. Johnson was my 12th grade homeroom teacher. He also taught industrial arts, or shop.

Mrs. Esther Harden, my 10th grade English teacher, counselled me that I was not applying myself and I could do much better. I tried, but the one topic I could not seem to master was how to diagram a sentence. To this day I have no idea how I ever did that, but I might try again using artificial intelligence as my teacher.

Mr. Rhaney taught me geometry, and maybe algebra? Again, I loved this subject and enjoyed mathematics immensely. He might have also introduced us to trigonometry, but I think I might not have had this course until I was enrolled at Morehouse.

Ms. Willie Mae Patterson taught me American history, or world history, or both. I don't remember us covering the Civil War history to the extent that I have studied this history in my later years. I think all people of African descent should study this history to recognize it when we see it and to keep from repeating it.

I am not sure what Ms. Lydia B. Mabry taught me but one of the life lessons that I still use from her teaching was for us to always sleep with the window cracked a little bit, even in the winter, to breathe in some fresh air. Since I suffer from various kinds of allergies, I find this advice to be even more helpful.

Ms. Miriam F. Grant taught me biology, but I admit that I was somewhat squeamish when it came to dissecting the frog!

I might have had a music class from Mr. Peter J. Smalls, but I was not a member of the choir. I cannot sing.

I think Ms. Gwendolyn H. Hallman taught me Algebra, but I don't remember which grade I was in. Math was one of my favorite subjects.

I tried out for track and made the team, but I don't think Coach Joe Greene ever called on me to participate in a track meet. There were other boys much better than me. Nevertheless, I enjoyed being a part of the team. Margaret Brown, Edwin's sister, was also extremely fast.

I also made the football team but did not play in a game. In practice one time, Edwin emerged from the bottom of the rubble after Gus Hall had collided with him and smiled to reveal a broken front tooth.

I seem to think that Mr. Brownlee and Mr. Smith (both Clarence) coached football and track, respectively. Mr. Brownlee was a Tennessee State graduate and was probably a major force in Edwin's decision to go to Tennessee State. As I was going off to Morehouse College in Atlanta, this would be the first time that when we graduated from high school, we would be separated since the 7th grade.

I participated in several other activities.

Some of us were learning to drive during this period. We also had an instructor to teach us how to drive. I'm having trouble trying to remember his name - Mr. Holman (?) brown skinned man, starting to bald, nice person. Lieutenant Fink from the Savannah Police Department also taught us, taking us driving and teaching bicycle riding safety.

11th Grade

As I was writing this on 23 December 2023, I don't remember what happened in 11th grade.

12th Grade

I am blessed to have a copy of my 12th grade report card, duly signed by my dear mother. In those days, we were obliged to give our parents our report cards. Mr. Lester B. Johnson, my homeroom teacher, noted that on 05 May 1957 that I graduated with honors.

Except for 1 B, I received all As in chemistry, taught by Mr. Raymond Washington, physics, taught by Mr. Charles Johnson, and mathematics, taught by Ms. Hallman?

I earned a mixture of As and Bs in the rest of my subjects: English, taught by Ms. Hallman? Shop, taught by Mr. Roscoe Riley, Family, taught by Ms. Dorothy Lampkin. Ms. Hallman taught me something. I see her name on the card, but I am not sure if it belongs in the English line or not. I also see that I took American History and Algebra, but I cannot make out the teacher's signature.

One time there was an explosion in the chemistry lab. Mr. Washington asked me if I could find the cause. My conclusion was some kind of dust had been ignited and that caused the small explosion. I supported it with some research on what caused certain kinds of explosions. He accepted that conclusion.

In the shop, I made a cedar chest for my mother which she kept in my parents' bedroom to store things. I also made a corner table for her. The cedar chest still exists, but I do not know what happened to the corner table. I enjoyed working with the various kinds of tools and wish I could have kept it up.

The prom was and still is a mystery to me. I took the public buses to and from the prom, without a date, not like the elaborate transportation that they use nowadays, like limousines. Chris and his date, and his friend, Brett Duryea and his date rode in a limousine.

Many years later, after we had become adults, two of these teachers - JoAnn Mitchell's mother - Genevieve- being one of them - would tell some of us separately, of the fights they had had to try to equalize their salaries with those of white teachers. I was clueless at the time.

Our 1957 class slogan was "Achievement is our Aim; Success is Our Goal." I think I have done my part.

In April 1957, I placed second in a statewide oratorical contest, won by Verdell Lambert, who was in the 11th grade of the high school section. Her sister, Gladys and I were in the 12th grade. I think it was held in Macon or Columbus, Georgia.

I was inducted in the National Honor Society on 22 May 1957.

I graduated 15th in a class of 209.

Our graduation was held in the Savannah Municipal Auditorium on May 30, 1957. Our Principal Mr. Otha L. Douglas, who presided over the awards, gave me a $100.00 scholarship award from the Kappa Alpha Psi Fraternity. I was grateful for this award. Still am.

In April of 2022, 65 years later, I had the honor of being hosted at a luncheon at the home of Marguerite Tiggs Birt. Elizabeth Pryor Jackson and Gladys Lambert, two of our classmates, also attended the luncheon. At the luncheon, Verdell Lambert, Gladys's sister, reminded me that when I was serving as counsel for the IBM facility in Brooklyn NY, she joined that facility as a public relations/human relations manager and that I had encountered her there. I asked Marguerite if Margaret Brown, Edwin's surviving sister, could also attend the luncheon. She agreed and we all had an exceptionally enjoyable time. Marguerite's baked salmon was my favorite – delicious. While we were there, we discovered that Marguerite had written a very moving biography of her father, who had suffered serious injuries during WWII, and was hospitalized for 16 years, in New York, I think, before he was able to rejoin his family in Savannah.

The title of Marguerite's book is *Our Father, An African American Soldier: His life and Legacy Paperback – May 12, 2021*. She wrote "James Hill Tiggs was our father; an African American man, and a WW ll soldier in the United States Army. This historical, nonfiction account is written as a lasting tribute to our father. I am unable to keep to myself the proof of his determined spirit: finding ways to side-step segregation as a young man, committing himself in marriage to our mother, providing for our family, and serving his country overseas. As you read this testament, you will recognize Daddy's character was not diminished by his experiences of perpetual institutionalized racism – instead his character was ennobled by it."[25]

I highly recommend her book. In the appendix of the book, she lists all the places that she has travelled to; some of which I have also visited.

Preliminary, Marguerite had read a piece that I had written for publication in the Botswana Guardian during Black History Month. I had sent a copy to her. After reading it she came up with the idea of having a luncheon in my honor in Savannah when I visited. Her work in this regard involved contacting several of the Class of 1957 surviving members, as well as soliciting contributions to pay for the luncheon and to print the program. For those gracious efforts - which she described as being of service - I am forever indebted to her.

This luncheon was held at the Red Lobster on West Montgomery Cross Road in Savannah. Some of the attendees appear below.

---

[25] https://www.amazon.com/Our-Father-African-American-Soldier/dp/B097XB7D77 (Accessed 22 December 2023)

Top photo L-R Seated-my sister Gloria, Me. Marguerite Birt, 1st row standing L-R -Elizabeth Pryor Jackson (dec.), Mary A. McPherson, Nephew Darren, Unknown Gentleman, Vernelle Moultrie (in yellow), two Unknown ladies, Nieces Susan, Monica and Dina; 2nd row standing L-R Gladys Lambert (obscured in red jacket in front of Susan), Last Row L-R Vernelle's husband, Leon Grant.

Bottom Photo of actual classmates - L-R Elizabeth Pryor Jackson, (dec.) Me, Vernelle, Leon, Gladys and Marguerite.

When it came to selecting a date, I recommended April 9. The reason I selected this date was because it is the date that Robert E. Lee surrendered at Appomattox, Virginia to end the Civil War. I wanted to give my classmates some related history that most people know nothing about.

That history concerned the courageous rebellion of the 112 black cadets at the U.S. Army Military Academy West Point, New York in 1972 to defeat then President Nixon's order to have a monument erected at West Point honoring confederate soldiers. This was part of his southern strategy. They also achieved many other positive reforms at West Point. I was the civilian counsel to the black cadets and their supporters in successfully organizing and putting on a sickle cell anemia benefit at West Point.

An added historical note is that Lloyd Austin, the Secretary of Defense in President Biden's administration, was a plebe in the freshman class at West Point during that time. Born in Mobile, Alabama, he was raised in Thomasville, Georgia. I pointed this out to them at the luncheon.

On May 20th 1972, we successfully put on the sickle cell anemia benefit concert which was the first time in the history of all the service academies in the United States that one had been the forum for a charitable event.[26]

---

[26] I discuss this in greater detail when I discuss the events at West Point and the Sickle Cell Anemia Benefit held there.

Morehouse College

I had read that Morehouse was a very good college and that it had produced several outstanding black men who had achieved great things. But, since no one in my family had ever gone to college, I did not know who to ask. I think I probably got more information from my counselor, who nonetheless never told me that Morehouse had an early admissions program that I might have been eligible for. Some of the students at my high school were early admissions students.

I am aware of two histories of Morehouse. The first is Edward A. Jones, *A Candle In the Dark – A History of Morehouse College*, Valley Forge, PA, 1967The second is Benjamin G. Brawley, *History of Morehouse College,* Atlanta, 1917.[27]

Most people generally know that Rev. Dr. Martin Luther King Jr. is a graduate of Morehouse. However, I am going to single out just one other graduate of Morehouse and that is Maynard Jackson.[28]

In the photo below, I am seated in the first seat in the first row, and Maynard is seated 5th from the left in the front row. I cite Maynard, not to ignore the enormous contributions of many others in the photo, but because 1) he set me on the path to begin my personal visits which opened up my life to the people and places of the African continent, 2) Affirmative Action Programs: Dramatically increased minority

---

27 Dr. Brawley's History is cited in Appendix A to Dr. Jones's history.

28 It has been reliably stated that Maynard Jackson created more black millionaires than any other public official in history. Maynard Jackson: The Ultimate Champion for Black Business -; Maynard Jackson: creating a bully pulpit for black business; this bold politician used his city hall office to create black millionaires. - Free Online Library (Accessed 30 October 2025)

participation in city contracts and business 3) Airport Expansion: Oversaw the transformation of Hartsfield Atlanta International Airport into a major global hub—later renamed Hartsfield–Jackson Atlanta International Airport in his honor (this is now the busiest airport in the world by passenger traffic), 4) Olympics Bid: Played a pivotal role in securing Atlanta as the host city for the 1996 Summer Olympic Games and Police Reform: Implemented changes to improve community relations and diversify the police force.[29]

However, I must point out that Maynard is seated between Dr. Mays on his left, and Dr. Hugh Gloster on his right. Dr. Gloster succeeded Dr. Mays.

The other striking thing about this photo is that it shows Morehouse men across several generations and professions.

When I first entered Morehouse, I set the following goals, in my head, at least: (1) to win the physics achievement awards for beginning physics students, which I did, (2) to win a Merrill Travel Study Fellowship, which I did, (3) to win the departmental medal in chemistry, which went to my friend and colleague, Troy Story, 4) to earn a perfect

[29] I copied items 2-4 from CoPilot, 17 October 2025.

4.0 record during any one semester, which I consider met, since I achieved a 3.95 during the 1960 – 1961 school year, (5) to win an assistantship to graduate school, which I did (five).

,At Morehouse I would experience my first white teachers. They were as supportive of us as were the black, Asian, and Indian professors. Frau Rupert and Frau Axelrod for German, the Lockheed engineer for math physics, whose name I forgot, Mr. Mohanty for physics.

I remember my first set of interactions with white students. I think the need to fit in made it awkward to breathe when we were in close quarters, such as elevators. I recall some years later, that when Japanese started doing business in the United States and encountered whites in this country on a more frequent basis, they had the same breathing experiences. Akio Morita tells this story in his autobiography where he discusses the history of SONY. I don't think any of us felt threatened, it was just a new experience. I wonder if this is what happens when diverse groups of people interact for the first time?

I experienced another aspect of diversity at Morehouse. We had black male students from all over the United States and some from African countries.[30] This enabled us to interact with brilliant black men well outside of the environments that we were raised in our towns and cities in Georgia. This is one reason that we never felt inferior. We knew that we had this great network of smart, brilliant men and women. On the other hand, we also observed a continuing cadre of ignorant, less brilliant white men.

We also witnessed a vibrant black business and professional community in Atlanta.

The one big disappointment that I had at Morehouse was that when it finally got a Phi Beta Kappa chapter many years after I graduated, I did not get my Phi Beta Kappa key retroactively. I think a few did. I am not sure if I and those in these earlier classes was even considered. I was the top science student in the graduating class of 1962 and was

---

[30] Dr. Edward A. Jones discusses this diversity in his book *A Candle in the Dark: A History of Morehouse College* (Judson Press) (1967)

3rd overall, out of 315 graduates. Joseph Rodgers (Foreign Languages - French) and Clark Everett (English) finished ahead of me. I understand that there were some keys presented to people who would have gotten them had there been a chapter at the time they were in school.

Morehouse College was a mostly all male college (we did have some female graduates over time). Our sister school is Spelman College, an all-female college diagonally across from Morehouse. Morehouse was founded on 14 February 1867, initially as Augusta Institute, at Springfield Baptist Church in Augusta, Ga., by the Rev. William Jefferson White, with the Rev. Richard C. Coulter and the Rev. Edmund Turney.

We were allowed to take courses at each other's schools.

Freshman Year

When I entered Morehouse in 1957, tuition was **$150** per year. If I made Dean's list, I could get tuition grants (of $75 a semester). Dr. Benjamin E. Mays gave me one or more tuition scholarships. Along with this, I had a student loan from Pickett & Hatchett to help fill in the gaps. This was a Columbus Georgia based organization. Contrast that to today's tuition of **$28,000.00-plus**, excluding fees. Of course, books and food cost considerably less as well when I was a student.

I first learned of the early admissions program sometime after I had arrived at Morehouse. This program allowed students to enroll in Morehouse before they graduated, some as early as the tenth grade. Although some of the students at Alfred E. Beach High, my high school, knew about the program, I was not made aware of it as far as I can remember. Nevertheless, I think I graduated higher in my class at Morehouse than any other student from Savannah had ranked before me. I was third overall, and the top science student.

The fear of flunking out was the greatest motivating factor for me. I did not want to let my parents down. Besides, I enjoyed learning new things.

Chemistry – My major. Dr. Henry C. McBay was Chairman of the Department. McBay's reputation was widely known as a very brilliant, but demanding teacher. Teaching the freshman class, he scared the hell out of us, by using the look to your left, your right, back and front tactic telling us that 3 of them would not finish with a chemistry major. To be sure, some of these students took freshman chemistry, but when I graduated in 1962, only 8 people graduated with a chemistry major. There were 125 students in the freshman chemistry class. Some took chemistry as a prerequisite for medical school or other professions. Dr. McBay also taught several other chemistry courses.

He was a genius, as were most of our other teachers. Our first lecture was on "The Particle In the Box" which enabled Dr. McBay to derive the equation for the behavior of ideal gases , i. e. PV = nRT Many years later, I glanced at Dr. Troy Story's rendition of the same lecture using more sophisticated mathematics. By this time, the math he used had become incomprehensible to me.

Troy had been a classmate, housemate, and close friend to the day of his passing on June 18, 2025. He had sent me birthday greetings 2 days before. Among other things, he made Dean Brazeal aware that I had been left out when, at graduation, he called out the names of the 4 top graduates in our class, but he had overlooked me. Dean Brazeal left us standing in front of the place where the top five graduates' photo would be taken, went back to his office, checked his records, and came back to announce that I was the 3rd highest ranking graduate in the class. I am forever grateful to Troy for urging me to ask Dean Brazeal to check his records.

Likewise, in his monumental Morehouse history, *A Candle in the Dark*, Professor Jones omitted me from the list of the top graduates, although he did mention that the University of California had awarded Troy and me teaching assistantships in chemistry.[31] He also did not

---

[31] A Candle in the Dark, A History of Morehouse College, p.226.

mention that I had graduated with high honors in chemistry and mathematics.[32] I do not hold that against him.

FIVE RANKING STUDENTS IN MOREHOUSE COLLEGE'S 1962 GRADUATING CLASS—Left to right: **Joseph J. Rodgers**, highest honors, with a grade point average of 3.97 (about A-), a French major who has been awarded a Woodrow Wilson Fellowship to Harvard University where he will study next year toward an advanced degree, having had to relinquish a Fulbright Grant to France (Rodgers has already studied for a year in France on a Merrill Scholarship) and a French Government assistantship to teach in a French lycee; **Clark H. Everett**, also highest honors, with a grade-point average of 3.80, an English major, who has been granted a Southern Education Foundation grant for study this summer and a Woodrow Wilson Fellowship of $1,600 plus tuition and fees, to study English in the Graduate School of the University of Wisconsin (both Everett and Rodgers achieved departmental honors in their respective departments, in addition to general honors); **Leroy Wilson, Jr.**, with a grade-point average of 3.60, who has accepted a $2,390 assistantship in chemistry (his major subject) at the University of California at Berkeley, after having had to turn down offers of assistantships from Pennsylvania State University, the University of Chicago, Highlands University of New Mexicoo — and a Southern Regional Woodrow Wilson Fellowship (Wilson graduated with double departmental honors in chemistry and mathematics); **Melvin Heard, Jr.**, with a grade-point average of 3.58 (with high honors and departmental honors in mathematics), who has accepted a half-time graduate assistantship of $2,300 at Purdue University, was forced to forego assistantships of $1,800 at Princeton University, Carnegie Tech, and the University of Michigan; and **Nathaniel E. Griffin**, with a grade-point average of 3.51, who has been awarded a research assistantship in mathematics for approximately $2,000 at New Highlands University in Las Vegas, New Mexico (during the summer Griffin, who also graduated with departmental honors in mathematics, will work as a forest ranger in Yellowstone National Park.

Rodgers is a native of Hopewell, Va.; Everett, of Blakeley, Ga.; Wilson, of Savannah, Ga., Heard, of Albany, Ga., and Griffin, of Tampa, Fla.

LEROY WILSON JR.
High Honor Graduate

Savannahian Graduates at Top of Class

Leroy Wilson Jr. of Savannah has graduated magna cum laude (with highest honors) from Morehouse College in Atlanta and plans to enter the University of California in September for work on his doctorate in physical chemistry.

The young graduate, whose four-year grade at Morehouse was 3.6 of a possible 4.00, was third in a class of 103. He earned a $2,390 teaching assistantship to begin work on his doctorate and had several other offers of scholarships. He also has qualified as an honorary Woodrow Wilson fellow after declining the Wilson followship.

Wilson was one of two men in the history of Morehouse College to receive honors in two departments, mathematics and chemistry. He is the son of Mr. and Mrs. Leroy Wilson, 1001 Richards St.

Left to right Joseph J. Rodgers (French), Valedictorian, Clark H. Everett (English), Salutatorian, Leroy Wilson Jr. (Chemistry), Melvin Heard, Jr. (Mathematics), Nathaniel Griffin (Mathematics).

Some years later, after earning his Ph.D. from the University of California at Berkeley, and after returning to Morehouse, Troy rose to become the Chairman of the Chemistry Department. Almost 60 years later, I could not comprehend the mathematics that my friend Troy was now using. I would be surprised if he would be using that level of mathematics in a freshman class and would expect to find this in a physical chemistry class. However, students at the time he was teaching had been better prepared.

[32] Id.

As I remember, I was not quite as well prepared in mathematics as I might have been. Dr. McBay would say often that mathematics was a language. This was one of my guiding principles. When I had to derive a formula, I would have a picture in my brain of what I wanted to say and using Dr. McBay's "first principles," I could come up with formula.

The other guiding principle was learning how to read English. In this respect, I think one of the reasons students have difficulty with solving problems in the physical sciences is because students do not understand the English (even where English is their first language), so that they are unable to create a picture in their minds of what the problem looks like.

In high school, my 10th grade English teacher, Ms. Esther Hardin, tried her best to teach us how to diagram sentences. I never quite mastered this discipline, but I managed to learn enough to help me solve my science problems.

This recalls how much I enjoyed all my classes, especially those in the physical sciences - chemistry, mathematics and physics. In chemistry, Dr. McBay graded us on the best 3 out of 4 test examination grades. He also gave us a lot of "pop" quizzes. Sometimes, I did not take the final examination, because I would have already earned an "A" for the course. Having made the "A" I took it easy and intended to watch the girls going to the library, except that all the girls were studying.

One of my proudest achievements was to win the first year General Physics Achievement Award. This award was a very thick reference book containing all kinds of scientific information, with my name emblazoned on the cover. I just like the way it looked. The award was a compilation of all kinds of scientific formulas, standards, physical constants and other scientific information. I was given the award as the top physics student of all those in the Atlanta University Center (4 colleges) who took this course. I loved physics and the discipline that the study forced upon me. There was nothing like the beauty in solving a complex physics problem.

I found that if I could draw a diagram of the description of the problem, I could get a picture in my head of what I was trying to do.

Many years later, after he had become a famous physicist, businessman, and educator, Dr. Walter Massey, who taught me freshman physics, did not remember me from that time. Oh, well!

Throughout my stay at Morehouse, I always had some kind of job earning a few dollars or credits. One was a work study program which allowed students to work and get credits against their college expenses. One of those was as library assistant. This job allowed me to study as well. In several of my courses, when I was assigned problems to solve at the end of a given chapter, I would sometimes read a book on the subject contained in that chapter and solve the problems in that book that I thought were pertinent or which looked interesting. This enabled me to learn how to solve problems from several different points of view.

During that first semester I also took physical education, freshman lectures, introduction to social science, humanities 1, English composition, and college algebra.

One of the things I learned from the social science class, which was taught by Mrs. Gladys Chivers, the wife of Professor Walter Chivers, both in the Social Science Department, was the importance of train schedules in the behavior of individuals. Up to that point in life I had no use for train schedules but somehow, I buried in my brain that I would need to remember how to use those schedules. Many years later (1974-1982), when I was working as a lawyer in Union Carbide's law department, at 270 Park Ave. in New York City, I carried a portable train schedule in my jacket pocket. Calculating the amount of time it took from my office to catch a certain train to go home was an important event in my life, as was the time to catch the train to get down to New York City and be on time for work.

During the second semester of my freshman year (now in 1958), I took courses in the history of appreciation of music, introduction to social science, trigonometry, English composition, physical education, freshman hygiene, general chemistry, and freshman lectures.

The first or second semester, I think Mr. Malthus taught the course in English composition. He was a very exacting taskmaster, but the most memorable experience that I had in that class was listening to a discussion between Joseph Rodgers and Mr. Malthus in terms of who was correct with respect to some obscure English rule that had come up with respect to the text of a paper that Joseph had submitted to Mr. Mathus. Joseph was telling Mr. Mathis that he simply would not tolerate a B, as Mr. Malthus had made a mistake on the point. Joseph won the argument, and Mr. Mathus changed his grade from a B to an A.

Joseph would later become the top-ranking student in our graduating class. I was third. I was the top-ranked natural sciences student.

I think I took algebra and trigonometry from Ms. Harriett S. Walton,[33] who was brilliant, and had a crisp, clean method of teaching.

Dr. Wendell Whalum taught my History of the Appreciation of Music class. He was Chairman of the Music Department and Fuller E. Callaway Professor of Music. The only thing that I remember about that class was his teaching us about a certain composition by Franz Joseph Haydn which required the right and left arms to extend fully to the right and left ends of the keyboard, while requiring at the same time playing a note in the middle of the keyboard. Wendell said that the problem was solved when Haydn or another musician played the key in the middle with his nose.

After I returned from my studies in Vienna in 1959-60, Wendell told me what a great thrill it had been for him to have been invited to play the magnificent pipe organ at St. Stefan's Dom (St. Stephen's Cathedral) in Vienna. The cathedral dominates the Vienna skyline.

I ended my first year at Morehouse with 5 As, 7Bs, and 2Ps (physical education)

---

[33] Later Dr. Harriett S. Walton. Dumas, Carrie, *Benjamin Elijah Mays – A Pictorial Life and Times,* Mercer University Press (2006), p. 147 .

Sophomore Year

In my sophomore year, first semester (Fall-Winter 1958), I took classes in general physics, analytical chemistry, analysis 1 (mathematics), humanities I, elementary German, and introductory sociology.

In the second semester (Winter-Spring1959), I took analytical chemistry, humanities II, general physics, analysis II (mathematics), introduction to sociology, and elementary German.

I wound up with 7As, 4Bs, and an "I," for the year.

I received the "I" for incomplete in the analytical chemistry course because I did not complete the limestone experiment, widely regarded as the most difficult of our experiments.

In one of the analytical chemistry courses, I was so confident in my experiment that the liquid we were to analyze was comprised solely of water, that I drank the sample in front of the class.

Of course, the physics, chemistry and mathematics courses were of the greatest interest to me.

It must have been around this time then I looked at some of the upperclassmen with great admiration seeing the slide rules hanging from their belts or in their hands. Little things matter. To me, that was the epitome of practical mathematics; however, shortly after I mastered the use of the slide rule, computers were coming into vogue. But I loved my slide rule and always thought my learning how to use it was a major accomplishment.

One night, when I was teaching chemistry to some of my colleagues in Sale Hall Annex, one of them called me "Bonehead." Over time it was shortened to "Bone," which I wrote in ink onto my slide rule carrying case and carried it with extraordinary pride. To this day, Troy, Marvin Anderson and Milford Greene call me Bone from time to time.

Some of my gifted classmates like Charles Meredith, Troy Story, James "Beatnik" Davis, Robert Allen, and Alfred Gilbert were also slide rule experts.

One of the brightest students in the class was James Williams, who now lives in Pensacola, Florida. James worked all night and showed up for class the next day, ready to discuss the analysis of any of our math or physics problems.

James Williams

Pop Dansby taught Analysis I-IV (4 semesters) which were all courses in Calculus , Trigonometry, and Analytic Geometry.

There was a rumor that President Mays wanted to hire a teacher with a Ph.D. in Mathematics at Morehouse, so he contacted his Alma Mater (Univ. of Chicago); they wrote back and said that Morehouse already had the best mathematics teacher they had - Pop Dansby, even without a Ph.D.

There was one problem that he gave us in calculus that I don't think anyone solved.[34] It had to do with a liquid flowing through a bottle

---

[34] Maybe Billy Joe, James or Herbert knows.

container of some kind. Like the Particle In a Box in chemistry, there was a name for this calculus problem, but I have forgotten it.

Merrill Fellowship

During my freshman year we were all required to attend "Chapel" in Sale Hall, to listen to speeches by famous people of all types, including students. Tuesdays were always special because that is when Dr. Mays delivered the address. Invariably, it would be related to a theme of our duty to help our people, and to advocate for justice. One of those student speakers was Sam Allen, an English major, as I recall. Sam was introduced to us in Chapel as a Merrill Scholar. Here I was, sitting in the audience, listening to a live Merrill Scholar.

Sam was so eloquent. I wanted to be like him.

Already pushed by my determination to excel and not to embarrass my family and those who supported me, I was now turbocharged to dare to hope that I could qualify as a Merrill fellow. Charles Merrill Jr.,[35] then the Chairman of the Morehouse Board of Trustees, made these fellowships available to enable black students to travel, study and learn about people in other parts of the world, something that white students do from family resources or from resources not available to blacks otherwise.

At the time, Mr. Merrill, Jr was also Chairman of Merrill Lynch. Dr. Mays had secured Merrill, Jr.'s financial expertise and funding, as part of a group of funders to increase Morehouse's Endowment. [36]

Many years later, I would learn that the fellowships were also intended to spur black students into a career in the foreign service. I did not know that at the time. Since that time, however, I have become more involved in foreign affairs and have developed somewhat of a reputation as a people-to-people international Africa expert. Since

---

[35] The son of the Merrill in Merrill Lynch Fenner and Smith.

[36] I am not sure who started it, but Morehouse has followed a practice of attracting to its Board of Trustees individuals who are experts in their fields. Mays certainly continued it.

2016, I have been a resident of Botswana, after visiting the country numerous times since 2004. I am also becoming more active in my relations with people in southern, western, and eastern Africa.

This is how it happened. One day when I was doing an experiment in the lab, I was called into a meeting chaired by Dr. Melvin Kennedy, Chairman of the history department. I am not sure what kind of notice I received concerning the purpose of the meeting, but when I got there, I discovered that they were going to select the 1959-1960 Merrill Fellows at the meeting. Dr. Kennedy called off the names of the first 5 and I felt a keen sense of deep disappointment, but then, as if by a miracle, I heard Dr. Kennedy call my name as the 6th Merrill Scholar. I was thrilled beyond measure, but I had to get back to the lab or whatever else I was studying. I am not sure how I contacted my parents, but they were overjoyed for me.

Shortly after the announcement appeared in the local Savannah newspapers, which usually covered stories about white people, my father took me along with him to the bank. I did not know why he was taking me, but when we arrived, I learned that he wanted to take out a small school loan for me of some kind. During his conversation with the bank officer, my father reached into his pocket and pulled out his wallet, which contained a copy of the newspaper announcement of my selection as a Merrill Fellow - to help convince the officer to make the loan. He read the article. My father got the loan. I had no idea that he was carrying this article around with him, in his wallet. I was extremely humbled by that gesture and will never forget it.

There had been some uncertainty as to whether I would be even considered because by the time of the selection, I had become a young father. I think I had thought that the committee did not consider a candidate the year before because he was a young father. Nonetheless, the question never came up and I was selected.

The 6 selected at that time received travel study awards of about $3,000 each.

THE SIX 1959-1960 MERRILL EUROPEAN TRAVEL-STUDY AWARD WINNERS

Left to right: Joseph J. Rodgers, Nelson K. McMillan, Ashton G. Ward, Jasper C. Register, Leroy Wilson, James W. Compton.

The announcement read substantially as follows: "**JAMES W. COMPTON**, age 20, a junior from Aurora, Illinois, where he graduated from the East High School. Compton planned to major in history with a minor in education and political science. He planned a career in teaching or foreign service. At the time he proposed to study in England and/or France, **NELSON K. McMILLAN**, an 18-year-old senior and an early admission student from Monroe High School in Albany, Georgia, who majored in mathematics and minoring in German. He is currently looking forward to language teaching as a profession. He plans to study in Austria; **JASPER C. REGISTER**, 22, a senior and a graduate of Dasher High School in Valdosta, Georgia. His major is sociology and his minor is religion. He has chosen the ministry as a profession. He will probably study in Germany or France; **JOSEPH J. RODGERS**, 18, sophomore, a graduate of the J. E. J. Moore High School, Richmond, Virginia, who has a major in French and a minor in education and English. Rodgers plans to teach. He will study in France; **ASHTON G. WARD,** 17, a sophomore and a graduate of Westside High School in Chadbourne, N.C. Ward is a chemistry major with a minor in mathematics. He plans to become an industrial chemist. He expects to study in Germany; **LEROY WILSON**, 19, a sophomore, who got his secondary training at Beach High School in Savannah, Georgia. He has a major in chemistry and a minor in mathematics; and he plans a career in teaching or industrial chemistry. He, too, will probably study in Germany."

Also going to Europe with us was **JOSEPH PATTERSON**, 20, a senior from Brunswick, Georgia, where he attended Risley High School, and a chemistry major with a minor in mathematics, with the intention of becoming a research chemist. Patterson was selected as one of the six men last year to travel and study in Europe during the current year, but unforeseen circumstances prevented him from doing so; and the administration arranged for him to go with us.

Local Youth Receives Merrill Travel Award

Leroy Wilson, Jr. of 1011 Richards Street, received one of six Merrill Awards to travel and study in Europe during the academic year of 1959-60.

The awards are made possible by Charles E. Merrill, Jr., of the New York brokerage firm of Merrill, Luncy, Pearce, Fenner and Beane. Mr. Merrill is the present chairman of the Morehouse College board of trustees.

Awardees are selected by a faculty committee of Morehouse College on the basis of scholarship, personality traits, and campus citizenship records.

Mr. Wilson is the son of Mrs. and Mrs. Leroy Wilson, Sr., and a sophomore at Morehouse College majoring in chemistry and minoring in mathematics. The other recepients of the award are.

Joseph C. Register, 22, of Valdosta, Georgia; James W. Compton, 20, of Auroro, Illinois; Nelson K. McMillan, 18, of Albany, Georgia; Joseph J. Rogers, 18, of Richmond, Virginia and Ashton G. Ward, 17, of Chadbourne, North Carolina.

The Savannah Herald announcement that I had been awarded a Morehouse Merrill Fellowship

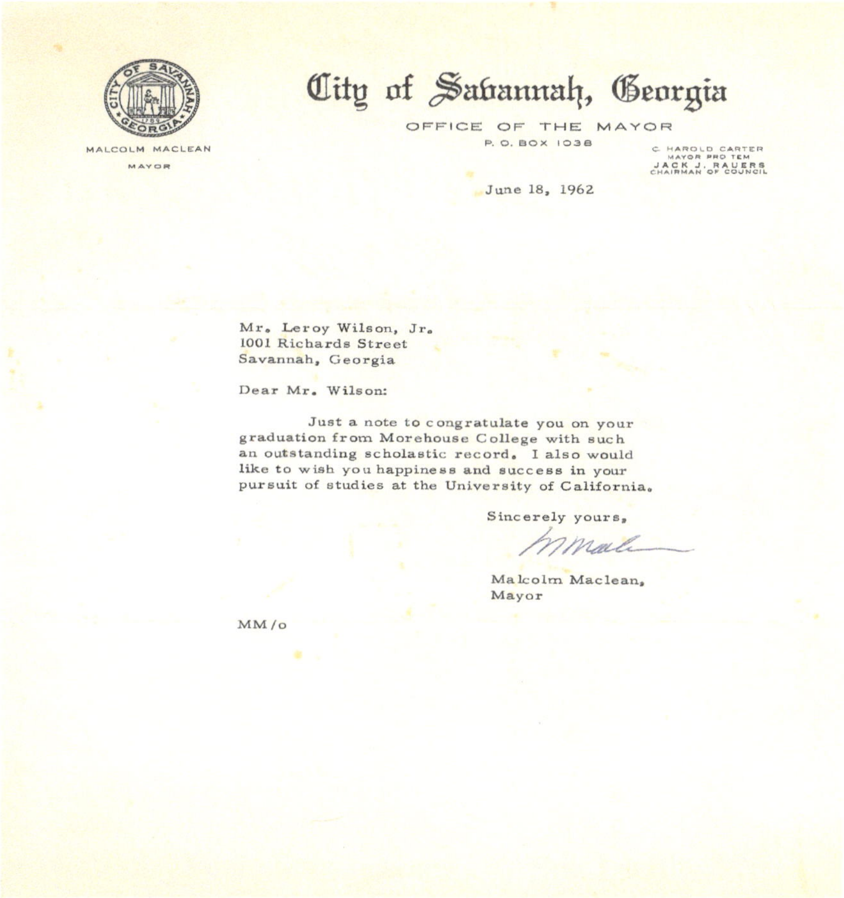
City of Savannah, Georgia

OFFICE OF THE MAYOR

P. O. BOX 1038

MALCOLM MACLEAN
MAYOR

C. HAROLD CARTER
MAYOR PRO TEM
JACK J. RAUERS
CHAIRMAN OF COUNCIL

June 18, 1962

Mr. Leroy Wilson, Jr.
1001 Richards Street
Savannah, Georgia

Dear Mr. Wilson:

Just a note to congratulate you on your graduation from Morehouse College with such an outstanding scholastic record. I also would like to wish you happiness and success in your pursuit of studies at the University of California.

Sincerely yours,

Malcolm Maclean,
Mayor

MM/o

Mayor of Savannah's letter of congratulations on graduation at top of class.

Thank goodness that I had studied elementary German for two semesters.

Itinerary On the Way to Vienna, Austria and Rest of Europe

My first passport was issued 30 March 1959.

Fortunately, I had saved all my passports and therefore, I have a record of where I was when.

On our outward-bound ship, the S.S. Amsterdam/Rotterdam, as I remember, about 4 or 5 Morehouse Merrill Fellows were on board. Ashton and Nelson were two of them. I think Joe Patterson was also on board. There was also a fellow from Detroit - not from Morehouse- who had discovered where the bakery was.. However, every morning at about 4 AM, he would go down and get us some delicious fresh rolls and other baked goods. I have no idea how he found out where the bakery was. He also travelled lightly. When I asked him why, he said that he would buy clothes as he needed them.

We first stopped in Boston but did not get off the ship. The trip across the Atlantic ocean took about seven days. What a beautiful boat ride! I was thrilled at some meals when the ship would roll with the waves. One minute I saw sky; the next minute, I saw the ocean. It was a bit too much for Nelson, who obligingly threw up from motion sickness.

31 August 1959 Ireland and England

We landed in Cobh, Ireland on 31 August 1959, where we were met by a very strange language (Gaelic) and English, several people stopped to stare at what one little boy described as "a full-grown black man." We were novelties to some people. Gene (Ashton) Ward and I made our way up to Trinity College in Dublin to visit Prof. Ernest Thomas Sinton Walton, who had been one of the distinguished visitors to Morehouse College whom we had met when he visited. He was the first Nobel Prize winner for physics that I had met. He was an Irish physicist and co-recipient, with Sir John Douglas Cockcroft of England, of the 1951 Nobel Prize for Physics for the development of the first nuclear particle accelerator, known as the Cockcroft-Walton generator. He graciously received us, answered our questions, and showed us some of the work he was doing at the time (1959). I was honored by the time he spent with us.

Growing up in West Savannah, Georgia, i could have hardly imagined that one day I would meet a Nobel prize winner, let alone, study chemistry and physics from two others while I was a student at Berkeley.

Fearing that we would need to refer to our chemistry, math and physics books while we were in Vienna, I had loaded mine in a footlocker, which proved something of a challenge when the place we stayed in in Dublin was a 5-story walkup. The books were heavy. We didn't have Google in those days, and I felt I might need these books for references.

Overall, our stay was pleasant and all the people we met were kind and helpful. I don't recall knowing anything about "The Trouble" between the Protestants and Catholics at that time.

We travelled from Ireland to England by boat, arriving 16 September 1959 in Harwich. We made our way to London where I was fascinated by the number of people riding bicycles.

I spent four days out of London, sightseeing famous places that I had read or heard about: Canterbury Cathedral, where Thomas – a -

Becket was murdered by order of King Henry II, for becoming more priestly than the priest.[37] Before, they had been very close friends before the King had appointed him archbishop; Stratford on Avon, home of Willliam Shakespeare, where I was privileged to sit in a too - close - to - the stage in the front row seats. I witnessed one of the last performances of Paul Robeson, the great scholar, actor, all American football player (from Rutgers University), peace and civil rights advocate, and one of my heroes. He portrayed Othello;[38] Peggy Ashcroft played Desdemona.

Our visit to Winchester Cathedral added more history; the Germans did not bomb it because that is where they had planned to crown Adolf Hitler if they had won the war.

After being used to seeing black men as military men, scores of people were surprised to learn that we were students, studying and travelling on scholarships at that. This travel was taking place after the showdown between Dwight D. Eisenhower, as President of the United States, and Orval Faubus, Governor of Arkansas.

Orval Eugene Faubus was an American politician who served as the 36th Governor of Arkansas from 1955 to 1967. He is most famously known for his role in the Little Rock Crisis of 1957, where he ordered the Arkansas National Guard to prevent nine African

---

[37] The assassination of Thomas Becket in Canterbury Cathedral on 29 December 1170 changed the course of history. Becket was one of the most powerful figures of his time, serving as royal Chancellor and later as Archbishop of Canterbury. Initially a close friend of King Henry II, the two men became engaged in a bitter dispute that culminated in Becket's shocking murder by knights with close ties to the king. It is a story of betrayal, of the perceived abuse of power and those who fall for standing in the way of the Crown. Here we explore Becket's rise and fall, and unpick the events that led to the murder that shook the Middle Ages...https://www.britishmuseum.org/blog/thomas-becket-murder-shook-middle-ages (Accessed 27 December 2023)

[38]"It's 60 years ago, in April 1959, that one of the most momentous events in the history of the theatre in Stratford-upon-Avon took place. Paul Robeson, the great American singer and actor, became the first black Othello in Shakespeare's town in the twentieth century." https://theshakespeareblog.com/2019/04/stratford-upon-avons-first-black-othellos/ (Accessed 27 December 2023)

American students, known as the Little Rock Nine, from entering Little Rock Central High School. This action was in defiance of the U.S. Supreme Court's decision in Brown v. Board of Education, which declared segregation in public schools unconstitutional.[39]

Faubus's actions drew national attention and led to President Dwight D. Eisenhower sending federal troops to enforce the court's ruling.[40] The troops were there to protect the young black students from the hostile crowd.

Eisenhower was pressed to demonstrate the supremacy of federal power. The civil rights movement was in full swing at the time, so people were naturally curious to talk to us. American whites wanted to know from us 20-year-olds if blacks wanted to marry whites and whether we really wanted integration. We engaged them in civil conversation.

After the election of Donald R. Trump in 2024, he and his government are trying their best to revert education policy to the states, with no federal standards or support. Black people did not fare well when education policy was left to the states before the civil rights movement and Brown v. Board of Education decisions in 1954 and 1955.

We face a very uncertain future if they succeed.

September 1959 The Netherlands

I am not sure but would guess that we arrived in the Netherlands in September 1959.

Rotterdam had been called an open-air museum. Many of the city center buildings had been destroyed during WWII; several were newly rebuilt, among them the Rijn Hotel and the YMCA. We were surprised to be asked to join Queen Juliana for the opening of the new YMCA.

---

39 https://en.wikipedia.org/wiki/Orval_Faubus?form=MG0AV3 (Accessed 07 NOV 2024)

40 https://www.britannica.com/biography/Orval-Eugene-Faubus

The first time I had met royalty of any kind, but her, being royalty and all, treated us nicely and warmly.

The Germans had bombed and destroyed thousands of homes and stores, many warehouses and other structures. This destruction was symbolized by "The Destroyed City" bronze sculpture which shows a man with a hole where his heart was supposed to be, symbolizing Rotterdam without its historic heart. The sculpture was created by the Russian- born artist Ossip Zadkine. It was quite an impressive sight.

At the time, Rotterdam boasted the most state – of – the – art seaport.

As I travelled throughout Europe on my way to Vienna, I kept notes and otherwise reported on my travels to The Herald, our local black newspaper in Savannah. My accounts follow.

Amsterdam held many surprises for us, including a "red light" district where women earned their living sex workers. They were on display in the windows, of assorted sizes and shapes, but all white. Some were naked. The same is true today. This was their way to earn a living.

On the cultural side, we visited the famous Rijks Museum, where we saw the world's largest collection of Rembrandts, Vermeers and Halls (?). Of course, we spent a few minutes looking at Rembrandt's famous "Night Watch" painting. This painting was revolutionary at the times because his use of light and shadow gave the illusion of a 3-dimension painting.

At the time, we learned that the Netherlands had an extraordinarily strong economy but there was a severe housing shortage. This caused them to drain water from huge lakes, which enabled them to build houses on the bottoms of the drained lakes.

22 September 1959 Belgium

We arrived in Belgium on 22 September 1959 at Wuustwezel. Of all the places we visited in Belgium, Bruges impressed me the most. At the time, I wrote that some of the Gothic architecture and older buildings, when combined with the many canals, narrow streets and night lights combined to make this a beautiful, enchanted city.

September 24, 1959, France

The first thing that impressed me about Paris is that it was rainy and overcast, like London was supposed to be, and London had been sunny and bright, like Paris was supposed to be. I think we arrived in France on 24 September 1959 (Surete Natle. R.G. Halluin -Route)

At the time, France was dealing with two significant issues - the war in Algeria and American foreign policy. I did not know too much about the second one of these, but I was somewhat familiar with the war in Algeria, At the time Gen. Charles DeGaulle was the towering French military figure.

On this visit, the Parisians seemed rather unfriendly. It could have been because of the American/French foreign policy issues. However, the fact that I had not studied French also contributed to the lack of communications. I learned that the French were proud of their language and decided that upon my return I would take some courses in French. I managed one semester. I was not able to take any further courses because I had to finish my analytical chemistry course. The analytical chemistry schedule conflicted with the French course.

When I visited France in 1989/90 with my late wife Jane the people were much more friendly and helpful. We had traveled to Cannes and Paris, France to honor an invitation that had been extended to us by Madam Celine Tabary. She was a client of mine, and we spent a considerable amount of time with her in Cannes and Cabris. She was the fiduciary and sole distributee of her husband's estate. We discuss this further when we discuss some cases that I handled later in this book (Estate of Maurice Eugene Tabary).

Jane had studied French and knew some, so, one day when we were standing before an imposing monument and I was trying to make out the French language description on the monument, Jane was rattling off what it said. Little did I know that her side of the monument displayed the description in English.

Of course we visited the well-known sights of Notre Dame, the famous Shakespeare & Co. bookstore, the Eiffel Tower, the Louvre, Sacré-Cœur Basilica, Hôtel de Ville, the Pantheon, Versailles, the Jeu de Paume museum, the Arch d'Triomphe, and strolled along the Champs de Elysee, and many other famous sites in Paris.[41] At the Jeu de Paume, I viewed works by some of the greatest impressionists: Degas, Renoir, Pissaro, Monet, Manet, Gauguin and others.

We also listened to some fabulous jazz at Le Petit Journal.

At the Louvre, we did spend some time watching the Mona Lisa. I noticed that in some places, there were artists painting copies of famous paintings. At that time, I think Mr. Pei's pyramid entrance had not been installed as the entrance to the Louvre. In later years, I discovered how his pyramid bathed the entrance with sunlight as one descended the stairs to the entrance of the Louvre. I had read about the entrance before I saw it and wondered what all the fuss was about. Now I saw it.

The pyramid did not disappoint.

I also saw the shroud of Turin on display in the Church of the Sacred Heart ("Sacre Cour"). There is an imprint or outline on the shroud which some have said is the face of Jesus. I don't know what the status is now. Many years after my student days, in about 1989/90 Jane and I had seen the church from what appeared to us to be a short distance at the time. It was at night, and the church was bathed in light. We took off on foot to walk to the church. It was much longer than we had expected, and the climb from the ground up the stairs was no joke.

---

[41] https://dreamsinparis.com/famous-buildings-in-paris/ (Accessed 17 March 2025)

Germany

I am not sure when Ashton and I arrived in Germany, but here we were able to practice some of our German.

We were now young men in the land of Kant, Schiller, Heine, Marx, Goethe, Planck, Einstein, Hitler, and World Wars I and II.

We were greeted with architecture that was quite different from what we knew at home. In the City of Trier, we saw an enormous Middle Ages bathhouse, which could accommodate 2,500 patrons at the time. We understood that this is where a lot of socializing took place. The bathhouse was heated by means of steam that had been created within huge coliseum structures. The steam under the water was 15-20 feet beneath the floors of the bathhouse and in this way, the bathhouse was heated.

We visited Bad Godesberg, the Bonn suburb where Chancellor Conrad Adenauer lived. In Bonn itself, we visited the Bundestag (Parliament) along with some 92 other students, where we heard a lecture on how the German government functioned. After having lunch there, we returned to Bad Godesberg, to prepare to leave for Heidelburg, by way of Cologne. (I think by this time, we must have met up with the American students who would be joining us at the Institute for European Studies in Vienna, our destination).

In Cologne, we visited another in the long chain of cathedrals we would visit on this trip. From Cologne, where we visited the cathedral, we took a boat ride down the Rhine river and were treated on board by a group of German travelers with the Song of the Lorelei.

The Lorelei itself is a collection of cliffs overlooking the river. The beauty of this river is augmented by the mountains, cliffs and castles rising on either side. The story is told of a beautiful maiden who combed her hair and exchanged waves with the sailors returning from battle. Savannah, Georgia also has a similar story with a statue of a waving maiden overlooking the Savannah River; however, at the time, this was the first I had heard of this kind of story, The Lorelei Song itself is quite beautiful.

After a brief stopover in Heidelburg, we made our way to the beautiful city of Rothenburg. In 1593, Field Marshall Tilley, under orders from his emperor, was ordered to take the town. He did so, and the population dropped to its knees to beg for their freedom. Tilley wanted some wine, and the townspeople accommodated him with a 3- and 1/4-liter pitcher to drink. Realizing that he could not finish, he promised the townspeople that he would free them if there was someone who could drink the 3 and 1/4 liters without taking the pitcher from his mouth. One Georges Nusch took the challenge, drank the wine without taking it from his lips and Tilley freed the townspeople.

As distinguished guests, we were given the same challenge. None of us could replicate what Nusch had done, although we tried. At the time, we were college aged students. At lunch, our hosts placed a bottle of wine on the table between each of two of us. Not being used to wine with lunch, a bunch of us got very sleepy. Fortunately, there was a nice hill with soft grass which served as my bed for a short, blissful nap.

We left Heidelburg for Munich. I think we were travelling by bus.

Having arrived in Munich, the Hofbrau House in Munich was impressive. This beer hall and restaurant was 3 stories high and occupied almost one full block. A liter of beer cost 30 cents.

At that time, the Germans in Munich seemed to be friendlier than the French in Paris. they were very patient as I flipped through my dictionary to try to construct a sentence. I had asked one clerk in German, if they had American cigarettes. She replied in perfect English, saying that they did not - the American cigarettes were too expensive for them to carry.

I distinctly remember at one point being on a bus in Switzerland high up in the mountains. I looked down, and I could not see the road beneath the bus. We were on the edge of the road.

Austria

Although we passed through Salzburg, Vienna was our destination. It was to be our home for the next academic year. At the time, Vienna had the reputation of being the cultural center of Europe, by virtue of fusing together so many diverse cultures from surrounding countries. It was a link between East and West.

Ashton and I studied at the Institute of European Studies/University of Vienna in Austria. Dr. McBay, my chemistry professor, had wanted me to study at the University of Heidelberg in Germany, but they required Latin as a prerequisite, which I had not studied. Dr. Christiansen, our physics professor, wanted me to study in Russia. I did not like this idea, because I had not studied Russian and from what I understood, it got very cold in Russia, a foreboding invitation for a young man from the sunny south of Georgia.

We joined a group of 85-90 other American students who were to be the group that would study at University of Vienna/Institute for European Studies for the upcoming academic year and travel throughout Europe. Ashton and I were roommates in Vienna.

This was the first time that I had dated a girl of a different race. She was American, part of our travel-study group. There were no African American girls in the group of American students of which we were a part; in fact, Gene and I were the only two black people in the group. German speakers often referred to us as die Beiden Herren (the two gentlemen).

I doubt if we saw more than 6 black people in the everyday population Vienna, while we were there.

Most of the students studied political science. There were a few who studied math, and I think Gene and I were the only ones with chemistry and math as our main disciplines. The two math students were from Boston College. I think they were Herb and Dan.

As best as I can remember, we arrived at the Institute of European Studies (IES) in Vienna, where we received our initial orientation. We met Anna Lisa Weismeyer, from Denmark, Uncle Andy from Hungary. We already knew Herr Fink (who conducted the history lectures on a lot of our tours across Europe). All the staff were supportive and took exceptionally good care of all of us.

In Vienna, Gene and I roomed with a wonderful Austrian family - Herr Hubert and Frau Heidi Reitler and their two young sons (Johannes and Harry) at 34/8 Gumpendorferstrasse in Vienna.

Reitler Family - Much later photo – years later.

We entered the building and walked to our apartment (not sure which floor).

This gave us a chance to speak German at home, although both of them were fluent in English. After having full breakfasts in Ireland and England, I was excitedly looking forward to the "continental breakfast."

We discovered that continental breakfast was basically some rolls and coffee. You can imagine how I thought I was going to starve to death after eating the full breakfast. Of course, we also ate some full breakfasts at the Reitlers. One morning, Frau Heidi Reitler fooled me. From time to time, she had asked me if I wanted to eat some Gehirn (brains). What! No! So, one morning she served me these delicious tasting eggs with something mixed in. You guessed it - brains. Not bad tasting. A new learning experience.

Our hosts spoke perfect English, helped us with our German and in general made us feel welcomed and at home. One feature that I noticed was the high-ceilinged lights burned only small wattage bulbs. I understood that this was a conservation holdover from World War II when Viennese had to conserve energy.

Breakfast was generally a continental breakfast, consisting of freshly baked rolls and breakfast coffee. The bakery was right downstairs from where we lived at 34/8 Gumpendorferstrasse. Frau Reitler would go down and fetch the rolls. We also ate eggs on a regular basis.

We usually ate lunch at school, as I remember. We had a variety of foods for dinner, although potatoes found their way into many meals. To this day, I have a fondness for Weiner schnitzel, what appeared to be a fried breaded veal cutlet. Succulent. Of course, there were the usual sausages.

Vienna is a city blessed with great natural beauty. It is surrounded by the Ring, a circular train railway that transits around the city and links several streets around the city, like the spokes of a bicycle wheel.

The Staatsoper or Opera House is in the center of the Ring. At the time, there were 26 kinds of museums, lots of theatres, palaces, cathedrals and parks. One of the most famous cathedrals is St. Stefensdom, or St. Stephens cathedral, which houses one of the most famous pipe organs in the world. Sometime later, after I had returned to Morehouse, Wendell Whalum, who had been one of the great music professors at Morehouse, told me what a wonderful experience he had when he was invited to play, and did play that pipe organ.

The Staatsoper was the only place in Vienna where I found a banana split. Expensive in 1959 at $5.00 a serving.

By the time we arrived in Vienna, we had already traveled through 8 countries -Ireland, England, France, Belgium, Holland, Luxembourg, Switzerland, Germany and Austria. I would follow these visits throughout the academic year by trips to former Yugoslavia, Hungary, and Greece.

We traveled to Hungary after the Iron Curtain was lifted. At the time my passport was issued, there was a big, imprinted stamp that read "This Passport Is Not Valid for Travel in Hungary." However, there was a big red stamp over this notice which read "VOID."

It was also not valid for travel "to the following areas under control of authorities with which the United States does not have diplomatic relations : Albania, Bulgaria (crossed out), and those portions of China, Korea, and Viet-Nam under communist control.

It contained a red ink stamped notice saying that it was valid for travel to and in Bulgaria.

Studies at Institute of European Studies/University of Vienna.

Morehouse had enrolled Ashton and me in a joint University of Vienna/Institute of European Studies ("IES") program where some of our classes would be taught in English and German at the Institute and German at the University. They would cover the 1959-60 academic year.

IES was headquartered in Neuer Markt Platz in Vienna. I don't remember, but I think most of our IES courses were taught in the same building. The University of Vienna courses were taught on the University campus. During the winter Semester, I studied European Art, Ontology, Principles and Instruments of Psychological Testing, Clinical Psychology, German and Beginning Russian (which Dr. Krutschera taught in the German language at 7 am, at the IES facility) and Theory of Functions I (at the University). Professor Hlawka, who taught this course, later taught at the Princeton Institute for Advanced Studies.

Many years later when I was a student at Berkeley, I met Anne Feder (who married Chung (Lee later) whose grandfather, Hans Kelsen, was the principal drafter of the Austrian Constitution. Kelsen's legacy extends far beyond Austria. His legal theories shaped constitutional jurisprudence across Europe and Latin America, and his work remains foundational in international law and legal philosophy.[42] I later read some of his brilliant essays, although I cannot remember if I agreed with what he had written.

In October 2021, Anne and her son Geoffrey represented the family in Vienna, Austria at the celebration of the 100th anniversary of its Federal Constitution and the 140th birthday of Hans Kelsen, the principal architect of that Constitution.

I thought all my professors were brilliant. I had the good fortune of learning from brilliant professors at Morehouse, IES/University of Vienna, and the University of California at Berkeley in chemistry, mathematics, physics, humanities, social science, and in law.

In higher mathematics, Prof. Hlawka arrived at the classroom and begin writing on one of the 4 or 5 whiteboards which slid up and down. One of the most scintillating examples of his brilliance was to substitute "Q" for all the mathematical symbols on one of the huge boards, continue with his writing, and then after he had filled that board with more symbols and continued to the next, he arrived at a board where he substituted "Q" back in. The net effect was to cause several of the symbols in the equation to be deleted. Remarkable!

He was later invited to join the faculty of Advanced Studies in Princeton, where Albert Einstein had also been a member.

It was a thrill to study in a foreign language, even more so to be taught Russian using the German language at 7:00 A.M.!

For the Spring Semester, I studied Intermediate Russian, two German language courses and Epistemology (at IES), and Theory of Functions II, Differential and Integral Calculus II, Inorganic chemistry of metals, and analytical geometry II (at the University).

For the 1959-60 academic year in Vienna, I earned 5As, 1B and 1C (the only C on my total undergraduate record). I took 4 courses for no credit.

[42] From my conversations with Anne, and access to CoPilot 26 October 2025.

I was struck by the Austrians reliance on first principles to solve problems, For example, in chemistry, the students performed experiments with chemicals instead of using machines for analysis. To be sure, we did the same thing at Morehouse, but not as much. I remember in a math class being fascinated by what one professor did with algebra.

One weekend, I was listening to a discussion on the radio about the lack of interaction between the Austrian students and foreign students. That program had the desired effect because on Monday, when I returned to the University, curious students swamped me. One of the delightful problems that they had was trying to figure out where I was from. This is because there are so many-colored people from various places in the world. One of these students was a young woman - Heidi - who graciously helped me practice my German and took me to see some of the places in Austria.

I had been hesitant to speak German because I was not sure I would say the right thing. I could read and understand long before I felt comfortable speaking .Then, one night, we went to a wine cellar in Grinzing, on the outskirts of Vienna. The wine was enough to loosen my tongue. From that night forward, I was not afraid to speak.

We had a month-long semester break in January/February 1960.

Ashton and I decided to travel during this school break.

January 1960 Yugoslavia

We arrived in former Yugoslavia with a scene of very few cars on the streets. I think this was the first time I had seen Russian built automobiles. When we got off the train in Belgrade, former Yugoslavia, I remember walking through the train station doors only to be greeted by 2 AK-47s across my chest by soldiers on either side of me. They removed the weapons immediately as they saw that we were not from whatever groups they were guarding the station against.

At the time, the city appeared grey and grim. Somehow., I wound up in a private residence headed by an Italian family. There was a boy in the house about seventeen years old. He spoke Italian, Yugoslavian and English. He was pretty much like us, enjoying things American, but especially jazz, rock, and roll. He told me that at that time students were required to select their vocations after the eighth school year, and that the government pays for their education for the chosen vocation. After listening to Harry Belafonte and Elvis, I took a walk, winding up at three museums or historical sites.

The second site was a park built around military armaments, one of which was a Nazi airplane, still kissing Mother Earth as it had in WWII. There was an overturned tank, anti-aircraft guns, and other weapons of American, Soviet, Italian and Spanish origin, on display.

As I walked back towards the center of town, I saw for the first time people who had been described in literature as peasants, very poorly dressed in rags for clothes, and shoes that looked like they had withstood many generations of wear. There were some children who appeared ill-fed and ill-clothed but like children everywhere, had joyous laughter about them as they played and teased each other along their journey.

As I continued to travel over the next few decades, I learned that all children everywhere had that spark within them to find happiness with whatever games, stories instruments, tires or toys might be available to them. Happy laughter filled the air.

We see this scene playing out now in the tragedies in Sudan, Haiti, Gaza, and the many miserable refugee camps in Africa and the middle East. How I wish we could eliminate poverty, lust for power, and man-made hatred.

Several Yugoslavians lamented the fact that I had not visited in summer; they said that things and appearances now were drab, but I should see the place in summer. Later in life, I observed that this mindset was also true in other countries, Uganda in 1979 being the prime example (but Uganda looked beautiful to my untutored and inexperienced eyes.)

February,1960 Greece

During our vacation break, Gene and I had intended to travel to Israel, but couldn't work it out, so we went to Greece instead. We traveled down through former Yugoslavia and visited Thessaloniki as the first Greek city. Athens greeted us with its vast collection of historical buildings. Of course, we visited them all.

At the time, I was still interested in architecture and learned that there was an agropics institute in Athens. As I understood it at the time, this institute studied the relationship between architecture and people living in buildings. I enjoyed that visit but lost my primary interest in architecture over time.

In Athens, Ashton and I met Peter Mejas, an American of Greek descent. Pete taught us a few words of Greek, and I thought that it was him who took us to visit a Greek family for tea which included figs and honey. We had some fun among some of the Greek population as Pete would say something in Greek, which required us to respond yes or no in Greek. the Greeks were puzzled because when they asked us or Pete where we were from Peter would say the "Peloponnesian" islands. Of course, this made no sense to the Greeks because the people from those islands were very fair skinned, not African. Many years later, in one of his speeches, President Reagan would refer to a Peter Mejas who was somehow responsible for giving President Reagan the "Shining City on the Hill" slogan. I do not know if he was the same person.

When I returned to Austria from this vacation break, my landlord or landlady (Frau Heidi and Herr Herbert Reitler) told me that the American Embassy had contacted them looking for me and that I should visit their offices upon return. I couldn't imagine what kind of trouble I was in. When I went to the Embassy, they told me that my dear mother had contacted them and that she was worried because she had not heard from me. She was concerned because there was a great controversy about the political situation in Berlin and she did not know where I was. What had happened is that I had written a letter to my parents to tell them I was going to Greece and other countries during the break, but I had left it in my suit jacket pocket and had forgotten to mail it to them. Whew, on both ends!

May 1960 - Hungary

Our group traveled to Hungary not long after the US lifted its ban on travel to Hungary. At the time it was issued, my passport had carried a stamp or legend saying that it was not valid for travel in Hungary, and Bulgaria (later lifted), and the "following areas under control of authorities with which the United States does not have diplomatic relations: Albania and those portions of China, Korea and Viet-Nam under Communist control."

Although Gary Powers's U-2 reconnaissance airplane had been shot down on May1, 1960 over the Soviet Union and had caused great embarrassment for the United States, a few days before we visited Hungary, I detected no animosity or tensions between our group and the Hungarians. Powers was captured, sentenced to prison for espionage, but was released two years after conviction in a prisoner exchange for Soviet officer Rudolf Abel. We spent a few hours with some Hungarian students talking about a wide variety of topics, among them, the Powers incident. It became apparent that they knew a lot about this incident. This was in marked contrast to what we knew at the time because the US government had been trying to cover up the incident.

However, we were in store for a bit of embarrassment ourselves when the Hungarian students demonstrated a broad and in-depth knowledge of American heroes; we did not know very much about theirs. I remember that one of them was named Kossuth.

With the advent of Google AI and social media, students should try to learn as much as they can before they visit a country. As I remember, there was no tension in the room. Helped along with vodka and strong cigarettes of the level of Gauloises French cigarettes.

I was anxious to learn what the Austrians thought about the position of the United States and the west during the Hungarian crises. When we returned to Austria, I discussed this issue with my very erudite landlord and his equally erudite wife and learned that they were so close to the situation that it was impossible to be objective. It seemed to them that the west stayed out because of commercial interests while the communists launched a cold-bloodied attack to crush the revolutionaries in Hungary. The Austrians were more concerned about the political and humanitarian aspects of the revolution.

Herr Reitler told me about the large number of refugees who had escaped into Austria and how they were received, saying that within the first 24 hours of the revolution, in Vienna alone, the Austrians had given 400 automobiles, trucks, 50,000 gallons of petrol (gasoline), 150 tons of food, 15,000 articles of clothing, shoes underwear and so forth, and about two tons of medicine and bandages to them. Six- and seven-year-old children came to the refugee office to help. Old people with only $20 monthly income contributed without expecting any compensation.

The Austrians hoped that the west would do the same, but only the Red Cross and similar organizations helped. He said that the US government had only kind words and that months and after the loss of many lives, when the help did come it was so little.

I learned that on the racial issues that existed in the United States, he said that most Austrians accepted people as individuals without regard to race, religion or national origin. He further explained that for many years Austrians had felt what it was like to live under the construct of a superior race (the Nazis) and themselves as being thought of as slaves.

He said that he thought that albeit, more than a century earlier, the reason Beethoven composed the Ninth Symphony (the Choral), to express these views only after he had resided in Vienna, by using

Schiller's lyrics "Seid und umschlungen millionen einen Kus die ganze Welt." ("Let us embrace all the peoples of the world and send them a kiss of friendship")[43]

As I write this book, I sometimes listen to the Ninth Symphony, with the Chicago Symphony Orchestra, Riccardo Muti, conducting.

1959 Christmas in Vienna

Since Mr. Adams, owner of the Herald, had given me such a nice Christmas greeting in this article, and because of the importance of this holiday, I set out the entire article below:

Editor's Note: The following article written by Mr. Leroy Wilson, Jr. now an exchange student in Europe, tells us about his experience in Vienna during the holiday season. However, he states that since most of the article was dictated to him in German by his landlord, some of the flavor might have been lost. He also sends greetings of the season to all at home.

CHRISTMAS IN VIENNA begins four days before Christmas. This period is called the Advent Period. It is during this time that the preparation for the arrival of the Christ Child on the Holy Night is made. It is also during this time that the Festival of the Holy Nicholaus is celebrated. This figure is the Austrian counterpart of the American

---

[43] Ludwig van Beethoven's revolutionary Ninth Symphony is, without question, one of the greatest works in classical repertoire. "The Ninth is the culmination of Beethoven's genius," says Classic FM composer and Beethoven expert, John Suchet." He uses solo voices in a symphony for the first time, setting the words of Schiller's poem An die Freude. It is the longest and most complex of all his symphonies, which we may regard it as the pinnacle of his achievement, because it is his last symphony – but he was working on his Tenth when he died." For almost 200 years, the famous hymnal theme to this symphony's finale – the 'Ode to Joy' – has symbolised hope, unity and fellowship – across borders and through conflicts. https://www.classicfm.com/composers/beethoven/music/symphony-no-9-d-minor/#What%20Are%20The%20Lyrics%20to%20%E2%80%98Ode%20to%20Joy%E2%80%99? (Accessed 28 December 2023)

Santa Claus. But unlike Santa Claus, this figure appears on the 6th of December instead of the 24th. One also finds the figure of Krampus, who represents the devil.

This pair, St. Nicklaus and the Krampus' are symbols for Good and Bad. St. Nicklaus commands the children to be good ·and scolds them for the sins they have committed during the passing year. They promise him to be good, and he gives them tiny gifts such as chocolates, nuts, fruit, pastries and many other useful things. During the Advent Period, the Geshaftsstrassen (the streets on which department stores, etc., are located), are decorated with strings of lamps, bells, and other symbols of Christmas.

At various places in the city, one finds huge Christmas trees which are lit up in the evening and can be seen at quite a considerable distance away. In former years all the stores were closed on Saturdays at midday and all day on Sundays. Now, however, these days some 10 thousand people crowd the main streets to buy gifts for their loved ones. The rush to buy is especially tremendous during these days because every worker in Vienna receives an extra month's pay ·as a Christmas gift and can buy more than what would otherwise ·be possible.

Almost 60 years later, I learned that this concept of the 13th check is also a part of Botswana culture.

The Christmas celebration in Vienna self is celebrated in the circle of the family and this celebration begins on Christmas Eve. The streets are almost empty, and the theatres and movies are closed. In every family, whether rich or poor, one can find a Christmas tree. It is decorated with candles, glass figures, angels, stars and sweets. The celebration begins with the lighting of the candles, singing Christmas carols and prayer. It ends with the reading of the Christmas scripture which itself ends: " Glory to God in the highest, peace on earth and goodwill to men Merry Christmas and a Happy New Year!"

As a student, I visited several tourist sites in Vienna.

The winter in Vienna was brutal. One of the reasons I elected not to study in Russia was because I had read about the severe winters there. I remember one day I accompanied Frau Reitler on a visit of Hannes to see the doctor. It was biting cold.

February 1960 Lebanon Embassy in Greece

I have a curious entry in my passport which says that I paid a fee in Athens, Greece for a visa to visit Lebanon. I did not go to Lebanon, but I think something must have piqued my interest to visit. One possibility is that one of my Morehouse classmates from the John Hope family had visited/been a student there and told me something about Beirut, Lebanon. I think it was James Hope.

John Hope was an important African American educator and race leader of the early twentieth century. In 1906 he became the first Black president of Morehouse College—the alma mater of Rev. Dr. Martin Luther King Jr., Mayor Maynard Jackson, me, and others—in Atlanta. Twenty-three years later, in 1929, Hope went on to become the first African American president of Atlanta University (later Clark Atlanta University).[44] He was Richard O. Hope's grandfather. Richard was our Class of 1961 President. He is now late, having passed away in December 2023.

---

[44] John Hope - New Georgia Encyclopedia

Leaving Austria and Returning to the U.S and Morehouse

After June 22, 1960 - Leaving Austria (My IES Certificate in scrapbook folder says I was in Vienna on this date)

I am not sure what my exact exit route was, but as near as I can tell, sometime during the summer of 1960, I visited Germany, Switzerland, Denmark, and Sweden.

I discussed most of my 1960 visits to Germany and Switzerland under the heading Lisle Fellowship/Aarau/Ketterschwang.

Lisle Fellowship/Ketterschwang/Aarau

Before I left Austria in the summer of 1960, I learned that I had been awarded a Lisle Fellowship to spend some time in Germany and in Switzerland. How this came about is still a mystery to me and my great hope is that one day I will learn what happened. It could be that I knew, upon inquiry at the time, but I had forgotten. The website at www.lisleinternational.org/history explains that the Lisle program was started in 1936 by Dr, DeWitt and Edna Baldwin, who were former missionaries in Burma, who wanted to "develop an educational experience - multicultural, interracial and interfaith - to foster increased interaction between U.S. and international students studying on college campuses." For this experience, I think I must thank Morehouse or IES.

The program, as they envisioned it, had the intended effect on me. I met many fabulous people and broadened my horizons far beyond the then small hometown city of Savannah, Georgia. After completing my studies in Vienna, and while I was still in Vienna, I was somehow awarded a second fellowship from Germany that allowed me to participate in summer work experience settings. I remember being in Ketterschwang, Germany part of the summer, and in Aarau, Switzerland part of the summer.

In Germany or Switzerland, I learned a little about a guest worker program and listened to discussions on immigration, which were matter of fact and not fraught with the acidic discussions around the topic today. I saw the guest worker program as being beneficial. I also learned a bit about the European community. On one of our field trips, we visited a steel factory. I will never forget the day when we had to run and scatter like mad when a vat of molten iron slipped from somewhere and liquid iron sprayed across the floor. Luckily, none of us was injured.

In Switzerland, I stayed with the Bachman - Sweitzer family of Aarau for a few weeks. I helped in the fields, but as I remember, I did not learn how to milk cows. I helped drive the milk by cart to the diary. I enjoyed my stay with this lovely family.

I felt an even closer affinity to Aarau after reading "Einstein" by Walter Isaacson during the Spring of 2016. I learned that he had also stayed and worked on a farm in Aarau.

I remember hitchhiking through Germany, up to Copenhagen, Denmark, and Sweden. At some point in Germany, I was introduced to the Volvo, being driven at considerable speeds through the Bayern countryside. This was the other extreme of the experience I had when I caught a ride in a very tiny two-person 3-wheeled automobile travelling on the highway.

July 1960, Denmark

I arrived in Gedser, Denmark on July 3, 1960. One puzzle is that I remember listening to a Patterson - Johansson prizefight on the ferry going from Germany to Denmark. The fight was broadcast in a mixture of English, German and Swedish or Danish. However, according to my research, the Patterson-Johanssen fights took place on June 26,1959, June 20, 1960, and March 13, 1961, at Yankee Stadium, Polo Grounds and Miami, respectively. This leads me to believe that I must have heard a re-broadcast, as I was still in Austria on June 20, 1960, and the other 2 dates are irrelevant.

Johanssen won the first fight, but Patterson won the last two.

However, it was the first time that I had heard the broadcast of the fight. The fight was significant because when Patterson defeated Johansson on June 20, 1960, it was the first time that a former heavyweight champion had regained the title. Of course, I was proud, as the only black person on the ferry. I don't know how I got out of Germany into Gedser, Denmark, because there is no visa stamp in my passport for this part of my trip. I exited Gedser and returned to Germany on July 11, 1960, via Grossenbrode.

While I was in Copenhagen, Denmark, I was sitting on a park bench when a young student approached me to ask for a light. We struck up a conversation and I learned that his name was Ole Ejby Larsen. We talked and he invited me to visit some of his friends - Benny Pedersen being one of them. I am not sure where we went to first, but I remember at one of their apartments, as I walked in, I saw a painting (or portrait) of a very strikingly beautiful black woman hanging on the wall, and Louis Armstrong or Ray Charles playing in the background.

So, I considered myself among friends.

Even though I was paying only 14 cents per night, Benny told me I could save the money and stay in one of the empty bedrooms in his apartment since his parents were away. I moved in and over the next few days, they introduced me to several people. I remember a discussion group of some kind, where I saw a woman smoking a pipe for the first time. Someone gave me a beautiful pipe which, alas, after I had returned to the States, I broke the pipe as it fell from my pocket and crashed on the ground. They also took me to see Oscar Pettiford in concert. He was a brilliant African American jazz double bassist, cellist and composer. I later learned that was one of his last performances as he died on September 8, 1960.

Ole turned out to be quite a painter. After I returned to the US, I visited Ms. Virginia Kiah, my high school art teacher, and told her about some of his work. He sent number of his paintings to her to tour the United States in an exhibition she was showing. After the exhibition tour ended, I asked him how to ship them back. Ole responded by making a gift of them to me saying that he was happy to say that they were in a collection in the United States. Except for one, in 2024, I sold all his paintings to a physiotherapist while I was downsizing in Gaborone, Botswana for a nominal sum, with the idea that his paintings would live on.

Of course, Benny and Ole took me to see the statue of the Little Mermaid, and a park that contained a beautiful fountain.

Sweden

After visiting Copenhagen, it was on to Sweden. I wanted to visit Sweden because Philip Townes, a student from Morehouse, had stud ied there and said some good things about the place. I also wanted to visit Uppsala, Sweden because of a science university there. Years later, there would be a student from Upsala, Bjorn, who became a part of Dr. George Pimental's chemistry group at Berkeley, of which I was a member.

One day as I hitchhiked to Upsala in the rain, a kind couple stopped to pick me up and take me home with them for dinner and return me to the road. That is when I learned the value of coffee in digesting a meal. After feeding me starters, which I thought was the main course, the wife invited me to eat dinner! I was full to bursting. Seeing how full I was, she offered me coffee to settle my stomach, after which I enjoyed a delicious pot roast and potato dinner. Then it was time for them to return me to the road, as it had stopped raining. Unfortunately, I do not have a record of their names as far as I know.

Return to the United States

I think I must have spent July 11 - August 3, 1960, in Ketterschwang, Germany, as a Lisle Fellow, and then from August 3 to August 14 in Aarau, Switzerland. My experiences on the farm in Aarau mirrored those of Albert Einstein there that Walter Isaacson described in his monumental book "EINSTEIN."

On August 17, I left Le Harve, France by ship for the return trip to the United States arriving at Quebec, Canada on August 24, 1960, and at Rouses Point, N.Y on August 25.

It so happens, that after I arrived in Canada, I met Thelma Washington, who it turns out, was related to the Jenkins family at the corner of Scarborough and Richards Street in my neighborhood in West Savannah, Georgia. I would later learn that Thelma lived in Westchester County, New York where I lived from 1968 to 2016. She was active in the White Plains Greenburgh branch of the NAACP, where I was a life member.

When I returned, I was 21 years old.

Return to Morehouse

Upon returning to Morehouse, I was headed for a double major in Mathematics and Chemistry and a double Minor in Physics and German. Because I had not completed my limestone experiment in the qualitative chemistry analysis class, Dr. Henry Cecil McBay made me repeat the entire course and would not settle for me simply doing the experiment. As a result, I had to drop 2 or 3 of my other classes because of scheduling conflicts..

Before we left NY for travel throughout Ireland, England, France , Belgium, Germany, Switzerland, and Leichtenstein on our way to

Vienna, I had not finished the so-called "limestone" analysis in analytical chemistry. As usual, I also enjoyed this course. But, because I had not finished this experiment, I was forced to drop additional studies in physics and French.

I had elected to teach a class in freshman German instead of working in the chemistry lab. I think this upset Dr. McBay a little and he told me there was nothing he could do about the conflict with the times the physics and French courses were offered and the time I would need to be in the chemistry lab to finish the limestone experiment. I was a bit upset and considered changing from chemistry as a major to mathematics. Word got out and I encountered Dr. Kimuel Huggins in the stairwell of the chemistry building. He told me he had heard the news and encouraged me not to make this change. At the time he was my organic chemistry teacher. I loved that course. After listening to him, I decided to stay with chemistry, but I graduated with a double major in chemistry and mathematics after Morehouse gave me some credits for the courses I had taken in Austria.

I felt much better when Dr. McBay told my parents at graduation that I was one of the brightest students he had ever taught.

Young Fatherhood

Before I left, my childhood sweetheart, Helen Odum, gave birth to our daughter Andrea. When I returned, I found that while I was away, Helen had become pregnant again and given birth to a second child, a boy. I did not know what to do, but ultimately, we were divorced. Helen and Andrea have now passed away; Andrea had two daughters, Altonaise and Natasha, and a son, Flavius. I did not contact Flavius until 2024, even though I had spoken to him many years ago. He now has a family – Nicole, his wife, and two daughters, Mary and Denise, and Tiny, the chihuahua.

Daughter Andrea with Jason and Christopher circa 1978 when we lived on Park Avenue in Mount Vernon.

Natasha, Leroy, and Altonaise 2005 in Savannah

Flavius Josephus, grandson, son of Andrea ca. 2024

I was able to spend some time with Altonaise and Natasha a few years back. Maleta and I met with them. They were lovely, grown young ladies with their own families.

Altonaise has one daughter, whose name is Arden and is in talented and gifted classes at school. She was born on April 11th, 2012. She also has twin sons Jayden and Courtney, who were born on March 17th, 2013.

Thanks to my brother Donald, I first saw these great grandchildren when they were toddlers but have not been able to connect again. Altonaise and I were almost able to have a reunion again when I was in

Savannah in 2021/2022 and she was in Savannah, but we had conflicts and were not able to meet. At the time she was a resident of Florida.

We message from time to time using social media.

We tried to meet again in the summer of 2025 when the Shepherd family reunion was held in Orlando Florida. She was living about 1 hour away, but that did not happen.

Natasha and I did not meet again until May 25, 2022, just before I left Savannah to return to Botswana by way of Washington DC with my son Christopher and Eastchester NY with my son Jason.

Christopher, ever looking out for the welfare of his father had driven his Jeep Cherokee down to Pooler GA so that I would have a way of getting around without paying the heavy Uber bills. He and I went over to visit Natasha in Savannah where she lived with her young children. I remember a very lovely visit with them.

Natasha's children's birthdays are Kiyimba Athena Foster born February 17, 2015 (pink pants), Keyaire Andrea Foster born March 2, 2016 (black pants, King Major Royal April 15, 2018 (sitting on my lap), and Prince Is'real Hanon Royal July 8, 2019 (sitting between me and Christopher).

When I visited Savannah in 2023, I contacted Natasha, but she had scheduling conflicts that prevented me from seeing her and the children.

Junior Year at Morehouse, Graduation and Graduate School

Winter Semester 1960

I took English Fundamentals, Mathematical Physics, Analysis III, Advanced College Algebra, Advanced German Prose, Elementary French, Organic Chemistry, and Physical Education.

Without slighting the other courses, Mathematical Physics was when I discovered that I could see mathematical formulas dancing in space. The course was taught by an engineer from Lockheed.

Dr. Kim Huggins taught organic chemistry. An older man, but when he hit the blackboard with his equations, he could make them sing. What I think I learned from him was regardless of how complex the molecule was, the important things were to learn which site of the molecule was active and what they electrons were doing.

Spring 1961 (second semester, 1960-61)

I took Theory of Equations, Ordinary Differential Equations, Organic Chemistry, Physical Education, Analytical Chemistry, and Public Speaking.

I enjoyed all of them. The dynamic Billy Johnson taught differential equations, and I wondered how someone who was so young could be so smart. I think the equally brilliant Ms. Harriett Walton taught theory of equations.

G. Lewis Chandler taught public speaking. I maintained that anyone who studied his course could deliver speeches or sermons like Dr. Benjamin E. Mays, Rev. Dr. Martin Luther King Jr., Rev. Dr. Howard Thurman, Rev. Jeremiah Wright of Chicago, or Rev. Frederick Douglass Haynes, III of Dallas, Texas, or Otis Moss, Jr., of Cleveland, to name a few of our great Morehouse orators.

I earned 3 As and 3 Bs.

Senior Year (1961-1962)

For the first semester, (Fall 1961), I took Religion, Thermodynamics, Physical Chemistry and Advanced Calculus

I think Rev. Roswell Jackson taught the course in religion, which exposed me to many of the religions in the world. I was the grader for the course.

I don't remember who taught the course in Thermodynamics, but I am happy I took it, as an introduction to the course I would take later at Berkeley.

Of course, Dr. McBay taught physical chemistry, and Dr. Lonnie Cross (later Lonnie Shabazz) taught the course in Advanced Calculus. Dr. Cross would later convert to Islam and became Minister Lonnie 4X. He was an extremely brilliant man.

I graded the student exam papers for Rev. Jackson and Dr. Cross.

Apart from the calculus, one invaluable lesson that I learned from Dr. Cross was to always try to remain in your own skin; i.e., don't let your surroundings make you become uncomfortable. This advice came in handy many times years later, but I remember one time when I went to Milwaukee to represent Union Carbide in a sophisticated acquisition of one of its distributors. We went to the Milwaukee club for lunch with the participants on both sides. The club is billed as a premier social and business club. A table had been reserved for us in front of the dining room, which meant that we had to walk the length of the dining room to reach the table. I could hear heads turning in the starched shirt collars of white men as we walked the length of the dining room. After we sat done, I unobtrusively scoped the room to see that I was the only black person seated at a table. Thanks to Dr Cross and my Morehouse foundation, I was not rattled.

I think my business hosts were proud to march me through the members of their exclusive club.

Senior year was full of anxieties about what would happen after graduation. I would apply to several of the leading universities and see if I could get some kind of financial aid. At the time, Georgia had an out -of- state aid program which gave financial assistance to black students to study out of the state if they could not find a program that would admit them within the State of Georgia. Little did I realize at the time that the program was designed to get as much of the black intellectual talent out of the state of Georgia as possible.

All seniors in the chemistry department were required to pass a comprehensive examination before we were allowed to graduate. My examination was to explain what I had learned about kinetic theory from freshman through senior year. Although I had not specifically prepared for this topic, I knew the area so well from having excellent teachers throughout my stay that I was able to pass with flying colors.

Several professors were present for my examination - I remember Drs. McBay, Mr. McCray, and perhaps Dr. P.T. Groves - all of them left during my examination with Mr. McCray saying that he was wasting his time because I had such a comprehensive and fluent command of the subject. That simply boosted my confidence. The exam was oral and lasted about 3-4 hours as I remember. I enjoyed the process and surprised myself by how much I remembered.

Berkeley - On December 21, 1961, Berkeley offered me a $2250 teaching assistantship and admitted me to their Master's degree program, and upon satisfactory completion of the first year would allow me to change over to the Ph.D. program. I passed the master's comprehensive examination and was accepted into the Ph.D. program. Alas, I would not complete the Ph. D. program because of my emotional upset about breaking up with my fiancée and could not prepare myself for the oral examinations. Looking back, I was more disturbed than I realized at the time. That was a big disappointment for me personally, and because I could not join my two Morehouse colleagues - Charles Meredith and Troy Story, who would be awarded their Ph.Ds. But I persevered and went to law school at Berkeley instead. I received my J.D. (Juris Doctor) degree from the University of California's Berkeley Law School in May 1968.

By all accounts, I have made Morehouse and my parents proud.

Penn State - On November 25, 1961, Penn State offered me a graduate teaching assistantship for 3 terms for $2250, noting that this was higher than their normal stipend of $1710. I was pleased with this recognition of all the studying and hard work I had done. I declined this generous offer and accepted Berkeley's.

University of Chicago - On January 4, 1962, The University of Chicago offered me a teaching assistantship of $2100 plus tuition of $1410. I really wanted to accept this one since it was Dr. McBay's alma mater, but in the end chose Berkeley because at the time its graduate program in chemistry ranked a bit above the program at Chicago.

Southern Education Foundation/Woodrow Wilson Fellowship – on March 22, 1962, the Woodrow Wilson Foundation notified me that had I been awarded a joint SEF-WW fellowship. The SEF portion of the award would pay the cost of my full tuition, room and board, and fees for the summer of 1962 after I graduated. However, the award required me to enroll at either the University of Oklahoma, University of Kentucky or the University of Texas. It encouraged me to continue my further graduate studies at the university that I would have chosen for my summer studies.

The Woodrow Wilson portion of the award we have allowed me to study at any Graduate School in the United States or Canada.

I also turned down the Southern Education Foundation -Woodrow Wilson Fellowship because all the information I had at the time said that the University of California at Berkeley was higher ranked for my program of study.

MIT turned down my application.

University of Wisconsin - I don't think I have their letter, but Wisconsin rejected me. I applied there because we used the physical chemistry textbook that had been written by one of their professors. On my way to Berkeley, I traveled by train via Wisconsin, because I wanted to find out why they had rejected me. The department head was absent at the time, but another professor sat down with me and went over my subjects and grades. After we finished talking, he said he did not understand why they rejected me.

However, I am pleased to note that when Billy Jo Evans (from Morehouse) applied to Wisconsin the next year, he was admitted, received his doctorate, and went on to become an outstanding professor of chemistry at the University of Michigan. I am not sure my visit had anything to do with it, but I was sure happy for Billy Jo. Some years later, my youngest son Chris graduated from Michigan undergraduate and law school and became friends with Billy Jo while he was a student there.

Graduation from Morehouse and Reunions

I graduated from Morehouse on June 5, 1962, with High Honors, and a double major in chemistry and mathematics. Ashton also graduated with double departmental honors in chemistry and mathematics. Morehouse gave us credit for some of the courses we had taken in Vienna.

Troy graduated with departmental honors in chemistry.

During Senior Week, when the outstanding students for a given discipline would make speeches to the lower classmen, I delivered the speech for the chemistry department on May 23, 1962. Troy received the chemistry departmental medal.

Morehouse awarded honorary degrees to Milton King Curry, Jr. (Laws); Ralph Emerson McGill (Humanities), and Nathan Pusey (Letters). Pusey was President of Harvard. He gave the commencement address.

Afterwards, Ralph McGill wrote an article for the Atlanta Journal – Atlanta Constitution shortly after our graduation entitled "A Door Begins To Open," which recited the names of those of us who were awarded scholarships or positions that prior to that time were closed to black Americans.

Ralph Emerson McGill (February 5, 1898 – February 3, 1969) was an influential American journalist and editor.[45] He is best known for his work as the editor and publisher of the **Atlanta Constitution**, where he used his platform to advocate for civil rights and social justice. McGill was a vocal opponent of segregation and played a significant role in promoting racial equality in the southern United States.[46]

Morehouse President Dr. Benjamin E. Mays, sent us off into the world with the following charge:

THE PRESIDENT'S CHARGE TO THE CLASS OF 1962

When I graduated from college in 1920, careers for Negroes were highly restricted. Teaching at $25 a month in schools that ran three and four months a year made you a Negro leader, and one highly respected among Negroes. It was expected that we would farm, preach, teach, and do menial labor. Law was

---

45 https://en.wikipedia.org/wiki/Ralph_McGill?form=MG0AV3 (Accessed 12 November 2024)

46 https://www.britannica.com/biography/Ralph-Emerson-McGill (Accessed 12 November 2024)

impossible. A doctor of color was a *rara avis*. It was even dangerous to aspire to something higher.

But you are graduating at a time when new opportunities are beginning to emerge in Industry, Government, Education, Science, Politics, and Foreign Service. You no longer compete with men in a designated racial group. Whatever the handicaps of the past or the barriers of the present, you are in competition with all men everywhere.

We hope we have prepared you to meet whatever competition lies ahead and motivated you to pursue excellence, so that you will face the future with courage, confidence, and hope.

If we, teachers and administrators, have failed you in any particular, we pray forgiveness. I hope we have done the best we could - shall I say - with what we had.

Whether we failed you or whether we did not, *we do not expect you to fail Morehouse College, yourselves, your parents, and your friends.*

We expect you to do well whatever you touch and to make a creditable, honorable mark in the world. From now on, you bear the stamp of Morehouse. You will reflect either glory or dishonor upon your Alma Mater. My prayer is that you will reflect glory.

May the years ahead be gracious and kind to you and bring you success.

June 5 1962

By all accounts I reflected glory.

Benjamin E. Mays was an educator, leader, pastor, and civil rights activist. He was born on August 1, 1894 in Greenwood County, South Carolina, the youngest of eight children of former slaves Hezekiah Mays and Louvenia Carter Mays. Mays wrote a book called "Born To Rebel" which describes the impacts of racism on the black communities in America. He served as president of Morehouse College for twenty-seven years and as the first black president of the Atlanta School Board.[47]

As I have written above, Ralph McGill broadcast the transition of Morehouse men to new opportunities in his Atlanta Journal column titled "A Door Begins to Open" that Dr. Mays had described.

McGill recites the names of some of those who have these new opportunities, in addition to my own, which notes that I won a $2000.00[48] assistantship in chemistry to the University of California along with Troy Story Jr., Ashton Ward accepted a similar teaching scholarship at the University of Illinois.

The other names he cites in this transition are George Anderson who would begin to work at IBM as a systems engineer, Clark Everett who received a Woodrow Wilson fellowship in the amount of $1600 plus tuition and fees to study in the graduate English department at the University of Michigan, Nathaniel Griffin, with honors in mathematics, will be a research assistant in math with a $2000 award at New Highland University in Las Vegas, Melvin Heard Jr. with mathematics honors will be a graduate assistant teacher and student at Purdue with a salary of $2300, Donald R Hopkins will go to the university of Chicago medical school with the help of a national medical - Sloan Foundation scholarship of $2000, and Joseph Rogers, Jr., with highest honors won a competitive Fulbright scholarship which he passed up to accept a Woodrow Wilson fellowship to study French at Harvard.

Donald R. Hopkins, M.D.,[49] who McGill mentions, later became a MacArthur Fellow and was the Vice President and Director of Health

---

[47] The Life of Benjamin E. Mays Born to Rebel: The Life and Legacy of Benjamin E. Mays · AUC Woodruff Library Digital Exhibits (Accessed 13 NOV. 2024); Dumas, Carrie, *Benjamin Elijah Mays – A Pictorial Life and Times,* Mercer University Press (2006)

[48] $2250.00.

[49] For a quick overview of his accomplishments, see Killing off deadly diseases: The legendary Donald R. Hopkins | News | Harvard T.H. Chan School of Public Health (Accessed 13 NOV. 2024)

Programs at The Carter Center. At one point, Donald contracted malaria in Sierra Leone and became critically ill.

He also played a significant role in the eradication of smallpox and did significant work in the fields of Guinea Worm Disease, River Blindness (Onchocerciasis) and Measles Control.

Dr. Hopkins has served as the deputy director and acting director of the Centers for Disease Control and Prevention (CDC) and has been a professor of tropical public health at the Harvard School of Public Health.

Dr. Hopkins has authored numerous articles and books on public health, including his book **"Princes and Peasants: Smallpox in History,"** which was nominated for a Pulitzer Prize.

I returned to Morehouse for a few reunions in my early days, but the ones that stand out for me now are the 50th anniversary of our 1961 graduation held in Atlanta, the ad hoc 51st reunion of the Class of 1961 held in Greenwood, S.C., and our 60th class reunion held in Atlanta, GA.

Troy Story, Me, Marvin Anderson, George Crawford at 60th Morehouse Reunion in Atlanta (2022)

I remember Roulette Smith being present for the 50th reunion of the 1961 class in Atlanta.

In August 2012, George Grant, publisher of the Gray Tiger, sent out an announcement to convey the invitation of Dr. Joseph D. Patton, Director, and Loy Sartin, curator of the Benjamin E. Mays Historical Preservation Site in Greenwood, S.C. for us to attend the 51st reunion, and unveiling at the Site. https://www.mayssite.org/

George tells us that 33 classmates and their spouses attended the 50th reunion in Atlanta in 2011.

The September 2012 Greenwood program was in two parts.

First, the unveiling ceremony:

"Welcome & Opening Remarks	The Honorable Claude Thomas, Chairman GLEAMNS Board of Commissioners Member/Abbeville County Council
Invocation	Rev. Dr. Danny Webb Pastor, Old Mt. Zion Baptist Church
Remarks	The Honorable Gonza L. Bryant District #3 Councilman, Greenwood County Council
Remarks	The Honorable Welborn Adams Mayor, City of Greenwood
Remarks	Dr. Marshalyn Yeargin-Allsopp Great Niece of Dr. Mays
Letter from	Dr. Tracy Power Coordinator of South Carolina Historical Marker Program Read by: Ms. Trentsie Williams
Remarks	Dr. Richard O. Hope President, Morehouse Class of 1961 Alumni Morehouse College Hymn - Audio CD
Unveiling and Closing Comments	Dr. Joseph D. Patton, III CEO, GLEAMNS Human Resources

	Commission, Director of the Benjamin E. Mays Historical Preservation Site
Dismissal	Rev. Dr Danny Webb"

Several of us arrived for the unveiling and ceremonies to mark the permanent placement of the memorial plaque at the memorial park.

September 12, 2012 – Class of 1961 attendees, Dedication of Banjamin E. Mays Memorial Park

Left to right Marvin Dunn., Charles Edward Smith (Smitty). Walter Grady, Richard O. Hope, George Grant, Leroy Wilson, Jr., [a classmate from Georgia whose name escapes me], and Charles Willie, several of whom we Ph.D.'s, Douglas Rucker (a dentist not shown).

There were also spouses: Eleanor, Smitty's wife, Alice, Richard's wife.

Second, in the afternoon, we were treated to a film, an afternoon panel discussion, and book signings recorded for television by ETV South Carolina

The film is titled *Benjamin E. Mays: "Born to Rebel, Driven to Excel"*

The Discussion Panel focused on *"Personal Reflections of Dr. Benjamin E. Mays"*

The panelists were:

Dr. Samuel Dubois Cook, President Emeritus, Dillard University

Member, Morehouse College Class of'48; Mays's Eulogist

Dr. Charles V. Willie The Charles W. Eliot Professor of Education Emeritus Graduate School of Education, Harvard University; member of Morehouse College Class of '48

Dr. Marshalyn Yeargin-Allsopp Medical Epidemiologist and Chief, Developmental Disabilities Branch at the National Center on Birth Defects at the CDC; great-niece of Dr. Mays

Mrs. Billye Aaron, Teacher; Television Personality; Philanthropist and Wife of baseball great, Hall-of-Famer, Hank Aaron

Mrs. Sally Warner, Secretary for D, r. Benjamin E. Mays

Ms. Tawana Wimbish Great, great niece of Dr. Benjamin E. Mays

Ms. Carrie Dumas, Program Coordinator for Alumni Affairs, Morehouse School of Medicine

Dr. George C. Grant.....................Owner, Grant House Publishers; houseboy for Dr. and Mrs. Mays from 1959-61

Member, Morehouse College Class of 1961

Dr. Randal M. Jelks.......................Author, Benjamin Elijah Mays, Schoolmaster of the Movement: A Biography

Dr. John H. Roper................................Author, The Magnificent Mays: A Biography of Benjamin Elijah Mays

Dr. Orville Vernon Burton Distinguished Professor of Humanities, Professor of History and Computer Science at Clemson University; and the Director of the Clemson Cyber Institute

Moderator: Mr. Loy Sartin, Curator, Mays Museum and Historic Site

The book signings were by the following:

Dr. Randal M. Jelks, who wrote *"Benjamin E. Mays - Schoolmaster of the Movement* (May 2012)"

Dr. John H. Roper, who wrote *The Magnificent Mays: A Biography of Dr. Benjamin E. Mays* (August 2012)

_____________ Dinner

_____________Lunch

As usual, Dr. Mays was always trying to inspire us. Several books have been written about his remarkable life.[50] I bought a few of these when I attended the 51st Morehouse Class of 1961 reunion in Greenwood, South Carolina.

Saturday, 08 September, was devoted to a symposium on the life and contributions of Dr. Mays. There was a full video of the proceedings.

Among the reunion attendees at this event were Richard Oliver Hope[51] and his wife Alice, Douglas Rucker, Marvin Dunn, George Grant, Smitty and his wife Eleanor.

---

[50] Some are Carrie M. Dumas, with Julie Hunter, *Benjamin Elijah Mays, A Pictorial Life and Times* Mercer University Press (2006)("Dumas") ; Jelks, Randal Maurice, *Benjamin Elijah Mays, Schoolmaster of the Movement*, a biography, The University of North Carolina Press (2012) ("Jelks"); Roper, John Herbert Jr., *The Magnificent Mays*, A Biography of Benjamin Elijah Mays, The University of South Carolina Press (2012)("Roper")

[51] As I was writing this book, I learned from Alice that Richard passed away at home December 1, 2023. They had moved to Chicago to be near Leah, their daughter, a long-standing anchor at ABC 7 TV in Chicago.

At the Sunday this weekend, Richard was sitting across from me, and Marvin was sitting to my right. Richard and I were discussing our relevant South Africa experiences. He had been very much involved in assisting part of the transition as a Woodrow Wilson Foundation officer. He told us how he and President Mandela met, and his promise to try to get the Foundation to support the new government. Richard was heavily involved in developing the Public Policy Partnership Program in South Africa, which aimed to support various initiatives during the transition from apartheid to a democratic society.

Richard was successful in getting the Woodrow Wilson Foundation to make a financial contribution to President Mandela in South Africa, which he personally delivered to President Mandela. What made this also significant was the debate at the foundation on whether the foundation could contribute to support a program outside of the United States.

During the luncheon Richard made us aware of late Amb. Edward Perkins's autobiography "Mr. Ambassador," which I promptly purchased. President Reagan appointed Amb. Perkins as America's Ambassador to South Africa from November 27, 1986, to May 22, 1989, during apartheid. He was an African American who did a lot of work quietly. And some, not so quietly.

He told us that President Reagan charged him with the responsibility of dismantling apartheid.

Two of my recollections from the book are the fragile and frightful situation in Liberia when Sgt. Doe took over the government, and the times he attended the Delmas treason trials in South Africa. The first told of how he and his family were under imminent threat of deadly bodily harm; the second was the "most important political trial since that of Nelson Mandela two decades earlier."[52]

---

[52] Edward J. Perkins, with Connie Cronley, "Mr. Ambassador, Warrior for Peace" University of Oklahoma Press p. 5 -6 (2006)

I subsequently read a book about the Delmas trial.[53]

Joseph Huggins, who was the United States Ambassador to Botswana when I met him in 2004, told me in 2024 that he met Amb. Perkins in 1983 in his first Washington assignment in the Bureau of African Affairs. Amb. Perkins was Director for West Africa. He gave Amb. Huggins the "Black in Foreign Service" talk and recommended that Amb. Huggins read the Art of War by Sun Tzu and the Book of Five Rings by Miyamoto Musashi.

Amb. Perkins hosted Black officers at his house monthly to support each other.

During that luncheon discussion, Dr. Marvin Dunn joined us to tell of some of the work he had done in South Africa and in the townships during the period we were discussing. Richard told us that , as things turned out, he was aware of Marvin's work as he had funded Marvin's activities without Marvin's knowledge at the time. We would, discover that we had been living up to Dr. Mays's charge to all of us.

As I wrote at the beginning of this book, among Dr. Mays's many sayings are the following:[54]

"It is not a disgrace to read for the stars, but it is a disgrace to have no stars to reach for. Not failure, but low aim is sin," and

"Whatever you do, strive to do it so well that no man dead and no man yet to be born could do it any better."

So, it is easy to understand how every Tuesday morning when Dr. Mays delivered his chapel address, for a period of 4 years, we were inspired beyond measure.

---

[53] Id. The Delmas trial was held in a remote location, about a one-hour drive from Pretoria (now Tshwane). This is like what the authorities did in the trial of Jomo Kenyatta., as well. However, a member of the famed Leakey family was disqualified as an interpreter after a member of the audience pointed out to the Judge that he was not interpreting correctly. See Calvin Slater's book "*The Trial of Jomo Kenyatta.*"

[54] Dumas, pp. 5 and 34, and the Epilogue, respectively.

I also attended the 50th reunion of the 1962 class in Atlanta. There I would re-connect with Troy, Dr. Milford Greene, and Dentist Dr. George Crawford, who brought along his daughter. We all had a delightful discussion in George's suite..

At the September 2012 Mays symposium in Greenwood I had the pleasure of meeting and having dinner with the brilliant historian, computer science expert, educator, and voting rights expert, Dr. Orville Vernon Burton,[55]Georganna, Vernon's wife, and Frank Wideman who was President of the Self Family Foundation.[56]

Contemporary history of Morehouse can be found in the online copy of the Maroon Tiger at https://maroontigermedia.com/.

---

[55]Distinguished University Scholar – Professor of History and Computer Science-Clemson University. Orville Vernon Burton | Profile Information (Accessed 13 NOV 2024)

[56] Self Family Foundation – Legacy Community Opportunity (Accessed 13 NOV 2024)

AFRICA

Growing up in a segregated society, I developed an early interest in affairs affecting black people in the United States and other parts of the world, mainly Africa.

I devoured anything that I could read about black people, especially the black print media. In those days white newspapers and, with very few exceptions, white magazines, did not cover black people.

As I stated, I couldn't wait to read the next issue of Ebony magazine, Jet and the Black World magazines. Among newspapers, I read the local Savannah black press, which were the Tribune and The Herald. The Pittsburgh Courier, the Afro American, and the Chicago Defender were the black newspapers that we received that were printed outside in the state of Georgia. The founder of the Chicago Defender was Robert Sengstacke Abbott, and he grew up in Savannah, Georgia.[57] The paper's reach extended nationally, thanks to Pullman porters who distributed it across the South.[58]

One of the stories printed in 1951 in Ebony magazine that I remembered figured prominently in my decision to travel to Botswana with the National Bar Association in 2004, where I now reside; I cover that below.

---

[57] Abbott founded The Chicago Defender in 1905, launching it from a small kitchen with just 25 cents and a press run of 300 copies. The paper became one of the most influential African American publications in U.S. history, playing a pivotal role in the Great Migration by encouraging Black Southerners to move north, Chicago in particular, for better opportunities. Accessed CoPilot 26 October 2025.

[58] Id.

August 26-31,1973 - World Peace through Law Conference Coté d'Ivoire

By the time I had received the invitation to attend the World Peace Thought Law Conference in 1973 (the "Abidjan Conference "), I had already had the experience of traveling in Europe, and living and studying in Vienna, as a Morehouse Merrill Travel Study fellow in 1959 to 1960.

I would not travel outside of the United States again until 1973, when I attended the Abidjan Conference in the Coté D'Ivoire.

After I had become a lawyer (admitted NY 1969), Charles W. Meredith, my close friend and Morehouse classmate, made me aware that Maynard Jackson, a Morehouse man and first black Mayor of Atlanta,[59]had told him that Dean Rusk, former U. S. Secretary of State under John F. Kennedy, was interested in having more African Americans enter the foreign service. Dean Rusk, a fellow Georgian, was not a stranger to Morehouse.

My moment came when somehow I received an invitation to attend the Abidjan Conference. Charles Rhyne was President of the World Peace Through Law Center; Judge William "Turk" Thompson was its Secretary General. I telephoned Dean Rusk and relayed what I had heard about his interest, that I wanted to go, but I needed funds to attend. Without making a commitment, he told me that he would "see what he could do." I then heard from Turk that they had secured funds for a sizeable number of African American lawyers to attend the conference. I was included.

---

[59] First Term: 1974–1978, Second Term: 1978–1982 (reelected), Third Term: 1990–1994

To date, I never mentioned my role in this process, not knowing if my call to Dean Rusk anything had to do with our attendance.

Among these lawyers was Haywood Burns,[60] a brilliant friend and outstanding lawyer. Haywood was instrumental in negotiating the ultimate resolution of the tragic Attica riot. He was later named the Dean of the law school at the City University of New York. In 1997, I

---

[60] Burns served as general counsel to Martin Luther King Jr.'s Poor People's Campaign and was one of the founders of the National Conference of Black Lawyers. He represented Angela Davis and prisoners after the Attica prison uprising. After meeting with Nelson Mandela in Harlem, Burns was a legal advisor to the drafting of South Africa's interim constitution in 1993. Tragically, Haywood was killed in a car accident in Cape Town, South Africa in April 1996. https://en.wikipedia.org/wiki/W._Haywood_Burns (Accessed 30 December 2023)

became the Chair of the New York State Bar Association's Civil Rights Committee.[61] One of the things I accomplished was having the bar establish an award in Haywood's name.

At its annual meeting on January 28, 2004, I received the Haywood Burns Memorial Award from Peter Sherwin, whom I encouraged to become a part of the active bar. Peter was now the Chair of the Committee. He had been reluctant to actively participate because he thought the bar would not befriend him because he is openly gay. It is now awarded annually, and Peter is very active.

I had not seen Haywood for most of the conference, so I asked him where he was. He responded, "in the bush."

I knew Turk from my participation in the National Bar Association, which I had joined in 1970. The NBA became an important part of my life.

At the time of the trip to the Conference in Abidjan, my late wife, Jane and sons Jason and Chris, lived at 415 Gramatan Avenue, Mount Vernon, New York.

I was a lawyer in the Office of Vice President and General Counsel in International Business Machines (IBM) at the time.

We arrived in Abidjan on August 25, 1973. The flight was overnight, and I remember getting goosebumps when I looked out of the airplane window and saw the coast of Africa for the first time.

The Conference was held at the Hotel Ivoire, a modern skyscraper of a hotel. Some of the delegates stayed there, but some of us stayed at the Hotel Mediterannee (although from my passport, I think we were first scheduled to stay at the Hotel Tiama), which had one or two stars less than the Hotel Ivoire.

---

61 1997-2000.

This is the assembly hall where the majority of our general meetings were held in 1973. At the 2025 meeting of the International Law Section at Quarles law firm, the present Cote d'Ivoire Ambassador to the United States said I should visit soon to see the changes.

Charles Williams and I were roommates. Thereafter, he would assume several historical positions in New York, including Secretary of State.

The President of Côte d'Ivoire at the time was His Excellency Felix Houphouet – Boigny.

The President of the Supreme Court of Côte d'Ivoire was The Honorable Alphonse Boni. There were 3 chambers.

Left to right The Honorable Alphonse Boni, President Supreme Court; Driver; The Honorable Lucien Yapobi, Vice President Supreme Court; Attendee ostensibly from California

The World Peace Through Law Center established policies through an Executive Committee comprised of Honorable Charles S. Rhyne, as President, The Honorable Sansern Kraichitti, as Vice President for Asia and Australasia, The Honorable Roland Barnes, Vice President for Africa, The Honorable Albert Brunois, Vice President for Europe , The Honorable Fernando Fournier, Vice President for the Americas, and The Honorable William S. Thompson as Secretary - General.

The World Association of Judges had its own officers and Executive Council. Its officers were: Honorary Chairman The Honorable Earl Warren, Chief Justice of the United States (Ret.), Vice-Chairman for Asia and Australasia The Honorable Kasuo Ishida, Chief Justice, Supreme Court of Japan (Ret.), Vice-Chairman for Africa, The Honorable C.O.E. Cole, Chief Justice, Supreme Court of Sierra Leone, Vice President for Europe, The Honorable Ilija Dosen, Chief Justice, Supreme Court of Yugoslavia, Vice-Chairman for the Americas, The Honorable Warren E. Burger, The Chief Justice of the United States, Secretary, The Honorable Marielies Geyser, Federal Civil Court of Germany, Treasurer, The Honorable Sir William Randolph Douglas, Chief Justice, Supreme Court of Barbados.

After the Opening Ceremony on Sunday, August 26, which featured an African Law Exhibit, Hon. Alphonse Boni, President of the Supreme Court, Côte d'Ivoire, treated us to a reception, which was followed by a Proclamation of World Law Day by Hon. A.H. Zaire, Chief Justice Supreme Court, Afghanistan.

Ten Center Sections carried out the formal programs of the Center programs.

The US attendees included Hon. Earl Warren, the Chief Justice of the United States (Retired), Hon. Thurgood Marshall, Associate Justice of the United States Supreme court, Hon. Wade H. McCree, Jr., Federal Circuit Judge, Hon. Barbara Watson, Department of State, U.S., Hon. Jacob K. Javits, Hon. Raymond Pace Alexander, Hon. Clarence Clyde Ferguson, Jr., Department of State, U.S., Hon. Norman Redlich, Corporation Counsel, NYC, Prof. Henry J. Richardson, Indiana University, Hon. Damon Keith, Haywood Burns, Esq., among others. Other attendees were Heads of State, as well as highest ranking members of the Judiciary and legal profession from many countries.

It was a pleasure to be able to have informal conversations with these important people.

The formal name of the program was "Abidjan World Conference on World Peace Through Law and World Assembly of Judges."

Monday called us to attention to the Inaugural Ceremonial Session with addresses by Hon. Alphonse Boni, Charles S. Rhyne, Hon. Earl Warren, H.E. Felix Houphouet-Boigny, and messages from the Heads of State.

The cavernous main auditorium was large and accommodated all the delegates without a problem. The frescoed carvings that adorned the walls were of African animals (otherwise Africa themed).

After Luncheon, the World Association of Judges presented several distinguished speakers on the status of the Universal Declaration of

Human Rights: 25 Years Later. The Hon. Lucien Yapobi, Vice President Supreme Court, Côte d'Ivoire, presided.[62]

The Honorable Lucien Yapobi resembled my father, and I resembled his son. The resemblance was so striking that one of Mr. Yapobi's friends mistook me for his son. With those introductions, Mr. Yapobi assigned his driver to drive me around and show me some of the sights of Abidjan.

The Government Lawyers Section, Honorary Chairman Hon. Emile Abou – Kheir, Chief Justice Supreme Court, Lebanon, presented a seminar on International Control of Dangerous Drugs, presided over by Leo M. Pellerzi, Esq., U.S.

The Law and Computer Technology Section, Honorary Chairman Isaac E. Hayatali, Chief Justice Court of Appeals, Trinidad & Tobago, presented a seminar on Recent Developments, presided over by Stephen J. Skelly, Esq., Canada

The session ended with a computer demonstration by the I.B.M. Paris Office.

At the time, coincidentally, I was employed in the Office of Vice President & General Counsel, Armonk, NY as Staff Attorney, Antitrust Law, and later as a Staff Attorney for Environmental Law. I was I.B. M.'s first environmental lawyer, because of my additional background in the study of chemistry.

At 7:00 p.m. local time, H.E. President Felix Houphouet – Boigny hosted a scrumptious reception for us at the Presidential Palace.

On Tuesday, August 28, we woke up to a continuation of the session on the International Control of Dangerous Drugs, which ran concurrently with the Human Rights Section's Seminar on Human Rights for Refugees, Hon. Chairman Nagendra Singh, Associate Justice International Court of Justice, India, presided over by H.E. Felix Schnyder, Ambassador to the United States, Switzerland Formerly United

[62] Speakers in many of these sessions produced Work Papers.

Nations High Commissioner for Refugees, and continuation of the Law and Computer Technology Section.

A session on a new topic was introduced at the 9:00 A.M. hour simultaneously – Special Study Committee on Revision and Strengthening of U.N. Charter, Hon. H.T. Lee, Grand Justice Republic of China, Presided over by Dr. Max Habicht, Switzerland.

The Hon. Thurgood Marshall, Associate Justice Supreme Court, U.S. was the luncheon speaker.

The afternoon bought with it the Criminal Law Section's concurrent session on Terrorism, Hon. Chairman Rolv Ryssdal, President Supreme Court Norway, presided over by Marut Bunnag, Thailand.

The concurrent Multinational Business Law Session, Honorary Chairman Hon. T. Akinola Agouda, Chief Justice Supreme Court Botswana,[63] on Development Law for Developing Nations, presided over by Prof. Tokusuke Kitagawa, Tokyo Metropolitan University, Japan.

Another concurrent afternoon session was the Section on Intellectual Property, Honorary Chairman Hon. Torwald Hesser, Justice Supreme Court, Sweden, presided over by Prof. Svante Bergstrom Uppsala University Sweden.

The Committee on Expanding the Jurisdiction of the International Court of Justice presented an interesting seminar by Honorary Chairman S. Azu Crabbe, Chief Justice Supreme Court Ghana, presided over by Lee S. Kreindler, Esq., U.S. (Kreindler later became known for his work in airplane disaster cases)

---

[63] During this period, by virtue of having one of the largest developed bars in Nigeria, Nigeria had loaned several Judges and lawyers to other developing countries. Botswana was one of them. However, the High Court of Botswana is now the court of plenary jurisdiction, with the Court of Appeal as the apex court. In his seminal article Chief Judge Elias tells of Nigeria's many contributions to the bar and bench around Africa as African nations became independent. See n.64, below.

The Trial Lawyers Section treated us to a Demonstration Trial: International Skyjacking. Chairman was Tafari Berhane, Ethiopia, with Hon. T.O. Elias,[64] Chief Justice Supreme Court, Nigeria presiding.

Wednesday, August 29 continued the session on Development Law for Developing Nations.

There were concurrent morning sessions on Problems of Urban Development, Honorary Chairman Hon. Hamoodur Rahman Chief Justice Pakistan, Presiding Officer Hon. Esther Tchouta-Moussa Ministry of Justice, Cameroon. and the Section of International Education on Africa and the Development of Legal Education, Honorary Chairman Hon. Brian A. Doyle, Chief Justice Supreme Court, Zambia, Hon. Raymond Pace Alexander, U.S., presiding.

In the afternoon, the Urban Law and Development group presented a concurrent seminar on The Environment with the same officers.

The other afternoon seminar was presented by the Law of the Sea group, discussing the Blue Revolution, Honorary Chair Keba M'Baya, Chief Justice Supreme Court, Senegal, with Dr. Milenko Milic of former Yugoslavia as the Presiding Officer.

That evening, Hon. Konan Kanga, Mayor of Abidjan, hosted us at a reception. The New York Times reported[65] that:

> ABIDJAN, Aug. 25 (UPI) Hundreds of lawyers and judges from about 115 countries are about to try again to advance programs aimed at replacing war with law.
>
> The World Peace Through Law organization will hold its 10th anniversary convention there beginning tomorrow. More than

---

[64] On August 1, 1985, Judge Elias presented a seminal paper on *Organization and Development of the Legal Profession in Africa, in particular the ability of the Bar and judiciary to uphold the rights of both the citizen and the state.* See The Denning Law Journal at 49 (ca. 1985). It is an essay explaining how the convenors established the African Anglophone legal systems. It is noteworthy that none of the 300 judges and lawyers at the London conference were black Africans.

[65] https://www.nytimes.com/1973/08/26/archives/peace-through-law-group-meets-today-in-ivory-coast.html (Accessed 12 December 2024)

100,000 of the world's one million lawyers are working in its program.

So, you see, the receptions were full of people.

Thursday morning , August 30, 1973, would bring the Criminal Law Section's discussion of the Report on International Criminal Court , Honorary Chairman Dr. Kamal Hossain, Minister of Foreign Affairs, Bangladesh, Presiding Robert K. Woetzel, Esq., U.S.

Mr. Woetzel presented a paper on "Draft Convention on International Crimes; Draft Statute for an International Criminal Court."

Fifty years later, Kim Hall, my best friend in Botswana, where I was now living, had occasionally mentioned her friend Helen and Helen's husband, Professor Nsereko., who she had befriended when they lived in Botswana. Helen is an American and Daniel is a Ugandan.

I was intrigued by her description of the Professor, and her friend Helen, so she sent me the cover of one of his books, "To the Hague from Nabinene." So, on 12 December 2024, I asked the clerk at Exclusive Books in Gaborone if they carried the book. She said no. I then found an excerpt from the book on google books.[66]

Judge Daniel David Ntanda Nsereko played a significant role in the formation and development of the International Criminal Court (ICC).

Judge Nsereko's advocacy of using indigenous languages to teach students, including science, is a topic of current conversation, not only in schools, but in legal judgments, as well. He argues that students do not need to be taught in foreign languages, such as English. He argues that Chinese, Korean, Japanese and Thia children do not have to forego their "native languages for the sake of being able to communicate with the rest of the scientific community of the world. See how scientifically advanced they are!"[67]

---

[66] https://www.google.co.bw/books/edition/To_the_Hague_from_Nabinene/T9XcEAAAQBAJ?hl=en&gbpv=1 (Accessed 12 December 2014)

[67] Id. at 14.

On the other hand, as Dr. Churchill L. Onen, my physician here in Botswana, also from Uganda, says that this would not work because many of the scientific concepts and words do not exist in Setswana, the language of most of the Batswana. The languages of China, Korean, and Japanese are far older than that of Botswana.

Recently however, in the legal world, some of the South Africa courts are issuing their judgments in local languages.

'Groundbreaking' labour judgment written in Sesotho

By Daily News Published on Wednesday, 07 December 2022 Tags: #Litigation

---

A Truworths cashier fired for short-changing the company won't be going back to her job at the fashion retailer after the Labour Court found that her dismissal was lawful, reports **News24**.

In a groundbreaking judgment penned in Sesotho by Acting Judge Smanga Sethene, the court disagreed with the CCMA's ruling that overturned the company's decision to fire Maphasha Mochekgechekge.

Sethene reviewed and set aside the CCMA decision, stating that the 'arbitrator misdirected himself and failed to take into account the evidence that was before him'.

The acting judge started his judgment by explaining why writing the judgment in Sesotho was essential.

He quoted Judge Neville Holmes, who in 1958 penned a judgment in Afrikaans and said: *One's experience is that the winner is usually content to know merely that he has won. But the loser likes to know the reasons why he has lost. I proceed to give judgment in the language of the losers.'*

Sethene said Mochekgechekge had first asked for a Selobedu and Sepedi interpreter, and when they were not available, she opted for a Sesotho interpreter instead.

The Acting Judge said: 'With that in mind, it dawned on the court that when the judgment is handed down written in the language of King Charles III, Ms Mochekgechekge may not understand why she lost. In the circumstances, ***I considered it apt to write this judgment in the language of King Letsie III, which is Sesotho, for the benefit of Ms Mochekgechekge and many others who have never seen or read a judgment written in Sesotho*** *since the dawn of democracy. (Emphasis in the original)*

https://www.southafricanlawyer.co.za/article/2022/12/ground-breaking-labour-judgment-written-in-sesotho/ (Accessed 13 DEC 2024) (Originally brought to my attention by my South African colleague Edward Lesufi on 13 DEC 2022)

I had the reverse history. When I was in graduate school chemistry, in the 1960s, I needed to understand what the great scientist Edward Teller had written. He wrote his paper in German. My native language is English. Having studied in Vienna for a year, including math and chemistry, I knew enough German to understand what Teller had written. Teller is the father of the hydrogen bomb and a founder of nuclear physics.[68]

As I began to read, some of Judge Nsereko's history. I realized that in 1979 I had visited the general area that he comes from. It was clear that I was intimately familiar with some of the events he described, as I was counsel to Godfrey L. Binaisa during that time. I met Mr. Binaisa in 1977 in Mount Vernon, New York, and we became good friends. I

[68] Omitted, information generally available.

visited when Mr. Binaisa became interim President of Uganda in 1979 -80.I

Returning to the International Criminal Court (ICC), Judge Nsereko was instrumental in laying the groundwork to establish the ICC in 1998. He worked on this project while working full time as a professor and administrator at the University of Botswana. He attended the 1998 United Nations Diplomatic Conference of Plenipotentiaries that approved the Rome Statute which established the ICC.

On 03 December 2007, Prof. Nsereko attained the necessary votes to become a Judge of the ICC.

His book provides a rare "insider's perspective on the workings of the ICC: the Court's historical roots, its purpose, functions, powers and limitations."[69]

Prof. Nsereko, as well as Kofi Annan, have issued staunch defenses against those who argue that the ICC was set up to selectively prosecute Africans.

His story demonstrates the benefits of having a vast network of friends.

The Thursday, August 30, 1973, concurrent session at the Abidjan Conference also brought with it the continued Section of Legal Education on Africa and the Development of Legal Education, continued, Honorary Chairman Hon. T.O. Elias, Chief Justice Nigeria, presiding.

I cited Chief Judge Elias's seminal 1985 presentation on this subject which explains the creation and evolution of the organization of the legal profession in Anglophone Africa. I highly recommend reading this article to anyone who wishes to have a comprehensive understanding of this historical development and how today's (2025) Anglophone legal structure came about in Africa.[70]

---

[69] Id. at xvii (Preface by Dr. Cosmas Gitta, Former Assistant Director for Policy and UN Affairs at the UN Office for South-South Cooperation, UNDP)

[70] See n. 64 supra.

On this last meeting day, there were several meetings by various organs of the conference: Center Associates, Presiding Officer Marion Dentzel, World Association of Judges, Presiding Officer Hon. Earl Warren, The Chief Justice of the United States (Retired), Standing Committee on Law of Outer Space, Presiding Officer, Dr. I, H. Ph. Diederiks-Verschoor, Netherlands, followed by a Center Associates Luncheon which saw us witnessing the *"Pax Orbis Ex Jure" Awards.*

After the Luncheon, we attended the closing Plenary Session to hear the Presentation of Reports of Rapporteurs and Recommendations on conference Resolutions.

This was followed by the usual scrumptious, elegant African Reception and closing Gala Banquet.

I note that the comprehensive Conference Standing Orders provided that the official languages of the conference were English, French and Spanish, with simultaneous interpretation.

Before I left the US, I had asked my friend Lloyd Lynch, an electronics expert, to prepare a briefcase for me which would be voice activated so that I could sit in my seat and record the proceedings. I did some of that, but I soon saw that no one was interviewing the attendees. So, I started interviewing them.

I must have done a surprisingly good job because some of them lined up to be interviewed. Amazing. One even called me the next Walter Cronkite. Quite a compliment.

I think this man is the first one that I interviewed. I think he was from former Yugoslavia

I saw what surely must have been part of the apartheid South Africa security regiment, because these were the biggest men that I had ever seen. Years later, I would learn that some Afrikaners are quite big.

One peculiar thing happened. There was an African American who gave me his card with a Carson City, California address on it. He had been videotaping some of the conference. He told me that if I gave him my recordings, he would put a package together and send it to me. I never heard from him and was never able to contact him through the contact information he gave me. As a result, I lost this historical information.

Naïve at the time, I concluded later that he must have been on someone's payroll.

I am not sure if I recorded the following conversations, but Chief Justice Earl Warren told me that the "one-man, one vote" decisions were the most important that the US Supreme Court handed down during his tenure.

I was also able to tell Judge Damon Keith how I had used his analysis in the City of Hamtramck urban renewal case to stop the wholesale relocation of black and poor people from within the city limits the City of Newburgh, New York to somewhere outside of the city limits. This was proposed by a developer who wanted to use the riverfront property for building a high-end residential, commercial and industrial area.

The Hon. Clarence Clyde Ferguson, Jr. told me how he had smuggled Archbishop Luwum out of Uganda in the boot (trunk) of his official limousine when the Archbishop's life was in danger. Amb. Ferguson served as the American Ambassador in Uganda from 30 June 1970 to 19 July 1972.

Allegedly, Idi Amin murdered the Archbishop in February 1977 by shooting him in the mouth and by torturing him.[71]

These exchanges with these officials enriched my life.

I was 34 years old then.

I am 86 now.

---

[71] https://www.facebook.com/watch/?v=1495069054120980 (Accessed 21 DEC 2024)

Remembrances of the life, death, and state funeral, of late President Godfrey L. Binaisa, Q.C., Esq. of Uganda

There are few Americans who have witnessed first-hand so many of the issues involved in the affairs of an African state. Because of this, I have tried to give an extensive account of my activities and interactions.

The State Funeral for President Godfrey Lukongwa Binaisa

Godfrey Lukongwa Binaisa and his eldest daughter, Nakalema, 2002

On Thursday, 5 August 2010, I received an early morning telephone call from Lillian Nkoba telling me that Godfrey had passed away. Her call came at about 8:00 a.m. (3:00 p.m. Uganda time). She told me that he had passed away in his sleep. He was 90 years old. I had lost a great friend.

I immediately began to change my scheduled trip to New Orleans (where I was to be inducted into the National Bar Association Hall of Fame) and to head, instead, for Uganda to attend his services and to comfort his family as they had now lost their second parent.

I did not have a visa but wanted to get one before I left New York. I telephoned Joan Mack at the Uganda Mission to see what I needed. She told me and directed me to the Mission website, from which I downloaded an application. She also gave me the name of Pan Express, at my request, because I wanted to use a booking agent familiar with travel to Uganda.

At that time, no funeral arrangements had been finalized, except that Nakalema, his eldest daughter, later contacted me to tell me that there would be a State funeral, after 2 days of mourning (later extended to 5) and a national holiday. Pan Express could only get me out on Tuesday, August 10, at the earliest, because I thought I would not be able to get my papers and proof of medical coverage to the Mission before Monday.

I could get the visa in Entebbe, but I did not want to take the chance. I located Dr. Eduardo S. Granato, M.D., a travel medicine specialist in Eastchester, New York, after I was unsuccessful in getting the Typhoid vaccine administered on Thursday, 5 August 2010 by Dr. Valiere Alcena in White Plains I went to Dr. Granato a few years earlier to get my travel medicine. Dr. Granato could only see me on Friday at 2:30 p.m., 6 August 2010.

I kept the appointment, received the vaccine, and took off for the Uganda House in New York City after picking up a $60 money order from the Post Office to pay the visa application fee. I was not sure we could make it to the Uganda Mission in New York City from Dr.

Granato's office in Eastchester in time. My wife, Maleta, thought we should try, so off we went. We arrived at a parking garage across the street from Uganda House at 4:15 p.m. The visa office was scheduled to close at 4:30 p.m. I asked Maleta to dash across the street to present my visa application as I looked for parking. I had known Joan from the first time I visited Uganda in 1979.

I walked into the office, and Maleta was engrossed in a lively discussion with Joan and Duncan Muhumuza-Laki, First Secretary. Having been raised in a Botswana diplomatic family, Maleta had unsurpassed people communication skills.

Duncan believed I should travel sooner rather than later, as my KLM flight would put me into Uganda on Wednesday night. Joan processed the application without delay, with Duncan's blessing. He had asked a very pertinent question to which I did not have the answer – what the legal status of Godfrey's Rev. Moon's sponsored bride Tomako Yamamoto was.

After I arrived in Uganda, Gordon Wavamunno, Godfrey's close friend, told me that he had not been able to find a filed marriage certificate for Godfrey and Tomako, and thinks one was never signed. This raised the question of whether they were legally married. It is not clear that if they were, did they get an effective divorce?

Visa in hand, but tired as the dickens, I left New York City and set out to return to our residence in New Rochelle, New York. My clear-headed wife asked if we shouldn't try Pan Express to see if they could get me on a Saturday flight. Sunny (Pan Express) was able to do so.

I left Maleta in the car while I went to pick up the ticket upstairs in the building that housed the travel agency. An excellent driver, she was deathly afraid she would have to drive in New York City traffic jams, for the first time, away from the parking space I left her in. You see, in Botswana, her country, people drove on the other side of the road, and there was not nearly the same number of vehicles. Thankfully, the traffic officer passed her by.

Pan Express's Sunny brought the tickets down to the car and we headed home. Had I kept the original flight schedule, I would have missed the State funeral. It took place on Wednesday morning, and I would have arrived on Wednesday night. No food, so we stopped, ate, and started to pack. Maleta did a fabulous job with 2 pounds to spare. The airline had begun to charge for everything, including excess baggage.

Meantime, we had been scheduled to go to New Orleans on 8 August 2010 to attend the 85th National Bar Association ("NBA") annual meeting. In fact, I had drafted two resolutions and emailed them to Beverly Baker Kelly, Co-chair of the International Law Section ("ILS") and to Norma Hutcheson, Chair of the Resolutions Committee. The purpose of one was to link the various bar associations of color around the world to the NBA website and vice versa. The second was to call upon Rwanda to allow attorneys participating in the Genocide trials to do so without intimidation and arrest. Beverly later told me that both resolutions passed without amendment.

Maleta and my sons, Jason and Christopher, were left with the task of cancelling the various flight and hotel arrangements we had made for the trip to New Orleans. This was especially painful since I was scheduled to be inducted into the NBA Hall of Fame after 40+ years of practice. Working through my friend, Maurice Foster, Deputy Executive Director of the NBA, I thought the NBA had agreed to post pone my induction to the 2011 convention scheduled to take place in Baltimore, MD. Instead, they inducted me in abstenia. I was inducted in person the next year in Baltimore.

2011 Inductees left to right back row: Daryl Parks, Ed Gray, Taylor (?) Thelma Wyatt Cummings Moore, Jim Cole, me and Alice Bonner; front row: Alvin O. Chambliss Jr. (Forgot next two) Robert Bell, and Billy Murphy

Before I left, I sent a text message to Nakalema Binaisa, requesting the opportunity to make a few remarks at Godfrey's State funeral. I learned before my arrival that the children had decided that it would be understood that I would be allowed to speak and deliver one of the 13 eulogies.

When the Requiem Funeral program was printed, I saw that I was the only foreigner (except for Charles Njonjo, former Attorney General of Kenya) and untitled non-family member who had been selected to give one of the eulogies. The rest were Ugandans except for Mr. Njonjo, who was not able to make it.

Ironically, Godfrey had told me that in the early 60's when he and Njonjo were Attorneys General of Uganda and Kenya, respectively, Mr. Njonjo was reluctant to face Godfrey in court in a case where Kenya had arrested some Ugandans on weapons charges. Kenya's President Jomo Kenyatta told Mr. Njonjo that the prestige of Kenya was on the line and that if Mr. Njonjo refused to go to court to face Mr. Binaisa, then Mr. Njonjo should order the men to be released. He refused. They were released.

I would later learn that Mr. Njonjo was also friends with Sir Seretse Khama, first President of Botswana, where I now reside, stemming from the days when they were both students in England.

Off to the airport with 3 hours to spare. The dutiful wife that she is, Maleta saw me off by taxi. I almost missed the plane, KLM Flight, because the taxi I was riding in did not have E-Z Pass. E-Z Pass would have allowed us to pass the toll gate without stopping. We were forced to use the cash only lane. I got there just in time. The friendly attendant asked me to use the kiosk to get my boarding pass. I did so. I sat in my preferred aisle seat, but the kiosk gave me the option of changing my seat. I did so, to what I thought was a two-person row. Mistake! It was a middle seat.

I concluded that the kiosk displayed the seating plan for another airplane. I dreaded a middle seat trans-Atlantic , trans-Africa flight and paid the $105 to upgrade to the last remaining aisle seat. However, this seat was next to a huge Capetonian. He had overly broad shoulders but had managed. Besides his wife, our other row seatmate was a fellow Georgian whom I later met after we had exited the plane. Turns out he is well-traveled and is now the conductor of the Norway Opera. He and the Capetonian did not really talk to me, but it was obvious to me that I was at least as well-traveled as them, and except for the conductor, knew considerably more than the others about the opera. After all, I had attended the Vienna State Opera in 1959-60; the San Francisco opera in 2003, and the New York Met several times. I had also been a patron of the Met.

The flight was uneventful, but Schiphol, the airport in Amsterdam, was impeccably clean, well-organized, and very people - friendly, at all ages. There were ample eating and seating facilities. There were places to stretch out and relax. The chairs and sofas were tastefully decorated and had soft cushions, not the rigid plastic and steel uncomfortable bottom bashing chairs that you find at the pathetic New York airports of LaGuardia and JFK. In later years, they have improved the seating a bit.

I was pleasantly surprised to meet Joel Mugambwa and his family at the at Schiphol Airport in Amsterdam. Joel is the brother of my good friend, Ralph Nyakawbwa-Atwoki. Joel's family is Juliette, a development economist with the U.N. in New York, Oyo, a boy, and Catabe, a girl. Ralph and Joel were two of Godfrey's brothers-in-law, brothers of Irene, Godfrey's predeceased wife. They hail from the Kingdom of Toro, originally. We joined together to eat a freshly prepared breakfast at the airport, flap jacks, French fries, bacon and juice

Some of their relatives met us at Entebbe Airport, 08 August 2010, on a Sunday night. The Sheraton van lady allowed me to cancel my previously scheduled shuttle reservation. We were able to get underway after I recovered my bag which I thought I had lost. The bag had been before my eyes all the time, whirling round and round on the baggage belt. I was looking for a grey band wrapped around a bag, but my darling had forgotten to tell me that she had removed it.

Margaret, one of Ralph's sisters and a veterinarian I had met before, and another Joel, gave me a lift to the Sheraton in Kampala, while Juliette's niece took Joel and his family. Margaret had also worked a while in Botswana but was discouraged when the government began to reduce the emoluments for expatriates.

Since I had a breakfast plan at an excellent rate ($165/night w/o taxes), I took my breakfast at the Sheraton Kampala. The hotel seems to favor the government paper, New Vision, over The Daily Monitor, an independent paper. I read both but felt the latter was fairer to Godfrey. At least we got differing viewpoints. I also read Andrew Mwenda's "The Independent". Of the accounts that I read on how Godfrey was selected to be President, the account that Muniini Mulera Mulita[72] gave was more in accord with what Godfrey had told me.

Later, at the burial ceremonies at Nateete, President Museveni, speaking in English, said that he was the person who identified

[72] The Saturday Monitor November 6, 2010.

Godfrey for the National Consultative Council as being suitable for the Presidency and Chairman of the Council after they had forced Prof. Yusufu Lule to resign. He also said, in Luganda, which I would later understand after translation, that he was the person who initiated the removal of Godfrey from office.

I do not remember right now where I ate, or if I ate, dinner on the night of our arrival. It was late after I arrived at the hotel. I think I ordered a bowl of delicious clam chowder soup with some very tasty sourdough bread from room service.

The next morning, I viewed the scene from the eighth floor and discovered that I had a genuinely beautiful view of the City of Kampala. I took some photos to compare the view with the ones that I had observed in 1979/1980 and in 2002.

9 August 2010

On Monday, 9 August 2010, we were to go to Parliament where Godfrey lay in State. There was a mix-up at the time someone was to pick me up. When I spoke to her, Nakalema told me to stay put, but then forgot to pick me up. I think Margaret picked me up in the afternoon just after the body had been taken into the Parliament Building. Joel and his family saw the cars and hearse en route (and I think they arrived before the casket.) So much rested on the shoulders of Nakalema, I can see how she would forget.

Meantime the Sheraton hotel events board showed that the Uganda Christian Lawyers Fraternity was having a luncheon at the Sheraton at 1:00 p.m. Since they were lawyers, I invited myself in and was graciously received. Eunice Nabafu, The Project Director/CPD Coordinator received me. I also met Paul Asiimwe, one of the lawyers who had attended an Intellectual Property CLE in Boston. I also met Titus S.M. Kamya, Sekabanja Kato, Martin Erone, and Hon. Dickson Ogwana.

Then a man walks up to me and introduces himself as "I am the American lawyer." I responded by saying, "So am I." It turns out that this lawyer, Sam Casey, is the Executive Vice President and General Counsel of Advocates International, which is somehow affiliated with the Uganda Christian Lawyers Fraternity. I would learn that his organization quickly sponsored this luncheon to honor five of the Fraternity members who were called to the High Court. Since it was his luncheon, he gave a speech, citing various scriptures to support his thesis on how the new judges should conduct themselves.

Of course, I thought this was utterly inappropriate.[73] The issue of religion in the courtroom has been raised starkly at the International Court of Justice in connection with the Israeli genocide case, Justice Julia Sebutinde saying "The Lord is counting on me to stand on the side of Israel,"[74]

I thought silently that Sam Casey was invading Caesar's world. I thought that the counterpart to our judicial training centers would undertake this responsibility in New York. He told me that they were involved in the mediation of land disputes in Uganda. I thought this was a bit strange, since the land issue in Uganda was so complicated, even for Ugandan lawyers, let alone Americans. It reminded me of what Jomo Kenyatta had said about Kenya land in relation to Christian missionaries. He said that when the missionaries arrived, the missionaries had the Bible and the Kenyans had the land; now, the missionaries have the land, and the Kenyans had the Bible.

We will see.

I figured the luncheon would end by 2:30 or so and I could fill the time while I waited for Margaret (Ralph's sister) to pick me up at 3:00

---

73 The deleterious result of this fusion of religion into the law in Uganda may be seen by the ICJ judge from Uganda in "Many people puzzled why the Ugandan judge on the International Court of Justice was often the only one to vote with Israel. She explains: "We are in the end times" and "the lord is counting on me to stand on the side of Israel." https://x.com/kenroth/status/1956305663061000365?s=12&t=t8tiVe1b9XH7tBO-4aVuWw (Accessed 17 August 2025)(Read comments in this link).

74 South Asia Journal – Sebutinde reveals religious bias; Justice Info – Sebutinde's background and reactions

p.m. We were to go to the Parliament Building where Godfrey lay in State.

Margaret arrived; we ascended the stairs and went into the Parliament Building. Had I known it was so close to the Sheraton, I would have walked over. Ironically, Godfrey's daughters Lena Nakalema Akiiki (Nakalema), Irene Naluwembe Atwooki (Nalu), Rosemary Nakabiri Amooti (Kipuchu), and Maazi (Kutchi) were all wearing beautiful black and white dresses. I had worn my zebra black and white shirt Patrick Mulwale had given me, and my white linen pants. Patrick was Dineo's husband. Dineo was Maleta's cousin. They live in Indianapolis. Maleta and I attended their wedding in Indianapolis.

As I stood in front of the casket viewing Godfrey's body, I was overcome and the tears began to flow, copiously. My exhaustion did not help. After a few minutes, I turned and Amooti received me, whereupon we let loose rivers of tears. Then followed embraces by Maazi and Nalu. Nalu was accompanied by her son Kwame, a bright, well-behaved 13-year-old. We had a lively discussion about the study of chemistry and mathematics, both of which he enjoyed. I majored in chemistry and math at Morehouse College in Atlanta. I had also studied math and chemistry in Vienna, Austria in 1959-1960, as a Merrill Fellow. I later earned a master's degree in physical chemistry from the University of California at Berkeley, California, one of the world's preeminent universities, in addition to my Juris Doctorate degree

We sat for several hours, Nalu and I holding each other's arms and hands as we sat, her right, my left. Maazi left to order some food, and we were treated to freshly cooked chicken, chips and Fanta orange soda. Incidentally, this soda tasted better than the Fanta we drink in New York.

While we were sitting there, an alarm sounded continuously, which prompted someone to say that Godfrey would have quipped, "What's with this alarm? I thought I was supposed to rest in peace!" The funeral director had done an excellent job, for Godfrey's body looked as if it would spring out of the casket at any moment.

At some point, before I arrived, I think Nakalema had called to ask if I had prepared a will for Godfrey. I told her I did not think so but would look in my files when I returned to New York. She told me that they searched and asked the Uganda lawyers but could not find out who had done so. She told me that Godfrey Lukongwa Binaisa had transferred title to all of his property to her, but that she knew he had promised to give me some land (1 acre she said) but I told her that I told Godfrey that it was impractical because I did not live in Uganda, but he insisted that I have it anyway. In fact, in 2002, he had taken me, and my sons Jason & Chris up to Mutundwe Hill to see the property. He pointed to what was supposed to be my land. There was at least 1 TV or radio station on that hill at the time. During this 2010 trip, Ralph pointed out Mutundwe Hill to me from Entebbe Road on the way to the airport. Now there were 3 towers on the property.

Nakalema told me she intended to honor his wish that I get this property, but that I might want to have her buy my interest for about $85,000.00. She also told me she intended to honor his gift of property to Mary.[75]

Godfrey told me that the military had used his Mutundwe Hill residence as a place of operations during the 1986 (?) civil war. When we visited the property in 2002, we saw that the military had trashed it. A lot of the structures had been destroyed and there were animals walking through the various rooms. I could see that Godfrey was heartbroken.

The government had promised to restore it, but the last time I mentioned the topic to Godfrey, he told me that they had done nothing and were also dragging their feet on providing him with the benefits of his office as a former Head of State under The Presidential Emoluments And Benefits Act. On this trip someone told me that the government had offered him the option of rebuilding his house or paying him $250,000 to compensate him for the loss. The realtor told me that Godfrey opted to take the $250,000.00. At the time we visited in 2002,

---

[75] Not sure who this is or if it is a typo, meaning Maty = Mutundwe

he was living in a large, leased house that the government had provided. That house was in Mukindye. This was the first time that I had been in a house with movable iron safety doors embedded in the walls to protect the occupants from intruders.

Incidentally, Lillian Nkoba, a friend with whom Godfrey lived just prior to his last return to Uganda in 2001, told me that he had told her he had given me some property and that because he had done so, he must have really loved me because Africans do not part with their land. Godfrey had also showed me some property he wanted to give me overlooking Lake Victoria.

On this visit, Francis Burungi (Irene's son) said something to me about Godfrey's giving me some property overlooking Lake Victoria. But I digress.

Godfrey's body lay stately and dignified in the casket, reminding me of the times when he would tuck his chin into his chest and assume the Presidential strut, which I teased him about. The body language of the guards guarding the casket suggested that they were not quite sure of what to make of this non-Ugandan shedding tears for their fellow President. They understood even less the apparent easy familiarity with which I interacted with the Binaisas and relatives who were present. The Binaisa women placed me in a seat between Nalu (Irene) and Amooti (Rosemary). Kwame sat to the left of Nalu and Maazi sat to the right of Amooti. Three of the Baganda whom I thought were princes or elders sat to the left of Kwame, separated by a couple of seats.

Throughout the vigil, the Police Service Band and Choirs played mournful funeral dirges all night. The Prison Service band played until midnight, and another band continued to play after midnight. I think I left about 1:00 a.m. In the interim, Maazi, who had written "Heaven in Your Handbag," had said a prayer with those present linking hands.

At one point, I went over to sign the Condolences Book.

I did not know most of those who came by to show their respects, but I did remember Mr. Emmanuel Tumusiime-Mutebile, then

Governor or the Bank of Uganda and he recognized me from my visits and residence at State House in 1979-1980. I walked over to him as he signed the Condolences Book. He had become heavier, and his neck pitched his head forward and downward. He related that he had some health issues but did not reveal the source or nature of his illness, so I do not know if it was temporary or more chronic.

Someone had said that he had become a bit bent over because of his constant reading of books and records. With the passage of time, he had become much heavier than he had been in 1979 when I first met him. He died 23 January 2022 (aged 72) in Nairobi Hospital, Kenya.

In 1979 -1980, Mr. Tumusiime had been Ben Dramandre's assistant. My interaction with them had always been cordial and pleasant. A few days later I would now see them together again at the Binaisa residence. My recollection is that Mr. Dramadre was Godfrey's Chief of Staff. I remember them both as being resolute and diligent.

Of the people I met that night, Chris Kaddu, a lawyer, and I became friends. He would later give me a lift from the burial location to the Binaisa residence. He referred a Ugandan widow of an American serviceman to me to see if I could assist her to secure her survivor benefits. I was able to contact Mr. Daniel Griffin to secure her veterans' survivors' benefits. As it happened, Mr. Griffin, a program specialist with the Veterans Service Agency was located in Westchester County, where my law offices were located, about 5 minutes away. Mr. Griffin was able to secure her benefits.

10 August 2010

The next day I went back to Parliament, and we sat for vigil again. This time it was suggested that I sit in the second row, lest mourners confuse me for being Patrice Binaisa or Godfrey Binaisa, Jr.

The speaker's procession was supposed to enter Parliament at 2:00 p.m. Members of Parliament kept Uganda time, and this processional started late. But this was only the second time Uganda held a State funeral for a former President, so this was understandable. Maazi gave me a copy of the program for Parliament and at the then slipped appointed hour, they wheeled Godfrey's casket into Parliament. By this time, we had all gone upstairs to the visitors' gallery, except the immediate family, which was allowed to sit in a special set of seats downstairs in the Chambers, first floor, where the members of Parliament sat. Seated with them was Gordon Wavamunno, a close family friend, and another man, whom I did not recognize.

The business of Parliament on that occasion was to move and debate a resolution of Parliament to pay tribute to the late Godfrey Lukongwa Binaisa.[76] The debate was orderly and thought provoking, although some who listened to it thought they heard an interplay of geographical politics.

The Rt. Hon. Prime Minister Leader of Government Business in Parliament, Professor Apolo R. Nsibambi, moved the resolution. He noted in the resolution that Godfrey had served the nation in many capacities and that as President, he had sought to unite all Ugandans! I had met him on my initial visits to Uganda in 1979/1980. In fact, I have a photo of me, him and Prof. Ssali, in front of Makerere University where I had gone with Godfrey to listen to a lecture delivered by Prof. Ssali. Sometime after this visit, Prof. Ssali tragically lost his life in an auto accident.

Hon. Prof. Morris Ogenga Latigo, Leader of the Opposition in Parliament, was the 1st Seconder and Hon. Oliver Wonekha, MP Bududa District, was the 2nd Seconder of the motion.

Several members talked about serious need to come up with a procedure to govern State funerals, covering such things as the number of days of mourning, how flags were to be flown, where the decedent should be buried, and so forth. James Akena, the son of the first President of the Republic of Uganda, H.E. the late Milton Obote, recounted the uncertainty that surrounded the funeral arrangements for his late father.

---

[76] See Resolution at the Appendix.

In fact, Nakalema did not know what the arrangements were going to be with respect to some of these items, as she related them to me before I left New York. She had been told that there would be two days of mourning and at that time they did not know when the funeral would be held, and I think she said that they were uncertain as to where he would be buried. In Godfrey's case, the question was whether he should be buried at the Kololo Field of Heroes or a place that the family selected. In the end, he was buried at Nateete Mackay Church of Uganda where his parents were buried.

This issue was a serious one for the children. Nalu (Irene) discussed it with me to some extent and told me how important it was to have a discussion with one's children beforehand so they would know what the parents' wishes were and to know what to expect. At the age of 81, I took her words to heart. There had been several people who gave conflicting reports of where Godfrey said he wanted to be buried. Mr. Wavamunno said in a television interview that Godfrey had expressed to him the desire to be buried at the Kololo Field of Heroes. I never had this discussion with him, but it could be that one heard different conversations at various times, depending on the circumstances.[77]

I would later learn that one would need permission to visit this Kololo Field of Heroes gravesite; even relatives. Joel Mugambwa pointed out to me that one fear that some people had expressed was that a government could arbitrarily decide that they wanted to use the land to build on, exhume the bodies and re-locate them. He said it had been done before, although I am not sure where he was referring to.

Part of the funeral program at the cathedral, which lasted about 4 hours, called for the laying of wreaths on the casket. Various people did so – family members, the Rt. Hon. Speaker, H.E the Vice President (he was listed but I don't remember if he did so or not) the Rt. Hon.

---

[77] Mr. Wavamunno discusses the issue of where he is to be buried in his book *The Story of an African Entrepreneur.* He gave me this book on one of my visits to Uganda.

Deputy Speaker of Parliament, the Rt. Hon. Prime Minister/Leader of Government Business, the Leader of the Opposition and others.

I was given the honor of also laying a wreath on his casket. I did so.

At the end of the service, the casket was delivered to the family resident in Mukindye.

When I arrived, with Margaret I think, huge white tents (marquees as they are called in Botswana) had been erected on the property to receive visitors.

My great friend Ralph Nyakawbwa-Atwoki was there. This was the first time I had had the chance to speak with him on this visit. He enthusiastically began to introduce me to several people, some of whom I had met in Uganda in the past. Included among these were Ben Dramadre who was recently retired as the Chairman of the Electricity Rates Commission and Emmanuel Tumusiime – Mutebile, who was now the Governor of the Bank of Uganda, and Princess Bagaya of Toro.

I understand it was she who oversaw the acquisition or building of Uganda House, next door to the United States Mission building to the United Nations. I think this was during President Amin's time and the rumor was that he wanted Uganda House built so that it would be taller than and overlook, the United States U.N. Mission Building across from the United Nations. He wanted Uganda to look down on the United States.

Ralph also re-introduced me to his daughter, Charlotte Karungi Mafumbo. When I first met Charlotte some time ago, she was thinking about a career in conflict resolution. She later became the Academic Director of the Uganda Studies Abroad program at Makerere University.

Also there was Gordon Wavamunno, who Godfrey had introduced me to in 1979.

We met again in 2002, when I took my sons to visit the Binaisas in Uganda. On that occasion, he graciously invited us to dinner through Mr. Binaisa. His residence was eye opening.

Me, Godfrey and Gordon in a sitting room in Gordon's mansion (2002)

The house had 64 bedrooms, two Olympic-sized swimming pools, an exceptionally large parking lot, and an in-house elevator. The beautiful dining room tables give some idea of this tastefully opulent residence:

The beautiful dining room of Mr. and Mrs. Wavamunno's house, with children to be seated at the smaller children's tables in front.

Hundreds of people congregated at Godfrey's residence where his body lay in one of the rooms of the house. I marvel at how some of them made it. Many came with their new 4-wheel drive Mercedes and others. Given the state of some of the pot-holed, eroded, red clay roads, I wonder how they made it, especially if they took the back routes. The main road leading to the house was in better shape.

The food was plentiful and delicious.

The man who presided over this informal visit was Q.C. himself, Godfrey Lukongwa Binaisa, who lay in his casket in the lounge of his residence. I say he presided because there was a lot of chatter about him throughout the tents.

Brian Kaggwa, a lawyer whom I met later, did a reasonably excellent job of keeping the food processional moving in an orderly fashion. Godfrey was counsel to Brian's firm in Kampala. Brian would later tell me that he was looking for an American lawyer with oil and gas expertise, as commercial quantities of oil had been discovered in Uganda. This discovery was around Lake Albert (renamed Lake Sese Seko) which was where Godfrey had told me he suspected oil deposits in 1979. There were seepages of oil from the ground.

After I returned to the United States, I set up a meeting among Brian, and Ben Wilson, Chairman of Beveridge & Diamond, P.C., who invited Steve Hill, and Shemin _______to discuss Brian's need for oil and gas expertise and to introduce him to a wider range of American lawyers. The meeting took place at Ben's offices at Beveridge & Diamond, P.C. in Washington, D.C. on September 2, 2010

Although we knew there was a possibility of oil production, the question was whether it could be extracted commercially. It wouldn't be until 2006 that commercial quantities of oil were discovered.

Decades later, in August 2014, at the USA-Africa Summit in Washington, D.C. hosted by President Obama, I had a discussion with one of Uganda's engineers who told me that one outside consultant- oil company had concluded that the oil could probably not be extracted commercially, because the oil was too heavy, Uganda had no pipeline or refinery and so forth. He said President Museveni then got a second opinion from its own Uganda engineers who disputed part of the findings, and concluded they could extract the oil, build a pipeline and refinery and heat the oil so that it would flow thought the pipeline. I understand that construction was scheduled to start late 2025.This would be the last night that Godfrey would spend in his home. I had intended to place one of my cards in Godfrey's lapel pockets which I had discussed with Maazi or Amooti at the Parliament Building, but somehow, I forgot to do it. I placed one in his casket at the residence.

Of all the people Godfrey had met in the United States, I think I was the only one who attended the funeral ceremonies. They might not have known as none of the major newspapers or wire services reported his death. Also, because things moved so swiftly, they might not have been able to make travel arrangements in time.

Joel Mugambwa and his family dropped me back at the Sheraton. I had asked the Binaisa young women earlier that day what time I should be at Namirembe Cathedral where the funeral services would be held at 10:00 o'clock the next morning. They said they were going to be there at 8:30 a.m. but I should try to get there earlier. At one time, Canon Reverend Ananiya Jjukko "Ssalongo" Binaisa (1892-1995), Godfrey's father, had been the priest of this Cathedral.

Namirembe Cathedral 1979-1980

Because of the need to go through security, since they had expected H.E. the President Yoweri K. Museveni to be there, Joel suggested I should get there by 7:00 a.m. I compromised and ordered a taxi for 7:15 to leave the hotel. We travelled with ease. I had the greatest fear of getting stuck in traffic or the security line and not being able to deliver my eulogy. Extra police and military personnel were on duty that morning since President Museveni was expected to be present. The program that we received later listed him as one of the eulogists.

Guess what? I was the first person to arrive. Already there was a very heavy police and military presence. I walked into the cathedral – where I had visited before – to be greeted by a somewhat startled priest, who told me that morning prayers had just ended and that I was a bit early for the 10:00 a.m. funeral service. However, this gave me the opportunity to rehearse my remarks and make some last-minute changes. I was just following their example. I continued to make changes right up to the time I was called up to speak, adjusting to consider some of what the first few speakers had said.

There had been some reports (including the published program for the burial of Godfrey) that the service was going to start at 9:00 a.m. and this was probably the reason that Jon Qwelane, the South African High Commissioner to Uganda, arrived with his wife at 8:45 a.m. Since the Rt. Hon. Speaker had announced the time as 10:00 a.m. the night before, I felt confident that 10:00 a.m. was the correct time.

I introduced myself and told him that I was also a friend of H.E. Jerry Matjila, his counterpart and South Africa's Permanent Representative of South Africa to the UN and International Organizations, Geneva. I later learned that H.E. Qwelane had been an accomplished journalist in South Africa.[78]

The cathedral was filled with people, but H.E. Yoweri K. Museveni did not show up. Later, he explained at the burial services that something had come up that he as President, had to deal with so he could not be present at the services at cathedral. The sizable number of security personnel and the sweeping the cathedral with sniffer German Shepard also had indicated that he was coming.

I was honored to be seated with the family. I had already made certain that I knew where the loo was, given the anticipated length of the service. My body was spent. We sat on the left side of the nave facing the pulpit.

Seated to the right of us were the Rt. Hon. Prime Minister, Apolo Nsibambi, the Rt. Hon. Speaker, the Rt. Hon. Chief Justice, H.E. Gordon Wavamunno, (Honorary Consul of the Republic of Hungry), James Zikusoka (who had designed the Entebbe Airport), and others.

[78] Later still, in about 2012, I learned that Mr. Qwelane had written an editorial for the Sowetan Sunday Star November 24, 1986, titled "Dear Mr. Perkins, you are just not welcome. "Ambassador, *Warrior for Peace, p. 260-261, 537 n.2.* At the time, President Ronald Reagan had named Mr. Perkins as the first black American Ambassador to South Africa, with the secret mandate to dismantle apartheid. None of the South African press was friendly to Mr. Perkins in the beginning of his tour.

The beautifully designed Programmes for the Burial of the late Godfrey Lukongwa Binaisa, Q.C. with his photo on the front in a blue suit against a pale-yellow background and Uganda colors, closed the last outside cover page with Revelation 21:4. Below is one of the program photos.

Godfrey Lukongwa Binaisa, Q.C., Esq.

The Programme outlined the events for 7-11 August 2010.

PROGRAMME FOR BURIAL OF THE LATE GODFREY LUKONGWA BINAISA Q.C. – FORMER PRESIDENT OF THE REPUBLIC OF UGANDA

Wednesday, 11th August 2010: Funeral Service at Namirembe Cathedral

9:00 a.m.	-	Mourners take their seats
9:30 a.m.	-	Arrival of Family/Relatives of the deceased
9:45 a.m.	-	Arrival of the Casket of the deceased
10:00 a.m.	-	Funeral Services
12:00 noon	-	MC announces Programme
		(Hon. Kabakumba, Hon. Wabudeya)

Laying of Wreaths

Order:

- Family members
- H.E. the President
- H.E. the Vice President
- Chairman NRM
- Speaker of Parliament
- Chief Justice
- Prime Minister
    - 1st Deputy Prime Minister
    - 2nd Deputy Prime Minister
    - 3rd Deputy Prime Minister
    - Dean of the Diplomatic Corps
- Other VIPs

Speeches: (Master of Ceremony invites the)

- Representative of the Family
- Rt. Hon. Prime Minister
- H.E. the Vice President
- H.E. the President
- Final Prayers

2:00 p.m. Burial Grounds at Mackay Church of Uganda, Nateete

(Master of Ceremonies, Hon. Kabakumba Matsiko)

Laying of the wreaths by:

H.E. the President

- VIP and other Mourners
- Speech by the Family Representative
- The Rt. Hon. 2nd Deputy Prime Minister/Minister of Public Service
- H.E. the President addresses the mourners at Nateete
- Final Prayers

  The similar Funeral Order of Service and the Requiem was beautifully designed, this time with Godfrey appearing (above) in a stylish brown coat with a dark blue tie, with animals on it against a light blue shirt, as he looked away while tugging at his right ear lobe. The back cover shows a photo of Godfrey in his Queen's Counsel dress,[79] sitting alongside Irene M.K. Binaisa, his late predeceased wife.

For the funeral itself, we were given the official printed program and a typed hand-out of the Programme for the burial of the late Godfrey Lukongwa Binaisa, Q.C. – Former President of the Republic of Uganda.

When I first saw the handout, which I received before the printed Programme was handed out, I became alarmed because my name was not listed, and I am afraid to say, my anxiety which had culminated from all the things that could go wrong, required that I speak to relieve it.

I had not had the opportunity to write any remarks before I left home and during the first few hectic, sleep-deprived, jet-lagged days, I

---

[79] He was The First Black QC in East Africa. https://medium.com/@barbenchafrica/godfrey-lukongwa-binaisa-the-first-black-qc-in-east-africa-1121a5e2683a (Accessed 13 DEC 2024) [This article also quotes then President Milton Obote and Godfrey Binaisa discussing why and how the 1966 constitution came about.]

also had no chance to write. I arrived on Sunday, and the funeral was scheduled for Wednesday.

I had had some of those premonitions that Chris, my son had, when he accompanied David Kotz, the SEC Inspector General, to give his report to Congress on the Bernie Madoff Ponzi scheme matter. Chris envisioned himself tripping as he approached his seat behind Mr. Kotz, spilling something all over him. I thought that if I did fall as I went up to speak, at least my remarks could be delivered with some coherence if they had been written. I thought the delivery would be better from a written statement since this was a State Funeral and I wanted to honor my friend by not being too disorganized or too wordy.

I didn't succeed though because it took me about ten minutes to deliver that 3-page speech. After watching the DVD that Mr. Gordon Wavamunno had given me, I was happy with the product and the delivery.

I had somehow managed to write some remarks but emailed them to Maleta for her observations since she had had extensive experience with official state functions, and because I have a great deal of respect for her ability to write well. She wrote a guide to the official protocol address and order for me and re-organized the document, for both of which I am eternally grateful. I now had, at least, a decent statement to read. The night before I rehearsed it aloud, once, underlining where I thought I should put specific emphasis. As I said earlier, I revised the emphasis and the speech right up to the last minute as I sat and listened to the two or three speakers who spoke before me.

The handout schedule was incorporated into the official programme schedule, and according to the handout, the President was supposed to be one of those to lay a wreath and to speak.

Thirteen people were selected to give eulogies. I was listed as the 8th person. Mercifully, the Mistress of Ceremonies changed the order, so I was called much earlier. Merciful because my jet-lagged, exhausted body was breaking down into more trips to the toilet than I had ever experienced before. I wondered if I was going to be able to stand there and deliver my eulogy. Looking back on it, she must have seen and understood my evident stress.

I read my statements at a cadence designed to get the message across, since I was the only one there who could give an account of his two stays in New York. As I scanned the audience, everyone seemed to have been connected to what I was saying.

The listed eulogists were Right Rev. Wilberforce Kityo Luwalira, the Bishop of Namirembe, Representative of his Majesty, the Kabaka of Buganda (I understand he was present but did not speak). Right Honorable Katikiro Engineer J.B. Walusimbi, Mr. Gordon Wavammuno, Chairman of the Spear Group of Companies, Mr. Emmanuel Tumusiime-Mutibele, Governor of the Bank of Uganda, Honorable Charles Njonjo, Former Attorney General of the Republic of Kenya, (who was a no show), Mr. Andrew Kasirye, Uganda Law Society, who did not make it as he was in Southern Sudan to help train its judiciary. Bruce Kyerere,[80] then current Uganda Law Society President, spoke instead, Mr. Leroy Wilson Jr., New York Bar Association, (I was amused that someone gave me this description which I did not know about beforehand, but out of an abundance of caution, asked Maleta to telephone Pat Bucklin, Executive Director of the New York State Bar Association that I had not misused the Bar's name), Dr. Edward Kayondo, Old Budonian Society, Nakalema Binaisa, eldest daughter, His Excellency General Yoweri Kaguta Museveni (who was prevented from coming to the cathedral because of the press of official business)[81]

My outline is as follows:

> TO THE BINAISA FAMILY, I SAY TO YOU PUBLICLY WHAT I HAVE SAID TO YOU PRIVATELY. YOU HAVE OUR DEEPEST SYMPATHY AND CONDOLESCES. AS

[80] Many years later, in 2023, I would meet Bruce again at the Pan African Lawyers Conference in Livingstone Zambia.

[81] He would later speak at the internment.

YOU KNOW, YOU ARE NOT ONLY MEMBERS OF THE BINAISA FAMILY. YOU ARE ALSO MEMBERS OF THE WILSON FAMILY.

HIS EXCELLENCY PRESIDENT YOWERI MUSEVENI

YOUR EXCELLENCIES, HEADS OF STATE AND GOVERNMENT

THE CHIEF JUSTICE

SPEAKER OF PARLIAMENT

HONOURABLE MINISTERS,

MEMBERS OF PARLIAMENT

YOUR EXCELLENCIES MEMBERS OF THE DIPLOMATIC CORPS

HONOURABLE CHIEFS AND REPRESENTATIVES HERE PRESENT

(FIND OUT HOW THEY ARE ADDRESSED IN UGANDA – AT HOME WE WOULD SAY HONOURABLE CHIEFS AND SUB CHIEFS)

REVEREND CLERGY

DISTINGUISHED LADIES AND GENTLEMEN

WORDS CANNOT BEGIN TO EXPRESS THE SENSE OF LOSS THAT I FEEL FOR MY FRIEND OF THE PAST 33 YEARS, H.E. THE LATE GODFREY LUKONGWA BINIAISA, Q.C. AND IF I MIGHT ADD, "ESQUIRE." IN AMERICA AND IN NEW YORK LAWYERS ARE KNOWN AS "ESQUIRE."

I MET GODFREY BINAISA IN 1977 IN MOUNT VERNON, NEW YORK, WHEN HE AND HIS FAMILY MOVED INTO AN APARTMENT BLOCK IN WHICH ME AND MY FAMILY WERE LIVING.

MY SONS JASON AND CHRISTOPHER MET AND BECAME FRIENDS WITH HIS CHILDREN PATRICE, NAKALEMA, NALU, KAPUCHU, MAAZI, GODFREY AND FRANCIS; AS WAS THE CASE WITH MY LATE WIFE JANE AND HIS WIFE IRENE. IN FACT, NAKALEMA AND PATRICE, AT SEPARATE TIMES, STAYED WITH US FOR A PERIOD TIME, AFTER WE HAD MOVED FROM MOUNT VERNON TO NEW ROCHELLE, NEW YORK.

I AM NOW MARRIED TO MALETA LUNA-ROSA MOGWE, A BOTSWANA CITIZEN. I HAD THE GREAT PLEASURE OF INTRODUCING HER TO GODFREY OVER THE TELEPHONE, WITH THE INTENTION OF BRINGING HER TO UGANDA TO MEET HIM, BUT THE SCHEDULE OF FLIGHTS FROM BOTSWANA TO UGANDA AT THAT TIME MADE THE TRIP IMPOSSIBLE.

OVER A PERIOD OF TIME, I HAVE GOTTEN TO MEET MEMBERS OF HIS IN-LAWS FAMILY, MANY OF HIS FRIENDS AND COLLEAUGES, BOTH HERE AND IN THE UNITED STATES.

FROM THE FIRST DAY WE MET WE TALKED ON A DAILY BASIS FOR A YEAR. THE FOLLOWING YEAR IT WENT FROM THAT TO EVERY OTHER DAY RIGHT UP UNTIL THE NATIONAL CONSULTATIVE COUNCIL APPOINTED HIM AS INTERIM PRESIDENT.

DURING THIS TIME, I WAS THERE FOR HIM AND HIS FAMILY AS A RESOURCE AND AS SOMEONE HE COULD SPEAK TO KNOWING I HAD HIS BEST INTERESTS AT HEART AND HE HAD MY EAR IF HE NEEDED IT.

I CAME TO UGANDA IN 1979 AND 1980 AND TRAVELLED WITH HIM AROUND THE COUNTRY AS HE

TRIED TO UNIFY VARIOUS GROUPS AND TO LIFT THEIR SPIRITS.

HIS MAJOR PREOCCUPATION WAS HOW TO RECONCILE THE VARIOUS INTERESTS OF THE COUNTRY AFTER THE DEPARTURE OF MR. AMIN AND THE REMOVAL OF DR. LULE.

HIS SENSE OF HUMOR IS LEGENDARY. HE HAD AN ENCLYCOPEDIC KNOWLEDGE OF HISTORY AND WORLD AFFAIRS. WE HELD DISCUSSIONS ON A WIDE VARIETY OF LEGAL ISSUES, INCLUDING THOSE THAT INTERSECTED UGANDAN AND AMERICAN LAW.

IN OUR 33 YEARS OF FRIENDSHIP I CAN STAND HERE TODAY AND SAY GODFREY NEVER DIRECTED A CROSS OR UNKIND WORD TOWARD ME.

ALTHOUGH WE MAINTAINED SEPARATE OFFICES (OR CHAMBERS AS YOU CALL THEM), IN 1995 WE FILED A MAJOR LAWSUIT IN THE UNITED STATES DEALING WITH IMPORTANT ISSUES OF WHEN THE UNITED STATES AND THE UNITED NATIONS COULD TAKE OVER A PERSON'S PROPERTY IN A FOREIGN COUNTRY AND NOT COMPENSATE THEM FOR IT. THE CASE WAS ULTIMATELY DISMISSED BUT PROVIDED THEORIES THAT SOME LAWYERS MIGHT BUILD ON IN THE FUTURE.

GODFREY BINAISA WAS A PATRIOT OF THIS COUNTRY. HE ALWAYS PROMOTED UGANDA WITH LOVE WHEN HE WAS IN THE UNITED STATES. HE WOULD OFTEN EXPRESS TO ME HIS DESIRE TO RETURN TO UGANDA SO THAT HE WOULD BE LAID TO REST IN HIS NATIVE SOIL. I AM HAPPY TO BE HERE TODAY TO HAVE OUR LAST CONVERSATION.

AND SO, MY FRIENDS, I END BY ASKING WHO OF THE HISTORIANS AMONG YOU WILL TELL HIS DEFINITIVE STORY TO INSPIRE YOUNG UGANDANS AND SHINE THE LIGHT ON AFRICA'S BRILLIANCE FOR ALL THE WORLD TO SEE?

WE WILL ALL MISS HIM GREATLY, BUT AS HIS STAR NOW ASCENDS INTO THE HEAVENS, LET US REMEMBER THAT IN HIS OWN WAY, HE TRIED TO LEAVE THIS WORLD A BETTER PLACE THAN THE ONE HE FOUND.

FAREWELL MY DEAR FRIEND, FAREWELL!MAY YOU REST IN PEACE.

The handout schedule was incorporated into the official programme schedule, and according to the handout, President Museveni was supposed to be one of those who had a wreath and to speak.

Amooti sang a moving solo – Amazing Grace. She also asked me to lay one of the wreaths which had not been sent by a specific person or organization which I gladly did. I am grateful to her for that. She would later refer to me as "Pops".

I left the stage to return to my seat. Rt Hon Professor Apolo Nsibambi, Prime Minister and Leader of Government Business in Parliament, reached out and took my hand, pulled me toward him and told me he liked what I had said. He was now governor of the Bank of Uganda. I had been called to speak before him, sort of reversing the protocol order.

Prof. Emmanuel Tumusime-Mutebile, whom I had met in 1979 in Uganda as One of Godfrey's personal assistants, gave a genuinely nice tribute at the state funeral. He was now Governor of the Bank of Uganda. It read as follows.

REMARKS BY PROF. EMMANUEL TUMUSIIME-MUTEBILE AT

THE FUNERAL SERVICE OF THE LATE GODFREY BINAISA,

NAMIREMBE CATHEDRAL, 11 AUGUST 2010

I want to testify that before us lies a man of incredible complexity, yet with the simplicity of Spartan proportions, an erudite (well learned) man who was willing to listen to uneducated people; a man who was decidedly social democratic without being anti-business; a man of laws and high politics who had the time for his family and especially the kids. Here lies a man who loved his tribe without being a tribalist, and a man who was so humorous that those who did not know him well would take him for not being serious, and lastly a man who was so confident as to live [sic] the affairs of his office almost entirely to a technical staff whom he had not personally selected, and indeed a staff whom he had not personally previously known, and a staff drawn from all parts of Uganda.

On the night when the Honourable Binaisa QC was asked to be President, I was by the Secretariat of the National Consultative Council to work on the staff of the new President. In fact I was the first staff that Mr Binaisa was given. I am proud to say that I have never regretted this decision and I know none of the other staff who have ever regretted being selected to work for him. He did not know us but within weeks anybody who found us working for President Binaisa thought that he had known us personally for a long time.

We came to find out that this cross in the man's natures, that to work with us was part of the call of duty. Other people can speak of his accomplishments in the anti-colonial struggle and indeed in my other calls of duty that he had to answer. I will only speak about two. The first, in the 1966 crisis, because it showed the man for the nationalist that he was. Following the crisis between the President and the Prime Minister, the Honourable Binaisa as Attorney General presented to the Prime Minister the Republican constitution which he wrote to save the country. This was a triumph of patriotism from a man who nonetheless recognised the long held traditions of the Buganda Kingdom.

The second call of duty was the night in June 1979 when the National Consultative Council called upon him to replace Professor Lule. Following his assumption of office, the most important single driving force in everything Binaisa did was to unite as many of the political groupings as was possible. That was the origin of his politics of One Umbrella. He had no other motive. Although he has been accused of trying to use his office for business, I can say without fear of possible contradiction that President Binaisa did not use his office for making wealth, even if a number of business people no doubt tried to use him to do so. President Binaisa was a man of integrity to an extent that was rare in the chaotic times following the politics of Mafuta Mingi under Idi Amin.

Personally, I have wonderful memories of President Binaisa who remained my friend after he was deposed, although I continued to work for his successors. He made me a friend of his family and I came to know the family very well. Even over these sad days, I was sharing some jokes that Godfrey used to regale us with.

Finally, let me say that Uganda is so much the poorer because of the death of Godfrey Binaisa. May his soul rest in Eternal Peace.

After the service ended and we were entering the aisle to leave the cathedral, I handed the Prime Minister two of my business cards and asked him if he would have his staff send me a copy of his speech. He said he would. I also shook Mr. Wavamunno's hand and spoke to him but did not have a conversation with him at that time. When I mentioned to Maleta that I was not sure if any of my old friends were there, she told me that I had now became a "Big Man" and that I would have to invite them up to see me (even though I didn't know if they were there.)

We exited the church en route to the burial ground. I travelled with Joel and his family. His wife's niece was driving, and Joel, backseat driving a bit, managed to get us lost. He was trying to take the back routes.

When we arrived at the Burial Grounds at Mackay Church of Uganda, Nateete, the military/police were directing traffic. Somehow, they managed to get the various vehicles into the parking lot.

There was a very loud 21-gun salute.

President Museveni appeared at the Mackay burial grounds and made some remarks; some in English and some in a language that I did not understand, so I missed some of what he had said.

However, the audience was merciless. If he (or anyone else) mispronounced a word, they would loudly correct his mistake, in unison.

I have seen that there is a societal hierarchy. in Uganda and in Botswana. At the Mackay Burial ground, there were two or three VIP tents, which they call marques. I was sitting underneath one of these tents with the family and other relatives. After President Museveni made remarks to the crowd, he motioned for the family to move to the actual plot where Godfrey would be buried alongside his parents.

Since the announcement said that only family members would be allowed to go to the burial gravesite, I remained seated. President Museveni recognized me and came over and motioned to me to come and go with the family. As I stood up to go in that direction, he gave me a broad smile and shook my hand. I am eternally grateful to President Museveni for this warm gesture.

I had seen him once since my visits to Uganda in 1979 and 1980, and that was at the gala dinner of the ANC centenary celebrations in 2012 in Mangaung, South Africa. I also greeted him on that occasion.

We proceeded to go to the burial plot and several of us took hands full of sand to throw onto the top of the casket and, there might have been a few flowers thrown in as well.

Earlier, at the funeral ceremonies in Namirembe cathedral I noticed that there was a television camera recording the event and the same happened at the Mackay location. I happened to mention to Mr. Wavamunno that I wondered if I could get it copy of the DVD. He said you will have a copy this afternoon. I later learned that the reason he could speak so authoritatively to my request is that he owned the television station. I have that DVD along with my collection of other DVDs.

After the services, the Uganda Parliament passed a resolution honoring Mr. Binaisa for his service. Because his service encompassed the history of the things he did, I set out the full resolution in the APPENDIX, i. e. MOTION FOR A RESOLUTION OF PARLIAMENT TO PAY TRIBUTE TO THE LATE H. E. GODFREY LUKONGWA BINAISA QC, FORMER PRESIDENT OF THE REPUBLIC OF UGANDA

When I returned to the Sheraton after the services, I took the elevator downstairs to the in-house dry cleaners in the basement to thank the man who had prepared my suit, tie and shirt for the funeral. I was thrilled when he told me that he watched the ceremonies on television and when I appeared he said to his family members "you see that suit, tie, shirt? I cleaned and pressed them!"). He was excited. I was happy.

My History, Visits and Counsel to President Godfrey L. Binaisa in Uganda

In 1977, Henry Flagg came up to my apartment on the 6th floor of the building we were living in on Park Ave. in Mount Vernon, New York. He told me that he had just moved in a lawyer from Uganda into the 5th floor and that he thought we should meet. Henry was the proprietor of Flagg Brothers, a local moving company.

I went down to the 5th floor, knocked on the door of his apartment, and that is how I met Godfrey Binaisa. From that day forward, for the first year after we met, Godfrey and I spent some time talking every evening after dinner. The next year we talked about every other day about several issues involving Uganda, Africa, world affairs, and the practice of law.

At that time, Godfrey, his wife Irene, and children Nakalema, Nalu, Amooti, Maazi and Patrice were living in their apartment. I am not sure if Francis and Godfrey Jr. lived in the apartment at that time.

At some point in 1979, there was a shortage of petrol, and we had to line up at filing stations to purchase gasoline. Since I would have to wait in line to purchase gasoline, I went into the 7-11 store and purchased the local newspaper to read while I waited in line. I was astonished to read a short piece on the front page saying, "Mount Vernon Man elected President of Uganda."

Godfrey served as President of Uganda from June 1979 – May 1980.[82]

I went into the line and waited to purchase gasoline. After that I went to his apartment to see what was happening with his family. Irene and I placed a call to State House in Uganda. Godfrey asked if I was surprised. I said yes and was shocked. So, we began to discuss the return of his family to Uganda.

At the appointed hour, we all gathered at the airport at JFK for the flight to Uganda. Unfortunately, there was not enough room for me. So, I remained behind. I think the plane was a Gulfstream II.

I would take a flight into Kenya on October 14, 1979, via London's Heathrow airport, and traveled on to Entebbe, Uganda on 16 October 1979.

Union Carbide allowed me time off to assist Godfrey. I think this was helped along because sometime before Godfrey became President, I had invited him to lunch at the Union Carbide cafeteria with me and Joseph Geoghan, my boss at the time.

When I arrived, Godfrey entrusted me to Ralph Nyakawbwa - Atwoki, Irene's brother, to look after me.

Left to right Minister of Labor, Ms. Kalikwani, Dr. Kalikwani (a breeder of prized cows), and Ralph, who remains an exceptionally good friend to this day.

---

[82] For one account of how Godfrey came to occupy his office, see *Rise and Fall of Binaisa,* **The Monitor (Kampala)**, May 12, 2002, Posted to the web May 12, 2002 - Part 1

Ralph is an electrical engineer and all-around brilliant person. He was known as "Mr. Fixit," because every time something stop working, the call went out to Mr. Fixit. One humorous incident occurred when we were all sitting in the President's private quarters and someone hit the on power button for the TV. Nothing happened. Ralph looks at it, but all we got was snow. Godfrey , ever quick, quipped "at least that is a miracle here in darkest Africa ."

As we would go from place to place, it was quite common for people to stop us on the streets to greet us. Invariably, at that time if we were going to an administrative office to get something done, Ralph would ask the greeter about the ethnicity of the clerks. I don't think it mattered because we were always able to get what we wanted.

When we went to Kitgum and Gulu, Ralph would point with pride to some of the electricity equipment and distribution wires that he had installed or supervised.

Initially, Godfrey assigned two soldiers to safeguard us, armed with AK-47s. I never saw any hint of us being harmed and so I said to Godfrey that I thought we did not need the guards anymore because they could attract attention to others who think I was someone important. He agreed but left me with one guard.

I think my sense of the tasks that I was working on – 29 projects – kept me focused on what I was doing, so I never had any fear, including the night when one of the police officers was driving Frank and me and the filmmakers to a place where we would spend the night in Kitgum. The officer's vehicle was loaded with weapons.

Out of the dark, a group of armed soldiers appeared and began to question the driver. Ralph, Kacu as we call him, spoke with the soldiers, who were inebriated, and they let us pass.

It was significant that the policeman recognized the roadblock – not the elaborate things we see here, but it could be a stick, trig, rock, etc., as I learned from time to time.

Living at the statehouse in Uganda was another unforgettable experience. Again, everyone that I encountered, including the Tanzanian palace guard, were nice and kind. They also saw that their President Binaisa and I interacted very freely as close friends.

The then existing Statehouse was a huge building on beautiful grounds, overlooking Lake Victoria, the first or second largest lake in the world at the time. This was the residence of the President. There was a dining hall, a large formal reception area, sleeping quarters, other space, and a wing where he conducted official business.

Front, back and grounds of the Statehouse as they existed in 1979-1980.I understand that there is a newly constructed Statehouse.

In the dining room, the regular dining tables were arranged in a "T" fashion, with 4 chairs seated at the top of the T, and a long table leading up to it. Meals were served at specified times.

Godfrey and his wife Irene would sit at the head of the head table, I would sit to his right, and across the table from me would sit whoever he granted audience to. I was privy to remarkably interesting conversations. I will describe two.

One was with the Russian Ambassador. Godfrey and the Ambassador had a very pleasant conversation throughout. They reached the point where the Russian Ambassador asked Godfrey when Uganda was going to pay Russia for some the weapons it had supplied to Idi Amin. Godfrey looked him in the eye and said, "we are not going to pay you one red cent for the weapons you supplied to Amin to kill our people." That was that. The conversation continued.

The second I will recount was with a New York Times Magazine reporter. The reporter interviewed Godfrey at the table. It so happened that I returned to New York shortly after that interview. The report portrayed Uganda in a poor light. He wrote just the opposite of what the situation was at the time. I do not remember if Godfrey protested the deceitful report, but I learned to try to read or listen to more than one source regarding any given situation. In this respect, Botswana, where I now live, is a Godsend because I have so many channels of news about African countries as a whole.

Seated at the long table were Ministers and the President's cabinet, relatives, friends, and people who arrived between the time I went to bed and the time for breakfast. I would ask Godfrey "where did these people come from?" He said, "I don't know my dear, they just show up." Some were looking for a little money; others were looking for a meal. One request I heard over and over was for "a little piece of pork and an ice-cold beer." I don't remember the taste of the beer, but I do remember the taste of the most succulent pork I have ever tasted. My sons often tease me about this request, as they remember it as well, from their visit to Uganda with me in 2002.

During my 1979/1980 visit, Uganda started an exercise to change over its currency by removing Idi Amin's face on it. To do this Godfrey ordered the borders to be closed and to announce a schedule within the country for the changeover. Throughout the country, people started exchanging the old currency for the new currency.

Somehow, the message from the Uganda Minister of Finance to the Kenya Minister of Finance that this exercise was about to take place, and the borders would be closed never got through. Uganda or Tanzanian soldiers closed the borders on the Uganda side. This buildup of troops alarmed Kenya. So, Kenya began to beef up its side of the border.

Since tensions were building up, Godfrey decided to discuss the situation with President Nyerere of Tanzania over the telephone.

Nyerere asked Godfrey what he was going to do if certain contingencies occurred.

Jokingly, Godfrey replied "I will switch off their electricity. They will have to eat in the dark."

Finally, the word got through and Godfrey did not have to order the electricity from the Owens Fall Dam to be switched off to Kenya. The dam supplied electricity to both Uganda and Kenya.

Some people were bringing sacks full of noted to exchange.

One of those was Tiny Rowlands, the CEO of Lonrho, "who operated like a soldier of fortune."[83]

Rowlands arrived at night with an airplane load of currencies. His plane needed fuel. He was allowed to re-fuel, but Godfrey would not allow him to off-load the currencies. I do not remember the reason. He had to leave.

---

[83] Perkins, p.394 . n. 120

The 2002 Visit

In April 2002, I learned that I contracted prostate cancer. The cancer was discovered when my internist noticed a discrepancy between what his lab results were showing and the results obtained that my urologist had reported. It was this discovery, and the willingness of my urologist to re-take samples that led to a biopsy and the discovery of the prostate cancer.

Top photo - Glenn A. Davis, M.D., my internist

Bottom photo – Arthur L. Burnett, II, M.D.

My surgeon, Arthur L. Burnett, II,[84] told me that he could not operate right away because it would take some time for the tissue to heal that was damaged from the biopsy. So, I decided it would be a good time to re-visit Uganda and to give my family some appreciation of the African continent. We scheduled the operation for 23 August 2002, so I had some time to travel. My wife Jane was not able to join us.

Chris had always felt squeamish about flying, especially long distances, but he came through ok.

We had learned that the least expensive way to fly to Entebbe would be to buy round-trip tickets from NY to London and then round trip from London to Entebbe.

I made a day reservation for a room at the Ibis budget hotel to take naps upon our arrival in London, but after we arrived, we decided we did not need the rooms. We arrived early in the morning but would not leave London for Entebbe until 9:30 pm.

Godfrey was so happy that we arrived. We, on the other hand, were very jet-lagged. That did not stop him from taking us immediately to visit the One2Net exhibition booth at the Kampala Sheraton Tech Show. His daughter Maazi was a part of the One2Net group.

---

84 Patrick C. Walsh Distinguished Professor of Urology, The James Buchanan Brady Urological Institute Department of Urology The Johns Hopkins Medical Institutions . Dr. Burnett is the gifted surgeon who is the son of late Judge Arthur Burnett, Sr.. Judge Burnett had been active in the NBA for years, and I knew him. Dr. Burnett was one of the creators of Viagra, working on a project for Pfizer Pharmaceuticals. He is a professor of urology at Johns Hopkins University and a leading expert in erectile dysfunction. After I listened to his presentation at an NBA Men's Health retreat that Clyde Bailey organized, I said that if I ever needed the operation, he would do it. That is what happened.

On2Net group with Maazi just over my right shoulder, and Godfrey just over my left shoulder (2002)

By this time, the government had provided a secure house for Godfrey and his family. This is where Jason, Chris and I ate our first lunch in Uganda in 2002, with Godfrey and Nakalema, his daughter.

Jason, Christopher and Godfrey coming down the stairs of his residence at the time.

Godfrey's chef was also named Jane. Jane somehow always had food available, regardless of who came and what time they came.

We visited Mr. Maciah, Godfrey's friend and his guests. Jason, Chris, Nakalema, Maazi, Godfrey, his driver Leewombe, and me, constituted our little travel group. John, a gentleman from the information office in the government accompanied us, as had happened with the 1979-80 trip.

We reached Ssezzebwa Falls, not as impressive as Kabelaga Falls, or Bujagali Falls, but impressive and beautiful, nevertheless.

Left to right - Left of Jason were 3 of Mr. Maciah's visitors, Jason, Maazi (squatting) Christopher, Godfrey, Nakalema, Mr. Maciah is the tall man at the back, John, (squatting with my camera bag) 3 visitors in front of Mr. Miciah.

We would also get a chance to visit the structures of a rondaval for the first time. The walls were made of mud and cow dung, with thatched roofs. I would later see many in Botswana and South Africa, including one on the premises in Cathkin Park, near Drakensberg Mountains, South Africa, which had been converted into an office.

By 2002, the Jinja Municipal Town Council had erected a tastefully designed sign telling the history of the mouth and source of the Omigga Kiyira (Nile River). It read, as follows.

Once again, we see, in 1862, the British appetite for misappropriating other people's property by naming the Falls, "Ripon Falls" after the head of the Royal Geographical Society in London. The local people called them Bujagali Falls.

There was also a cadre of young drivers of rowboats fitted with a motor to carry us out to the actual source of the Omugga Kayira.

Origin of the White Nile River in Lake Victoria in Uganda

Godfrey accompanied us in the rowboat. The driver then took us for a short ride up the river to the mouth of the Omugga. When passersby on the bank of the river realized that the man they saw was the former President of Uganda, they waved and greeted us in a warm Uganda fashion.

Godfrey, who had an unmatched wit and sense of humor, sitting in the row boat (fitted with an outboard motor), along with Nakalema, with Jason and Chris on the way to join them.

The Omugga flows some 6,500 km through Uganda, Egypt and the Sudan on a 3-month journey to the Mediterranean sea.

White water rafting was available.

We visited the Bulange (boo-lah-ngeh) building in Uganda. It houses the Lukiiko (Parliament) of the Kingdom of Buganda, and the Kasubi Hill in Kampala which is the site of Kasubi tombs. The Kasubi tombs are an active spiritual area holding the burial chambers of the four late Kabakas of Buganda.

These weapons and shields are part of the ceremonial and historical display at the Kasubi Tombs, the royal burial site of the Kabakas (kings) of Buganda in Kampala, Uganda. They reflect the martial heritage, authority, and spiritual symbolism of Buganda's monarchy. The Kasubi Tombs are displayed below.

We also visited Saint Paul's Cathedral Namirembe, commonly and locally (Uganda) referred to as Namirembe Cathedral, is the oldest Anglican cathedral in Uganda.

As I pointed out above, Godfrey's father had been the Canon at Namirembe during his lifetime.

It is also the first place where we worshipped when I first visited in 1979-80. One of the most unforgettable experiences that I had at the time was to observe that when the Namirembe choir began to sing, they started to sway from side to side in the same rhythmic motion that I had observed in the black church choirs singing in the United States. This was a Kunta Kinte moment for me, seeing the two cultures joined this way. [85]

Lastly, Nakalema and Maazi took us to a tailor to have them make a dress or outfit for Jane. Here, Jason is trying to describe her size for the tailor, using hand signals. I think the young lady in pink in the photo was about the size of Jane.

---

[85] The Inspiration – The Kunta Kinte-Alex Haley Foundation

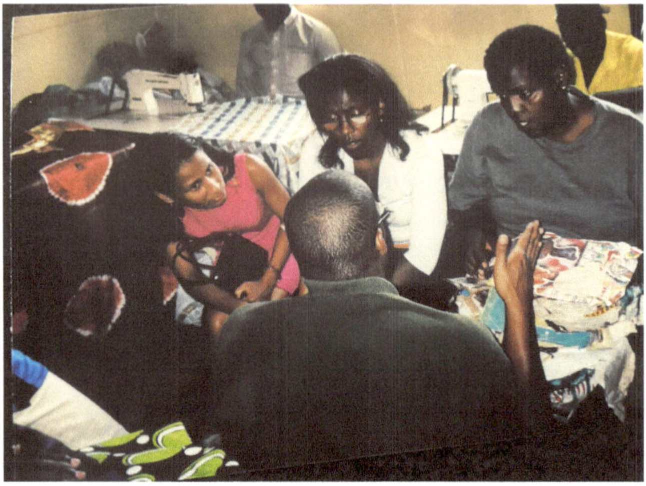

Uganda had imported Nigerians to teach Ugandans how to make certain garments because the Ugandans had not been trained to sew the intricate Nigerian type patterns. It was amazing to see how many different sewing tools and needles there were to make certain designs.

The outfit did fit Jane when we returned home.

Celebrations in Kitgum and Gulu after Ouster of Idi Amin

On 02 November 1979, there was a big celebration in Kitgum, followed by a similar celebration in Gulu.

I developed an uneasy stomach while I was on this trip and was examined by the doctor who always travels with the president. He told me to drink some tea that he asked the chef to prepare for me. Of course, being from the United States, I wanted to know where the pills were. Somewhat skeptical, I drank the tea, and my stomach calmed down. Frank Mingo, the film crew and I had been awake most of the night before, listening to the drums.

Meantime, Godfrey met with the Elders all night.

Members of various clans came from all over to celebrate and to play their drums. The same people you see in their traditional outfits below would be dressed in their suits of more business-like attire when they went to work or on other occasions.

Godfrey took the position that the people had been deprived of expression under Amin, so they should be allowed to celebrate and let off steam.

The title for this celebration was "PROGRAMME FOR THE CELEBRATION OF THE LIBERATION WAR AGAINST DICTATOR IDI AMIN, ON THE 2ND NOVEMBER 1979."

Following protocol, the events were laid out in detail, showing the times for music from the school children's bands, the UNLA[86] band, followed by the spaced arrival of dignitaries, and starting at 8:00 a.m.

Godfrey arrived at 10:00 a.m., with the singing of the Uganda National Anthem, just after the arrival of the Prime Minister of Tanzania, and the introductory speech by Hon. A. Ocaya.

I was a part of the Presidential delegation.

At 10:30 a.m., President Godfrey Binaisa cut the tape to rename Vali Mohammed Road to become Archbishop Janani Luwum Road.

The Archbishop was allegedly assassinated on the orders of Idi Amin[87]

---

86 Uganda National Liberation Army

87 https://en.wikipedia.org/wiki/Janani_Luwum (Accessed 16 DEC 2024)

Janani Jakaliya Luwum was archbishop of the Church of Uganda from 1974 to 1977 and one of the most influential leaders of the modern church in Africa. He was arrested in February 1977 and died shortly after. Although the official account describes a car crash, it is generally accepted that he was murdered on the orders of then-President Idi Amin.

Since 2015 Uganda has a public holiday on 16 February, to celebrate the life of Janani Luwum.

Luwum was born in the village of Mucwini in the Kitgum District to Acholi parents.

In the afternoon, the Prime Minister of Tanzania gave remarks, as did Godfrey. To my great astonishment, he asked me to say a few words. The crowd accepted my remarks with cheers and applause. There were sequential interpretations of my remarks into 4 different languages or dialects. A beautiful experience.

Among the many activities of that day was a friendly football (soccer) match. In about 2010, I came to understand how deeply ingrained soccer is to the psyche of Africans. In fact, civil wars have been paused so that teams could play a match, with the war resuming after the match.[88]

The programme activities recessed at 7:05 p.m. By strict invitation guests closed out the evening with a State reception and dinner at the Hilltop Hotel.

An official entourage saw us off the next morning for Gulu.

Heady stuff for a young black lawyer from West Savannah!

My internist in Botswana comes from Gulu.

---

[88] https://www.bing.com/search?q=List+the+civil+wars+that+were+stopped+so+soc-cer+match+could+be+played&form=WSBEDG&qs=SW&cvid=a4af09e77ace47cb8d5b5dbf888e7de8&pq=List+the+civil+wars+that+were+stopped+so+soc-cer+match+could+be+played&cc=BW&setlang=en-US&nclid=5818987FB4D68F5BAD3F221AD7D26E69&ts=1734362971955&wsso=Moderate (Accessed 16 DEC 2024)

Film to Show to Outside World

When I first arrived in 1979, I asked Godfrey why he didn't tell me that Uganda was as beautiful as it was. He replied that if he had told me, I would not have believed him.

I suggested to him that since people were afraid to come to Uganda, because of the reputation Amin had given the country, we should take Uganda to them. He agreed.

Before I left for Uganda, I introduced Godfrey to Frank Mingo, who headed an advertising/public relations firm (Mingo-Jones Advertising) in case the need should arise to publicize Uganda.

After I arrived, he gave me the ok to ask Frank if he could get a film crew to come to Uganda and make a film to be used for many purposes – promote tourism, domestic and foreign investment, industrial and commercial development, artifact and archeological research, education, public relations and similar uses.

Meantime, Hon. Elly Karuhanga of the Attorney General's chambers had advised Godfrey to create a company to make and exploit the film.

We incorporated Pan Africa Associates, Inc. in the State of Delaware to produce and exploit the film.

Frank Mingo arrived with two filmmakers, and we traveled by helicopter and land to make motion and still film. They arrived with a lot of equipment, but no sound equipment, so they missed the authentic music and drumming of the local people in Gulu/Kitgum. When they were editing the film, after they returned to New York, they dubbed in sound from somewhere else.

They took the film to New York, edited it down from a 4-hour film to a 1-hour film, but we never got to do anything with it because Godfrey was overthrown in a bloodless coup and placed under house arrest by Tanzanian soldiers in May 1980.

After Frank died, we were unable to get access to the film.

Frank Mingo and one of the filmmakers he brought with him, standing in front of Statehouse.

Godfrey was ultimately placed under house arrest in a bloodless coup by the Tanzanian soldiers stationed at Statehouse.

The Tanzanian soldiers allowed me to continue to communicate with him during his house arrest concerning his family and other personal matters.

During the Christmas holidays, in December 1980, Godfrey escaped to Kenya, with Irene , his wife, and Kuchi, their youngest daughter.

Cotton

While I was there on this visit, I was discussing some 29 different projects with Godfrey, one of which was the establishment of several large cotton fields. He said that Uganda produced a long cotton fiber like Egyptian cotton. He arranged for me to visit Nyanza Textiles in Jinga. There I saw how textiles were made from raw cotton to the finished dyed or imprinted textile. An Amazing experience.

When I returned home with the textiles that they gave me as a gift, my sister Gloria made some cherished sleeping gowns for me. I wore those out, and I think I gave some fabric to sisters Gloria and Deloris.

Tom Wood and Amb. Andrew Young's Last Official Trip

Tom Wood, an African American businessman,[89] had gone to Uganda to try to lease or sell 200 trucks to transport coffee beans from the farms to the Coffee Marketing Board in Kampala, and then to shipping points.

Photo of Tom talking with the Minister of Transportation on Statehouse lawn, with me looking on (1979/80).

[89] https://aalbc.com/authors/Tom+Wood (Accessed 17 Aug 2025) (He discusses the opening of doors in his experience, as well)

During this process, General Motors sent representatives to Entebbe to meet with us.

Me at the Coffee Marketing Board where coffee beans are delivered from the farms (1979-80)

Photo of Tom Wood and Godfrey on State House lawn.1979/1980] on his first trip to discuss the trucks before I got involved.

Tom was also interested in the cobalt pile (which is what we called it). He was an electrical engineer and had calculated the value of the cobalt pile. I will discuss that later.

The first time Tom met with Godfrey, time was short, and Tom was a stranger, so Godfrey directed Tom to me to discuss his proposal, and thereafter, Godfrey would ask me to brief him on Tom's proposal enroute to Cuba via New York to the Non- aligned Nations Conference Tom returned to New York, called me and that is how we met.

After we met, Tom was part of Amb. Andrew Young's final diplomatic mission. On September 5, 1979, Amb. Young led a business delegation to Africa. Originally scheduled to visit 7 countries, the number was increased to 8, resulting from a telephone call I received from Tom while they were in flight. He wanted to know if they diverted the flight to Uganda if I could arrange a meeting with them and Godfrey. I did so, but I do not know what they discussed.

Someone in the group complained that Godfrey had them waiting while other people came and went. From what I recall, Godfrey wanted to consult with various interested parties about the subject of the meeting.

I regarded this as part of the consensus building process that happens in some African contexts.

Godfrey and I were able to discuss Tom's proposal when Godfrey passed through New York on his way to the meeting of the 6th Summit of the Non-Aligned Movement which took place on 3–9 September 1979 in Havana, the capital city of Cuba. 93 countries took part in the summit.[90]

---

[90] https://www.bing.com/search?q=When+was+the+meeting+of+the+non-aligned+nations+in+1979&form=WSBEDG&qs=SW&cvid=040c634ab74541efabae51dbfc1362b5&pq=When+was+the+meeting+of+the+non-aligned+nations+in+1979&cc=BW&setlang=en-US&nclid=5818987FB4D68F5BAD3F221AD7D26E69&ts=1734529329960&wsso=Moderate (Accessed 18 December 2024)

This is what some have referred to as person-to-person diplomacy; i.e., my friendship with Godfrey, which developed before he became President. Our common professions as lawyers, his participation in and knowledge of American affairs, and my knowledge of African affairs helped develop this relationship.

Photo of me and Godfrey reading JET magazine's report of the Andrew Young trip in Godfrey's office.

The New York Times reported on the beginning of the trip,[91] and how the trip increased the numbers of countries they visited from 7 to 8, but they did not know that I made the diversion possible. The Times reported:

> The Young trip, which lasted 17 days, eventually encompassed eight, not seven, countries because the group made a stopover in Entebbe, Uganda, at the invitation of President Godfrey L.

[91] *Young Begins Trade Mission to 7 African Nations*
Young Begins Trade Mission to 7 African Nations https://timesmachine.nytimes.com/timesmachine/1979/09/06/issue.html (Accessed 18 December 2024)

Binaisa, who told the American delegation how eager he was for fresh doses of Western investment in his war-ravaged country.

During the Ugandan stopover, another member of Mr. Young's party, Thomas A. Wood of New York, signed an agreement under which his company will provide 200 trucks to enable Uganda to ship out its coffee; it has been lying in warehouses since last spring when Tanzanian soldiers ended the tyrannical rule of Uganda's President, Idi Amin. Mr. Wood's agreement, for $25 million, also includes a provision under which he will lease 66 roadgrading machines to Uganda.

***

For businessmen on such trade missions, the advantage is that they get to meet the top officials on various countries with a minimum of hassle. During the Young trip, for example, the group met the following: President William R. Tolbert Jr. of Liberia; Gen. Olesegun [sic] Obasanjo of Nigeria, then head of state, and his successor, Shehu Shagari, who assumed the Presidency last Monday; President Julius K. Nyerere of Tanzania, and President Godfrey L. Binaisa lsic] of Uganda.

"We know that sometimes when businessmen arrive on their own, it takes weeks for them to set up appointments and weeks more for them to get to see people," Mr. Young said. "On trade missions such as these, it's right to the top."

https://www.nytimes.com/1979/10/08/archives/business-aided-by-african-trip-youngs-trip-to-africa-aided-business.html (Accessed 18 December 2024)

We met with the Uganda Minister of Transportation, but he favored a Kenyan company for the trucks deal.

I do not have any notes of my conversations with Tom about the cobalt pile.

Uganda Cobalt

Uganda started extracting copper from the Kilembe Mines in 1948, located in western Uganda, along the border with the Democratic Republic of Congo. Since that time, it was estimated that the waste products from the mine constituted a pile of about one million tons of waste, including cobaltiferous sulfides (the "pile").

Because the spot price of cobalt was attractive at the time, several global businesses were interested in it. Professor Lule , Godfrey's predecessor, had sold or promised to sell 100K of the pile to a Swedish company. I do not know what the result was.

However, Godfrey wanted to build a hydroelectric dam at Kabalega Falls, also known as Murchison Falls, to use the hydropower generated to extract the cobalt from the cobaltiferous sulfides, and to power the Kilembe mines downstream. Then he would convert the sulfides into sulphuric acid and combine the acid with superphosphates deposits to make fertilizer. We could not get that project off the ground before he was overthrown in a bloodless coup on 12 May 1980.

As part of trying to understand the project, I visited Kabalega Falls by helicopter, and Kilembe Mines by airplane in January/February 1980.

The helicopter crew – Me, Co-pilot, Pilot (ranked first in class in Italy), Security, Frank Mingo.

On Thursday, 31 January 1980, Ralph and I visited Kilembe Mines, where Lt. Col. (Ret'd.) Wm Ndahendekire gave us a tour and explained how the mine worked. John Stephens[92] was with us; I remember John explaining the mathematical formula for the power of water to move the large rocks and boulders. I was impressed.

Of course, Ralph was with me on these trips.

On our return from the Kilembe Mines at night, a departing airline pilot radioed to our pilot that they had switched off all the lights at Entebbe airport and his was the last plane to leave. I was concerned because we were flying over territory occupied by troops, and I didn't know if they knew who we were. The ever-brilliant Ralph, who was an electrical engineer, radioed to someone on the ground to please ask Captain Sandy to re-open the airport because we were returning.

He did so.

A large contingent of troops met us when we landed.

Meanwhile, Mr. Eugene Dibble of Chicago, had visited Uganda while I was there. I met him when he made an appointment to see the President, H.E. Godfrey L. Binaisa. I am not sure if I attended the

[92] John A. Stephens, owner of Excel Minerals and Diatomic Chemical Company in California. He would serve as the mining expert in our group.

meeting with them, but he had seen me on the official side of the reception desk in the President's office.

After he returned to the U.S., Mr. Dibble called me to say that he was associated with some people in the mining business and that they wanted to meet with me in New York on Super Bowl Sunday[93] to discuss their interests in the pile. Initially, at 9:00 A.M. I met with Mr. Dibble at the Pierre Hotel, where he was staying. He wanted to give me an overview of the people we would be meeting and to discuss how we could earn commissions if we were able to make a deal on processing the pile.

Dibble and I then went across the street to the Plaza Hotel to meet the team of people who would take the lead in pulling together the resources we would need. At 10:10 A.M. we met at the Plaza. Present were Eugene Dibble, John A. Stephens, owner of Excel Minerals and Diatomic Chemical Company in California, Clarence Avant, a businessman from Los Angeles, California, John Wilks, who had secure ties with the Republican Party[94] and Robert Jablonski. We ate breakfast and met in Clarence's room. After some discussion, I suggested we call Godfrey to see if he would agree to meet with them. Luckily, the call went straight through, and we all were able to speak with Godfrey on a speakerphone.

Godfrey told them that several businesses were interested in the pile, but since I was calling on their behalf, he would not make any commitments until he had met with them. Except for the mining engineer, I cannot remember who went but they were impressed and the group that John was associated with agreed that they would send Uganda $200-300 million right away to help with the governments cash needs with more to be sent later. Idi Amin had looted the treasury of foreign reserve currencies.

---

[93] January 20, 1980

[94] President Nixon had appointed him as Deputy Assistant Secretary of Labor for Compliance and Director of the Office of Federal Contract Compliance on August 13, 1969. I had met John before our 1980 meeting as he had had a business connection with Jefferson Beaver, my father-in-law, my wife Jane's father.

Unfortunately, the TELEX machine was in the public waiting room next to the President's office and I think someone must have read the message.

John Stephens had significant contacts within the mining and oil industries, with the President of MIT (who was from Santa Barbara), Union Oil, , and several political and non-political contacts that could be helpful

Someone in this group suggested to Godfrey that they form a joint venture with the Ugandan government, earn a reasonable rate of return and split the profits on a 50-50 basis. On the American side John A. Stephens said he had solid relations with large oil companies, and he indicated that he would approach them as a joint venture partner. Godfrey was deeply knowledgeable about the issues they were raising, as he had studied geology. He had also been Uganda's first African Attorney General after independence, and the first African Queens Counsel (Q.C.) in sub-Saharan Africa.

Some of the questions that were asked were 1) what was the magnitude of the copper reserves in the ground, 2) how long would it take to do a survey, and 3) what kinds of records did Uganda have?

He also suggested that they could explore oil/energy and technology initiatives.

Dibble suggested to John Stephens that he should pay me a small amount for making the introduction. John did so. I had spent a considerable amount of time working on this matter without any compensation from them or my small law practice. However, I had the contact that they did not have. Eugene Dibble's meeting me when I was behind the desk at the State House added to my credibility.

Dibble called me a few days after the meeting to assure me that John was very well connected, was involved in joint ventures in Guangzhou China, and Maylasia, and had been a part of Andy Young's Africa trip but had to leave the trip after Nigeria.

He also told me that Noranda Mines (Canada) and Union Oil were interested in the Kilembe Mines project.

On 29 and 30 January 1980, we met with David P.M. Hadoto, Senior Geologist, at the Geological Survey office, and one with the Commissioners of Mines. David was a brilliant encyclopedia of knowledge about mineral resources. I am not sure who was at that meeting.

On an earlier trip, I met David at the Geological Survey offices.

On 08 February 1980, Godfrey signed a letter of intent, on behalf of the Republic of Uganda, with me and Clarence Avant[95] in the State House, subject to a comprehensive agreement, to find financing for a joint venture with the government of Uganda to process the pile and to make fertilizer.

The Republic also intended to negotiate with us regarding gold, wolfram, tin, beryl, tantalum, kaolin and sheet mica.

One of the conditions for our participation would be to raise $300,000,000.00 payable to the Republic at the time a comprehensive agreement was signed. We never got to this stage, although John Stephens had arranged for this initial payment.

On February 11, 1980, W.J. Daffron, a Mining and Geological Consultant, prepared a 7-page report "at the request of Mr. John Stephens, Excel – Mineral Co., W.J. Daffron has made an examination of the surface plant, underground mine, engineering and geological records, and cobalt-bearing pyrite concentrate stockpile of the Kilembe mines, Ltd. at Kilembe, Uganda."

Among other things, item 7 estimated that it would take about $60-70,000,000.00 in phases over an extended period, to conduct exploration, rehabilitation and construction of the cobalt processing plant.

Mr. Daffron wrote that there were three other significant challenges: 1) lack of senior European staff, 2) lack of supplies, lack of

[95] In 2024, when I discovered the signed letter of intent while decluttering, I was so excited I wanted to share the discovery with Clarence. When I telephoned his office and spoke to him, Clarence denied ever having visited Uganda. This was very strange to me. A few months later, Clarence had passed away.

transport, and 3) unrestrained search and seizure by Tanzanian soldiers.

Daffron thought there was a copper ore body that extended some 60 miles, 5 million tons of copper reserves.

Throughout this process, several major corporations were interested, including Union Oil, Noranda, Falconbridge (however, Falconbridge wanted to ship the pile to Norway for processing), and Leon Templesman and Sons.

John sent a TELEX to Godfrey saying the $300 million would be forthcoming. Somebody read the TELEX; shortly thereafter he was ousted from office in a bloodless coup.

The Uganda or Tanzania military announced over the radio that they had removed Godfrey from office and taken over the government.

After the overthrow of President Godfrey Binaisa in 1980, a Military Commission took over the leadership of Uganda. This commission was headed by Paulo Muwanga, with key members including Yoweri Museveni, Brigadier Oyite Ojok, Maj. Gen. Tito Okello, and Colonel Zed Maruru.[96]

They placed Binaisa under house arrest along with his wife and youngest daughter, Maazi. His other children were elsewhere. I think during this period Nakalema and Patrice stayed with us at separate times, and the rest were in England or Uganda.

A Ugandan group comprised of people in the United States organized a petition to ask Tanzania's President Nyerere to spare Godfrey's life. Grace Ibingira was part of that group, although I never met him.

However, the Commission allowed me to continue to talk with him throughout the period of house arrest. With Irene and Maazi, Godfrey

---

[96] https://www.ugstandard.com/archive-museveni-takes-centre-stage-as-military-commission-takes-charge-of-uganda-affairs/?form=MG0AV3 (Accessed 16 NOV. 2024)

escaped to Kenya during the Christmas holidays while the soldiers were celebrating.

Joel Mugambwa and I were communicating about his whereabouts. The U.S. State Department called me and asked if I knew where he was and I told them I did. With our information, the State Department arranged a flight for Godfrey, Irene and Kuchi (the youngest daughter) to the United States and the Attorney General admitted them on parole. I am not sure who all played a role in this process, but as near as I can remember, this is what happened.

Unfortunately, during the period that he was in the United States, Godfrey had a tough time finding employment. None of his good friends from his days as Attorney General and in private practice would hire him. At that time, I am not sure that any of the Wall Street firms had a member of his stature.

He told me that Rogers & Wells offered him a position with a salary in 1977 equal to my starting salary in 1968. He turned them down. Looking back, I think this might have been very shortsighted of them, given his relationships with lawyers and jurists within the continent of Africa and the global explosion in commercial development since then.

Godfrey landed a position with the Office of the Corporation Counsel for the City of New York. However, he was let go with thousands of other city workers because of the fiscal crises.

Ralph also introduced me to many aspects of Ugandan life and culture. I also visited sugar factories, tea plantations, zoo, botanical gardens, Owens Falls Dam, Kasubi Tombs, the resting place for the late Buganda kings of Uganda, and so forth.

Marriage To Jane Marie Beaver

In the Spring of 1967, I along with few other graduate students at Berkeley, decided to have a party so that the unmarried black male and female students could meet each other. As I was leaving the party, I noticed a beautiful young woman sitting on a throw pillow reading a book. The light fell onto her hair at just the right angle. I went over and introduced myself and we started talking. I asked her out to celebrate my 28th birthday which would fall due next week. She accepted, although she later told me that she was shocked that I would be 28. I have never looked like my age. I am 86 now and most people always think I am much younger.

A few years ago, I was being examined by a lovely optometrist in Blackheath, Johannesburg, because I was seeing less distinctly than I thought I should be. During the examination, she exclaimed "What, no wrinkles!" This recalled for me the saying "black don't crack!" She was able to explain to me what I was experiencing. My eyesight is now much better only a few days after using the treatment that she recommended. She is Ms. Esthé Lee. At the time of her birth, she was presented to the heavens during pouring rain and acquired that nickname "Mma Pula." Pula means rain in Setswana.

Speaking of birthdays, Jane's birthday was November 10, 1944. She was born in Children's Hospital in San Francisco. Her father was Jefferson August Beaver, and her mother was Fanny May Ansley (maiden name), both Social Workers at the time.

They had four children, Jane, Jeffrey, Jonathon, and James Michael who died of tuberculosis in infancy. Michael died when they were living in New York. For many years, Jeffrey did not know where Michael's grave was. Once, when Jeffrey visited us in New Rochelle, NY, after Jane had died, Jeffrey, Jason, Chris and I went to the cemetery where James was buried and located his gravesite. I think Jason or Chris first found the burial site which had been obscured by a large tree.

They were one of the prominent San Franciso families.

Jane's father, Jefferson, received a B.A. degree from the University of California at Berkeley, and studied further at Springfield College in Springfield Massachusetts, and one year at Golden Gate University Law School. He began his banking career by co-founding Transbay Federal Savings and Loan in 1949 and Golden Gate National Bank in 1961. I tell this story in a separate chapter entitled "People I have Met Along the Way." Particularly important is his description of how exceedingly difficult it was to meet the capital requirements for creating a bank and the hardships that he endured. He also covers how the black bank was able to expand the ownership of property by the Chinese and Japanese population in San Francisco at the time by lending these communities when white-owned banks would not.

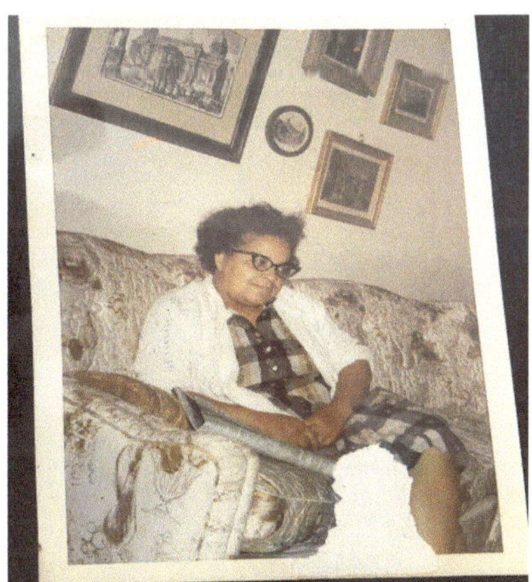

Jefferson August Beaver, Jane's father
Fanny Ansley Beaver, Jane's Mother

By the time that I met Jane, I had graduated from Morehouse, spent a year traveling and studying abroad, and was a year from graduating from law school. We celebrated my 28th birthday at the Trident Club in Sausalito, where I heard Vince Geraldi for the first time. I think I might have also heard Dave Brubeck on records about the time. I was not a big jazz fan then, but Don Hopkins, who was a student at University of California at Berkeley law school (Boalt Hall, now called Berkeley Law), was a great fan. Listening to jazz in his apartment, tried as I might, just seemed like noise to me. Now I am a great fan and have amassed quite a collection.

After my 28th birthday celebration at the Trident, Jane and I continued to date. I think our second date was a lovely day at Santa Clara, California beach. I was living at 2455 Byron Street, in Berkeley and Jane resided with her parents on Los Palmas Drive, on the side of Mount Davidson in San Francisco.

Jane and Leroy newlyweds at the first apartment at 2455 Byron Street, Oakland, CA (1967)

They lived in a community of accomplished black people, which included Dan Collins, a physician and member of the Board of Directors of HarperCollins Publishing Co., and Willie Brown who lived down the street. Willie would go on to establish himself as Mayor of San Francisco and Speaker of the California Assembly, and a well-known political commentator. Less well known were his talents as a babysitter for Jane (and Jeffrey and Jonathan?).

I was always fascinated by the way the fog would flow through their dining room when they opened the window. The house was located on the side of Mount Davidson on Los Palmas Drive. Mount Davidson was the highest natural point in San Francisco. I had many pleasant memories of that house. It had a sunken living room, which, many years later (1978) would warm my heart when we were house hunting in New Rochelle, New York. Our New Rochelle house had a sunken living room and many unusual amenities. My son, Christopher now owns that house, out of his lifelong desire and Jane's last wishes.

We were married November 18, 1967, in their living room by Judge Joseph Kennedy, one of the few black judges in California at the time. The wedding was very well attended. Lonnie Poindexter was my best man, assisted by James Page, Sam Toney, Walter Toney, and probably Bob Toney;[97] Mimi Rodgers was Jane's Maid of Honor, assisted by Lynette Carter, Barbara Ann LeGall and Pat Forneret. My parents were able to join us from Savannah, Georgia. I was so happy that they were there. I am even happier now. As I look back on it now, they must have attended at great financial sacrifice.

Champagne flowed throughout the afternoon.

Our first apartment at 2455 Byron Street, where I had been living, was a block from San Pablo Boulevard in Berkeley or Oakland. This was a one-bedroom apartment with just enough room for the two of

[97]All three of these Toney brothers served in the Navy, and all achieved the rank of Commander, except that Bob went on to rise to the rank of Admiral of the half-staff.

us. Our location was convenient to the bus line to Berkeley's campus for me and to transit for Jane to the Emporium store in San Francisco.

Jane read a wide variety of books, magazines, and other reading materials. She was brilliant. She worked at the Emporium in San Francisco, one of the premier department stores. I had gotten my first law related job, as a law clerk at the San Francisco Neighborhood Legal Services organization. The indomitable, brilliant Ben Travis led the organization. Sammy Dukes and George Mason were other law clerks.

Jerry Glass was one of the attorneys. Ken Hecht was another. I remember Jerry because he was composing his legal arguments on an emergency motion, while I was reading out cases to support him as we walked to the courthouse. Ken was more laid back than Jerry. Also, this was the first time that I had seen a male secretary, who typed all our documents.

Jane and I moved from California to New York after I graduated from law school.

In my 3rd year of law school, I read a recruitment ad in Ebony magazine about job opportunities at International Business Machines Corp. ("IBM"). The ad expressed an interest in recruiting and hiring black people, so I contacted them and was interviewed in San Jose by Robert Ransom. Bob was a magnificent individual and was one of my guardian angels at IBM. During the interview, we talked about a variety of things, but I remember particularly his great concern about the Vietnam War. I did not understand at the time what his intense interest in the war was. He would later lose a son in that war, and it pained him deeply. I think I remember him losing a lot of weight because he once told me about fitting into a suit that he had been able to wear only long ago.

Jane graduated from Lowell High School in San Francisco and had entered Howard University with the thought of majoring in Geology, only to find out late that Howard did not offer a degree in Geology. Her main interests then were geology and anthropology. She finished her undergraduate studies at the University of California at Hayward with a B.A. degree in Sociology.

Our sons, Jason and Christopher, were born in February and December in 1969 in White Plains at St. Agnes Hospital..

As Jason and Christopher grew into teenagers, Jane would go on to Pace University Law School in White Plains, New York and become a member of the Law Review.

Both sons also became lawyers with advanced degrees; Jason, with an MBA from Columbia University School of Business where he met his wife Michelle, and Christopher, with an LL.M in Securities Law from Georgetown University School of Law. He is still single.

Jason earned his B.A. degree from Princeton, and his Juris Doctor degree from the University of California at Los Angeles (UCLA); Chris earned his B.A. degree and his Juris Doctor degree from the University of Michigan. Chris finished undergraduate school with honors in three years.

L-R at Chris's Michigan undergraduate graduation with his Mother Jane, cousin Teddy, Grandfather Wilson, brother Jason, Grandmother Wilson, Chris, and Grandfather Beaver. I am taking the photo.

Jane wanted to become a tax lawyer, so she applied to the Internal Revenue Chief Counsel's office in New York City for a position. She went through a round of interviews but heard nothing. After interviewing her, the man who was to become her boss, Bob Marino, called and asked Jane what the status was since he had heard nothing. She told him she had heard nothing.

Jane contacted Joseph Hairston, a member of the National Bar Association ("NBA") to find out what to do. Joe was one of the first, if not the only black senior executives in the Internal Revenue Service at that time. Jane met him through her attendance at NBA meetings. An investigation ensued and it was determined that someone had tossed Jane's application into the rubbish bin.

Things were put back on track; she was hired and rose to the position of Deputy Regional Counsel for Criminal Tax matters for the northeastern region of the United States. That region is comprised of 11 states. She had also been cross designated as a special assistant US Attorney for Criminal Tax matters in the US Attorney General's office for the southern district of New York, leading to several convictions for tax fraud. She worked closely with U.S. Magistrate Lisa Smith. Lisa Gave remarks at Jane's memorial service.

Jane as Deputy Regional Counsel for Criminal Tax

9/11 and the World Trade Center Attacks on Tower 7

Jane's IRS home office was in Tower 7 of the World Trade Center. There were two terrorist attacks on the World Trade Center Complex (WTC) during the time that she worked there.

Eighteen minutes after noon on February 26, 1993, a bomb exploded in the basement parking garage below the north tower of the WTC. The massive explosion killed six people and wounded more than 1,000, with some 50,000 people forced to evacuate the twin towers as smoke and flames spread upward into the buildings.[98]

Jane had gone outside the building to buy a cup of coffee. As she was walking back to her building, she heard a noise and felt a bump that slightly lifted her off the pavement, but she did not know what had happened. Of course, she later found out. That this was a terrorist attack on the United States via the first bombing of the World Trade Center.

I received a telephone call from Jonathan, Jane's younger brother, in San Francisco, asking if she was all right. I later reported to him that she was.

At the time, I was headed to Surrogate's Court in Queens. As I drove across the bridge, the radio went off and I couldn't get it back. I would later learn that "Also as a result of the loss of power, most of New York City's radio and television stations (save for one, WCBS-

---

[98] https://www.history.com/news/world-trade-center-bombing-1993-facts (Accessed 30 December 2024)

TV (channel 2)) lost their over-the-air broadcast signal for almost a week, with television stations only being able to broadcast via cable and satellite via a microwave hookup between the stations and three of the New York area's largest cable companies, Cablevision, Comcast, and Time Warner Cable. Telephone service for much of Lower Manhattan was also disrupted.[99]

The 1993 bombing was a precursor to the 9/11/2001 attack that brought down the twin towers at WTC 1 and 2 and Tower 7 where Jane worked.

That morning, I had returned home after dropping Jane off at the Scarsdale, NY train station for her to take the Metro North commuter train down to New York City. Since I had a few minutes before heading to my office, I followed my usual practice of laying back down. I was listening to the radio when the announcer said that a small airplane had crashed into the WTC. A few minutes later, Jeffrey, the older of Jane's two brothers, called me from Seattle, where he lived, telling me it was not a small plane, but a big plane. So, I rushed downstairs to the family room where we kept our television, three levels down. As I stepped onto the second level, Jeffrey phoned again, telling me that a second plane had crashed into the towers, and he thought this was a terrorist attack.

As I switched on the television, there were frantic reports of a terrorist attack. This bombing also disrupted telephone communications. The communication towers were built atop the WTC towers. My calls to Jane did not go through.

So, following my thought practice, I would sit in one stationary place – at home – so I would be reachable in case she or someone else called.

All I could do was sit, watch television, and wait.

---

[99] https://en.wikipedia.org/wiki/1993_World_Trade_Center_bombing#Attack (Accessed 30 December 2024)

Finally, about mid-afternoon, I received a call from Jane telling me she was ok.

She told me that on the way down from Grand Central Station to her subway stop, the New York City subway that she normally took from Grand Central Station to Fulton Street Station stopped before reaching her station and announced to all passengers that the subway train would not be traveling further, and that all passengers needed to exit the train. The conductor did not tell them why they needed to exit the subway train.

She told me that she exited the station and walked toward her office because she was scheduled to attend a meeting. I think her office was on the 25th Floor of Tower 7.

However, as she rounded the corner, she saw people running toward her who looked like ghosts. They were covered with debris. She then turned back and started walking from lower Manhattan, where the WTC was located, to Grand Central Station in the middle of Manhattan, about 3 and ½ miles. Of course, transportation was also disrupted. Grand Central Station was packed, but she managed to catch a Metro North train. I drove to the Scarsdale commuter station to pick her up.

We spent the rest of the afternoon watching the after effects of the airplane bombings. At about 5:20 p.m., We witnessed the collapse of Tower 7, with her office and mementos in it. One was a photo I had taken with Bill Clinton. I think Eric Clay was also in the photo, showing Clinton walking down the receiving line. In his Autobiography *My Life*, Clinton wrote that he appointed Eric to a position on the United States Court of Appeals for the Sixth Circuit. Eric's firm represented one of my clients in Michigan when I was at Union Carbide. I, in turn, later represented Eric's uncle's estate with respect to New York legal issues.

The IRS would eventually relocate to Maiden Lane in lower Manhattan. They probably stayed in lower Manhattan because that is where most federal and state courts and offices were located.

On June 15, 2003, after a truly epic fight over six to eight months, Jane succumbed to lung cancer. We still suffer this great loss. Dr. Valiere Alcena, M.D., F.A.C. P., a medical oncologist, told us that the kind of cancer that Jane had was unrelated to those caused by the 9/11 fallout.

A year earlier, in August 2002, Jane nursed me back to sound health after my prostate operation. I was well enough to travel to Savannah for Christmas and a reunion with my 1957 high school class. They selected me to give dinner remarks. I decided I would talk about prostate cancer. However, as I was about to make my speech, I received a call from Jane, telling me that my brother Vernon had passed away in New Rochelle. I gave the talk. I felt bad because I was not in New Rochelle when he passed away. We had a very severe snowstorm before I left for Savannah, so I could not get to the hospital, but I could get to the airport, so I went. I had said to myself that I would see him when I returned. Jane made the arrangements to ship his body to Savannah.

Sadly, she would be stricken with lung cancer a year later.

She was a great, loving wife and mother who seemed to know what to do with Jason and Chris and the right time to do it.

Throughout this complete process, Carmen Baerga, Jane's close friend and professional colleague, was invaluable in assisting Jane and me.

Sadness would return in May 2021; Carmen would also pass away, survived by Peter, her son.

Before her career as a criminal tax attorney, Jane served as the first Director of the Westchester County, NY Women's Center.

Jane's graduation from Pace Law School, with Jason and Chris

Jason's graduation from law school (UCLA)

Christopher's graduation from Law school (Michigan)

Marriage To Maleta Luna-Rosa Mogwe

After the death in 2003 of my wife Jane Marie Beaver, I met Maleta Luna-Rosa Mogwe, a divorcee, on the National Bar Association's (NBA's) annual international trip in 2004.

Maleta Sep 7, 2004, Birthday with Roses I sent shortly after I met her.

In 2004, the trip was scheduled for South Africa, Seychelles, and Zimbabwe, all places that I wanted to visit.

Then the NBA substituted Botswana for the Seychelles. I was not as enthusiastic about visiting Botswana, as the only thing I knew about the country was contained in a June 1951 EBONY magazine article I had read.

My friend, Beverly Baker Kelly, who was Chair of the International Law Section of the NBA, tried to persuade me to go. I searched for the article again, read it, and decided that I would go.

In Gaborone, the capital of Botswana, we stayed at the Gaborone Sun Hotel (now Avani).

Joseph Huggins, the American Ambassador to Botswana, scheduled a dinner reception for the NBA delegation at the Maharaja Indian restaurant in Gaborone, the capital of Botswana.

Even though the air in South Africa and Botswana was clear, I think I detected some pollutants in the air because my allergies started bothering me in South Africa.

I decided that I wanted to nurse my headache, so I elected to sit at a table in the back of the restaurant. At the front of the restaurant, Maurice Foster, the NBA's Deputy Director, with Clyde Bailey, NBA President looking on, presented Amb. Huggins with a copy of the NBA's directory of its members.

Maurice presents NBA Members Directory to Amb. Huggins

As my table began to fill up, Maleta sat down, and we went around the table introducing ourselves. She asked, "How are you?" and I replied "Ok." She followed up by saying "How are you really?" I told her about my allergies, and she said she had some tablets in her handbag that could help. Out came the Demazin antihistamine pills: they helped immediately.

I recognized her as a staff member of the American Embassy from our NBA visit earlier in the day at the American Embassy.

Then she offered to get me a plate, which I thought was nice. I am not sure what the motivation was, but I later learned that younger people assisted older people in such situations and in case there was a queue (line), they would walk the older person to the head of the queue. There was deference to the Bagolo.[100]

An amusing aside happened one day when I had gone grocery shopping with a friend and she mentioned that it was unusual to see a

[100] Plural of Mogolo, An elderly person, a senior; an adult. (Setswana English Setswana Dictionary, p. 251, Macmillan Botswana (2004))

mogolo out shopping, as they are usually living in the village, while the young people go out to the shops. After 8 years residing in Botswana, I had somehow noticed in my subconscious that it was rare for me to see an older person in the shops. The toddlers were especially intrigued and often rewarded me with an engaging smile when they realized that I saw them watching me.

A very brilliant , engaging and diplomatic person in her own right, Maleta enriched my life by teaching me the ways of the Batswana, and a lot of the history of southern Africa.

As with Jane, as I learned some time later, Maleta also came from a prominent Botswana family. We were married in 2006 in Lobatse, Botswana in St. Mark's Anglican Church. Her dad, Archibald M. Mogwe, had served in many ministerial capacities in Botswana, and was Botswana's Ambassador to the United States in the late 1990s. Her mother, Lena, was active in her own right.

Maleta being escorted by her father, Archibald Mogwe, into St. Marks Church on our wedding day, February 25, 2006, in Lobatse, Botswana

One day, after we had left the farm, I was speaking to Amb. Andrew Young by telephone from Botswana. During that conversation, he told me of all the people he had met, he would never forget Archie Mogwe. My father-in-law arrived during that call, and I was able to have them greet each other over the telephone after such a long time, stretching over several decades.

During her 6 years at the American Embassy as its media specialist, Maleta advised and assisted the Public Affairs Officer (PAO) on all media-related activities and under PAO's direction organized and implemented Embassy sponsored press events.

While she was there, she interacted with her counterparts in the Botswana Office of the President, the Botswana Department of Foreign Affairs, and other Botswana Ministers and their ministries; other Members of the Diplomatic Corps present in Botswana. She was the protocol contact in Botswana among the various United States establishments ranging from the White House to private companies. She also served as a liaison between the various American Ambassadors and the local population to ensure effective communications.

When she resigned her position, she was the longest serving Media Specialist at the American Embassy since it opened diplomatic relations with Botswana in 1967. She assisted Laura Bush and later George W. Bush when they visited Botswana.

Maleta, Laura Bush, First Lady of the USA, and Maleta's supervisor, PAO Karen Morrisey. Not shown is Air Force One parked on the tarmac behind them.

Maleta had achieved a number of "firsts."

One of her crowning achievements was her successful grooming of Mpule Kwelagobe to win the Miss Universe Pageant in 1999. Maleta acquired the Miss Universe license for Botswana for the specific purpose of using the pageant to create an awareness campaign internationally and to try and stop the spread of HIV/AIDS in Botswana. She also used the pageant to encourage tourism to Botswana.

As a result of her efforts, this was the first time an indigenous black African woman had won any international beauty contest.

Because of her skills and personality, The Gaborone Broadcasting Company recruited her to become the first Motswana television news anchor for GBC. She worked at GBC for 5 years before being recruited away by the American Embassy.

She was the first Editor for Motswana Woman Magazine, the first woman's magazine in Botswana.

The Botswana Society for the Arts was Maleta's brainchild. She was its co-founder as well as its first Chairperson. She was part of the committee that introduced art lessons to prisoners, inspired the government to introduce the arts into the schools, encouraged the government to require all expatriate teachers (in any subject, such as physics, English and so forth) coming to Botswana to be skilled and learned in the arts so that Batswana students would graduate and earn a living as artists. She resigned due to her heavy schedule while working for the US Government.

At the same time, she also served as Vice Chairperson for Ditsala Tsa Maitisong - the national arts promoting body which also hosts the National Arts Festival (the Maitisong Festival) at which international performers are invited. She resigned from this post because she moved to America to live there with me.

While holding these volunteer positions, she was also Vice Chair for the Botswana Music Camp for 9 years. They ran a camp for students who would otherwise not have been exposed to or needed further tutoring in all disciplines of music, both traditional and international.

Maleta worked independently with street children in Botswana, managing to persuade a group to register their skills for parking, watching, cleaning cars.

She was also Chairman of the Lobatse Tennis Club and a member of the Board of Directors for the Botswana Lawn Tennis Association, among others.

Right after we were married in 2006, she moved from Gaborone to New Rochelle to be with me. Practicing law as a solo practitioner did not give us too much of an open window to get things done.

Trying to find a position in the United States was very trying for Maleta. Invariably the online applications would stop her process when she arrived at the screen that asked if she was an American citizen.

Colleagues she had known in Botswana also were not responsive in helping her.

In August 2008 Maleta attended The Protocol School of Washington and received certification as a Corporate Etiquette and International Protocol Consultant. Her training consisted of how to succeed in the international arena, how to outclass the competition, public relations and public speaking. At the end of the program, she also received certification in Dining Like a Diplomat.

In November 2009, having been invited to join the United Nations Women's Guild by Ms. Elizabeth Ntwaagae, wife of Botswana's Ambassador to the United Nations, Maleta was the Mistress of Ceremony at the United Nations Women's Guild 60th Anniversary, "Brides of All Nations" Gala.

Maleta presiding as Mistress of Ceremony at the Brides of All Nations fund-raising event.

Mrs. Mmasello and Botswana UN Ambassador Charles T. Ntwaagae at the Gala

The Gala was held at the New York Botanical Garden in the Bronx. United Nations Deputy Secretary General Asha-Rose Migiro was in attendance together with a host of Ambassadors and their spouses.

In 2011, she relocated from the United States to Botswana to accept the position of Press Secretary to H.E. Lt. Gen. Dr. Seretse Khama Ian Khama, the President of Botswana. Given her background, I thought this would be an excellent position for her to demonstrate her skills.

She related several pleasant and remarkable experiences she had while working as Press Secretary. I forwarded a set of notes to her daughters Natasha and Daniella, so that they will have some of this history of their mother's life. I kept a running diary of episodes she told me about in her encounters with domestic ministers, parliamentarians and foreign diplomats.

Her father, Archibald Mogwe, was always astonished by the number of people Maleta knew in the country of Botswana.

In 2016, I relocated to Botswana, where I now reside.

Tragically, the center did not hold. We were divorced in May 2025.

When I was looking for an apartment in 2022 after I had returned to Botswana after the Covid-19 pandemic had subsided, I was fortunate that Prof. Monageng Mogalakwe referred me to a friend of his who owned a 6-unit apartment building. Amazingly comfortable, quiet, secure quarters where I can sit on my balcony overlooking the jacaranda tree and enclosed, but wide-open patio, pool, and garden. From time-to-time singing birds drop by. It is a perfect environment for me.

I can also walk in the garden without regard for my personal safety. Botswana is generally safe, but there is an increasing amount of robberies and burglaries, some during the daytime.

Maleta is the eldest of three children, with siblings Alice and Hugh.. Sadly, Hugh passed away on Christmas Eve in 2012.

Sons Jason and Christopher

Michigan, Seville, and Princeton

After graduation from Berkeley Law, Jane and I moved into a garden apartment complex known as Wyndover Woods, White Plains, New York, not too far from Jane's Cousin Theodore ("Teddy") and his family in Parkway Gardens, Town of Greenburgh, New York, a suburb of White Plains.

Parkway Gardens is a middle-class community in Westchester County where several African American notables moved to after leaving Harlem. For example, Gordon Parks lived one street over, and Moms Mably one block behind Teddy.

Teddy's family came from Macon, Georgia. He told us that they took the surname "Life" after they were freed from slavery.

Jason was born on February 3, 1969. While we were visiting Teddy, but getting ready for Jane to deliver, Teddy, being the astute observer, yelled "You had better take Jane to the hospital or Jane is going to have this baby right here in the living room." We sped off to St. Agnes hospital in White Plains, located across the street from the then headquarters of General Foods. Jane was in labor a few hours, but, as fate would have it, the bar review course was to begin that evening at the Statler Hotel in New York City. This was a 45–60-minute train ride away, but I decided to drive.

The name of the Dr. who was to deliver Jason escapes me. Dr. Tennyson Phillips was the pediatrician. The doctor told me that he could not tell when she was going to deliver and that I should go to the review course. This was important because at the beginning of most of the courses that I have ever attended the lecturer would tell us what the course was about and how to get the most out of it.

The purpose of the bar review course was to prepare us to take the bar examination.

Well, Wendy, Jane's cousin Teddy's daughter, had a charm school appointment for that evening, so I picked her up and off we went to New York City. I dropped her off in Harlem at Ms. Ophelia DeVore's charm school and went on to the Statler Hotel to attend the bar review course.

During the break, I telephoned the doctor to find out how Jane was doing. He congratulated me on the birth of a baby boy. I didn't know anyone who was taking the bar review course, so I had no one there to tell. I'm not sure if I telephoned Jane or my parents then. I left the hotel, picked up Wendy, dropped her at her house and the sped off to St. Agnes.

When I went in to see Jane she was doing fine. She asked if I had seen the baby, and I said no. I did see him and promptly bought (or had bought) a 35 mm camera that I learned how to operate on the spot. I took some photos of Jason and kept them with some others as he grew along and gave the photo album to him a few years ago. I would later do the same for Christopher. Hence, they both have some photographic history of their lives.

Incidentally, when I dropped Wendy off or picked her up, I encountered Marguerite Tiggs Birt at the DeVore charm school in Harlem. Marguerite is my 1957 Alfred E. Beach High school classmate from Savannah, Georgia.

We would share another auspicious occasion when she organized a luncheon for me on April 9, 2022, over 60 years later..

Jason and Christopher's illnesses, schools and education

Fortunately, Jane had educated herself and me on how to take care of children. They received the usual inoculations and had the usual childhood illnesses; however, there were a couple of unusual ones that stood out.

For the most part, the boys tended to get sick on the weekends. We were living in Newburgh at the time when Christopher had a scary episode. One Sunday, when I was working from home after I had been assigned to the law department staff at IBM's chip processing facility at East Fishkill, NY, I heard one of those sounds coming from the boys' bedroom that a parent could not ignore. When I entered the bedroom, Chris was frothing at the mouth. I was wearing a pair of shorts at the time. Holding up the shorts with one hand and grabbing Chris from his crib with the other, I ran for the car and Jane grabbed Jason.

Normally, I had trouble trying to start the Mercury cougar.

Fortunately, this time it started right up. I raced towards St. Luke's Hospital and rounded the corner of the street that the emergency room of the hospital was on, sideways. At some point, a police vehicle raced behind me. When we entered the ER passageway, I jumped out of the car, and, in my excitement, grabbed one of the doctors in one arm, who could see Chris was in distress. Thankfully, they were able to resolve the condition that he was being subjected to.

There were a couple of frightening episodes in Jason's young life, but I will cite only one. When Jason was about 5 years old, I think he had been given an injection or was being treated for something. Sores began to break out around his mouth. We rushed him to Lawrence Hospital in Bronxville, NY, where Dr. Tennyson Phillips, his pediatrician, recognized a nasty disease called Stephens Johnson syndrome. Sores ran throughout his alimentary canal (and as I remember, with spread on the outside as well as the inside of his body). He was not smiling.

On one of my visits, when I opened the door to his hospital room, Jason smiled through cracked lips. I thought it might have been painful because smiling caused the sores in his lips to crack. It broke my heart. He was feeling better. I was there when a nurse was about to give him an injection. For some reason, I asked what it was. She examined the labels and gasped that she was about to give him medication for an 80-year-old male patient. She then retrieved the correct medication. Jason survived his ordeal.

I now understand its meaning when people say "to God be the glory..."

Throughout their lives, we paid close daily attention to their experiences.

We started them out with children's books at home, although we would sometimes find them looking at the print on some of our books. Then came enrollment in the Montessori School in Newburgh. Jason started first. Christopher couldn't wait to start. On the given day, we drove Chirstopher to start his first day. Christopher alighted from the car and his mother's arms and ran straight for the schoolrooms, without one lookback. He was so excited to be going to school. His mother was heartbroken, tears streaming down her face. I have forgotten our reaction when Jason first went to school. However, years later, while having a parting family dinner on Jason's orientation weekend at Princeton, I had great difficulty leaving him there. Jane was prepared and took our departure from Jason in stride.

After a couple of years in Newburgh, I left IBM for a few months. We moved to Mount Vernon and enrolled our sons in the Alcott Montessori School. Because we had been educated in public schools, we enrolled our sons in the public elementary school system. Unfortunately, the Montessori Schools had prepared them above the level of education these schools could give them.

Another example of the need to pay close attention to your children's education happened to Jason. He had skipped one grade in the Mount Vernon school, and they wanted to skip him to another. The grade he skipped is the one where they taught cursive writing. Since he didn't have that course, he printed everything. When I went up to get his report card, he had received an Unsatisfactory grade (U) for a subject which was somehow connected to writing. i asked the teacher to show me a paper written by someone that she had marked Satisfactory (S). She readily did so and showed me a paper that had been written by a Caucasian classmate. As it turns out, the writing was almost identical. She changed Jason's grade from U to S. During our discussion, she lamented the fact, showing me a stack of report cards, that too many parents did not show up to review their children's report cards.

We attended PTA meetings religiously to find out what their teachers thought of our children's progress.

It became apparent to us that we needed to find another school system. We decided to move to New Rochelle, NY. Fortunately, one set of our new neighbors, Judy and Bob Basis, were exceptional and we drew close to them from the time we moved in. Judy told us that she thought that the George M. Davis Elementary School was probably the best of the Elementary Schools in New Rochelle, NY, . We enrolled them in that school, within walking distance of our house on Stratton Road. They did extremely well at the new school. Again, several things stand out in following their daily studies.

Stratton Road House that Jason and Chris grew up in.

Top – 2024; Bottom - house after one winter storm

Christopher was dyslexic, but I didn't fully understand this condition. I think when he was in about the third grade, the school started giving him a series of books prepared by IBM with a bunch of funny looking letters. We worked with him to try to get him through his experiences. At some point, he told us that he was much better at processing things he heard, as opposed to those that he read.

When I later learned how difficult this was for him, I had great ad miration and respect for him when I learned that when he was tested at the University of Michigan, he was severely dyslexic. My admiration stemmed from his graduation with honors despite dyslexia.

We had put into place a system of rewards for good grades, so money much for an "A", "B" or "C". They made good grades, but the school determined that Chris should be transferred to the gifted and talented program at the Webster School across town.

Before he left, Chris had scored one of the highest marks on the ATP (tests) in Latin ever recorded at the school. This might reveal some connection between dyslexia and Latin. Later, while watching an interview on television of an annual football game between two high schools, the black interviewer asked the white captain about his academic plans but asked Chris about sports. That has rankled me to this day. The African American interviewer (who I remember as a VP at Woolworth's) seemed to succumb to the idea that black children were not pursuing academic careers.

After he transferred to the Webster School, Chris decided to run for School President. The Principal of the school told me that Chris did not have a chance as he was new to the school. As I remember, he won by about 6 votes. It so happens that there were a few Haitian students in the school at the time and Chris endeavored to speak to them in French. We think they gave him the margin of victory.

Chris and Jason would then attend Albert Leonard Middle School.

After leaving Albert Leonard, they attended New Rochelle High School, where Chris was again elected as President of the student body in his senior year. He had his own parking space for the old red Volvo that we gave him. Chris gave the President's speech at the graduation of his class.

Returning to Jason, while they attended Davis Elementary School, at about the time that the US Department of Education was trying to desegregate the advanced placement classes, and after he was tested and placed in the advanced math class, Jason's math teacher gave him some grades I thought he did not deserve. I telephoned the head of the math department at the school and asked for a meeting between her, us and the teacher. I knew she had marked him incorrectly because I reviewed his homework daily and knew his aptitude. I graduated with a double major in mathematics and chemistry from Morehouse College in Atlanta, studied advanced mathematics at the University of Vienna, and held a master's degree in physical chemistry from the University of California at Berkeley (and a J.D. degree in law). At the meeting, the head of the math department told me that she thought that Jason had been placed in a class that was too advanced for him.

After the meeting, the head of department telephoned me back that night after promising to investigate my complaint. She apologized profusely, told me that Jason had made the second highest score for placement in the class, and that teacher (Ms. L) began to teach him properly.

This is another example of why parents should pay close attention to what their children are being taught.

Jason and his wife Michelle have started my grandchildren Blake and Parker off on the same tracks. Both are doing very well in school. Parker is headed to Middle School at Iona, and Blake is getting ready for college, with Spelman being her likely first choice. In 2025 she spent 4 weeks in a summer program at Spelman. Spelman is the sister school of Morehouse College, my alma mater.

L-R Daughter-in-law Michelle, grandson Parker, granddaughter Blake, Jason standing, and Christopher, kneeling (Christmas 2024)

Jason was the first of our sons to go to college. He was one of two students Princeton accepted from New Rochelle that year. During his first weeks at Princeton, one white student said that Jason was admitted because he received an affirmative action preference. The white student retreated when he learned that Jason's admission test scores were higher than his. This is but one example of the ignorance of white people about the history of our country and of this institution.

Jason earned his B.A. degree in political economy from Princeton, a J. D. degree in law from UCLA, and an MBA in finance from Columbia.

He has worked as a lawyer in law firms, a securities firm, banks and as an officer in the Jockey Club, and as Chief Operating Officer of 1/ST Content to focus on innovative thoroughbred racing content. In the interim, he was Chief Operating Officer of Equibase, which keeps statistics on thoroughbred horse racing and publishes related magazines and newspapers throughout the United States. He is admitted to practice law in California and New York. Most recently, he was appointed as a Non-Executive Director at Total Performance Data (TDP), The World's Leading Horse Racing Data Provider

When Chris began looking at colleges, he wanted to go as far away from home as possible. He settled for the University of Michigan, and not California, which was a relief to us. I believe he chose Michigan because some of his good friends were enrolled there, and because it was closer to home.

It was while he was enrolled in Michigan that I read the first set of dyslexia test results which brought home to me the enormous academic achievements of Christopher even though he had difficulty reading. He managed to graduate from Michigan, a top ranked four-year college, with honors, in three years.

He also had the opportunity to study in Seville, Spain for a semester.

When Chris graduated, we gave him and Jason a trip to Europe. They were joined by Daniel Basis, the son of our neighbors, Judy and Bob, across the street. Among the many pleasures they enjoyed were the stories that Orlandus "Doc" Wilson regaled them with. Doc was not a relative, but he was one of the founding members of the Golden Gate Quartet in 1934/35. Doc enthralled them with stories about all the famous musicians that he knew from the States and throughout Europe.

The boys met Doc and Gun, his wife, in Paris.

Chris earned his B. A. and J.D. law degrees from Michigan, and an LL.M in Securities Law from Georgetown. His Georgetown class had the distinction of being the first commencement class that then newly installed Chief Justice John Roberts addressed.

Chris started out with me and then went on the work in various capacities at the United States Securities and Exchange Commission. I think the highlights of his career there was that he had been among the recipients of the 2010 Council of Inspector General's Integrity and Excellence Gaston L. Gianni, Jr.'s Better Government Award: SEC Investigative Team - Bernard L. Madoff Ponzi Scheme. (2010) and the Chairman's Award for Excellence, Senior Initiative Team. His last assignment was Special Counsel in the Office of Market Intelligence, Division of Enforcement (HQ - Point of Contact) for deciding whether various complaints should be forwarded for further investigation and enforcement.

Vacations

When the boys were young toddlers, Jane and I took them to visit their maternal grandparents in San Francisco.

When Jason was a toddler, we took him to visit them when they were living on Los Palmas drive, down the street from where Willie Brown used to live but I'm not sure that we ever took Christopher to visit them in that location. Willie is the former Speaker of the California Assembly, and Mayor of San Francisco.

However, when they were still at the big wheel stage, for some reason, we bought them big wheels in San Francisco which had to be assembled in San Francisco, then taken apart and reassembled after we returned to New York. My great friend Melvin Hodges helped us to do this. Mel and I are still great and close friends some 65 plus years after we met at Morehouse in 1959.

When Jason and Christopher were about 8 years old, I took them with me to visit Yellowstone National Park and a few other places in the northwest part of the United States. That is an exceptionally beautiful part of the country. We landed in Butte Mt where I rented a car to drive on to Seattle. What happened is that I had gone to a National Bar Association meeting in Seattle WA a few weeks earlier and decided that it was so beautiful that I wanted to take my family there for vacation. Jane's brother Jeffrey would later establish residence there where he would raise his family. At the time of our trip Jane could not accompany us and so we agreed that we would meet her in Seattle. Sometimes Seattle reminded us of San Francisco.

Shortly after we rented the car in Butte to drive to Seattle a pebble popped onto the windshield and left a little hole that we didn't pay much attention to. As we drove further the hole developed into a spider web which made it exceedingly difficult to see. We managed to get to some place so that I could change automobiles. We spent two nights in Yellowstone National Park where we saw the usual things - bison, the hot springs, and the upper and lower falls. As I looked at the photograph that I took sometime later, I saw that at the time I took the photos I had no idea that they were standing so close to the cliffs. Scared me to death.

As we continued our journey, we drove down the Cook Road Drive on the recommendation of Lynn, one of the young women who worked with me at Union Carbide. She recommended the drive because of its beauty. It did not disappoint. Lynn was also a photographer; she recommended that I use Fuji film at the time mainly because Fuji film contrasted the green colors more prominently than other films. I think that was the case.

When we reached Jackson Hole Montana, nestled in the Rocky Mountains, that was quite a sight to see. We rented a chalet, and I went out to get some hamburgers and Coca-Cola and soft drinks and when I returned, I was startled to see my well-mannered young boys jumping from the upper deck down onto the couch on the first floor. We managed to spend our time in Jackson Hole and continued through Idaho.

Our route took us through Coeur d'Alene, Idaho. I had some misgivings about driving through Coeur d'Alene because there had been some white supremacist activity there. Later the skinhead's organization which went under the head of the white Aryan nation, was based there, they killed one or two people, including an African American. His mother sued them and recovered, satisfying her judgment by taking their assets.

Arthur Fletcher-Assistant Secretary of Labor

On the other hand, I was curious because Art Fletcher had asked me if I wanted to relocate to Idaho to work as a lawyer for one of the paper companies. He had been the U.S. Assistant Secretary of Labor in the Nixon, Ford, Reagan, and George H. W. Bush administrations.

I met him at a convention when I noticed he was one of the speakers and this would be an effective way to meet him since I would not need to go through his gatekeepers at his office. I used this tactic many times when I wanted to establish contact with a person whose access was closely restricted when they were in their offices.

From those days, he took the initiative in requesting those white businessmen who sought his assistance, to bring African American lawyers with them.

One of the things that Art taught me was how to play what I call the inside outside game. I think this was after he became the Executive Director of the United Negro College Fund in 1972.

On one occasion I discussed with him the kind of letter he should send to a funding source that I was connected to asking for an increase in the funds the UNCF normally requested. I sent him a draft; he revised it and sent it to the funding source. UNCF received an increased amount.

I don't remember what the occasion was, but he was the person who taught me about people writing their own letters that needed the signature of someone else. Many years later, my wife Maleta was asked to write her own appraisal by one of her bosses which she found a bit unusual, but she had not been a student of this method of proceeding. I explained it to her long after the event had taken place.

From Art, I learned the art of "going to conventions." It happened when I was working with some people in Newburgh to try to create a new town in town in Newburgh, New York. I needed to speak to Art and to Sam Jackson to try to get the program funded. Sam served as HUD's Assistant Secretary for Metropolitan Planning and Development from 1969 to 1973.[101]

Art gave me a tutorial on how to operate in the environments I was interested in.

At a convention where they were both on a panel, I approached each of them and at least got a chance to make my pitch. Had I tried to make an appointment to see them I their offices, I think the gatekeepers might not have let me in.

On one such occasion, I knew I needed to approach a gentleman - an African businessman and philanthropist - I wanted to meet as soon as he came off the stage at President Obama's US-Africa Summit panel. I had become aware of him by reading Africa's Greatest Entrepreneurs, by Moky Makura. Gordon Wavamunno of Uganda, one of the subjects of the book, gave me a copy in 2010 when I went to attend Godfrey Binaisa's funeral.

As I anticipated, he would not have time to talk. He gave me his card and asked me to send him an email. We have exchanged emails since then.

101 https://www.nytimes.com/1982/09/29/obituaries/samuel-jackson-nixon-aide-in-housing-matters-is-dead.html (Accessed 04 JAN 2023)

The Presidents

Barack Obama

Barack Obama was first elected President of the United States in 2008. He was the first African American President of the United States. He accomplished several things during his two terms as President., despite Republican Majority Leader Sen. Mitch McConnell's threat that Mr. Obama would be a one term President. During the two terms of President Obama, whether as minority leader or majority leader of the Senate, McConnell did all he could to defeat Obama's proposals. He made this statement after a meeting with some of his cohorts in Washington, D.C. I think this meeting took place the night of the election.

McConnell then did all he could to defeat everything that Obama proposed. One of the most notable being to stifle Obama in his nominations of people for federal judgeships. Another was his refusal to even hold a hearing on the nomination of Merrick Garland as a Justice of the United States Supreme Court. Garland would later become Attorney General of the United States in President Biden's administration.

As Attorney General , Garland was a major disappointment, especially his two-year delay in investigating Donald Trump's attempt to overthrow the government as he sought to be elected to a second non-contiguous term.[102]

---

[102] In 2024, Trump was elected to a non-contiguous second term, after President Joe Biden's one-term.

Biden had been Obama's Vice President.

Obama was reelected for a second consecutive term. Enormous crowds witnessed his two swearings in, in freezing weather. I was in Washington for the first time swearing-in but decided not to go to the capital because of the very freezing weather. I watched it on television in Christopher's living room. However, I could truthfully say that I was in Washington at the time of Obama's swearing in.

In my opinion, there were many white people who could not stand the idea of a black President. This thought harkened back to a time when a large part of the white population could not stomach the idea of black people having equal political, social and economic rights. Then Chief Justice Roger B. Taney said as much in the infamous Dred Scott decision in 1857.[103] Taney said that this was the opinion of the white population of the world:[104]

> It is difficult at this day to realize the state of public opinion in relation to that unfortunate race, which prevailed in the civilized and enlightened portions of the world at the time of the Declaration of Independence, and when the Constitution of the United States was framed and adopted. But the public history of every European nation displays it in a manner too plain to be mistaken.
>
> They had for more than a century before been regarded as beings of an inferior order, and altogether unfit to associate with the white race, either in social or political relations; and so far inferior, that they had no rights which the white man was bound to respect; and that the negro might justly and lawfully be reduced to slavery for his benefit. He was bought and sold and treated as an ordinary article of merchandise and traffic, whenever a profit could be made by it. This opinion was at that time fixed and universal in the civilized portion of the white race. It was regarded as an axiom in morals as well as in politics, which no one thought of disputing, or supposed to be open to dispute; and men in every grade and position in society daily and

[103] Dred Scott v. Sandford, 60 U.S. (19 How.) 393 (1857)
[104] Id., 60 U.S. 393, 407

habitually acted upon it in their private pursuits, as well as in matters of public concern, without doubting for a moment the correctness of this opinion.

Some white people, then and now, look at black people as some kind of alien force within America. They simply ignore the patriotism of black people in this country, partly because they do not know the history of America. This ignorance is exacerbated by the Trump administration's Plan 2025 to erase as much of black American history as they can.

Thus, we have grown, white male crybabies, with all their privileges that flow from white skin color alone, whining about being deprived of their rights.

Obama was succeeded in office by Donald Trump, who falsely attacked Obama throughout his first presidency as not having been born in the United States. Obama was born in Hawaii. Trump argued that since Obama was not an American citizen, he was disqualified to serve as President. The great irony is that in 2023-2024, several states considered whether Trump was disqualified to be sworn in as President under section 3 of the 14th Amendment because of his prominent roles in leading the insurrection against the United States government on January 6, 2021.

However, there were many delays in the various cases pending against him, even as he took office. In two of the most significant cases, United States District Judge Eileen Cannon, in Florida, dismissed the classified documents case against Trump; In Washington, D.C., United States District Judge Tanya Chutkan dismissed the January 6, 2021, insurrection case against Trump without prejudice. Special Prosecutor Jack Smith moved to dismiss those cases because of new Supreme Court decisions embracing more of the imperial presidency theory of constitutional law.

On January 6, 2021, at his incitement, Trump urged his supporters to attack the Capitol to keep the election of Biden in 2020 from being certified by Congress. He went as far as to ignore public mob calls to execute Mike Pence, his Vice President. His supporters had even erected gallows on the west front of the U.S. Capitol grounds, specifically near Union Square and Independence Avenue. Trump claimed that the election was stolen from him, although some 60 federal and state courts had ruled it was not stolen from him.

He has acquired a wide-spread reputation for being a nimble, notorious, and prodigious prevaricator.

Many of the insurrectionists were convicted of various crimes thereafter. However, after Trump was elected in 2024, he pardoned all the insurrectionists, calling them "patriots."

Trump also made no secret of his affinity for white supremacists' people and organizations. This unleashed some nasty racist demonstrations throughout the country, the most notorious one being Charlottsville, Virginia. However, as nasty as it was - a vicious attack on Jews and blacks - the counter demonstrators turned out in much greater numbers. Joe Biden said that the white supremacists' events at Charlottesville are what caused him to run for President for a four-year term starting in 2020.

To some extent, the public reaction to the Charlottesville demonstration vindicated Joe Biden's position that racism in has no place in the American body politic.

Among other things, Trump used Twitter to communicate racial and religious hatred, as well as "policy" pronouncements. He continues to use social media and Executive Orders to do so. Many of the Executive Orders are facially unconstitutional and will need to be declared so by courts. Meanwhile, they have had the intended effect of intimidating a wide swath of people.

Trump could not stand the many successes of Obama and is trying to do all that he can to reverse and nullify Obama's policies and erase his accomplishments from history. One of the most prominent being Obama's success is getting nationwide health care insurance passed which covered millions of previously uninsured people. To add salt to this wound, late Senator John McCain, a Republican, who Trump had supremely disrespected, provided the deciding vote in the Senate to pass what has come to be known as Obamacare.

In 2025 Trump displayed his typical outsized egotistical mania to have the Nobel Peace Prize awarded to him, even though he was ineligible according to the Nobel Committee's rules. He also secured a number of nominations from people, organizations and other countries to get the prize. They had nothing to lose by currying favor with him by making such unseemly political recommendations.

True to form, he attacked the Nobel Committee when the Committee awarded the prize to Maria Corina Machado of Venezuela.

After Ms. Machado was awarded the prize, his administration denounced the Committee's decision. She telephoned Trump to say he should have gotten it for his efforts to support her effective advocacy to oppose Venezuela's President Nicolás **Maduro** Moros authoritarianism and to promote democracy. Since the Venezuelan government had forced her into hiding, she might not have been aware that while Trump called for democratic reforms in countries overseas, he is proceeding 180 degrees in the opposite direction in the United States to destroy as much of democracy as he can.

Jacob Zuma of South Africa (and Jerry Matjila and Toshio Akiniwa)

As I wrote earlier, I had developed an interest in events that were happening in the black world at an early age. When it came to South Africa, my interest intensified as I began to follow the trials and tribulations Nelson Mandela and the political prisoners under apartheid. That led naturally to what was happening in South Africa itself.

My earliest active involvement in affairs affecting South Africa were through various resolutions that I wrote and would introduce at National Bar Association annual meetings. All of them passed.

We came around to the 1980s and during that time I had met Johnny Makhathini, who was the African National Congress (ANC) representative in Manhattan. Johnny told me that he thought it would be helpful if the National Bar Association were to adopt a resolution calling for the freeing of Nelson Mandela and the political prisoners in South Africa being held under the apartheid regime. In those days there were no fax machines and no e-mail either. So, I wrote a draft of a resolution and met with Johnny at Newark airport to review the draft and make whatever revisions we decided on. I took it to the National Bar Association for adoption. The resolution passed.

Johnny also invited me to a reception for Oliver R Tambo, the president of the ANC, which was to be held at Uganda house. Uganda House housed Uganda's Mission to the United Nations. At the time I did not realize I was about to meet such a powerful historical figure. I attended the reception, and I met OR Tambo.

At that time Mr. Eldad "Eddie" Wapenyi was Uganda's Permanent Representative and Ambassador to the United Nations. President Binaisa called him Eddie. I was thoroughly familiar with Uganda house in 1988 because of my connections with Godfrey Binaisa from Mt. Vernon and Uganda, going back to the 1970s.

During the era of Idi Amin, Amin wanted to buy a building in New York City that housed the Uganda mission to the United Nations. The person who oversaw the purchase of that building was Princess Elizabeth Christobel Edith Bagaaya Akiiki of Tooro, Uganda. I later had a chance to meet her in person on two occasions, one of which was during the funeral preparations for Godfrey Binaisa.

As it turns out Uganda house was built right next to the United States mission to the United Nations. Rumor has it that Idi Amin wanted to be sure that Uganda House was higher than the United States mission building so Uganda could look down on the United States.

Because of my interest in the black world, and my ignorance of her stellar background, I think it is important for me to tell you about Princess Elizabeth from a published source.

> "After finishing elementary school from the present Kyebambe Girls' Secondary School, she was sent to Gayaza High School, a girls' boarding school in Buganda, followed by Sherborne School for Girls in England, where she was the only black student. "I felt that I was on trial and that my failure to excel would reflect badly on the entire black race," she later wrote. After one year, she was accepted into Girton College, Cambridge, the third African woman to be admitted to the University of Cambridge in the institution's history. In 1962, she graduated from Cambridge with a law degree. Three years later, in 1965, the princess became a barrister-at-law as a member of Gray's Inn, becoming the first woman from East Africa to be called to the English Bar.[105]

In 1988 South Africa was still under the control of the apartheid government. This means that there was not a South Africa owned property in New York that could receive O.R. Tambo. Many years later, in 2012, during the gala dinner in Mangaung which closed out the 2012 centenary celebration of the creation of the ANC, I learned why Uganda house had a special connection to the ANC. All the heads of state and presidents who attended the gala dinner told a story that was peculiar to that person's country. When Uganda President Museveni spoke, he told us that Uganda had been considered as one of the front-line states, something that I did not know up until that point. Many South African fighters trained in Uganda. I now understand why Mr. Tambo's reception was held at Uganda House.

There were many celebrities at the centenary celebration in Mangaung, South Africa, including Amb. Andrew Young and Reverend Jesse Jackson from the United States. Jesse Jackson was given a singular honor of being one of the three or four faith leaders (priests, imams and rabbis) who opened one of the largest events during the ceremonies at the huge Mangaung Rugby Stadium.[106]

---

105 https://en.wikipedia.org/wiki/Princess_Elizabeth_of_Tooro (Accessed 15 JAN 2024)

106 The successor name to Bloemfontein

I attended this centenary celebration at the invitation of Jean Bailey, Ph.D. USA -ANC Centenary Co-Chair, Graduate Professor and Chair, HURSAP (Howard University South Africa Research Project) housed at Howard University, and USA-ANC Centenary Co-Chair Joseph E. Harris, Ph.D. Howard University Distinguished Professor, (Emeritus). There was a delegation of professors from Howard, as well as NBA past president Yvette Simmons (2000 - 2001). Then NBA President Daryl D. Parks, also from Florida, was scheduled to attend, but travel arrangements caused a delay for him to attend this event.

Other members of the delegation were: Dr. Charles Johnson, Assistant Professor of History, Assistant Director of the South African Research and Archival (SARAP), Howard University; Dr. Judi Latta, Executive Director, Office of Howard University of Communications, Dr. Melbourne Cummings, Howard University Department of Communications, and Mr. Maurice Foster, Executive Director, National Association of Black Journalists.

Jean had arranged for us to stay at the Intercontinental Sandton Towers Hotel in Johannesburg, and the President Hotel in Mangaung.

She also had arranged for us to sit in the VIP section for the ceremonies at the stadium that day, from where we were to go into one of the private rooms to meet President Jacob Zuma.

L-R Dr. Charles Johnson, Maurice Foster, Rev. Walter Fountroy, President Zuma, Dr. Jean Bailey, me, and Dr. Bain from Trinidad

At the time we met President Jacob Zuma, each person was asked to make a comment about that connection to South Africa or something similar. When it came time for me, I simply told him that that I was a friend of Amb. Jerry Matjila, who at that time was the Director General of the South Africa Department of International Relations and Cooperation. He ran the daily operations of South Africa's foreign relations.

Amb. Jerry Matjila and me at the Grand Palm Hotel and Resort in Gaborone on the occasion of President Zuma's later visit to Gaborone, Botswana (March 2016).

One of the things that I learned about Jacob Zuma during this visit is his ability to connect with human beings. Not only was this the case at the Mangaung stadium where he was very well received, but at one of the political rallies through his telling stories, dancing and singing. He was a highly effective communicator.

While we were meeting with President Zuma in the VIP lounge, Jerry wanted me to meet Mr. Toshio Akiniwa. At the time, Mr. Akiniwa was 88 years old. I cite his age because he gave me the strongest bear hug that I had ever experienced.

Mr. Akiniwa had been the long-standing Representative Director of the Japan Asia Africa Latin America Solidarity Committee based in Tokyo. An extremely cute female Japanese interpreter assisted us. With him and Jerry, I experienced a Kunta Kinte moment. I learned from Mr. Akiniwa that he had followed our meetings and activities in the newspapers and other sources when our NAACP delegation visited Japan in 1989.

During the ceremonies, on 26 October 2012, the government of South Africa awarded the Order of the Companions of O.R. Tambo to Toshio Akiniwa, the president of the Japan Asia Africa Latin America Solidarity Committee (JAALA), for his unconditional support for the African National Congress (ANC) during the apartheid era.[107]

Toshio Akiniwa with his Honors awards

[107] ANC supporter awarded for role in struggle - The Japan Times

During our 1989 visit, I was part of the NAACP delegation that went to Japan to discuss the racist remarks that some then present or former highest ranking Japanese officials had made about African Americans. We met with Mr. Yukio Okamoto who was director of the foreign ministry's First North America Division, which guided U.S.-Japanese relations, and with Kazuo Nukazawa, senior managing director of the Japan Federation of Economic Organizations (Keidanren).

In 1989, I did not know that Jerry Matjila was running the ANC office in Tokyo; he had also followed our NAACP visit through the media while we were there. When I first met Jerry some 20 years later in Westchester County, New York, he told me that some of our visit had an influence on Japanese officials and private organizations to cause them to pay more attention to what was happening in South Africa as well.

Heidi Malesa, a friend of Maleta's asked us if we could come over to her house to meet her uncle, who turned out to be Jerry.

Jerry and I became fast friends. A few years ago, when the National Bar Association annual meeting was held in New York, Jerry, and his wife Flo invited me to stay with them at the South African UN Ambassador's penthouse in New York City to save me from the time-consuming commute from Westchester County to the City. Their daughter Bobo was the official doorkeeper and stayed up to let me in after the long- day NBA activities. I am forever grateful to them for this hospitality.

Mr. Akiniwa confirmed that it was his organization, the Japan Asia Africa Latin American Solidarity Committee that had raised the money to support the ANC office in Japan. Mr. Akiniwa seems to have had a very intense interest in human rights and has a special relationship with the ANC that dates from 1956 in Cairo. He and Jerry explained how helpful his organization had been to the ANC, through Jerry, when Jerry was the ANC Tokyo-based representative.

Meantime, I received an invitation which read:

His Excellency
The President of the Republic of South Africa, Mr. JG Zuma
Requests the pleasure of the company of
WILSON LE ROY JR
To the National Orders Wards Ceremony & Luncheon
At: SM Makgatho Presidential guest House , Pretoria

On Friday, 26 October 2012

At 12h30 for 13h00

I attended the luncheon.

Jerry and I sat together at the ceremony where President Zuma presented awards to people who had rendered service to the ANC during apartheid. One of them was Mr. Akiniwa.

The government of South Africa awarded the Order of the Companions of O.R. Tambo to Toshio Akiniwa, the president of the Japan Asia Africa Latin America Solidarity Committee (JAALA), for his unconditional support for the African National Congress (ANC) during the apartheid era[108].

Jakaya Mrisho Kikwete of Tanzania

President Kikwete of Tanzania is one of the many high officials that I met through my great friend, Charles Thembani Ntwaagae, who was the Permanent Representative of Botswana to the United Nations from July 2008 to 2018.

---

[108] https://www.japantimes.co.jp/news/2013/02/07/national/anc-supporter-awarded-for-role-in-struggle/ (Accessed 13 JAN 2024)

President Kikwete and me at the dedication of the Tanzania Chancery in Manhattan

Although I had read about President Kikwete, I did not meet him until about 2016 at the opening of the Tanzania Chancery in New York City. I attended with Charles and his wife Mmasello as a guest of Botswana. He and I discussed the acquisition of Uganda House.

The next time I would see him was on television at the Nelson Mandela funeral , having a conversation with former President Kaunda of Zambia.

Kennedy, Clinton, Obama Inauguration Invitations

I received commemorative inauguration invitations for these 3 Presidents,

Festus G. Mogae, former President Of Botswana

On March 7, 2018, a remarkable luncheon happened.

Since 1988, H.E. Festus G. Mogae and I would meet from time to time at various social events. At the Memorial Service for late President Sir Quett K. Masire, we again exchanged greetings, and he said that now that I was living in Lobatse, Botswana, he would call so that we could sit down and talk. He said something like that earlier but had not followed through. Sometime later he did telephone me and asked if Maleta and I could meet with him for lunch the next day at Caravella's in Gaborone. Yes, of course.

To prepare for the meeting, I had 3 things that I wanted to discuss with him. One was the conception and building of the Arapa diamond sorting plant and operations, because of a dinner conversation that I had had with Harold Hester who had helped design the plant. I thought that a documentary on this process would be great, since I had not viewed one; I would later learn at a diamond exhibition in Botswana in 2024, that there were films that told the story of the development.

Harold told me that he designed plants for sorting diamonds. They were called CARP & FISH =Aquarium. Harold had worked on creating and developing software to process minerals and sort diamonds. CARP did first part of process. FISH was the sorting plant. It was the world's first fully automated diamond processing and sorting plant, a project between Debswana and DeBeers.[109] Mogae referred to the

---

[109] Debswana is a mining company located in Botswana; It is an equal partnership between the Government of the Republic of Botswana and the De Beers Group of Companies. https://www.bing.com/search?q=what+is+debswana&form=WSBEDG&qs=U

venture as being like Siamese twins-one couldn't function without the other. The engineers developed a fully working prototype in South Africa. They took the Botswana government down to South Africa to see the prototype and explained how it would operate. The aquarium was built with separate monitoring controls in SA.

In 2024, Debswana had an exhibition at the Fairgrounds Pavilion which I attended. There I discovered many videos of mining operations. Debswana is the joint venture between the government of Botswana and DeBeers of South Africa to mine and sell the gem quality and industrial diamonds produced by Botswana mines.

"Botswana is a leading producer and the second-largest producer of diamonds, with annual output exceeding 20 million carats. The country's diamond wealth is centered around the Jwaneng and Orapa mines, some of the richest diamond mines globally.

Managed by Debswana, a joint venture between the government and De Beers, Botswana's diamond industry has significantly contributed to the nation's economic growth, funding healthcare, education, and infrastructure projects.

Known for producing some of the finest-quality diamonds, Botswana has also positioned itself as a leader in ethical mining practices." [110]

The Pavilion Restaurant, which is a part of the Pavilion complex, houses a closed inside restaurant and an outdoor restaurant. The restaurant, including the bathrooms, is always clean. The staff is

---

T&cvid=8dc4d452910d4ef3877b646bb6dcc0c5&pq=What+is+Debswana&cc=BW&setlang=en-US&nclid=5818987FB4D68F5BAD3F221AD7D26E69&ts=1736160820851&wsso=Moderate (Accessed 06 January 2025.) The De Beers Group is a South African–British corporation that specializes in the diamond industry, including mining, exploitation, retail, inscription, grading, trading and industrial diamond manufacturing https://en.wikipedia.org/wiki/De_Beers (Accessed 06 January 2025)

[110] https://www.brimco.io/mining/diamond-producing-countries/#:~:text=Botswana%20is%20a%20leading%20producer%20and%20the%20second-largest,mines%2C%20some%20of%20the%20richest%20diamond%20mines%20globally. (Accessed 03 APRIL 2025)

exceptionally welcoming. I thoroughly enjoy the setting and eat lunch there frequently so I can enjoy the fresh air while I eat lunch.

I am the only American who eats lunch there on a regular basis. The combination of being a Mogolo (older person) and an American has caused the staff to adopt me. I think it is more because I am a Mogolo, in keeping with Botswana customs to look after old folks.

Aone Mabote, one of the waitresses, has dedicated herself to seeing that I am well taken care of as "her" customer. We have gotten to the point where I telephone or text her that I am coming in for lunch. She texts the menu to me, I tell her what I want, and when I arrive, there is a sign on the table saying "RESERVED." She will have fixed the plate and kept the food warm until I arrive. Another of the waitresses says Aone treats me as if she is my first-born child. So, I feel quite special.

Returning to the luncheon with President Mogae, to help prepare him for the meeting, I sent H.E. Mogae a copy of my resumes and history to prepare him when I asked him to identify some place where I might get some consulting work.

We had a lovely discussion among Maleta, me and Uncle Festus (as she calls him). He leaned over, looked me in the eye and said he wanted me to be his legal adviser. He said he knew I was a practicing attorney in New York, but he did not know of my extensive background until he read my material. I explained that I was not a member of the Botswana bar, but that I was in the process of petitioning the High Court and had also made the American Embassy aware that I was about to do so.

The attorneys for The Law Society of Botswana and the Attorney General told me that if I withdrew the High Court petition, and instead made an application to Chief Judge Terence Rannowanne, they would not object. The Chief Judge never acted on my application. I should have stayed my application in the High Court, instead of withdrawing it, pending the decision by the Chief Judge.

In May 2018, we expected the Chief Judge to act within a few weeks. My application showed that my credentials were far more than what now retired Judge President of the Botswana Court of Appeal wrote would be necessary for the admission of a foreign lawyer. Judge President Ian Kirby suggested those requirements in the case of Chessie Dow, an applicant who had been educated in n the United States, a non-commonwealth country.

I retained Eddie Bayford, a brilliant local attorney, to represent me. He told me that the Chief Judge told him that he was not sure how to act on the application. I know from researching the legislative history of the Legal Practitioners Act of 1996 that here were two schools of thought. One thought that admitting a foreign lawyer would cause unwelcome competition; the other thought that the foreign lawyer could exchange complementary information with the local lawyers and could bring expertise that local lawyers did not have.

Then, in 2022, while still awaiting word from the Chief Judge, Covid-19 hit New York. On March 02, 2022, I arrived in New York, to try the long-running Brisbane case which we had started in 2005. Because of the no fly and other travel restrictions, and the timeline for developing and administering a vaccine, I was stuck in the United States from 02 March 2020 to September 2022.

By the time I returned, the Chief Justice had not acted; Eddie contracted long Covid and was no longer practicing.

After this experience, and after sitting in on a few hearings, I slowly concluded that I would pass on asking the Chief Judge to act, because I did not want the primary responsibility for the limited clientele that I would serve. I also realized that if I were involved in litigation, I might have trouble following testimony because I might not understand some of the names of the litigants, witnesses and Judges as a case progressed in trial. Also, many of the participants, including Judges, spoke so softly that I could not hear them.

Then, in 2024, the Botswana Democratic Party (BDP) lost the elections . The 54-year-old Advocate Duma Boko, of the Umbrella for

Democratic Change (UDC) , replaced President Mokgweetsi Masisi, after his Botswana Democratic Party (BDP) lost by a landslide for the first time in 58 years.

Advocate Duma Boko appointed a new Chief Justice. I decided not to pursue admission to the Botswana Bar.

How I Met President Mogae

In 1988, I was a public member of the New York Banking Board. Vincent Tese, then Jill Considine, were successive Superintendents of the NYS Banking Department and Chaired the Board.

My appointment came about as follows.

Paul Williams, Esq. headed a group called black attorneys for Mario Cuomo and raised funds to support his election. After he won, Paul asked what I wanted to do in government. I told him I wanted to sit on the NYS Banking Board because I was interested in stopping or restricting deposits of New York bank customers from being used to support apartheid South Africa.

The Governor duly appointed me. I was successful in getting the Board to enact a regulation that forbade New York State chartered banks from investing in real estate in apartheid South Africa for a period of 2 years. I defined real estate to include mining operations. At the time, our banks were some of the largest in the world.

The New York State Banking Board with Vincent Tese Chairman, seated at table, second from the left. I am standing at the far left, next to John Torrell, then President of Manufacturers Hanover Trust (1983-87).

At the time of the UN General Assembly meeting in New York, I asked Vince, then Chairman of the Board, to extend an invitation to the members of the Southern African Development Coordination Conference (SADCC) so that they could discuss New York State charted banks investments in the SADCC community.

We extended the invitation, and the meeting was held on the 101st floor of one of the World Trade Center Towers.

At that time, I met Sam Nujoma,[111] who would become President of Namibia in 1990, and Festus Mogae, who would become President of Botswana in 1998. There were several others, but I had discussions mainly with these two.

At the time of our meeting, Nujoma was the head of South West Africa People's Organization (SWAPO), an anti-apartheid organization, which had formed the PLO, a military wing. The military wing

[111] Mr. Nujoma died 08 February 2025.

was formed only after negotiations with the UN and South Africa failed.

Festus G. Mogae was Botswana's Assistant Minister for Finance and Development. We enjoyed a discussion about the transfer of know-how and technology. He thought that the level of education of Batswana at the time was not at a level that could support advanced technology. I told him of my experiences with these kinds of transfers when I worked at IBM's computer chip making facility. In East Fishkill, N.Y.

In between the time of the SADCC meeting in 1988 in New York, and the March 2018 luncheon in Gaborone, he and I would meet several times. Our New Rochelle, New York residence was 10 minutes from the residence of H.E. Charles T. Ntwaagae, Botswana's Ambassador to the United Nations and his wife Mmasello. My wife, Maleta, had known them (and many other Batswana) for many years, as her father, H.E. Archibald M. Mogwe,[112] was Botswana's Foreign Minister from 1974-1984, and had served as the first Permanent Secretary of Sir Seretse Khama, first President of Botswana. As a result, many Batswana learned under him. Charles was Ambassador from 2008-2018. He holds a master's degree from Penn State.

Our families exchanged visits frequently, most of the times informally, but on many occasions my wife Maleta and I assisted Ambassador Ntwaagae and his wife Mmasello in welcoming and entertaining delegations from Botswana. This included delegations led by former President Mogae, the late Vice President, Mr. Mompati Merafhe, former Attorney General Athalia Molokomme and the former Attorney General and Foreign Minister, Mr. Phandu Skelemani and his wife.

In 2024, Mr. Skelemani also completed his service as the Speaker of Parliament.

---

112 He also held many other important posts, including Botswana Ambassador to the United States in 1995-1999. https://yourbotswana.com/2019/04/07/15-facts-that-every-motswana-should-know-about-one-of-botswanas-founding-fathers-archibald-mogwe/ (Accessed 17 JAN 2014)

Before Charles came to take up the post as Botswana's Ambassador to the United Nations, Maleta and I had paid a courtesy call on then outgoing UN Ambassador Alfred Dube and later assisted incoming UN Ambassador Sam Outlule and his wife to welcome a Botswana delegation at the Ambassador's residence. H. E. Mogae led the delegation on that occasion. My wife, who is a protocol specialist, took over the sequence of who would be served when. A member of the delegation who told her he admired the way she handled things and asked if she was a general in the Botswana military.

I particularly enjoyed the swimming pool at the Ambassador's residence. One feature that it had was a built-in seat at the far end of the pool, so after swimming some distance one could sit down at the deep end of the pool.

Maleta and I also hosted a dinner for President Mogae at our residence in New Rochelle, and we traveled to Washington, D.C. in 2009 to serve as his "family" when he received an honorary doctorate degree from Howard University, Washington D.C. Later, we accompanied President Mogae at dinner in his honor after he received an award from the Schomburg Museum in New York City.

I also attended several functions at the Botswana Embassy in Washington, D.C.

President Mogae at our residence in New Rochelle, New York

Stalled Application for Admission to Practice Law in Botswana

In about 2017, I had started researching the cases and the Botswana Legal Practitioners Act to see what I needed to do to apply for admission to the Botswana bar.

Although I had secured a work permit to allow me to act as a legal and business consultant, I became more wary of this route as the Law Society had objected to some people being engaged in the "unauthorized practice of law." My approach would have been to tell the client that I would analyze a problem and then recommend that we meet with a Botswana lawyer to review my analysis and give the client a legal opinion on whether the analysis met the requirements of Botswana law. I would be free to give an opinion if the question needed to be answered according to my background and experience in New York law, and the laws of the United States. I did not want to see my name attached to the headline of one of those stories.

By August of 2017, I had gathered enough material and done enough analysis that I thought I could prepare a draft of the petition under the Legal Practitioners Act. As it happens, I was in New York at the time, but Attorney Eddie Bayford was visiting Maleta at our residence in Lobatse on an issue that he needed her help with. I had read the judgment in his case for petition to the Botswana bar, and about that time, I had contacted Chris du Plessis, the attorney who represented Eddie on his petition to see if he would represent me. Mr. du

Plessis told me that he was not practicing anymore and recommended Eddie.

I met with Mr. Tebogo Moipolai, the Executive Secretary of the Law Society, to introduce myself and to see what was required.

When I telephoned Maleta from New York, she told me that she was in a meeting with Eddie, who had come to our house. Fortunately, I had left a draft of the petition on a table in the lounge and attached the backup documentation to the draft. I spoke with Eddie and asked him if he would review the draft with the possibility of him representing me.

He did so and represented me.

After a lot of factual and legal research, many drafts and compilations we filed the petition on 25 May 2018 in the High Court.

Unfortunately, when I returned to Botswana, Maleta told me that Eddie was suffering from long Covid. That really hurt, because Eddie is a nice person, in addition to being a first-rate lawyer.

As it turns out, Eddie enjoyed Dunkin' Donuts coffee, which was available in New York, but not in Botswana. I brought a bag back with me but was not able to see Eddie to give him this precious little bag of coffee.

Brisbane Case and Covid Plus Buffalo Soldiers

I practiced law in the State of New York, USA for almost 56 years, with stints at IBM, Union Carbide Corporation and private practice from my offices in White Plains, New York.

On 1st March 2020, I left Botswana to complete a few matters and try the Brisbane Estate case that we had been litigating for 15 years. I had intended to return to Botswana around 11th April 2020. Instead, I did not return until 15 September 2022, due to Covid travel restrictions and the timetable for development and administration of a vaccine.

When I landed on 2nd March 2020 in New York, I learned that the first Covid-19 case on the East coast of the USA was diagnosed in New York the day before I arrived. The victim was a man who attended a Synagogue about half a mile from where my son and his family were living. The authorities designated that whole area as a containment zone. The Governor imposed a 1-mile radius containment zone, closing various facilities in New Rochelle, and quarantining some people within the zone. I was not quarantined, although I acted as if I were.

Fortunately, my son Jason and his wife Michelle had a completely furnished basement, fashioned in the form of a sitting room, bedroom, and an office, so I was able to continue to work and to be isolated from the rest of the family to prevent potential cross contamination. I spent most of my time in the basement, coming up to join the family for meals. That worked out well.

After I arrived, I retrieved 10-15 banker's boxes of Brisbane case files from Hugh Campbell, Esq., my client, with whom I left them before I left to live in Botswana on December 31, 2015. It helped that Hugh was a very experienced and brilliant lawyer which made my life a lot easier in this case, with all its twists and turns.

Around 16th March 2020, the Courts were partially shut down, because of the Covid-19 pandemic. Shortly thereafter, most in-person court appearances were stopped. In the meantime, I, and the attorneys in the Surrogate's Court case,[113] with the telephonic help of Kevin Murphy, the Westchester County Surrogate's Court's Principal Law Secretary, were trying to resolve the case.

The process leading to this negotiation was a bit complex because by the time we got to this stage, we had first to resolve legal issues initially in the Surrogate's Court, then to retain counsel in New Hampshire to resolve legal issues there, to try valuation issues in the Bronx Supreme Court, then to prepare and argue a number of motions in the Bronx Supreme Court, one of which for summary judgment, argue an appeal, and thereafter return to the Surrogate's Court in 2021.

Meantime, on December 21, 2016, Bronx Supreme Court Justice Elizabeth Taylor decided the defendant's motion for summary judgment against us and dismissed our Brisbane case in that Court. A motion for summary judgment is essentially a paper trial where the judge decides the case by reviewing a voluminous stack of papers, determining the facts and the law. We appealed.

The appeal was scheduled for oral argument on December 5, 2018. I traveled to New York from Botswana to argue the appeal. I was happy to receive the Appellate Court judgment on January 10, 2019, overruling Justice Taylor by a vote of 5 to 0, and remanding the case

---

[113] Robert Damast, Esq., of Lauterbach Damast Garfinkel and Hollander, LLP who represented Richard Brisbane and Michael Friedman, Esq., of Kurzman, Eisenberg, Corbin &Lever, LLP, who represented Virginia Brisbane, the beneficiaries of the Estate of Emma Brisbane.

back to Bronx Supreme Court for "further proceedings on the issue of the value of decedent's estate's interest."

After Bronx Supreme Court Justice Doris Gonzalez restored the case to the calendar for trial, we began discussing settlement in earnest with her. Jeffrey Buss, Esq. represented Mr. James Alston, the defendant in the Supreme Court. After several discussions, just before trial we were able to settle the case with Justice Gonzalez. We were then required to return to Surrogate's Court so that the entire estate could be settled. We settled the Supreme Court case on August 26, 2020, by establishing a value of our deceased client's interest in the estate at a seven-figure number..

It would take a month or so to finalize the distributions and so forth. This brought us to autumn (in USA) of 2020, when Covid was surging in New York.

The overall hard-earned fee that I earned helped me greatly in my retirement, especially because of the favorable exchange rate, about 13.2 Pula to the dollar. This made my Botswana expenses and my expenses when I traveled to the United States bearable.

On 14th December 2020, the first Covid-19 vaccine was administered in the United States, in Queens, New York City to a nurse.

By this time, my Botswana residence permit had expired on 31st October 2020.

Also, during the COVID period, airlines service had been halted or severely restricted, so I couldn't return to Botswana, even if I had wanted to.

Around 14th February 2021, New Yorkers with underlying conditions or over 65 become eligible for COVID-19 vaccine. I was in this group, over 65 years of age.

I received the Pfizer vaccine, at the Centers for Disease Control and Prevention (CDC) recommended spacing as follows: 3rd February 2021, and 24th February 2021. Then followed a national debate over whether and when booster shots (jabs) would be available. After booster jabs were available, I got these jabs on 29th September 2021, and following CDC guidelines, took the last jab on 1st April 2022.

In the interim, and for many months to come, Covid-19 vaccines were not available anywhere in sub–Saharan Africa, including in Botswana.

Since I was in the United States, I wanted to attend the first in person annual meeting of the National Bar Association ("NBA"), after the onset of the pandemic, to be held in July 2022. Except for about 2 years, I had attended each of these annual meetings every year since 1970. I am a life member, and I have held several offices in the NBA.

Thereafter, since I had played a pivotal role in serving as legal counsel to the black cadets at West Point in 1972, in a unique history in the 187th year lifetime of West Point, the parties felt that I had an obligation to attend the 50th celebration of that history on 4th September 2022 where West Point was also going to honor the Buffalo soldiers who served at West Point.

Statue on Buffalo Soldiers Field (Placed 2021) I am there for the 04 September 2022 celebration.

In 1972, the black West Point cadets had defeated then President Nixon's wish to erect a confederate soldier monument at Trophy Point where West Point erected a statue to honor those service members who fought to save the union. The confederates had fought to destroy the union.

Nixon tried to do this in connection with his southern strategy, to try to win over the vote of white southerners.

I represented the cadets in connection with a sickle cell anemia benefit. Because no charitable event had ever been held on the grounds of any United States military academy there were various legal issues that need to be resolved. We were able to successfully resolve them.

I returned to Botswana on 15 September 2022, with a worrying demand by Maleta, my Motswana spouse, that I not return to our residence. I cover this separately, above.

Graduate School in Chemistry

Of the teaching assistantships that I was awarded, I accepted the one from the University of California at Berkeley. All the schools were rated at the top of world class teaching and research.

As we entered our senior year at Morehouse, forever optimists, we began to explore opportunities for graduate school study.

I feel that Morehouse and Berkeley are sacred institutions.

It was this indelible sense of self-worth that our pre-college schools had instilled in us, which Morehouse fortified, that enabled us to dare to imagine a future by applying to the best universities. Since I had been dreaming of California from an early age, the University of California at Berkeley was my first choice of the universities that had accepted me.

The first address that I remember as a student at Berkeley was 722 Alcatraz Avenue, Oakland, California. Oakland and Berkeley were contiguous cities. At the time I lived alone in my apartment. Somehow it dawned on me at the time that God was preparing me for the many times I would be alone in my life, and He was teaching me how to live alone and adjust to the loneliness.

Fortunately, I was a student with many different interests and kept myself busy by learning a lot of things. I also met a lot of people. My father (probably after discussions with my mother) thought that I should have a roommate. I met Lonnie Poindexter, from Arkansas through Clarence Hampton. Clarence had been in school with me at Morehouse. He was a year or two ahead of me.

In any case, Lonnie and I got along fine, although we had different fields of endeavor. Lonnie had been a dental assistant in the Navy, and he did something regularly that I wish I had done more of - flossed my teeth. Had I done so, I would have escaped the many regular, sometimes painful, teeth cleanings. Fortunately, I have an excellent, painless dentist here in Gaborone. She is Dr. Seema Chawla.

Lonnie would become the first black man employed by Al's Men Shop on San Pablo Avenue, in Oakland. He later became a very valued employee at Levi Strauss and Co. in San Francisco.

I had arrived in Berkeley by train. Fortunately, Leon Thompkins and Charles Meredith, from Morehouse, preceded me at Berkeley and were there to greet me and to welcome me and Troy into the Berkeley community. Leon would graduate from Berkeley and pursue a career in pharmacology at the Eli Lily Corporation in Indiana. Charles would return to Morehouse, head the chemistry department, create and head the Morehouse - Georgia Tech dual degree program which resulted in a Morehouse Man graduating with degrees from both schools. Charles become the Provost of Atlanta University. Troy would return to ultimately Chair the Chemistry Department at Morehouse.

Troy Story and I would become the 4th and 5th Morehouse graduates to be accepted into Berkeley's graduate chemistry program. From oldest to youngest were Adolphus Milligan (Morehouse '49, Berkeley '58), Leon Thompkins and Charles Meredith. Leon and Charles also received a Ph.D. degree.

At some point, I was assigned to Dr. George Pimental as my research director. George was a great director and supportive. My assignment was to experiment with phosgene and perhaps some other gas, to study certain molecule vibrations in a specific area of the spectrum. I did discover a few new peaks, but I forgot what they were. I remember having to translate one of Dr. Edward Teller's papers from German to do the experiments.

In the fall semester of 1962, I took a chemistry seminar of some kind, organic chemistry, inorganic chemistry, physical chemistry - thermodynamics. I earned 2A's and two Bs.

Leo Brewer taught the course in inorganic chemistry. By the halfway point, we had finished his assignments in the Heslop and Robinson textbook, in addition to a lot of handouts. It was in that course where I allowed myself to wonder if Doctor McBay had slightly misled us by telling us that we could compete with anyone. Nevertheless, I studied hard and earned one of my As in that course.

I think Brewer also taught me thermodynamics.

He was a fantastic teacher, who had lost one eye, but as Charles Meredith said Brewer saw more with the remaining one eye that he had than all of us with our two eyes.

In this spring semester of 1963, I again took a chemistry seminar, advanced physical chemistry, and quantum theory 1. I earned 2A's and an unprecedented D (in advanced physical chemistry).

Nobel Prize Laureates Dudley Herschbach and Emilio Segrè

Dudley Herschbach taught the quantum theory 1 course. Later, in 1986, he was awarded the Nobel Prize in Chemistry jointly with Yuan T. Lee and John C. Polanyi "for their contributions concerning the dynamics of chemical elementary processes."[114]

In the fall semester of 1963, I again took the chemistry seminar, advanced organic chemistry, research, and quantum mechanics 1. I earned 3 As and 1 B. This time, I took quantum mechanics from Dr. Emilio Gino Segrè. By the time I took his class, he had already been awarded the Nobel Prize in Physics. He discovered the elements technetium and astatine, and the antiproton, a subatomic antiparticle, for

[114] Dudley R. Herschbach - Wikipedia (Accessed 18 January 2024)

which he was awarded the Nobel Prize in Physics in 1959 along with Owen Chamberlain.[115]

I remember encountering him one day as he was about to board a local bus. It had been raining extremely hard, and he was soaked. I remember thinking how unusual it was that even Nobel Prize winners got wet when it rained. A weird thought, but that's what I thought. When he saw me, he recognized me and said hail to Morehead college (instead of Morehouse College). Nevertheless, I highly appreciated the gesture, and the fact that he had remembered my college.

During the time I was practicing law, I had the opportunity to spend some time in Italy. I wish I could have visited for an extended period before I met him so that we could have had discussions about his native Italy.

For his class, as with many others, I would always try to find textbooks on the specific subjects that we were studying. This helped me to better understand the subjects I was studying. It was my good fortune to discover the textbook in the physics library, from which Prof. Segrè took a few of his problems for us to solve in the classroom. One of my most prized possessions that he also required us to use was a small book that was handwritten by Enrico Fermi, also a Nobel Prize winner in 1938 in Physics.[116] I loved that little book.

For the Spring semester of 1964, I again took the Seminar, Quantum Theory 2, and research. I earned 2 As and 1 B. I think Dudley Herschbach must have taught this course, as well.

In the Fall semester 1964, and Spring semester, I took a seminar and did research for both semesters. I received two As for each semester.

Alas, I had a painful breakup with my fiancé around the time of my oral examinations for my Ph.D. I could not respond to any of the questions, like writing the symbol for the Hamiltonian, or where do you

---

115 https://en.wikipedia.org/wiki/Emilio_Segr%C3%A8 (Accessed 18 January 2024)

116 https://en.wikipedia.org/wiki/Enrico_Fermi (Accessed 18 January 2024)

need to shoot to strike a fish swimming in a barrel. The examination was re-scheduled, but I fared no better. I did not realize that I had really had a serious nervous breakdown. Had I known, I would have waited and aced the examination. I had mastered the subject matter, but I was disturbed to the point that I could not answer the questions.

My lesson here is that if one is scheduled to take an exam for the Ph.D., postpone the examination until you are certain that you are mentally prepared. I did visit the school psychologist/psychiatrist for one or two sessions, but the net result I got was that I was going to have to dig myself out of this hole by myself alone. I was not ready.

Law School

50th Law School Reunion (I am sitting at top in middle of back row)

In this part of the story, I have included the courses I took and the grades I earned. I thought it would be more interesting to read if I also included how I applied some of what I was exposed to in law school but learned in practice. I have done so to demonstrate that one does not need to finish at the top of the class to be successful.

From my improbable socioeconomic beginning I somehow was fortunate enough to be able to study the things that I was interested in. For example, I enjoyed studying chemistry, math and physics just for discipline and subject matter. However, when I was in the 10th grade, Cooper, a friend of Daisy's, gave me a copy of Black's Law Dictionary. I realize now that given our status then that this was really a remarkable thing to have happened to me. Daisy Swinton was my grandmother's adopted daughter. Cooper pointed to the pathway for my professional life.

I kept that dictionary for many years; it would come in handy when I went to law school. I decided to go to law school after the little girls we're bombed at the church in Birmingham. However, I had mixed emotions about getting a background also in business law.

On a given day, when I was in the chemistry graduate program at Berkeley, I decided that I needed to go to law school to practice law and do something about the mistreatment of black people. So, I went to the Dean's office at the law school on Berkeley's campus, then known as Boalt Hall; now known as Berkeley Law, because of a name change after the racist background of John Henry Boalt, the original benefactor, became known.

I walked over to the law school and met with David Walkley, who was the assistant Dean of the law school at the time. He told me that I was too late because the deadline had passed for applications and that they had no more application forms. Since he was reading a Scientific American magazine, and I was a scientist, I thought he was an OK guy. However, the next night, I saw a young lady at a party who had been in the office when I was meeting with Dean Walkley. She came over and asked me who I was and noted that she had seen me in the Dean's office the day before and asked me what had happened. And I told her what Walkley had told me; she expressed surprise and told me to come into the office again on Monday morning and to bring my transcript with me. I think I carried my Morehouse transcript as well as my University of California transcript with me when I revisited the office.

Joan Wolff was her name and either she or the Dean gave me the application papers. Dean Walkley looked at my transcript and took my application, but he couldn't guarantee that I would be accepted. I told him that if there was a finite chance of me being accepted then I wanted to submit the application, which I did.

The most remarkable thing about this episode is it after I was admitted I discovered that the law school had admitted only one other black student in my class James Page from the Compton area part of Los Angeles.

In any case, I found law school to be quite a challenge because first, in the sciences, we could calculate what the result would be to a problem and know that we have solved it. On the other hand, in law school, there was maybe this, maybe that answer. And, of course, the language was different. It took me some time to get used to this. The second hurdle that I had to deal with was I was not used to doing a lot of writing in the sciences, because most of the work dealt with calculations. We did have a young British professor who taught research and writing.

However, I learned to write clearly and persuasively after studying how to write on my own.

But I still felt that I was struggling with writing. It would be only after I started working at IBM that I began learning how to write, under the tutelage of Ed Buhl.[117] Ed was an extraordinary lawyer and human being. Perhaps he identified with disadvantaged people because he began his career at IBM, not in the law department, but rather in the mailroom of IBM World Trade Center at night. He joined the IBM law department in 1960, only a few years before I was hired in 1968.

Ed gave me the starting lawyers marvelous little book called "How to Take the Fog out of Writing," which helped a lot.

I also found the following references to be helpful, as I recall the topics: Legal Writing Style, by Henry Weihofen, The Elements of Style, by Strunk & White, and the U.S. Government's "GPO Style Manual: An Official Guide to the Form and Style of Federal Government Publishing."

Ed helped to draft the first United States affirmative action policy for businesses (1969) and negotiated IBM's position with respect to apartheid-era South Africa.[118] I think I was unaware of his role, but he

---

117 https://www.legacy.com/us/obituaries/nytimes/name/edward-buhl-obituary?id=21105470 (Accessed 18 JAN 2024)

118 Id.

did assign me to the task of analyzing how Executive Orders 10925 and 11246 applied to IBM's operations as a federal contractor. The focus was more on E.O. 11246, as it superseded E.O. 10925. President Kennedy's Executive Order 10925 (1961) established the President's Committee on Equal Employment Opportunity.[119]

President Johnson issued E.O. 11246 in 1965, three years before I joined IBM.

On January 21, 2025, President Trump issued E.O. 14173. The purported purpose of the order is "—Ending Illegal Discrimination and Restoring Merit-Based Opportunity." In my opinion, the Trump Executive Order was designed to undercut the benefits of affirmative action that E.O. 11246 granted to black people and others to partially correct the longstanding and deeply ingrained discriminatory practices against black people and other disfavored groups.

In the opinion of many of us, Trump and his loyalists at the federal state, and local level, are trying to erase black history and disparage the accomplishments of black people.

President Johnson's Executive Order 11246 (1965) prohibits federal contractors and federally-assisted construction contractors and subcontractors, who do over $10,000 in Government business in one year from discriminating in employment decisions based on race, color, religion, sex, sexual orientation, gender identity or national origin. The Executive Order also requires Government contractors to take affirmative action to ensure that equal opportunity is provided in all aspects of their employment. Additionally, Executive Order 11246 prohibits federal contractors and subcontractors from, under certain circumstances, taking adverse employment actions against applicants and employees for asking about, discussing, or sharing information about their pay or the pay of their co-workers.

---

119 https://www.presidency.ucsb.edu/documents/executive-order-10925-establishing-the-presidents-committee-equal-employment-opportunity (Accessed 07 JAN 2025); it also required equal employment opportunities by federal contractors.

For the first time, Executive Order 11246 charged the Secretary of Labor, a Cabinet–level official with strong enforcement authority, with the responsibility of ensuring equal opportunity for minorities in federal contractors' recruitment, hiring, training and other employment practices. Until that time, such efforts had been in the hands of various Presidential committees. Executive Order 11246 continued and reinforced the requirement that federal contractors not discriminate in employment and take affirmative action to ensure equal opportunity based on race, color, religion, and national origin.[120]

In the field of foreign relations, Trump continues to close the door on black people. Thus, when the foreign service did not look like America, Congress passed the Foreign Service Act of 1946. This Act, passed with unanimous consent, was designed to promote and establish a foreign service that looked like America. America's great statesman, Henry Kissinger, at the urging of junior foreign service officers Edward Perkins, John Gravely, and the Thursday Luncheon Group, supported this re-making of the Foreign Service in the mold of the American demographic makeup.

Kissinger elevated the EEO office to that of the Civil Rights Office, "headed by a deputy assistant secretary (which gave it clout), and installed a Foreign Service Officer to direct it... Mr. Ambassador, Edward Perkins, pp.154-157. It thus appears that President Trump violated this Act when on March 18, 2025, he issued an order that ""Fact Sheet: President Donald J. Trump Removes DEI From the Foreign Service, The White House, March 18, 2025. "So, apparently what was good enough for Henry Kissinger is not good enough for Trump.

[120] History of Executive Order 11246- https://www.dol.gov/agencies/ofccp/about/executive-order-11246-history (Accessed 07 January 2025)

First year or 1L

Fall Semester 1965

Since my last name started with W, I was assigned a seat in the back of the classroom, next to my friend from Texas, Jerry Wilson. I lost track of him, but I did see him again at the 40th Class reunion in Oakland's Jack London Square.

I took contracts, pleading and procedure, property, legislative and administrative processes, torts, and introduction to law. I earned a "C" for all these courses, except contracts and introduction to law, for which I got an "S. "C" was Fair, and "S" satisfactory or passed at a minimum level of B-.[121]

Pleading and Procedure in Civil Cases. Prof. David Louisell taught this course. The one thing I remember about him was his passion when he discussed the concept of the demurrer. Good God! Demurrer? To a black student form Savannah, Georgia? I survived and went on to understand a lot of the concepts in practice that I did not understand at the time I went to law school, even to the point of having judges tell me how well I applied the concepts of law practice and procedure and sitting as an Acting Surrogate's Court Judge in Westchester County New York.

Property. Prof. John Wilkins came from a very accomplished African American family. Once I left law school, I don't think I ever heard the concept of blackacre ever mentioned again. Blackacre for class purposes was our piece of fictional real estate. In my 55 years of practice,

[121] Transcript Information document, Office of the Registrar, University of California, Berkeley, California 94720-5404

I have never run across the term-but it gave me a run for the money when I was in law school.

J. Ernest Wilkins, Sr., John's father, was an Assistant Secretary of Labor in the Eisenhower administration. He was the first African American to be appointed to a sub-cabinet position in the United States Government and the first to attend White House cabinet-level meetings.[122] He had a falling out with James Mitchell, the Secretary, and resigned.

J. Ernest Wilkins, Jr., John's brother, was a nuclear scientist, mechanical engineer and mathematician. A child prodigy, he attended the University of Chicago at the age of 13, becoming its youngest ever student .

One of the defining memories of Prof. John Wilkins was his classic red Ford Thunderbird. I think he owned the only red 1955 Thunderbird in the Bay Area. I don't recall having ever seen another one, and it was rare to see them anywhere else in the United States.

Legislative and administrative processes. Preble Stolz taught this class. Prof. Stolz was one of those who congratulated us on being the brightest of the brightest. Nevertheless, he told us to look to our right and left, and front and back, and that at the end of the course 2 of us would be gone. Chilling stuff, but I survived.

Prof. Stolz introduced us to two concepts which were rather futuristic:

1) whether the government could require cigarette manufacturers to affix safety labels to their cigarette packages. That is eventually what happened.

2) then, he introduced the concept of the cashless society. I don't think debit cards existed in 1965, but this is what he was talking about. Now, in Botswana, at the end of 2024, banks here will no longer take checks.

---

122 To the White House", Time, August 30, 1954.

Torts. John Fleming taught me torts, the law governing civil injuries. If a person or her property was injured, then the wrongdoer could be held liable to pay damages. Well, torts was another unfamiliar word for me because I had never heard it before, of course. This was the first time that I would be introduced to the reasonable man standard. One of the debates in class was where did you measure these reasonable man standards? Whose neighborhoods? Professor Fleming's answer was the standards were to be determined in accordance with the morals and values of the community. Of course, this led to what community was one talking about. In New York, I did not handle many personal injury cases. Most lawyers welcomed serious personal injury cases because generally they would charge a contingency fee, which was a percentage of the recovery for the underlying case.

Contracts. Richard Speidel taught me first year contracts. One of the interesting parts of the course was this concept of consideration. If a contract was not supported by good consideration, then it was unenforceable. At one point, he asked the question of whether a peppercorn could constitute good and sufficient consideration for the formation of a contract. Well, of course he lost me on that because I had no idea what a peppercorn was. Throughout my law school career this was the case in several courses when concepts were mentioned that I had absolutely no idea what they meant. AI or Siri would have been extremely helpful at that time.

One time, he told me, in front of the class, that I articulated the points of law very well. I do not remember him ever commending another student in class.

Introduction to Law. I do not remember the name of the young Law Associate lecturer who taught us legal research and writing. He came from one of the islands in the United Kingdom, I think. Unlike a lot of people, I found legal writing and research to be interesting, especially research, because that is where you found the answers to your legal questions. Therefore, the time that you spent in the library doing research at that time paid off. We were introduced to the concept of Shepardization of Cases, statutes and so forth. This was a method which would allow us to determine whether a given case was still good law, or had been overruled, or had been modified.

In my later practice I found that legal research sometimes made the difference between winning and losing. Nowadays, with artificial intelligence and digital research, the game has changed. Nevertheless, it still pays to know how to use digital research tools. Once, when I was part of a NYS Bar Association Special Task force, I used a data processing program to organize and analyze certain issues dealing with some proposed rules changes in Surrogate's Court practice. Of the 20 or so lawyers who were a part of that task force, I was the only one who had mastered the operation of the data processing program which enabled us to filter and organize the information that the Office of Court Administration had sent to us.

Second year or 2 L

Spring Semester 1966

I took criminal law and procedure, pleading and procedure, property, torts, two courses in contracts and two courses in introduction to law. I earned a "C" for all these courses, except criminal law and procedure, for which I was awarded a "D," which means I barely passed[123] this last course.

Criminal law and procedure. According to the curriculum, this was a first-year course, which I took in the second semester from Professor Caleb Foote. The one thing I remembered about him is that it was rumored in one of the years before me, he gave Michael Tigar the lowest grade that Tigar ever received at Berkeley. It was said that he did so because, had he given Tigar a higher grade, it would supersede Foote's record as having the all-time highest grade point average in the school.

At the time, all of us knew who Michael was, because he was highly active in the issues of the law relating to selective service and the draft during the Vietnam War. He went on to distinguish himself as an exceptional trial lawyer working with the legendary Edward Benntt Williams, scholar and professor. He taught our class one day, and I remember being impressed.

Pleading and Procedure in Civil Cases. I think Professor Louisell or Professor Degnan taught the course this semester.

[123] Transcript Information document, Office of the Registrar, University of California, Berkeley, California 94720-5404

As far as the rest of the classes were concerned, I took the second half of the courses that I had taken in the fall semester of 1965.

I also see an entry find my transcript which says first 1st SS where I received a C for a course in the administration of criminal justice

From the notes on my transcript, I think that Berkeley switched over from a semester system to a quarter system because the terminology changes from semesters to terms.

Fall term 1966

In this term, I took basic corporations, constitutional law, legal history, estates and trust, and income taxation. I see that I continued to struggle as I earned 3C minuses, an S in estates and trusts and an A minus in legal history.

Business Associations. I took Basic Business Associations from Jesse Choper, with whom I have maintained contact over the past 58 years (1966 -2024). How much easier my understanding of this topic was when I started practicing law. When I went to law school, the civil rights movement was underway in full force. I wanted to practice civil rights law, but I also knew that the black community needed attorneys with some expertise in business and commercial law. So, I took this course.

At the time, Ebony magazine carried an ad saying IBM wanted to hire African Americans and told us how to apply if we were interested. Black corporate lawyers were rare at that time. In fact, I met only one. Lloyd Reed,[124] who lived on South Road in Greenburgh, N.Y., a White

---

[124] After his Army service, he was accepted to and enrolled in Harvard Law School, graduating in 1949. As an attorney, Reed was employed by the Mutual of New York Insurance Company and worked in the real estate department in New York City. He retired as a senior vice president.

Reed was a member of the Alpha Phi Alpha fraternity and a lifetime member of the NAACP. In his younger days, he was an active community member, serving on the Board of Education in Greenburgh [White Plains, NY suburb] where he and his family lived, and many other organizations, including the Urban League. https://www.theexaminernews.com/lloyd-reed/ (Accessed 20 JAN 2024)

Plains suburb. He worked at Mutual of New York Insurance Company.[125]

I thought a job at IBM would be a good opportunity for me to learn something about how businesses operate, so I applied. I was the only person in my graduating class who was offered a job at IBM. I was scheduled to attend an interview with Robert Ransom at the IBM San Jose plant.

Our interview was mostly about the Vietnam War. I think that at the time, I did not know that Bob had lost a son in that war.

Bob gave me the option of starting at IBM's San Jose manufacturing plant or its headquarters in Armonk NY. I elected to start working at IBM headquarters in Armonk NY because when I took the business organizations course from Professor Choper, I could not understand how General Motors could run all its operations which were described in the very skimpy two - or three-page certificate of incorporation that I read in that course.

Of course, after a total of approximately 7 years at IBM and then 7 years at Union Carbide Corporation, I became quite proficient in applying the laws relating to corporations and commercial transactions.

As I continue my quest for lifelong learning, I have found through a series of webinars sponsored by Morrison Foerster, a law firm with a branch in California that there are still a plethora of rules and laws that apply to financing business associations with which I am not familiar.

Constitutional Law. I also had the good fortune of taking constitutional law from Professor Choper. At the time he looked so young, but he had been a law clerk to the late Chief Justice Earl Warren, so I figured he had to be smart, but the truth of the matter is I think he was only a couple of years older than us. Actually, 5 years older. And he was very smart.

---

[125] Id.

One of the most fortunate aspects of being a constitutional law student at that time was we were still in the midst of the civil rights movement and the passage of new civil rights laws and questions regarding their constitutionality.

Many years later he told me that one of the most exciting exchanges that he had seen as a professor was the time when James Page, the only other black student in our class, and I, were arguing the pros and cons of affirmative action. I was in favor and Jim was not as much in favor as I was. Jim was from Compton California, and I was from Savannah, Georgia. This might have accounted for the difference in our perspectives.

Ironically, I had forgotten about that debate until Professor Choper brought it up when we were having a discussion after he had given an electrifying lecture at Pace Law School in White Plains NY, shortly after Bush v. Gore was decided in 2000.

I was in the audience, since my office was in White Plains, and I got up to ask a question. When he recognized me, he shouted "IBM." I had not seen him since I graduated in 1968. He did not remember my name initially, but he did remember that I had been accepted in the law department at IBM.

Some years later I would attend the reunions of my law school class and get a chance to talk with Professor Choper, and some of the other professors at that time.

At another time, I introduced my sons Jason and Christopher to Professor Choper on a visit to the law school.

A little later my son Jason, after spending some time in law firms and as counsel to a software company in San Francisco, wound up as the Vice President for business development for the Jockey Club in New York. At about the same time, Professor Choper told me that he served on the California horse racing board, and that I should tell Jason that if he needed any information or assistance from him to please contact him.

Several years later, I would contact Professor Choper once again, in connection with an issue that arose in South Africa. Some context follows.

As I have always had an interest in African affairs; by this time of this introduction, I had already begun making serious contacts with members of the law fraternity in South Africa. One of those contacts was Nano Matlala. I think I first met Nano in 2005-2006 at a National Bar Association meeting in Orlando, Florida. He was among the 12 or 13 members of the Black Lawyers Association of South Africa who attended that meeting.

Nano and I continued our association and from time to time he would ask me whether we had had any experience with certain constitutional legal issues in the United States.

Since South Africa is still a very new Democracy and it is still fleshing out the meanings of its constitution, these are very natural requests.

Some years before I met Nano, my friend and Chair of the NBA International Law Section, Beverly Baker Kelly, invited a small group of us to attend an in-promptu dinner with Penuell Maduna, the then Minister for Constitutional Development. I sat next to him; we had an interesting conversation about development of constitutional law.

Penuell Maduna worked with and under Professor Jack Greenberg (who, together with the late Thurgood Marshall of the NAACP Educational and Legal Defense Fund handled the litigation in Brown v Board of Education, Topeka, US 1954) at the Columbia Law School, Columbia University, New York, as a visiting scholar in 1986.[126] I would have a chance to converse with him again when the NBA visited South Africa in 2004.

Returning to requests from South Africa, there were several, but the only one that I will mention within this context was the time when an issue had come before the Constitutional Court of South Africa and

---

126 https://www.southafricanlawyer.co.za/lawyer/penuell-mpapa-maduna/1488865442/?form=MG0AV3 (Accessed 08 JAN 2025)

the Court did not have a quorum to hear the matter. The ConCourt is the highest court in South Africa.

Eight or nine justices of the 11-member Court had to recuse themselves, after it was alleged that two of them had been approached by the Judge President of a lower court who interfered in a case before them. They then told the others. The dilemma that now arose was how could the Court handle this matter if it did not have a quorum.

The Chief Judge's Chief of Staff then wrote a request to bar associations around the world asking for their views on 5 questions for guidance.

The National Bar Association received his request and sent it to me, or I received it directly from Nano. I somehow got involved. The Chief of Staff wanted to see what experience the American Supreme Court might have had in an analogous situation. I remembered that I had studied a case back in 1967/1968 concerning Alcoa Aluminum Corporation that might provide some guidance.

The United States Court of Appeals for the Second Circuit decided the case; the opinion was written by Judge Learned Hand. This happened because when this Sherman Act anti - trust case reached the United States Supreme Court, the Court could not hear the case because several justices owned stock ownership in Alcoa. They had conflicts of interests. So, since the Supreme Court did not have a quorum to hear the case, the case was sent to the Second Circuit and that is how it was decided.

Since our constitution gives Congress the power to define the jurisdiction of the federal courts, Congress passed a law to give guidance to the Supreme Court (and perhaps others) on what to do in cases where there was no quorum at the Supreme Court.

I called Professor Choper to discuss the request from the South Africans in the context of the Alcoa case. He surprised me by saying that I did not study the case in his course. I then surmised that I must have studied it in a course that I had taken on federal jurisdiction from Professor Michael Smith, but I did not know how to contact him. So,

I sent what I had found to whoever had requested the information. At the time there was no similar provision in the South African constitution like the one that we had in the American constitution giving our Congress the power to define the jurisdiction of the federal courts. The Constitutional Court sent the case back to the Judicial Service Commission. I do not know the eventual outcome.

Legal History. Professor John Noonan taught the course on Legal History. I loved this course, and, after many years of practicing law, I have said that I wish I had studied more history. The most interesting part of the course that I enjoyed was the history of common law. As far as I number, I do not recall any mention of the history of the civil rights history in the United States. I think that was just not a part of the curriculum.

On the other hand, I have been exposed to many of the cases and the legal structures surrounding slavery and the history of the law during the civil war period and after. Many of the issues with which we are currently confronted have their roots in the civil war and Reconstruction Era. Also, the Reconstruction Era United States Supreme Court that gutted the civil war amendments which were designed to place black men and women on the same level as white people.

Suffice it to say that had the nation been guided by the thoughts of President Ulysses Grant, we would not have proceeded to the disastrous and unprincipled voting rights decision in the case of Shelby County v. Holder.[127] In his March 30, 1870, Special Message to Congress,[128] President Grant wrote:

"To the Senate and House of Representatives: It is unusual to notify the two Houses of Congress by message of the promulgation, by proclamation of the Secretary of State, of the ratification of a constitutional amendment. In view, however, of the vast importance of the fifteenth amendment to the Constitution, this day declared a part of that revered

---

[127] 570 U.S. 529 (2013)

[128] https://millercenter.org/the-presidency/presidential-speeches/march-30-1870-announcement-fifteenth-amendment-ratification

instrument, I deem a departure from the usual custom justifiable. A measure which makes at once 4,000,000 people voters who were heretofore declared by the highest tribunal in the land not citizens of the United States, nor eligible to become so (with the assertion that "at the time of the Declaration of Independence the opinion was fixed and universal in the civilized portion of the white race, regarded as an axiom in morals as well as in politics, that black men had no rights which the white man was bound to respect"), is indeed a measure of grander importance than any other one act of the kind from the foundation of our free Government to the present day."

Meantime, as Congress passed civil rights laws to restore or grant voting rights to black people, for several years now, the United States Supreme Court has been doing everything in his power to restrict or abolish the rights Congress declared by those statutes, the most notorious of which has been the case of Shelby versus Alabama[129]. The NAACP Legal Defense and Educational Fund ("LDF") wrote[130] on its website:

> 'In 2013, the U.S. Supreme Court dealt its greatest blow to the Voting Rights Act of 1965 in its *Shelby County v. Holder* decision that gutted essential protections of the VRA. Shelby ushered in a wave of discriminatory voting and redistricting laws. From voter suppression to discriminatory redistricting, *Shelby County v. Holder* irrevocably changed the landscape of voting rights in the United States."

Around June of 2023, Carolyn Rankins Shields, J.D., President of the Shelby County Branch of NAACP wrote the following in her invitation to the members of the NAACP and the public to attend the Shelby v. Alabama Summit:[131]

> "Ten years ago, when the decision in Shelby v. Holder was released, it opened the floodgates for new legislation in many states, legislation designed to significantly suppress the vote of

---

[129] n. 130 supra

[130] How Shelby County v. Holder Broke Democracy (naacpldf.org)

[131] Home | NAACP Shelby Summit (alnaacpshelbysummit.org)

marginalized Americans. It is time to fight back! Democracy is slipping from our grasp. The slide downward started here in Shelby County, Alabama with this decision. We hope to start a movement right here that will stop the downward spiral and you can help!"

This is a clear example of history repeating itself in a most cruel fashion.

President Donald Trump is doing his best to continue this effort to deprive the descendants of former enslaved peoples of many of the constitutional protections as he can. To be sure, many of his odious executive orders will be reversed, but it will take some time. Meantime, he will have caused the civil rights community and society as a whole to use its scarce resources and time, and the civil rights of black people will have suffered enormous harm.

Estates and Trusts. Professor, later Dean, Ed Halbach taught that course. I don't know what the exposure level of my classmates was, but I'm sure that there were many more who understood the concept of an estate better than me. In that course we were to study the law of intestate succession and wills; the nature, creation and termination of trusts; future interests, powers of appointment and perpetuities; problems of construction; administration of trust and decedents' estates.

Around the 1980s/90s, I thought that this was an area of the law that I wanted to know more about, so I attended my first continuing legal education course for that purpose. Kings County (Brooklyn) Surrogate Bloom taught the course. I followed this with courses taught by Bronx County Surrogate Gelfand, and many others.

I had gone from being in a fog during my law school course to concentrating in handling these kinds of issues for the last 30 years of my practice. We were one of the few firms in Westchester County that litigated and tried estate and trusts cases.

I handled or personally supervised the settling of over 50 estates and trusts cases.

Of note in this area of law were 2 commendations in written opinions that I received from two separate Surrogate Court judges, and a judicial appointment by another.

In Estate of Trotman, on April 30, 1998, Nassau County, N.Y. Surrogate's Court Decision, Surrogate Radigan wrote: "In general, this court is satisfied with the thorough, professional, and fastidious effort by the Wilson firm in bringing this estate, with several difficult problems, to a conclusion." [132]

I had the pleasure of preparing and resolving this case with the assistance of my associate and son Christopher, who was also a member of the New York State bar, and the litigation services firm of Kehnle~Mayers Ltd.

One morning, I opened a piece of unsolicited mail asking if I needed any assistance in organizing files and preparing cases for trial, so I contacted them. By the time they finished organizing the files in the Trotman case, we were looking at 35 distinct categories of documents spread over 5 file cabinet drawers. They had organized the file so that on the outside of the steel file cabinet was an index of what was in the drawer. That helped me immensely.

As the work continued the file, fees and expenses took a toll on Eileen Kehnle. She feared that the Court would never approve of the fees we had generated, and that they would not get paid. In the end, the Court allowed practically all the fees and disbursements. I continued to work with Muriel Mayers in my cases. Her help was invaluable.

This was the only case where the estate was sizeable enough to draw an IRS audit. Since I had not handled such an audit, I quickly educated myself.

Mr. Richard Trotman had left a multi-million-dollar estate that was being handled by a colleague of mine whose office was in Queens County, N. Y. She had filed the petition in Nassau County because that

[132] New York Law Journal, May 13, 1998, Wednesday, SECTION: COURT DECISIONS; Pg. 32

is where he resided. After she was elected to the bench as a Supreme Court Justice, she referred his estate matter to me.

As an aside, one of his companies, Texas Trading, which did not play a significant role in our estate litigation, was a party to """one of the most enormous commercial disputes in history"[133] Because Nigeria's ports were clogged due to oversupply of cement, Texas Trading could not unload its rice. I did not represent Texas Trading in that case.

W. C. Handy case. In his June 11, 2002, Decision in the Estate of W.C. Handy, Westchester County, N.Y. Surrogate Scarpino wrote: "The affidavit of legal services… adequately demonstrate the… considerable skills and abilities of counsel in handling the difficult issues raised in this trust."[134]

This was a case where we represented one of the great, great granddaughters of the famous American composer. The bank trustee wanted to resign from its office but needed court approval. In this case, my background in corporate law departments and as a public member of the New York State Banking Board enabled us to satisfactorily resolve the issues that had been raised in this proceeding and for my client to receive a distribution. I also consulted "This Business of Celebrity Estates," written by my colleague Gregory Reed, Esq., an attorney based in Detroit, Michigan.

I will discuss other cases that might be of interest under the heading LAW PRACTICE AND CASES. I will also write about lessons that I learned in those cases.

Estate of Clarence Brown. In 1993, Surrogate Albert Emanuelli appointed me as the Acting Surrogate of Westchester County to hear an accounting case that had several aspects to it because it had also been heard in the Supreme Court and had been appealed twice. It pitted a daughter against her mother. The Surrogate had been sued in

---

133 Texas Trading v. Federal Republic, 647 F.2d 300, 302 (2d Cir. 1981).

134

federal court and the plaintiff there had obtained an order that prohibited the Surrogate or any of his staff from hearing the case.

I was quite surprised that of all the hundreds of lawyers practicing in Westchester County at the time, he selected me and went on vacation. Happily, when he returned, we had settled the case with the assistance of Joseph Accetta, Esq., one of the Court's law secretaries.

In that case, a well-known state legislator did not seem to be familiar with Surrogate's Court practice. He was one of many lawyers who are not aware that as a special court, there are some special laws and rules of practice that apply in Surrogate's Court that are different from those found in the Supreme Court, as well as some that are the same.

The procedure called for him to introduce the Account as his prima facie case; however, he offered an attachment to the Account, which would have doomed that part of the case. After I questioned him about what he was trying to do, he took the hint and then offered the Account.

So, the lesson here is to become familiar with the rules that govern the court that you are practicing in.

Income Taxation. I think I took this course from Professor Stone, who was visiting from Harvard. However, I missed the first lecture, and I missed the lecture on basis. Basis remained a mystery to me for a long time – until Jane went to law school and explained it to me. It would turn out that I would encounter the concept again when I worked at Union Carbide and it became an important part of the work I was doing in buying, selling and merging companies on behalf of Union Carbide. I drafted the agreements, then have them reviewed by Mory McDaniel, Esq., for securities issues, and by Jerry Robinson, Esq.,[135] for taxation issues. I also consulted with the finance and accounting people to clear accounting issues with them.

135 They were specialists in these areas.

Spring Term 1967

In this term I took constitutional law (C), comparative jurisprudence (B-), modern social legislation, (C+), state and local taxation (C+), and continued my estates and trusts course (D). As seen from the Trotman, Brisbane, Handy, and Brown cases above, I did much better later in practice than these grades indicate.

Constitutional law. Professor Jesse Choper was his usual self, making constitutional law interesting.

Comparative jurisprudence. Professor Ehrenzweig taught the course in comparative jurisprudence. This course was described as " a comparison of the world's legal systems with reference to their ideologies, historical bases, sources, and techniques; critical analysis of the "schools" of jurisprudence and of legal concepts; practical problems in comparative law "dealing with foreign cases" and jurisprudence (the laws of crimes and torts in the light of current reform).

Modern social legislation, He also taught the course in modern social legislation, generally described as the legal, legislative, and economic problems in legislation designed to ensure adequate minimum standards of living. I remember that his discussion of the German social legislation was a particular interest to me.

State and local taxation. Professor Sho Sato taught this course. I found the course to be interesting, but more interesting was his playing Jimmy Reed and the Blues when he had his students over at his house.

Estates and Trusts. I have already discussed this course.

Fall term 1967

In this term, I took commercial paper (B), conflict of laws (C+), family law (C), federal jurisdiction (C+), trial practice (B), and evidence (S).

Commercial paper. My transcript lists this course at #233; however, the curriculum for that year does not list this course. I took the course from Professor Hetland. I enjoyed this course immensely. It came in handy in the years that I was in practice both in corporate practice and when I represented individuals.

When I was in the Union Carbide law department, I found it extremely helpful when I dealt with a lot of commercial transactions that required the use of the law of secured transactions. We used a lot of promissory notes, security agreements, and in one instance, in my hometown of Savannah, GA. I used a hypothecation covering the use of packaged cylinders, some 15-20 years after I graduated. No one knew what a hypothecation was at the time we were in law school.

Conflict of Laws. I took this course from Professor Stefan Rosenfeld. It has been helpful in several situations. Generally, whenever one has an issue that involves 2 states or countries, territories, jurisdictions etc., one needs to consider the conflict of laws to solve the problem.

I will cite a few examples.

When I was in private practice in 1986, I handled the Estate of Maurice John Tabary, who was domiciled in France at the time of his death. Ruby McZier, a colleague whom I had met through the National Bar Association and who practiced in Washington DC, referred Mde. Celine Tabary to me. She was Maurice's widow, residing in Cannes, France at the time. Madam Tabary was an accomplished painter who had taught at Howard University where Ruby met her. When Maurice died in France, Madam Tabary contacted Ruby.

Incidentally, Madam Tabary was close friend and colleague of Professor Lois Mallou Jones, who also enjoys a professional reputation as a painter.

This was an interesting case because Maurice had executed his will in Washington DC in the 1960s, the witnesses to the will had died and the stocks and bond assets that we were concerned with were issued by New York corporations. The stockbroker who managed the various transactions was in Virginia. My first question was whether the Surrogate's Court in Manhattan had jurisdiction over his estate. The answer was yes because in this case jurisdiction was determined according to the headquarters of the corporation that had issued the bonds or stock. The corporation was headquartered in the State of New York. In this case, I determined that the assets were deemed to be situated in New York.

Since the witnesses to the will had died, I found a provision in the New York Estates, Trusts and Powers Act which allowed a sole beneficiary of a will to act as an administratrix for this estate. Hence Mde. Tabary was the fiduciary, as well as the sole beneficiary.

During the administration, we had to determine the role of a notary under French law, and, under New York law we had to submit a family tree. For this purpose, I contacted the mayor of the municipality that Maurice came from in France. Since I knew from my visit to France as a Morehouse Merrill Fellow that the French are very jealous of their language, I had my letter to the mayor translated into French and sent it to him. I think he appreciated the gesture because his response to me was in English.

In about 1989/90, Madame Tabary invited my wife Jane and me to visit her in Cannes, in the south of France. When we went, we first had lunch with her cousin Jean in Paris and thereafter spent several days with her in Cannes in the south of France. Jean also held an important government post.

She lived in a tastefully decorated apartment on one of the upper floors, which had a balcony. After I returned to the United States, I found that my knowledge of the layout of the apartment was helpful in terms of assisting her in responding to some of my questions needed in administration.

We stayed at the Ibis budget hotel in Le Cannet, a suburb of Cannes. By this time, Mde Tabary was not as mobile as she used to be, so we hit upon the idea of renting a car to take her around and to sightsee a bit. One of those places was Cabris, where we saw some of her paintings. She preferred to paint in Cabris because the quality of the sunlight was better there.

Madam Tabary kept a notebook which listed the names of all her various paintings. She called them her children. Her dream was to select frames for all her paintings and then to relocate to the United States in the DC area. When we visited, she was still recovering from surgery, so I don't know if she was ever able to fulfill her dream.

Our visit to her painting studio answered some questions that I have been wondering about for years, "what does the inside the houses that I have seen along the Mediterranean look like? " The mystery was solved when we went in and I saw that the lounge and related rooms were on one floor, the dining room on another, and some other rooms on yet another, with her painting studio being on the top floor.

Another memorable trip with her was to visit the "Palais des Festivals et des Congrès (Palace of Festivals and Conferences)" where the Cannes film Festival takes place. The Palace housed a casino, where we had great fun with her. She was so thrilled with the slot machines that we bought a small functional one for her to play with at home.

Our trip was delightful because of all the places that we were able to visit with her.

We also visited a perfume factory in Cabris. She also treated us to another unforgettable experience, in particular, was the spectacular restaurant on the side of a mountain in Cabris. The name of the hotel and restaurant was L'Auberge du Vieux Chateau.[136] (**Auberge du Vieux Chateau**)

Family Law. Professor Herma Hill Kay taught this course. As it turns out, I would later learn that she was a law school classmate of Robert L. Doan, when they studied at the University of Chicago. He told me this after he became my boss when I started working at Union Carbide.

Once, I remember misreading one of her assignments. The problem called for an analysis under the equal protection clause of the U.S. Constitution. I wrote the argument under the due process clause. Luckily, I was able to completely re-draft the paper before I made my oral argument in class.

Federal Jurisdiction. Professor Michael Smith taught this course that I took, even though the curriculum that I reviewed from the curriculum at that time shows Paul Bator as the professor to teach this course. I have shown how I was able to use what I learned in this course in my discussion of the issue in South Africa concerning the Constitutional Court.

I had quite an extensive practice in the federal courts, appearing before Magistrates Joel Tyler, Mark D. Fox, and Lisa Smith, Gabriel Gorenstein, and Judges John Curtin, Leonard D. Wexler, Lawrence M. McKenna, Gerard L. Goettel, Charles Brient, John Sprizzo, Barrington Parker, Jr., Lee P. Gagliardi, John Koeltl, Loren Smith, to name a few. I also argued a couple of appeals to the United States Court of Appeals for the Second Circuit-I remember panel members Judges Feinberg and George Pratt.

Following my interest in civil rights, I think my first foray into the Federal courts concerned employment discrimination and other civil rights cases. Along the way, I appeared in the United States District Courts for the southern, eastern and western districts in New York, as well as the United States Court of Appeals for the Second Circuit, and one case in the United States Court of Federal Claims. I will discuss

---

136 https://www.aubergeduvieuxchateau.com/

some of these cases in chronological fashion under the heading of private practice and cases below.

Trial Practice. I took trial practice from Mr. Heafy, Esq., and James Brosnahan, Esq., who were practicing trial lawyers. I think I had one for the fall term of 1967 and the other for the spring term of 1968. I don't remember too much about them individually, except for Mr. Brosnahan - I was enthralled by his ability to weave in some of the classic literary works into the topics that he was discussing.

I think the closest I ever came to using the classics was in a case before United States District Judge Milton Pollock. in 1974, When I was in practice with Fred Hayes, Esq., who fashioned himself after Frederick Douglass in physical appearance.

One of our cases concern a young man named Sean. Sean, a young African American teenager, was charged with a federal drug charge.

His case was assigned to United States District Judge Milton Pollock, a very experienced federal trial judge. Fred defended him in the pre-sentencing stages, and my segment was to argue for leniency in sentencing after his conviction.

Our appearance date was the day after Gerald Ford had pardoned Richard Nixon, as an act of mercy. Drawing on what I had learned in my trial practice courses earlier it occurred to me on that day to fashion an argument around Shakespeare's well-known poem from Shylock:

"The quality of mercy is not strained, by William Shakespeare.
The quality of mercy is not strained;
It droppeth as the gentle rain from heaven
Upon the place beneath. It is twice blest;
It blesseth him that gives and him that takes:
'T is mightiest in the mightiest; it becomes
The throned monarch better than his crown:
His sceptre shows the force of temporal power,
The attribute to awe and majesty,
Wherein doth sit the dread and fear of kings;
But mercy is above this sceptred sway;

It is enthronèd in the hearts of kings,
It is an attribute to God himself;
And earthly power doth then show likest God's
When mercy seasons justice. Therefore, Jew,
Though justice be thy plea, consider this,
That, in the course of justice, none of us
Should see salvation: we do pray for mercy;
And that same prayer doth teach us all to render
The deeds of mercy. I have spoke thus much
To mitigate the justice of thy plea;
Which if thou follow, this strict court of Venice
Must needs give sentence 'gainst the merchant there. "[137]

Judge Pollack sentenced Sean to 4 months in jail. He was facing 44 years.

After I finished my argument, the Federal Marshall assigned to the courtroom told me that he had been there for 15 years and had never heard an argument like the one I had just given. I felt that I had served our client well.

Evidence. This course related to the rules concerning presentation in court material for the tribunal by means of documents and the examination of witnesses. Professor Sherry taught this course. I don't remember too much about it except that we were introduced to the monumental authoritative work called Wigmore on Evidence and several texts by Prof. Bernard Witkin which were compendia of California law, and which were extremely helpful. Like several of the other courses, the course in evidence did not come to life until I started trying cases.

---

[137] Portia delivers this monologue to Shylock in Act IV, Scene I of "The Merchant of Venice." To save Antonio's life. Antonio was on trial for defaulting on a debt he owed to Shylock. https://poemanalysis.com/william-shakespeare/the-quality-of-mercy-is-not-strained/ Poem Analyzed by Sudip Das Gupta, First-class B.A. Honors Degree in English Literature (Accessed 23 JAN 2024).

Spring Term 1968

During the spring term of 1968, which would be my last term in law school, I took the following courses remedies (B-), antitrust law (C), trial practice (B), and evidence (C).

Remedies. Professor Ronan E. Degnan taught this course. This course was to introduce us to the various forms of judicial remedies, the principles governing their scope and availability, and consideration of grounds for choosing between alternative remedies, this includes general principles of damages, specific performance, and injunctions. Over the years I used all of these in my practice.

In federal court, I became adept at using the rules to accelerate discovery and the case by combining motions for temporary and permanent relief.

I also used that part of the rules which began or ended with "Except as otherwise ordered …," and I would ask for relief to "otherwise order" something that I wanted.

Antitrust Law. Richard Buxbaum taught this course. Like some of our other professors, he had joined the faculty of the law school in 1961, shortly before I enrolled. I am not quite sure why I took this course, but it had to do with business so I took it. The curriculum lists this as #270. It is described as "Government control of business, which tells us that the course deals with maintenance of workable competition under the antitrust laws and the control by federal, state and local governments over industries where regulatory measures are deemed necessary. Emphasis is placed upon the impact of technology and upon the patent system of the United States as well as the regulation of specific industries such as transportation and communication.

Although I did not have a lot of experience with the antitrust laws after I started practicing, I did have some exposure while I was at IBM and while I was at Union Carbide. As we all know, IBM was the subject of several major antitrust cases, including the case against IBM by the United States government that resulted in the 1956 consent decree and the very lengthy case involvement Control Data.

As in-house lawyers, we had to become familiar with the 1956 consent decree to ensure that we properly advised our businesspeople to comply with the decree. As I remember, in the Control Data Corporation case the issue was whether IBM failed to live up to a so-called "ironclad guarantee" of some kind.

I did have some personal experience with the application of Section 7 of the Robinson Patman Act as it might have applied to certain donations that IBM corporation was making. There were also issues that I analyzed under the Federal Trade Commission act.

With respect to the Federal Trade Commission Act, I was amused during an investigation of an issue by the Federal Trade Commission concerning Union Carbide. I am told that at some point the investigators wanted to know who Leroy Wilson Jr. was, because his name was popping up on so many different documents and commercial agreements.

A few years ago, at the 50th reunion of my law school class I had an opportunity to have a small discussion with Professor Buxbaum about certain situations that are taking place on the African continent in which he expressed an interest. I will have to revisit that at some time.

Trial Practice and Evidence. I will now supplement what I have said above about trial practice and evidence. I think most law school students majored in political science field or a humanities and arts field as undergraduates. I did not have that background; my background was in the physical sciences, mathematics, chemistry and physics.

However, it wasn't until May 2023 that Daphne Michelle Titus, a U.S. diplomat, and international consultant, said something that crystallized my experience from theory to practice.

We were part of the American delegation to open the American Voices Against Apartheid exhibition at the Apartheid Museum in Johannesburg. The indomitable Dr. Jean Bailey led the delegation.

One day when Daphne and I were talking on the club floor of the Sandton Towers Hotel, she talked about her math background and how mathematics had helped her in organizing matters in her practice of law and diplomacy.

At that point it occurred to me that my background in mathematics and the sciences is what enabled me to exercise greater logic in putting together arguments and analyzing issues than I might have had if I had not had this background. There were things that I did which seemed to me to be quite natural and normal; others would ask "how did you do that." To me it was natural, but to them it was something extraordinary.

I used the rules in such a way to lead to a preferred outcome in cases.

Private Practice and Cases

Since I am a lawyer, I suppose the reader might want to know something about the cases that I handled in practice.

When I first went into private practice, my office was located at 1 Water St. in White Plains NY. I rented office space and paid for the services of a secretary who served several people.

I outgrew that office and moved into 149 Grand St., White Plains, where Boyd Henson was the owner and landlord. Boyd had been a White Plains City Court Judge. There were three receptionists during the time I was there: "Jane" Zelensky, Marge, and Desiree Soares. Quinetta Benton worked for Herb Wolff.

Regina Zelensky, "Jane's" daughter, worked for me parttime, as a secretary for 4 hours every other day. Regina helped me overcome my fear of computers. At the time I had a Compaq computer which had 25 megabytes of storage; I thought that I would never need another computer. At the time I was using a MultiMate word processing program and one of the early line printers.

One weekend I was in the office using a MultiMate and I wanted to move a paragraph from one place in the document to another, but I was afraid to try to move it. When Regina came in on Monday, I asked her to show me how to do it and then from day-to-day, I would ask her how to do certain things and that is how I started using a computer in my work. I gradually got up to the point where I used about five or six programs on a regular basis and about another 5 or 6 less frequently. Of course, over the course of several decades, I became quite proficient in the use of various programs and the Internet in my law practice.

Throughout my years in White Plains, I also used the services of Barbara Niles and Virginia Salisbury. I wrote my documents in long hand at the office and dropped them off at one of their houses at night and picked up the furnished work the next morning.

Jim Henson, Joseph Kirley; partners Hans van Nes and Marshall Goldstein; partners Herbert Wolff and Joseph Latwin, "Joe" Swart; partners Arnold Rich and "Joe Doe" Dennis Light, and Bob Marino all occupied offices in the building during the time I was there,

Roni Jacobson joined me in the Grand Street office as a summer law student in about 2001 and became an associate in March of 2002. She eventually became my partner, and we worked together for about 12 years up to the time we closed the practice in 2011 to pursue other personal interests.

Roni was the technical expert, as well as a brilliant lawyer.

Before she joined me, Roni had had careers as a special education teacher and supervisor, and as a real estate agent. She would use all her background in the cases that we handled.

During most of the years that Roni and I practiced together, we rented office space from Henry Miller, one of America's great trial lawyers, and a wonderful human being. Our offices were in the prestigious building at the corner of Court and Quarropas Streets, known as the Inns of Court Building, 99 Court St., White Plains, NY.[138] All the lawyers and staff personnel were wonderful people. I dealt mostly with Susan, the office manager, and Susan, his secretary.

---

138 In 2008, there was a proposal at some point to rename Court St. after Christopher Ridley, a courageous Mount Vernon off-duty black police officer who was mistakenly taken for a person committing a crime and shot to death right outside our building. I had recommended to one of the proposers that the street carry both names because changing the name of the street would require a lot of changes to stationary and other items which carried the Court Street name. I don't know what happened in the end.

When I returned to the United States for my 2020 visit, John Rand, Henry's law partner, told me the unbelievable news that Henry had died from Covid. This Henry, who loved Clarence Darrow, and who would hold forth in his annual, well-attended all day one-man seminar during the New York State Bar Association meetings, simply called "The Trial." I was stunned.

So enamored of Clarence Darrow, Henry also performed a one-man theatre show, called "Darrow."

I learned in 2023, that Robert "Bob" Doan, Esq., had also died of Covid-19. Again, this hit me hard because Bob was my longest serving mentor at Union Carbide. I learned a lot from him.

IBM

When I began my career at IBM, in 1968, there were six or seven African American lawyers who began working there at about the same time as I did. They all worked in what I would call the general law part of the law department; the other part was comprised of the patent, copyright and trademark intellectual property lawyers. There was one African American patent lawyer who worked at the Watson research facility.

The lawyers who worked in the general law part of the law department were Geraldine Greene, who later became the California Commissioner of Corporations, Mario Baeza, Judge Dickson, Matthew Whitehead, James Cotton, and a few others whose names I cannot recall at present. Except for Matt, we were all located at IBM's headquarters in Armonk NY, but there was another one who worked in the real estate part. His name was Arthur "Doe.".

The one black lawyer who worked at the Watson research facility was Hansel McGee. He later resigned to become a Supreme Court Justice in the Bronx. During the time that he worked at the research facility I went to visit him to see what a patent lawyer did who had a background in chemistry because that was my background as well. However, after the visit I concluded that I would stay in the general part of the law department and not go over to the intellectual property law section.

I think we were the first generation of African American lawyers in corporate America.[139]

---

[139] Lloyd Reed, Esq., had been hired earlier. See n. 127

The one conspicuous thing that I noticed when I glanced at the law school credentials of the lawyers whose officers I visited, is that most were all graduates of Harvard or Yale law school. This might not have been universally true, but it seemed to be the case. As far as I know, I was the first law graduate of Berkeley Law to become a part of IBM's law department.

However, Ed Buhl had graduated from St. Johns Law School in Queens, New York. Matt Whitehead had graduated from the world-renowned Howard University Law School.

I worked at IBM on two separate occasions.

IBM 1968-1972
Armonk, NY

When I first started working at IBM in 1968, right out of law school, the legal issues that I worked on were associated with the internal operations of IBM itself.

I was in the little group that reported to Ed Buhl. Ed would gather his little tribe together and walk us down to the cafeteria where we would all have lunch. He earned his law degree from St. John's University Law School, during which time he worked nights in the mailroom at IBM World Trade in New York City. Hired by IBM as an attorney in 1960, Ed rose through the ranks, eventually serving as General Counsel for IBM Europe (1979-1983) and finally Assistant General Counsel. Ed worked under IBM General Counsels Burke Marshall and Nicholas deB. Katzenbach, and his career covered several notable legal initiatives, including helping to draft the first United States affirmative action policy for businesses (1969) and negotiating IBM's position with respect to apartheid-era South Africa.[140]

[140] https://www.legacy.com/us/obituaries/nytimes/name/edward-buhl-obituary?id=21105470 (Accessed 11 April 2025)

In July 2024, IBM appointed Anne Robinson, Esq., an African American woman, a brilliant, well-seasoned attorney, as its Senior Vice President and Chief Legal Officer[141] I never met her.

On Mondays, Ed would review the status of the various matters that we were working on. That was a particularly effective way for him to keep up with us and us to keep up with him.

After writing my first memorandum for Ed, analyzing the complicated social security benefits integration rules, he retuned my 33-page memorandum with his comments and observations bathed in red ink, and a cryptic note written in red in the upper right-hand corner "Brevity is a virtue. This document is 10 times the length it should be." Of course, that left me a little unsettled because I didn't know how I was going to distill these the contents of these 33 pages down into 3 pages. I managed.

However, Ed provided us with some help. He gave me a little book called "How to Take the Fog out of Writing. I went back to his little book. I also read Strunk & White's little book "The Elements of Style" on writing and Henry Weihofen's "Legal Writing Style." Later, I would add the U.S. Government's Legal Style Manual. I then made a concerted effort to apply some of the writing rules that I had learned in these references. I was able to reduce the memorandum from 33 pages to 2-3 pages.

At headquarters, Ed reported to Bob Ransom, who was part of the 3-person Corporate Counsel level, just below Burke Marshal, the General Counsel; the other two were Bill Russell and C.B. "Chet" McLaughlin. Their titles might have been Assistant General Counsel.

Janet Britto, Ed's secretary, was invaluable; teaching me how to navigate the paths of IBM when I had a question.

When I moved to New York from California, I took the New York State Bar Examination. I had to master Mr. Herbert Wachtell's thick

---

141 https://news.bloomberglaw.com/business-and-practice/ibm-hires-vanguards-top-lawyer-to-replace-retiring-legal-chief?utm_source=Email_Share (Accessed 11 April 2025)

book on practice and procedure under New York law[142], and the substantive New York law (who was entitled to what).

Fortunately for me, I had raised a question to Mr. Wachtell directly about something that he had written in his book. He wrote back and gave me a lengthy answer to the question I raised. Then the night before the exam, I reviewed 3 outlines of the substantive law areas. On the day of the exam, 4 of the questions asked for answers that I had reviewed from Mr. Wachtell and the outlines. So, I felt I had done rather good.

Mr. Wachtell asked me to apply for a job! He and others went on to form one of New York's premier law firms.

I cannot forget Bob Troup, IBM's top labor lawyer, and part-time Justice of the Peace in Pleasantville, NY.

On the morning that the results were published in the New York Law Journal of those who had passed the bar examination, I went into the law library at IBM, looked at the list and did not see my name. Crestfallen. On the way back I ran into Bob Troup. Bob said, "congratulations on passing that *** **** bar examination." I told him I had just reviewed the list, and I didn't see my name. He told me that I needed to look at the list of the people who had satisfied most, but not all, of the paperwork required, but who had passed the bar exam. That is where my name appeared. I was one happy soul. This is a good example of why one of Jane's law professors said, "read on."

Some of the areas that I worked in at IBM initially involved taxation, Fair Labor Standards Act, involving overtime pay, and others; Group Benefits (I was given an assignment to determine if the IBM retirement plans were properly matched with the Social Security integration rules) , stock transfer problems (dealing mainly with issues that arose from our shareholder relations department regarding the transfer of shares.) One of those issues was who was entitled to the transfer of shares from the estate of a deceased IBM employee who was domiciled

---

142 New York Practice Under the CPLR,

in Türkiye at the time of his death. This gave me the opportunity to apply Professor Ehrenzweig's teachings on conflicts of laws issues.

I also solved problems regarding the construction of wills, divorce issues regarding stock transfer, garnishments and wage assignments, sanctions against Rhodesia and the issues surrounding equal employment opportunity arising in the IBM Bedford-Stuyvesant Brooklyn plant. Lastly, I served as the Administrative Assistant to Vice President & General Counsel of IBM Nicholas deB. Katzenbach for the Brooklyn plant. This gave me the opportunity to have one on one discussions with him as he drove to and from the Brooklyn plant.

When I first started working at IBM, Burke Marshall was the General Counsel. He had been the Assistant Attorney General for Civil Rights for the United States in the Kennedy administration.

In 1969 after I had been working and IBM for about a year I looked up from my desk and there was Nick Katzenbach standing at my door. Katzenbach had been the Attorney General of the United States, as well as an Under Secretary of State. Of course, I was astonished to have been in the company of these two great men.

One day, when we were having lunch, Bob Ransom was sitting in the middle, between Burke Marshall on one side and Nick Katzenbach on the other. Both were soft spoken men. Bob told me that Burke said something to Nick, and it was so soft that he couldn't hear what it was even though the message passed across him from where he was sitting.

East Fishkill, NY

IBM manufactured computer chips at this plant.

After an initial period at IBM headquarters in Armonk, the new lawyers were then assigned to work had various IBM locations.

I was transferred to the East Fishkill chip manufacturing plant. Part of my re-assignment to the IBM East Fishkill plant was to translate the requirements of affirmative action under Executive Order 10925, and later 11246, into the operations of the East Fishkill plant.

Executive Order 10925, signed by President John F. Kennedy on March 6, 1961, required government contractors, except in special circumstances, to "take affirmative action to ensure that applicants are employed and that employees are treated during employment without regard to their race, creed, color, or national origin".[143]

For the first time, as the successor to Executive Order 10925, Executive Order 11246 charged the Secretary of Labor, a Cabinet–level official with strong enforcement authority, with the responsibility of ensuring equal opportunity for minorities in federal contractors' recruitment, hiring, training and other employment practices.

Until that time, such efforts had been in the hands of various Presidential committees. Executive Order 11246 continued and reinforced the requirement that federal contractors not discriminate in employment and take affirmative action to ensure equal opportunity based on race, color, religion, and national origin.[144]

Under E.O. 11246, Art Fletcher, an American government official and Republican politician. He was referred to as the father of affirmative action because of his goals and timetables which he created in the revised Philadelphia plan. He also served as the head of the United States Commission on Civil Rights from 1990 to 1993.[145] He was an African American. We became friends, as I explained above.

In East Fishkill, my boss was Area Counsel Matthew Maloney. Matt and I got along very well, and he was a very excellent teacher,

Joe Larkin, the Regional Counsel, was immensely helpful to me in teaching me how to deal with the managers I would be speaking to, since the concept would be new to some of them.

I continued to solve issues arising under Federal & State Labor Laws, EEO, contracts with antitrust ramifications (Section 2(f) of

---

143 https://en.wikipedia.org/wiki/Executive_Order_10925 (Accessed 31 January 2024)

144 https://www.dol.gov/agencies/ofccp/about/executive-order-11246-history (Accessed 31 January 2024)

145 https://en.wikipedia.org/wiki/Arthur_Fletcher (Accessed 04 JAN 2024)

Robinson-Patman Act), U.S. Commerce Department and State Department regulations regarding export of technical data, environmental law under the Clean Water and Clean Air Acts, and the Federal Safety & Health Act.

I was also assigned to work on environmental issues because I had an academic background in chemistry.

The problems arising under these laws gave me an opportunity to gain experience in what kinds of legal issues arose in the operation of a manufacturing facility.

IBM, West Point and Sickle Cell Anemia Benefit

After a brief foray into private practice, I returned to IBM, as Bill Russell had told me I could if things did not work out.

When I returned, I was initially assigned to work with Ed Wunderli, who reported to Chet McLaughlin on antitrust matters. I researched and wrote memos on various antitrust laws.

I remember one time I made a presentation to Chet McLaughlin on an issue which involved the Federal Trade Commission Act. I was not satisfied with my presentation, so I went back to Chet and apologized. Then, a bizarre thing happened. Chet told me that I would never be as smart as him. Here I was, a very junior lawyer, being told something like that. It was so bizarre that I went to Bob Ransom and told him about it. Then Bob told me that Chet did not like me for some reason, but not to worry because he would look out for me and protect me from Chet. That is the only out of character experience that I had during the total periods of time that I worked at IBM. Chet never said anything remotely close to that again.

IBM was soon faced with several issues that required more legal attention. Environmental laws were just coming into focus, and they needed someone with a background in chemistry and physics to handle them. Bill Russell asked me. It might have been very brazen for me, but I asked them for additional compensation because this called on additional knowledge outside of the law. Initially, Bill told me that I had just got a raise six months earlier, but he would look into it. IBM did give me a raise to handle the environmental law problems on an almost full-time basis. At that time, I was assigned to the real estate and construction division in White Plains or Rye Ridge as a staff attorney for environmental law. Office of Counsel, Real Estate & Construction Division, White Plains, NY. My title was Staff Attorney, Environmental Law. I reported to Richard Halliday, a very delightful boss.

Thus, I was IBM's first environmental lawyer.

Being aware of IBM's policy of being a community-minded employer, on February 8, 1974, I wrote a letter to Frank Cary, the CEO of IBM, asking IBM to contribute $1,000,000.00 to Morehouse College as part of the Second Century Development Campaign. I pointed out that 80% of our students came from families with incomes below $8,999.00 per annum.

I pointed out that Herbert Charles, another Morehouse Man who was now employed by Corning Glassware, had presented a check to Morehouse from Corning for $150,000.00.

Thomas R. Horton, was the Director of the IBM Office of University Relations. He wrote:

"Dear Mr. Wilson:

March 7, 1974

I am writing in response to your recent letter to Frank Cary on behalf of Morehouse College and its Second-Century Development Campaign. While I am in no position to make a specific commitment at this time, I believe that IBM will probably make a substantial contribution to Morehouse College during the second phase of its campaign, though probably not as large as the figure you suggest. You may be interested to know that during the local, first phase of the drive, IBM made a $25, 000 contribution, and earlier we had contributed $50,000 to Morehouse on an unrestricted basis. We hold Morehouse and its brother and sister institutions in very high regard. As you may know, IBM made a $100,000 commitment to Clark College last year and a similar commitment to Spelman, both in the context of their on-going capital campaigns."

He also wrote about other IBM contributions to Morehouse and her brother and sister institutions.

ORGANIZING THE SICKLE CELL ANEMIA BENEFIT AT WEST POINT – MAY 20, 1972 - President Nixon, a Confederate Monument, Black Cadets and The History Behind the Sickle Cell Anemia Concert

One day in January/February 1972, as I was sitting in my office at IBM's East Fishkill facility, I received a telephone call from Caz Neville, a friend of mine and fellow IBMer. Caz had recently returned from the Navy and became an exceptionally good friend. Both of us lived in Newburgh, New York, about 32 miles from West Point.

Caz told me that the black cadets at West Point needed some legal assistance to put on a sickle cell anemia benefit concert at West Point and asked if I would go down to meet with them. He told me that the contact person was Maj. Melvin R. Bowdan, Jr.

IBM had a policy of encouraging its employees to participate in the civic activities of their communities, so I told Caz that I would try to help.

I scheduled a meeting with Major Bowdan and drove to his house for a 7:00 o'clock p.m. meeting. Ironically, he lived at 150 Lee Road on the West Point campus. I think there were just the two of us. Lee Road was renamed to Grant Road, honoring President and General of the Armies Ulysses S. Grant (USMA 1843).[146] By contrast, Robert E. Lee commanded the southern confederate soldiers that wanted to break away from the United States and dissolve the Union.

Major Bowdan told me that there were 112 black cadets at West Point that the wanted to show their connectedness to the outside black community. Putting on a sickle cell anemia benefit to raise money for the Sickle Cell Medical Research & Treatment Center at Howard University, headed by Dr. Roland Scott, would be one way to do this. This

---

[146] https://www.westpoint.edu/naming-commission-report (Accessed 17 NOV 2024)

was a supplement to the Cadets Manifesto which listed 13 demands for change that the cadets made of West Point to oppose President Nixon's order to erect a monument to confederate soldiers at Trophy Point alongside the monument to Union Soldiers.

"The cadets provided Knowlton with a devastating argument that the Confederates were traitors who fought against their country. No other single foe in American history had killed more U.S. Army soldiers than the Confederate army. Yet, Nixon wanted to put a monument on West Point's sacred ground to the enemies of the United States."[147]

After defeating Nixon's order, the black cadets received Superintendent Knowlton's approval to stage a sickle cell anemia benefit at West Point.[148] Several more approvals would be needed.

Major Bowdan told me that the proposed date was May 20, 1972, Armed Forces Day, but they needed approvals from the Department of the Army and the Defense Department to use the 40,000-seat Michie Stadium. The Secretary of the Army had approved, but the Secretary of Defense needed to approve as well. We would need this approval before I could start contacting entertainers. Senator Edward Brooke of Massachusetts, the only African American member of the Senate, had approved.

Major Bowdan set up a meeting for the core team to meet on February 17, 1972. Present were Cadet Captain Percy Squire, the most senior black cadet leading this effort, Cadet Captain David Brice, Maj. Bowdan and Howard Shegog (sp.?) . I think a Col. Lough; Head of the West Point Law Department was also present. Maj. Bowdan told us that we needed the approval of Gen. Kirwin, who was at the Pentagon, and that we should hear something by the following week.

---

147 Ty Seidule, "Black Power Cadets: How African American Students Defeated President Nixon's Confederate Monument and Changed West Point, 1971–1976," The Hudson River Valley Review, 66, AUTUMN 2019

148 Id. at 71-72

Maj. Bowdan brought in Captain Frank Slaughter, and a staff of 30-40 people, cutting across all departments, black and white. These were divided into committees for Entertainment (Ernie Simpson, Gaines), Work Detail - Engineer Support (OIC – Capt. C. G. Clinger, Cdt Liaison- Cdt Mercer Ferguson), Information (Edwards, Twitty), Ushers & Tickets (McLaughlin, Blount); Mess Hall (Coleman, Fountain), Escorts (Christian, Dixie), Parking (Eric Olsen, Edgar Anderson), Stage (Coats, Bell), Seating (Sutton), Transportation (Colbert), Security and Traffic Control (OIC Maj. R. T. Donovan, CPT John Craig (Assistant), Cdt Liaison -Cdt Jim Libhart); Communications/ Electronics Support (OIC- Maj Walt Classon, Civilian Liaison – Mr. Frank Calamari, Cdt. Liaison- Cdt Bill Perry); Finance and Budget Advisor (OIC – Maj Ed Khoury, Cdt Liaison Cdt. Wayne Blount);Cadet Activities Office Support (OIC – LTC Sam Collins, Cdt Ernie Simpson); Legal Consultants (Civilian - Mr. Leroy Wilson, USMA – Maj Dan Shimek)

Also, we received assistance from Major General Harry W. Brooks, Jr. As a Lt. Colonel, he was appointed Army Director of Equal Opportunity Programs at the Pentagon in 1972. Some years later, in 1989, General Brooks joined the NAACP delegation to Japan as part of the Mutual Interest Tour.

By April 4, 1972, only Donald Byrd had committed to perform. Arthur Godfrey had agreed to come. When I spoke to him on March 27, 1972, Donald also offered to contact, through his office, Donny Hathaway, Roberta Flack, Bill Cosby, Jerry Butler .

At a meeting held on April 4, 1972, among Col. Jeter, Col. Marks, Maj. Bowdan,[149] and Col. Maj. Withers, Superintendent Knowlton dropped in to show his continued support.

By April 7, 1972, we decided that we would need to decide by Friday May 14, 1972, if we were still trying to go forward with the concert.

[149] In some places, the transcript spelled his name Bowden; I have corrected it here to Bowdan.

I don't think I fully realized what a huge undertaking this was until I read some of the staffing and background documents that Percy Squire sent to me after I listened to his 2016 video interview.

One of the most hilarious things I listened to about how I got involved is in Percy Squire's April 5, 2016, oral history video.[150] Percy said in 2016, he didn't know where I came from, but he did remember my first name-Leroy. He called me Leroy Johnson from Newburgh in the video.[151]

What made it so funny was me watching how he shrugged his shoulders and made the comment in total bewilderment. He gives me sole credit for securing Stevie Wonder and The Supremes to perform the concert.

Part of the official transcript of the video quotes Percy as saying[152]:

- Percy Squire:

  Hey, it evolved because first we started and we were failing miserably. Well then I don't know if it was the commandant or the superintendent, but first of all they appointed Major Bowdan to advise use, then Major Bowdan brought in Captain Frank Slaughter, and then there was an attorney from Newburgh by the name of - I think his name was Leroy Johnson.[153] He out of nowhere volunteered to help us. Buddy Bucha got involved with us and then there was also a professor in the social science department named Carl McCarden, and Carl took me down to Harlem and we got together with - there was a booking agent down there by the name of Jimmy Booker, was a big promoter, and we were floundering. But then Major

---

150 https://www.westpointcoh.org/interviews/in-the-shadow-of-the-civil-rights-era-one-cadet-s-story-of-promoting-equality-at-west-point (Accessed 17 NOV 2024)

151 He talks about me at about 1:12:16 to 1:13:45. A little later he discusses Stevie Wonder's mini-concert at Thayer Hotel the night before and the long time that Stevie played the next day.

152 At 1:09:25 – 1:17:24

153 Actually Leroy Wilson Jr, not Leroy Johnson

Bowdan got involved and Leroy Johnson got involved and the Academy put these resources behind it and the next thing I know, you know, they fly Aretha Franklin's brother up here. They brought him here, Cecil Franklin. I met, along with members of the Contemporary Affairs Seminar, with Cecil Franklin in Thayer Hall right upstairs.

***

Then finally Leroy Johnson got involved and the first person that agreed to come in was Donald Byrd from Donald Byrd and the Blackbyrds.

And then Leroy came down and he lined up The Supremes and Stevie Wonder.

- Interviewer:

  Wow.

- Percy Squire:

  Leroy Johnson found those people.

- Interviewer:

  Now this is the attorney from Newburgh?

- Percy Squire:

  The attorney from Newburgh.

- Interviewer:

  So he's got some connections somehow that -

- Percy Squire:

  He knew - he came - he volunteered. I don't know where he came from, but he came over here. He worked with Major Bowdan and they're the ones that put that together. We tried but we were never able to land the acts, but Major Bowdan and

Leroy Johnson,[154] and they got Donald Byrd and the Blackbyrds, they got Stevie Wonder and they got The Supremes.

***

- Interviewer:

  This is a huge undertaking here.

- Percy Squire:

  Right.

Around November 2022, after my son Christopher stumbled across Percy's history video, recorded some 50 years after the event, I watched it, I telephoned Percy and renewed our connection.

While we were trying to put together the concert, we identified the following potential entertainers. Flip Wilson, who told me that he was booked until June, Aretha Franklin, Isaac Hayes, Duke Ellington, Lionel Hampton, Marvin Gaye, The Supremes, Harry Belafonte, Bill Cosby, Sammy Davis, Jr., The Shi-Lites, The Delfonics, the Dramatics, Roberta Flack, Nikki Giovanni, Freda Payne, Ray Charles and Stevie Wonder.

Cecil Franklin, Aretha's brother, was a classmate of mine at Morehouse. We scheduled a meeting in New York. He was also going to tell me if he had gotten permission to give me the telephone numbers of other entertainers.

In the video, Percy relates the displeasure that Marvin Gaye's wife expressed when he called Marvin Gaye's residence because Cecil had given Marvin's number to Percy without Marvin's permission.

Around March 2, Maj. Bowdan told me he had received approval from the relevant authorities to contact entertainers.

From March 3 - May 18, 1972, I made several telephone calls - to Don Warden, who had preceded me at law school and who was a good

---

154 Actually Leroy Wilson, not Leroy Johnson

friend of James Brown. Don had a radio show in the Bay Area, as well. He knew a lot of entertainers. Don Warden told me he would contact James Brown on 2 February and get back to me; he also told me that he would stop by Flip Wilson's house to ask if he would come.

Unfortunately, James Brown had a conflict.

I contacted Junius Griffin at Motown; Juanita Poitier; Roy Campenella Jr., Stax Records; Ruth Bowen's booking agency (probably after Ken Hagood, Esq., gave me her contact information); Ike and Tina Truner who committed initially, but they ran into a problem and could not come; Dave Moore of the Collective Black Artists, Sammy Davis, Jr.; Fred Patmon, Esq.; John Harmon; Clarence Avant; Richard Campbell; Ossie Davis; Nick George; Rev. Hosea Williams; and Atlanta Mayor Maynard Jackson.

Ruth Jean Bowen was the first black female talent agent and the president of Queen Booking Corporation, the largest Black-owned entertainment and talent agency in the world. It represented many of the United States' top African American performers.[155]

Jerry Butler said he would like to do the concert if he was free.

We also contacted Jackie Robinson, Nikki Giovanni, Rev. Jessie Jackson, Thomas Todd, Redd Foxx,

For many of these calls, I either used Col. Collins's phone number or he made the calls, according to my chronology.

On March 27 I called Donald Byrd (and the Blackbyrds); they were the first to commit. He gave me a Donald Byrd refrigerator magnet which I attached to my refrigerator with pride for many years. I lost it in my many relocations.

We expanded the list of potential entertainers to over 50.

We also began to focus on publicity for the event.

---

155 https://en.wikipedia.org/wiki/Ruth_Bowen (Accessed 18 NOV 2024)

Bill Cosby had moved to Massachusetts, so we needed to trace him. At some point, Regge Life, my cousin by marriage to Jane, directed the Cosby Show.

Duke Ellington told us that he would be conflicted on May 20, because he would be in Houston.

Lionel Hampton would be performing at the Los Angeles Palladium on that date.

David Franklin returned my call on March 7 to tell me that Donny Hathway and Roberta Flack are booked from May 20 - June 5. David lived in Atlanta.

Tony Brown told us that he could possibly find us a spot on his show sometime before May 20th.

The cadets met Cecil Franklin on March 20, 1972, in the Thayer Hotel. He presented himself as Aretha's manager, in addition to being her brother. He said he would try to bring her if there was a second meeting. I am not sure if I attended this meeting, but I have 4 pages of typewritten notes which indicate that I attended this meeting.

Present at this meeting were Percy Squire, Joe Edwards, Ernie Simpson, David Brice, Jay, and perhaps others who do not appear in my notes.

Aretha was interested, but working out the terms was problematic. The cadets explained that from the people, colleges, of the surrounding area, and the fact that this was Armed Forces Day, we expected a huge crowd.

The cadets had already identified an enormous number of media outlets which would ensure widespread publicity. Johnny Carson committed to give us some airtime, Ernie and his group were prepared to send releases to 81 music magazines, local newspapers and magazines, eastern college newspapers, put up posters, the cadets would make personal appearances at various locations in New York, New Jersey, and possibly Philadelphia. Jay pointed out that within a 2-hour driving radius, there was a population of 15 million people.

Cecil suggested that Ray Charles and Isaac Hayes might also be available. He also discussed the possibility of bringing in Bill Cosby, as well.

There was a full discussion of what Aretha would need, including fees for her, her entourage (usually 25 people), a comedian she would identify, Ray Charles, Isaac Hayes, transportation, what equipment would be needed, any releases from record companies

In the end, Aretha's expenses and fees were more than the cadets could commit to.

My research for this book sheds light on the reasons we were having difficulty with Aretha's negotiations.

On March 28, 1972, I received a letter from George Crockett, III, telling me that he had delivered to Cecil some documents that I had given to him. They both lived in Detroit. We had all been classmates at Morehouse College.

The letter recites one of the reasons Aretha felt compelled to be paid as she "has been giving benefits since December of 1971 and has had no paid engagements during that time period. It is my understanding that the situation is similar regarding Ray Charles, The Temptations and several other entertainment personalities."[156]

Reading this letter in November 2024, I now realize what a severe financial crunch many entertainers were under in 1972.

In2025, as I watched Sunday Best documentary on Netflix, the story of the Ed Sullivan show, the entertainers appearing in the film also confirmed this state of affairs. The show details the behind the scenes hurdles that Ed Sullivan faced as he purposefully scheduled black entertainers to appear on the Ed Sullivan Show.

---

[156] Letter dated March 28, 1972, from George W. Crockett, III to Mr. Leroy Wilson, Jr., in my Scanned files folder titled Wilson Sickle Cell Personal Historical Files (West Point parent folder)

A few days before our meeting at the Thayer Hotel, Cecil also offered to contact Isaac Hayes, Smokey Robinson, Lena Horne, Lou Rawls and Quincy Jones.

March 23, Arthur Godfrey also offered to help with publicity and to come to the concert.

On this date, Maj. Bowdan sent me copy of the 9-page Disposition Form with attachments from LtC John R. Jeter, Jr., to DISTRIBUTION which documented the one-time exception that the cadets had secured to sponsor the concert:

> "the Department of Defense has approved a request submitted by USMA to permit concerned cadets to sponsor entertainment at Michie Stadium and to donate the proceeds to the Center for Sickle Cell Anemia Research, Inc. This one time exception to policy has been granted by DOD as an action to further racial understanding."

The document then sets out in detail how the concert was to be conducted and who was supposed to do what, including how to conduct the concert in inclement weather.

If Donald Trump had been President in 1972, this concert could not have been held. Nor would West Point been able to make the reforms it did concerning diversity, equity and inclusion ("DEI"). He issued Executive Order 14151 (E.O. 14151) which applied across all federal agencies and facilities, including West Point.

E.O. 14151 is titled *Ending Radical and Wasteful Government DEI Programs and Preferencing*. West Point responded by disbanding all 12 of its cultural and affinity clubs, among other things.[157]

On April 11, 1972, Maj Bowdan sent a follow-up DISPOSITION FORM to Distribution reiterating the Staff/Cadet responsibilities and requirements that each staff representative prepare weekly reports.

---

[157] Trump administration: West Point disbands cultural clubs to adhere to anti-DEI executive order – NBC New York (Accessed 28 October 2025)

By April 26, 1972, Nick George got involved, but I am unsure which entity he was connected to and what his role was. He must have been connected to Electric Lady Studios, who recorded the event.

I see from Exhibits "1" and "2" attached to the letter from me to Maj. Bowdan dated May 22, 1972 that Nick George and Michael Frank Jeffrey are named in an unsigned draft of an agreement for Michael to "make a 16 track master tape recording of suitable commercial quality to constitute at least one Twelve (12") inch, two (2) sided long playing disc at 33 RPM, of selected performances to be mutually agreed..." "based upon the performances and events which took place at, and in connection with the West Point Concert for the Benefit of Sickle Cell Anemia, (the "Concert") presented at the United States Military Academy at West Point, on May 20,1972, as follows..."[158]

I do not know if these documents were ever signed.

However, it appears from the question Maj. Bowdan asked me and the meetings referred to in my May 22, 1972, reply to Maj. Bowdan that Electric Lady Studios did record the concert.

Meantime, the Supremes were re-organizing, and we had not received a contract from them. I had put Maj. Bowdan in touch with David Weisbart, who managed the Supremes.

At various times over a period of several months by March 27, someone had collected the following fees numbers from various sources: Aretha Franklin ($25,000.00), Sammy Davis, Jr. ($25,000.00), Delfonics ($3,500.00), Ray Charles ($8,500.00), Dells ($5,000.00).

Well, about 40 days out from May 20th, none of us succeeded in getting any performers to commit to perform, other than Donald Byrd. As it happened, one Friday afternoon, we all met to see if we still needed to expend these resources to try to put on the concert.

Aretha's financial requirements were all over the place. Her normal fee at that time was $20,000.00 vs. 60% of the gross. In March 1972

158 Letter from Leroy Wilson, Jr., to Major Melvin Bowdan, dated May 22, 1972, with two exhibits attached. From Mr. Wilson's personal files.

we had hoped to raise from $205,000.00 - $250,000.00 in ticket sales alone for a full stadium. If we raised that amount, then the first $150,000.00 would go to sickle cell. Then the first $20,000.00 above $150,000.00 would go to Aretha.

We also considered scenarios where we talked about a fee of $15,000.00 plus expenses for her people. She was really interested. We also discussed whether Aretha would do the concert for an honorarium of $1,000.00, plus expenses of $4,426.00.

During a meeting on April 4, 1972, of Col. Jeter, Col. Marks, Maj. Bowdan, and Col. Withers, and me, we tried to reach Cecil on April 4, 1972, by telephone, but were unsuccessful.

The next day, I spoke with Cecil. Aretha had left for Paris, but he thought the honorarium idea would not work. He would call her later that night and call me back.

Ray Charles was not available on May 20; neither was Smokey Robinson, someone said Sammy Davis, Jr. would charge $30,000.00 but would donate it back. However, his secretary told us he was not available on May 20th.

On April 6, I received a call from Mr. Murray, representing Arethea, saying they wanted a guarantee of $20,000.00 plus 80% over $100,000.00, plus the expenses of two opening acts. If Aretha was the only way that the show could go on, then they would need a guarantee of at least $20,000.00.

Ike and Tina Turner said they normally did not do benefit concerts. They wanted a fee of $10,000.00. Their availability disappeared when Ike was arrested.

On April 7, we discussed the latest proposal. Nick George, whose name I came across a few times during this process, told me that he was willing to get involved as a producer. We never made in-person contact as far as I remember.

As time was closing in, we decided that we needed to decide on Friday, April 14, if we were still going to try to do the concert.

Representatives of the full set of West Point committees met on that Friday, and the decision was veering towards calling it off, when I asked how much lead time we would need to prepare to put on the concert. Someone said 30 days. I then said that 30 days would begin to run from next Wednesday April 19, so we should postpone our decision until then.

They agreed, as we still had not heard from a few people so I suggested that we wait to see if anything would develop over the weekend.

Monday morning came. I received telephone calls from the managers for Stevie Wonder and the Supremes, saying they wanted to volunteer to do the concert. By that time, Diana Ross had left the group and the Supremes who performed were Mary Wilson (no relation), Jean Terrell, and Lynda Laurance.[159]

A hilarious aside is that in November 2023, my son Christopher, came across a link to a West Point oral history interview of Percy Squire taken 5 April 2016, some 44 years later. In that interview, the interviewer asked Percy where they got this lawyer from who bought the concert to reality. His answer, shrugging his shoulders, with a look of puzzlement on his face, was "I don't now, he just showed up." I couldn't stop laughing.

Another noteworthy thing Percy said about the concert, of which I was unaware, or had forgotten, is that the night before the concert, Stevie Wonder arrived at the Thayer Hotel on the West Point campus, and someone told Stevie that there was a piano in the lobby; whereupon Stevie proceeded to give those present a mini concert before the next day.[160]

---

[159] One day several decades later, I found myself walking behind Mary Wilson on the streets of Manhattan. I wanted to remind her of West Point, but she was in an animated discussion, so I did not interrupt. I few years later, she was gone. I wished that I had said hello. I do have a prized photo that she, Jean and Lynda signed for me.

[160] https://www.westpointcoh.org/interviews/in-the-shadow-of-the-civil-rights-era-one-cadet-s-story-of-promoting-equality-at-west-point (Accessed 17 NOV 2024) at 1:43:44 – 1:45:12.

After watching the video interview, I contacted Percy after a 50-year hiatus. We re-connected.

The day of the concert was rainy and chilly. Someone had telephoned the radio station to say that the concert had been cancelled. Fortunately, the station called me and I told them the concert was still on. The Supremes, Stevie Wonder, Smokestack (or was that Blood, Sweat and Tears?), Ecstasy, Spirit, Chicago, Donald Byrd and the Blackbyrds and members of a few lesser-known bands performed magnificently.[161]

After the concert, Mary Wilson inscribed and gave me the prized Supremes personally autographed photo which all of them signed. See below.

[161] Donald gave me the beautiful refrigerator magnet that I kept for many years. It gave me immense joy to see it every day.

Ken Hagood, an exceptionally talented entertainment lawyer, helped me over those parts of the terrain that I had no experience in.

Approximately 10,000 people braved the weather and showed up at Michie Stadium for the concert. The Flyer advertising the concert listed $5.00 donations, with live Stadium opening and live music starting at 10:00 A.M.[162] The Flyer carried the legend "Sponsored by: The Black Cadets of West Point."

Throughout this process, Donald L. Miller, Assistant Secretary Of The Department Of Defense, was incredibly supportive. He was responsible for equal opportunity throughout all branches of the

162 Squire, Percy Flyer from his electronic files

military. We sat together at the concert. On 08 June 1972, he sent me a nice letter of thanks.

Lt. Col. Harry Brooks, Army Director of Equal Opportunity Programs at the Pentagon also sat with us.[163]

I don't remember all the celebrities who attended, but Congressman John Dow and Mrs. John Dow, as guests of Superintendent Knowlton, appeared, as did Cadet Sutton appeared with the Congressman and his wife, Ossie Davis , who gave a few remarks, and Al Freeman, Jr.[164], Eddie Williams, from CBS, was the primary Master Of Ceremonies; Attorneys Edward Howard or Kenneth Hagood introduced Eddie to me. They were members of the law firm of Covington. Grant, Howard, Hagood & Holland (Robert Rhone, of counsel)[165]. Frank Kingston Smith shared the MC duties with Ed.[166]

Merrill Roberts took several of the photos that appeared in the Mid-Hudson Herald and the New York Amsterdam News.

Lt. Col. Patrick Dionne and Capt. Leon T. Delorme, Jr., covered the media for the Academy; there was also a Mrs. Barclay present.[167]

Robertson from the United States War College was present, along with L. Col. Floyd McAfee, a member of the West Point faculty.

The stadium had a capacity of 50,000 people. I understand that all told, the concert raised about $41,000.00 having been supported by a discretionary Superintendent's fund. In today's dollars, which would be about $302,070.81. Cadets Percy Squire and John Vaccaro presented the first $20,000.00 check to Dr. Roland B. Scott, Director of the Sickle Cell Anemia Research Center Of Freedman's Hospital, in Washington, D.C.

[163] Later promoted to Major General. He was the 6th African American to achieve the rank of general in history. thehistorymakers.org; Category: Military Makers

[164] New York Amsterdam News, C10, June 3, 1972.

[165] The Mid-Hudson Herald First June 1972 edition.

[166] Intentionally

[167] Id.

38 June 4, 1972 SUNDAY RECORD

To fight a killer

Dr. Roland B. Scott, left, director of the Sickle Cell Anemia Research Center at Freedmens Hospital in Washington, accepts a $20,000 check from West Point cadets Percy Squire, center, and John Vaccaro. The money was raised at a cadet-sponsored sickle cell anemia benefit concert at the U.S. Military Academy at West Point May 20 -- the first benefit in the academy's 170-year history. -- UPI Telephoto

After the concert was over, West Point sponsored a reception in Thayer Hotel, which was extravagant and well laid out, to my inexperienced civilian eyes. I was impressed.

During the reception, Stevie learned that my young sons Jason (3) and Christopher (2) were present and asked Jane, my wife, to bring them over because he wanted to "see" them. We were all puzzled as to how this was going to happen, because we all knew Stevie was blind. Stevie solved the puzzle by feeling their faces and then telling them how handsome they were.

I had joined the firm of Covington. Grant, Howard, Hagood & Holland (Robert Rhone, of counsel) for a few months in 1972 after the concert. In my first case, I successfully represented Eddie Williams in a lawsuit. Ed was the Master of Ceremonies for the concert.

Gen. Sam S. Walker presented Stevie Wonder with a gift of a mounted West Point Sabre, with Percy Squire and an unidentified cadet looking on.[168] This mounted Sabre is the highest award that West Point Association gives to a civilian who is not a West Point graduate.

---

[168] The Mid-Hudson Herald, First June Edition 1972

To my great surprise and pleasure, West Point also gave me, the Supremes, Stevie, Maj. Bowdan and Captain Frank Slaughter (as I recall) a mounted Sabre.

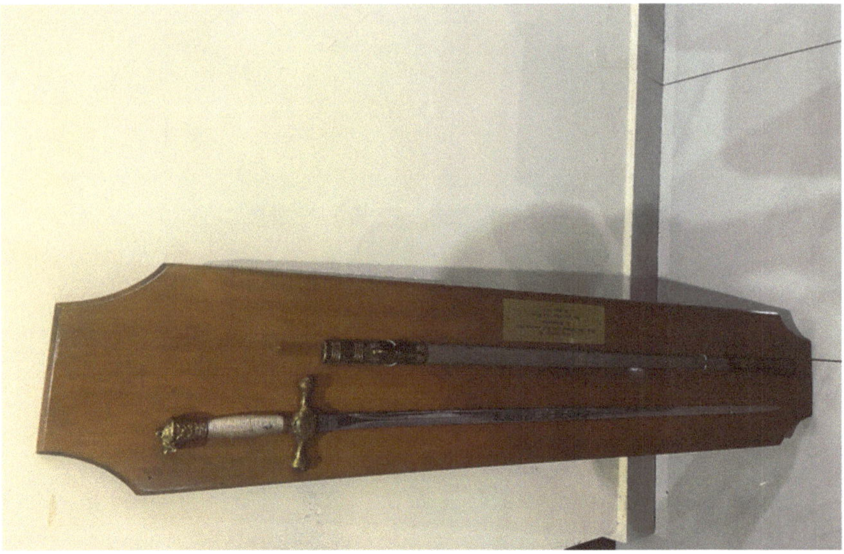

I was deeply honored to receive this award and regard my involvement in this history-making event to be one of the most precious of my life.

West Point had given this same Sabre to President Richard Nixon, entertainer Bob Hope, and Rev. Billly Graham, so this was rarefied company.

The Concert lasted for 9 hours.[169]

Ossie Davis presented gifts to the recording artists.

As I was writing this on 25 November 2024, I made a startling discovery.

As I was decluttering, I came across my hard copy of my 52-year-old West Point files.

---

[169] Mid-Hudson Herald

I discovered that I had written a letter to Maj. Bowdan dated 22 May 1972 suggesting that the concert was recorded, and that Motown owns the master.[170]

The letter begins:

> "Dear Major Bowdan:
>
> This letter is in response to your telephone request of Sunday, May 21, 1972 asking for the present status of the recording of the Sickle Cell Anemia Benefit given at West Point on May 20, 1972."

I wrote to Percy telling him that I did not copy him on that letter and that I did not know if he ever saw it.

Before I discovered this letter as I was writing this book, I did not remember in these later years if the concert was recorded or not. That first paragraph is proof enough that the concert was recorded

Now that I have read the letter and the attachments, I think the only reason I would have a copy of the Consent prepared by the Electric Lady Studios is that they did the recording.

Even now, because Jimi Hendricks gave his studio such a catchy name, I have a dim recollection of Electric Lady being mentioned at the time, of the concert. I still do not remember in what context.

The consent requested in Exhibit 2 , which was written on Electric Lady letterhead, caused me to research Electric Lady Studios. I learned that Jimi Hendrix had established and owned this state-of-the-art studio in about 1970. This suggests to me that Ken Hagood contacted Electric Lady. The reason being that at the time or about the time of the concert, Ken Hagood was the Administrator of Jimi's estate in New York, or he was counsel to the estate, and Ed Howard served in one of those roles.

---

[170] C:\Users\leroy\OneDrive\Documents\Personal\Leroy\MEMOIR and MOREHOUSE\Leroy's Autobiography Source Materials\West Point\Wilson Sickle Cell Personal Historical Files (Accessed 25 NOV 2024)

I remember writing an appellate brief in one of the Hendrix cases in New York while I worked for their firm.

They were partners in the firm of Covington Grant, Howard Hagood and Holland. These men had formed their law firm to try to compete with some of the more established white law firms. They opened their offices in what became known as the Gulf & Western Building, 10 Columbus Circle in the middle of Manhattan. They handled matters for some of the well-known celebrities of all time. I worked for them for about 3 months in 1972 after I left IBM for the first time. Ken, Ed, Al, Bob, and maybe others, have now passed away, and the firm has been dissolved.

Among others, Joseph L. Dozier, C. Douglas Dixon, and Marianne Spraggins were associates at the firm at various times during my tenure there.

Leo Branton, Wiley Branton's brother, represented Jimi's estate in Los Angeles. He and Ken and Ed knew each other.

This Electric Lady letter discovery reminds me of Questlove's description of the 1969 Summer of Soul film recordings found some 50 years later. He made a documentary of the entertainment events that took place "on six Sundays between June 29 and August 24 at Mount Morris Park (now Marcus Garvey Park) in Harlem, using professional footage of the festival that was filmed as it happened, stock news footage, and modern-day interviews with attendees, musicians, and other commentators to provide historical background and social context."[171]

> Speaking passionately from New York, [Questlove] explains how in 2017, out of the blue, two film producers, Robert Fyvolent and David Dinerstein, presented him with 40 hours of

[171] https://www.bing.com/search?q=Summer+of+Soul&form=WSBEDG&qs=SW&cvid=bf407f7d8f9d409b972534f7be995abf&pq=Summer+of+Soul&cc=BW&setlang=en-US&nclid=5818987FB4D68F5BAD3F221AD7D26E69&ts=1736852759577&wsso=Moderate (Accessed 14 January 2025)

footage from this festival, which took place over six Sundays from June to August 1969, in New York's Mount Morris Park.

He is keen to share the backstory, all of which was new to him.

"The Harlem Cultural Festival was an event thrown by two gentlemen, Tony Lawrence [who booked the acts] and by Hal Tulchin [who filmed it]," he tells BBC News. "They somehow managed to gather some of the mavericks of their day. We're talking about Stevie Wonder. Nina Simone, Sly and Family Stone, Ray Barretto, Olatunji, Hugh Masekela, Edwin Hawkins Singers, BB King, comedians, politicians, everybody was there."

'Sitting in the basement'

The reason why Questlove and so many others have never heard of this series of concerts, is what happened, or rather did not happen, next.

"The event is preserved professionally on tape and not one producer or outlet is interested in seeing the footage or making it worldwide-known or distributing," he continues. "So, what winds up happening is that this film just sits in the basement for 50 years."

This BBC description is the most complete summary of the events leading to the production of the Summer of Soul documentary.[172]

I did not find any documents in my files that tell us if Motown ever made the requisite commercial viability tests.

I learned from Greg Reed, Esq., my friend and colleague of many years, that Universal Music Group (UMG) acquired Polygram after Polygram had acquired Motown.

My first thought was to get the thoughts of Jason and Christopher, my sons who were both senior level lawyers, and businessmen, as well.

---

[172] https://www.bbc.com/news/entertainment-arts-57803091 (Accessed 14 January 2025)

After getting Jason's input, I sent a WhatsApp message to Percy Squire, to see how he thought we should handle this latest information. Percy was now a senior lawyer in Columbus, Ohio.

Before Percy could schedule a Zoom call among me, him, co-leader David Brice, and Ty Seidule, former Head of the Department of History at West Point, to deal with the master owned by Motown, President Trump issued E.O. 14151 which actively tried to wipe out any African American history at West Point as a part of American history. Given the ferocity of President Trump's many negative statements about race, diversity, equity, and inclusion (DEI), our next steps are now in limbo.

Through additional Executive Orders, Trump's erasure extends to museums, law firms, corporations, military academies, diplomacy, and libraries, whether these institutions are public or private.

So far, he has succeeded in cowering some organizations, while others have thwarted him or succeeded in defeating his takeover.

President Nixon, a Confederate Monument, Black Cadets and The History Behind the Sickle Cell Anemia Concert[173]

In 2023, Captain Paul Matthews, the Curator of the Buffalo Soldiers National Museum in Houston, Texas, invited me to give some remarks on the 1972 rebellion of the black cadets at the United States Military Academy at West Point. He was unaware of these events. I was the civilian counsel to these cadets in implementing one of those demands concerning the sickle cell anemia benefit concert.

He asked me to make the remarks at the Buffalo Soldiers 157th anniversary of the 9th and 10th horse cavalry association annual meeting on July 29, 2023, in Houston, Texas.

---

[173] Taken from Leroy Wilson, Jr., Esq.'s remarks for 157th 9th and 10th Horse Cavalry Association [Buffalo Soldiers] Annual Meeting - Houston, Texas, July 29, 2023

This account is based on those remarks.

In the Fall of 1971, Richard Nixon, was running for his second term as President of the United States. He visited West Point, where he would make an unpalatable request. As he toured the campus with Superintendent William Knowlton, they reached Battle Monument at Trophy Point. After seeing the monument to the memory of the union soldiers in the civil war,[174] Nixon asked Superintendent Knowlton why there were no monuments to the confederate soldiers in Trophy Point The superintendent told President Nixon that West Point honored those who fought to save the country, not those who fought to destroy it.

The superintendent also told Nixon that erecting such a monument would undercut West Point's efforts to recruit more black cadets to prepare them as army officers, and that it would harm West Point's image.

Nixon, not being satisfied, assigned Gen. Alexander Haig the task of seeing to it that the monument to the confederate soldiers was built at Trophy Point. When Knowlton told Percy Squire about Nixon's plan, Percy told the black cadets; they revolted.

The black cadets presented the West Point administration with a list of 13 demands. One of those demands was that West Point honor the West Point Buffalo Soldiers. A supplement to those demands was that West Point allow the cadets to have a concert at West Point to raise funds to support sickle cell anemia, to show that they were still connected to the black community.

After considerable debate within the West Point community, and with General Haig, General Haig informed President Nixon that his plan would not work; 111 /112 black West Point cadets had defeated the race-baiting plan of the president of the United States! This looked

---

[174] The inscription reads "In memory of the Officers and Men of the Regular Army of the United States who fell in battle during the War of the Rebellion this monument is erected by their surviving comrades." https://www.west-point.org/users/usma1951/18250/battle_Monument.htm (Accessed 25 NOV 2024)

like part of Nixon's Southern Strategy. They had mounted "most successful protest movement in the [170 year] history of the U.S. military academy."[175]

The superintendent and his administration proceeded to implement the 13 demands.[176]

With respect to honoring the Buffalo Soldiers, the next year, in 1973, West Point renamed its parade grounds Buffalo Soldiers field. However, it would take another 50 years, when Dr. Aundrea Matthews and others would finally get West Point to erect a monument to the Buffalo Soldiers who served at West Point. Aundrea is not related to Captain Paul Matthews. She is the granddaughter of Sanders Matthews, a former West Point Buffalo Soldier. She provided his specifications that Eddie Dixon used to sculpt the monument. Mr. Dixon has sculpted several other Buffalo Soldier monuments throughout the United States. He and Dr. Matthews are fellow/sister Texans.

The Buffalo Soldiers monument was dedicated on September 10, 2021.

After I had that conversation with Captain Matthews and with Dr. Aundrea Matthews (no relation), I decided that I needed to postpone my return to my residence in Botswana to attend the first in-person National Bar Association annual meeting after the outbreak of Covid, and to attend the wreath – laying ceremony and a fund-raising luncheon on September 4, 2022, at West Point, to honor the buffalo soldiers who served at West Point.

---

175 Ty Seidule. West Point and its cadets are not campaign props - The Washington Post (accessed 22 March 2023). B.G. Ty Seidule is the former Chairman of West Point's history department. See n. 82, https://www.westpointcoh.org/interviews/in-the-shadow-of-the-civil-rights-era-one-cadet-s-story-of-promoting-equality-at-west-point (Accessed 17 NOV 2024)

176 Incidentally, there is no mention of General Knowlton's role in the 1972 black cadets protest in his Arlington National Cemetery biography. William Allen Knowlton - General, United States Army (arlingtoncemetery.net) (Accessed 31 May 2023)

It was a sense of great pride that I could attend the event at West Point with my two sons, Jason and Christopher, also lawyers, who were then 53 and 52 years old, but were 3 and 2 years old when we attended the Sickle Cell Anemia Benefit concert together, 50 years earlier, together with their mother and my late wife, Jane. She was a criminal tax lawyer.

West Point Buffalo Soldiers Monument (Erected and dedicated 2021)

Union Carbide Corporation

270 Park Avenue, New York City

Richard Clarke operated a minority recruiting organization. His job was to identify black and other minority group candidates for employment at various companies. For a few years, even when I was at IBM, Dick was trying to recruit me to work for one of the companies he was trying to find talent for.

When he approached me to look at Union Carbide Corporation to see if I wanted to join the law department, I agreed and went to Union Carbide for a series of interviews by various people within the law department. Union Carbide was a chemicals and polymers company, headquartered at 270 Park Ave. in New York City, and the law department was on the 47th floor.

On August 4, 1999, the Dow Chemical Company bought Union Carbide for $11.6 billion in stock and debt in a deal to create the world's No. 2 chemical company.[177]

Robert L. Doan

The most important of these interviews was with Robert L Doan. He carried the title of Assistant General Counsel. Later I worked for Joseph E. Geoghan, also with the same title.

---

177 https://www.cbsnews.com/news/dow-buys-union-carbide/ (Accessed 14 April 2025)

Bob asked me if I had any interest in working with "small businesses?" Bob explained that Union Carbide was organized into several divisions, one of which was the Linde Division. Linde sold packaged gases that were stored in steel cylinders, (oxygen nitrogen, ethylene, and so forth) and welding products. Linde also housed medical oxygen. I later organized a corporation that we named Linde Homecare, and the operations of the medical oxygen group were transferred to that subsidiary.

Linde sold its products through about 267 industrial gas and welding products distributors throughout the country. These were the small businesses that Bob Doan was talking about. Union Carbide had distributorship agreements with all of them; it had invested in some, assisted in selling others, and recapitalizing some, either through equity investments or loans. My job was to research, interpret and apply the law as I drafted an immense variety of commercial agreements. Well, this was music to my ears because that is exactly what I wanted to learn how to do.

Bob Doan gave me some drafts of documents that he had prepared and used in the past to guide me; I created others. Bob taught me how to do cash for assets transactions, cash for stock transactions, stock for stock mergers, forward and reverse triangular mergers, secured loan transactions, drafting shareholder agreements, among other things.

I handled $14,896,000 in acquisitions; $731,000 in recapitalizations; $2,315,000 in divestitures, and $2,150,000 in loan agreements. I represented Union Carbide in transactions in various places throughout the country, with the assistance of local counsel.

For all these transactions, I would have in-house counsel Morey McDaniel review the draft agreements for securities law issues and Jerry Robinson review them for tax issues. In this way, I learned some of the more nuanced aspects of securities law and tax law.

The companies that I interacted with on a commercial level were in Greenburg, Pennsylvania, Oklahoma City, Oklahoma, Philadelphia, Pennsylvania, Milwaukee, Wisconsin, New Orleans, Louisiana,

Encino, California, New Milford, New Jersey, Las Vegas, Nevada, Toledo or Cleveland, Ohio, and Hampton Roads, Virginia.

After I was satisfied that the documents were in order, I would take them to the appropriate Union Carbide officer to sign; the corporation's Chief Executive Officer signed a few.

Nobody was concerned with my race or color, except that in the Toledo/Cleveland transaction, one man said he was glad to get to finally meet the Jewish lawyer who had drafted all these various documents. We had a good laugh. The money or stock was the primary interest.

In Philadelphia, we had retained Ballard Spahr, one of the well-known outside law firms. One day the partner that I was working with took me and his securities expert to lunch at the Union League Club, a private, members only club.[178] The partner was an older white-haired gentleman; the associate was a young man. As we approached the steps, there were two African American men polishing the brass handrails leading up the steps. When they saw me, they broke out with overly broad smiles, as if I was a celebrity.

Once we got inside, I understood the proudful smiles. The place was crowded. As we passed the rooms that I was able to glance into, I saw no women, and no person who was not white. It seemed as if the older white men were passing on knowledge and traditions to younger white men.

Above the landing at the top of the stairs leading from the first to the second floor, was a huge mural/painting which depicted men in Union uniforms and there was at least one black man. I don't remember if he wore a uniform or not. Of course, this peaked my interest in learning a little bit more about the Union League.

---

178 Union League Of Philadelphia founded in 1862 as a Patriotic Society in support of the Union is a private members only club. Building designed by John Fraser with additions by Horace Trumbauer has a vast collection of art, artifacts, and Civil War related items. https://www.youtube.com/watch?v=wElxSezYLOY (Accessed 21 January 2025)

As we continued to walk on the second floor as I remember, there was a huge room occupied by men smoking cigars and other forms of tobacco. There were no women present.

I closed 4 transactions in one week. Before the third of these transactions, I was not able to go home and get a change of clothes because closing dates had been set, and I had to be ready. I had been delayed by the first or second of these transactions.

As I was exiting a taxicab that I had taken from the airport to my office on Park Avenue, the seat of my pants just exploded, no nice rip along the seams but just an explosion! So, what to do? I checked into the Intercontinental Hotel on 48th Street in New York City, which was a couple of blocks from my office. Fortunately, there was a tailor shop and men's clothing shop downstairs in the hotel. I went in, told the man what the problem was and that I needed a new suit, new underwear, a new shirt and I might have needed a new tie by the next morning. He was great, prepared all of this for me and I was ready to go to New Jersey for the third of my transactions. When I got there, the transaction took less than 15 minutes.

However, I was now behind because I had not had time to draft the documents for the fourth transaction - a loan transaction that I was going to do in Las Vegas, NV. For that transaction I went to my office on Park Avenue, after I retrieved the documents from my office that I thought I would need to draft the loan documents for the Las Vegas transaction and booked a first-class ticket out to Las Vegas. I needed a first-class ticket the next day because I was going to have to draft the relevant documents on the plane and I needed the space.

My business delegation stayed at Caesars Palace. At that time, I think our team consisted of Bart Proctor, responsible for making business decisions, Myles Dempsey, responsible for financial decisions, and me for making legal decisions. I had prepared most of the documents on the airplane by the time I got to Las Vegas. However, I needed to have them typed. Fortunately, there was a secretarial service inside the hotel. I went to the woman in charge and told her that I would pay her double if she would close her office and just do typing for us that day. She agreed to do so and did so.

In Las Vegas, the parties to the second part of the transaction developed a conflict. The transaction called for Union Carbide to loan a certain amount of money to an individual who would be purchasing a Linde distributorship in Las Vegas. The second part of the transaction was between the seller and a third party.

I was relaxing in the beautiful pool at Caesar's Palace when after only about 15 minutes of my being in the pool there was an announcement over the public address system calling for me to report to someplace in the hotel. That's when I discovered there was an issue in the second part of the transaction. I told the other side that I would get up at 5:00 a.m. the next morning and draft the set of documents that would enable them to complete the second part of the transaction. I remember distinctly that to join the various parties; I created something which I called a joinder agreement. I somehow learned about joinder agreement when I analyzed the Social Security integration rules.

During the negotiations, I needed another $500,000.00. In those days wire transfers were new to me, and we had witnessed an earlier telex wire transaction involving Jimmy Carter's efforts to release the Iranian hostages which caused some confusion, so the Union Carbide officials were reluctant to wire the money. Instead, they put Don Morehouse on a plane with a $500,000.00 bank check to bring to me.

We successfully completed the transaction, but I did not get a chance to go back into the pool.

In 2024, the National Bar Association held its annual meeting at Caesar's Palace in Las Vegas. I was looking forward with great anticipation to getting into the pool and finishing my swim from 1982. Alas, it did not happen. Maybe one day?

Before me, there had been only one other black lawyer in the Union Carbide Law Department, William L. "Bill" Wood, Jr. I was the only one when I was there. My race was only incidental. Everyone was busy enough doing what they did. I was absorbed in leading the structure of these transactions. Fortunately, there was little to no discussion of politics.

Bill later went into private practice specializing in health and hospital law, with an office in Scarsdale, New York.

One day, when I was crossing the street in Manhattan, I encountered Sandra Marsh, a friend of mine. She asked me "what is was like to be working for the man?" I told her that it was great because I had access to enormous resources that I used to build human capital in myself.

As fate would have it, sometime later, Union Carbide hired her, and she became my secretary. Later, after she left Union Carbide, Sandra became a lawyer and was admitted to practice. Last, as I remember, she was a staff attorney at the Family Center.[179]

There was one interesting incident where John Stichnoth, Union Carbide's General Counsel, scheduled an on-premises interview with me and a man who was purportedly a New York University Professor who wanted to generally find out what I thought about the situation in South Africa. The Professor promised to give me a copy of his report of the interview. He never did. Sometime much later, I surmised that the real purpose of the interview was to get a general idea of how I would fare in apartheid South Africa, representing Union Carbide there. The interview would have taken place prior to March 22, 1982. This was during the apartheid era.

Joseph Geoghan

I continued to do the same work under Joseph Geoghan that I had been doing under Bob Doan.

[179] The Family Center's mission is provide holistic care and support to individuals and families affected by life-altering events to create a path to healing, stability, and a fulfilling future. https://www.thefamilycenter.org/who-we-are/ (Accessed 16 January 2025)

Sometime in the late 1970s, I introduced Joe Geoghan to Godfrey Binaisa, as a former Attorney General of Uganda. I'm not sure what the occasion was but I do remember that I made the introduction during our luncheon at Union Carbide. Godfrey was independent Uganda's first Attorney General under Milton Obote.

This would prove to be fortuitous because later, in 1979, the Uganda National Consultative Council (NCC) elected Godfrey as the interim president of Uganda. The NCC came into being after internal and external Ugandan and Tanzanian forces pushed Idi Amin Dada out of office. The NCC was to hold power until elections could be held. Godfrey wanted me to come to Uganda to assist him with a variety of matters.

Joe Geoghan graciously gave me some time off so that I could go to Uganda to assist Godfrey.

The importance of these connections was shown when a longtime friend and colleague of mine had done some work for the New York City Housing Authority. Bob Doan had resigned from Union Carbide and was now the general counsel at the Authority. The Authority was being slow to pay her; somehow in our conversation, she mentioned this. I asked her if she wanted me to intervene, and she did. I telephoned Bob and she received her outstanding money within a few days.

This was another example of being able to call on someone with whom one has always had a good relationship.

In 1982, Union Carbide moved from 270 Park Ave. in New York City to Danbury CT. They sold the building at 270 Park Ave. for $110 million. It later became the headquarters building for Chemical Bank. Chemical and Manufacturers Hanover merged with the surviving corporation later merged into JP Morgan Chase. JP Morgan recently opened its new headquarters at that location. They demolished the old building where I worked and built a new, super modern structure in its place.

In 1982, the new Union Carbide Danbury headquarters building was very modernistic.

This move proved to be problematic. My wife Jane had already established herself in Westchester County by doing several things, perhaps the most important of which was to lead the newly established Westchester County Women's Center. Jason and Christopher were also well established in terms of the schools that they attended. From a work standpoint, it would have been very inconvenient for me since I was traveling a bit, and the airports were some distance away.

Moreover, the question of where we would live in Connecticut became a problem. A relocation to Connecticut to the most likely city involved traveling along a two-lane highway. In the wintertime, which could prove to be very inconvenient, so we decided that we would stay put in New Rochelle.

Before the move, Union Carbide announced that it would pay staff a bonus if they remained with the company for at least three months after the move to Danbury.

As I wanted to go into private practice, Union Carbide and I agreed that I would continue to work for them as outside counsel under a 1-year retainer agreement. That was extremely helpful because it gave me some financial support as I was setting up my office in White Plains, and it would give them some time to find my replacement. General Counsel John Stichnoth signed the retainer letter. In addition to Joe, John Skislock was extremely helpful in getting me paid in a timely fashion.

March 22, 1982, was the date that Stichnoth, the General Counsel of Union Carbide agreed to hire me as outside counsel after I resigned from Union Carbide:

> This will confirm our understanding that you have elected to resign from the Law Department, effective April 1, 1982, for the purpose of opening an office for the private practice of law. To help us in maintaining a reasonable level of service during the interim until we are again fully staffed, you have agreed to

> provide legal advice and service to Union Carbide Corporation with respect to our participation in the financing, acquisition or sale of Linde Welding Products Distributors or with respect to other commercial or corporate law matters involving the Distributor Marketing or Welding Products business of the Corporation's Linde Division or the Cryogenic Equipment or Linde Homecare business of the Corporation's Engineering Products Division, all such assignments to be as designated by the Senior Division Attorney responsible for those Divisions, the Assistant General Counsel or the General Counsel...

There were some unanticipated problems in Danbury. As we were all adjusting to the new building, certain vapors were escaping from the carpeting and making some people sick.

On the second day after we moved in, workmen in the car garage accidentally set fire to some propane gas that escaped from the tanks that they were working with. This caused a tremendous fire. Someone called the fire department; however, since this had not been anticipated the fire engines were not able to gain access to the garage because they could not clear the opening entrance height. The engines were too tall. As a result, several cars burned up. Fortunately, mine was spared, but we had no access to the garage.

It was cold during that time and there was only one hotel in Danbury of any size, and it was already filled. So, I was faced with the problem of trying to get home in New Rochelle. I was able to get a taxicab from Danbury over to one of the adjoining towns and take the train down to the nearest New Rochelle station.

The new Danbury headquarters was designed with the environment in mind, and for that reason parking spaces were located within the building, and not outside to spoil the view. It was a nice arrangement because we could just drive in, park, get out of the car, and be in our offices within a couple of minutes, without having to walk from the parking lot to the building in inclement weather.

One of the great beauties of the move was that Union Carbide presented us with an array of office designs and furniture to choose from. That made a lot of us happy. Union Carbide had independently contracted my friend Hector Hyacinth to provide some, if not all, the office furniture that employees had selected.

As South Africa was preparing for its transition out of apartheid, Hector was a supporter Prince Mangosuthu Gatsha Buthelezi.[180] He wanted to know if I could support Chief Buthelezi's Inkatha Freedom Party (IFP). I had to turn him down, as I supported the African National Congress (ANC), the party of Oliver R. Tambo and Nelson Mandela.

I would later meet Chief Buthelezi in 2012 in an elevator in Mangaung, South Africa at one of the stadia celebrating the centenary of the founding of the ANC.

After overcoming several severe early life challenges, and serving his communities, Hector passed away Thursday, September 29, 2005, at the age of 72.[181]

---

180 https://en.wikipedia.org/wiki/Mangosuthu_Buthelezi (Accessed 03 February 2024)

181 https://www.legacy.com/us/obituaries/lohud/name/hector-hyacinthe-obituary?id=48168670 (Accessed 03 February 2024)

The National Bar Association

The purpose of the NBA, as stated in its articles of incorporation, is to "advance the science of jurisprudence, uphold the honor of the legal profession, promote social intercourse among the members of the American Bar, and protect the civil and political rights of all citizens of the several states and the United States."

I joined the National Bar Association (NBA) in about 1970/71. I have forgotten how I first heard about the NBA, but I knew it was an association of black lawyers. I think my first meeting that I attended was held in New York City. At that time, the annual meeting lasted for a week, with elections being held on Fridays.

Back then, campaigning for NBA office was a simple contest; by 2024 it had evolved into very spirited contests to the point where the Nominations Committee distributed a set of NBA Proposed Candidate Campaign Guidelines projected to take effect in September 2025. These proposals would include a limit on campaign finance spending.

In the early days, continuing legal education seminars were somewhat limited. Many had the title "The Negro and . . ." Many times, presenters spoke extemporaneously, with no handouts. That changed later, as State Bar Associations began to require presenters to submit written materials for attendees to get mandatory continuing legal education credits.

Today the NBA presents seminars that have moved in step with the new frontiers requiring new legal tools. Nowadays, especially with continuing legal education requirements, the seminars are far more sophisticated, using all the visual aid tools and the internet to hold in-person, and virtual seminars, domestically and internationally.

Mel Hodges and I established a ritual of taking a photo together at each NBA annual meeting, except we forgot to do so in 2025 in Chicago.

Top – me and Mel in 2016

Bottom - Mel and me in 2004.

Among South Africa attendees to our annual meetings in the United States are other past and current Presidents of the Black Lawyers Association of South Africa (BLA), also including Bayethe Maswazi, Lutendo Benedict Sigogo, Nkosana Francois Mvundlela, and Deputy Secretary General Khanyisa Mogale.

Members of the BLA Zintle Ngogodo and her twin sister, Siya Wotshela, Stanley Boikanyo, Michael Chauke, Peppy Kekana, Edward Mafori Lesufi, Puleng Keetse, Penelope Magona, David Netshitungulu, and Tshepo Shabangu.

Several high-ranking South Africa legal officials have visited our annual meetings (or other event in the United States) such as Pius Langa, Deputy Chief Justice, Dr. Penuell M. Maduna, and Jeff Radebe, th latter two being Ministers of Justice.

As I discuss below, I and fellow NBA members Herbert Moreira-Brown and Donald Watson attended some of the BLA meetings in South Africa. Beginning in 2012, I made solo presentations to the Law Society of South Africa (LSSA), followed by my colleagues in later BLA Annual General Meetings. My friend Nano Matlala was co-Chairman of the LSSA at the time. I shared the program with His Honor Mogeong Mogoeng, Chief Justice of South Africa.

Me and former Chief Justice Mogoeng Mogoeng after Nano made the introduction

From time to time, we also hosted other African lawyers in Washington, D.C. and New York City. In the mid-90s we hosted Harriett Busingye, John M.M. Mugisha and John Matovu from Uganda; Dorcas A.F. Coker-Appiah, Patrick Ambrose Dery Jones Victor Mawulom Dotse of Ghana; Mohammed Ismail, Mwandaidi Maajar, and Evarist Hubert Mbuya of Tanzania; Lucy M. Kambuni, Peter Mubia Mwangi, and Paul Matheri Wamae of Kenya. Maurice Foster, Deputy Director of the NBA , and I also assisted the East Africans in structuring the East African Bar Association.

More recently, in 2023 and 2024, we hosted Tewodros Getachew Tulu, President of the Ethiopian Federal Advocates Association and Vice President for the East Africa Region of the Pan African Lawyers Union (PALU). In 2025, Teddy was elected as President of the Pan African Lawyers Union. This is an important union of lawyers because it connects lawyers of African descent worldwide.

The Pan African Lawyers Union (PALU) is the premier continental forum for African lawyers and their associations, established in 2002. Its membership includes over 1,000 individual lawyers, more than five regional lawyers' associations, and fifty-four national lawyers' associations across Africa and the Diaspora. PALU aims to promote and defend the interests of the African people, focusing on areas such as institutional development, the legal profession, and the rule of law. The organization is committed to advancing justice, human rights, and socio-economic development in Africa.[182]

[182]The Pan African Lawyers Union (PALU)+4

Tewodros Tulu Getachew, current President of PALU, me, Kari ABDOUL BAGUI, immediate past President of PALU in Addis Ababa, Ethiopia 2024.

While I was there, I visited the ADWA Victory Memorial Museum, and the Makuta Law Offices. Also, the entertainment at Yod Abyssinia was superb.

"Battle of Adwa (1896): A decisive victory where Ethiopian forces, led by Emperor Menelik II and Empress Taytu Betul, defeated Italian invaders, preserving Ethiopia's sovereignty and inspiring anti-colonial movements across Africa.

Pan-African Legacy: The museum was built to ensure Adwa remains in the conscience of all Africans. As Ibrahim Shaddad of the African Minerals and Geosciences Centre stated, "Adwa is not a battle in a specific region, in Ethiopia, but rather the battle of all Africans for liberation"."[183]

---

[183] CoPilot description accessed 23 October 2025.

Tewodros accompanied me on our group tour of the museum, in the bus, and the park at Mount Entoto, the highest point in Addis.[184]

Me and Tewodros ("Teddy") at top of the highest point in Addis Ababa (Mount Entoto)
Mount Entoto is not only the highest point but also has historical and cultural importance. It houses ancient Orthodox churches, including the Church of St Mary, as well as palaces associated with Emperor Menelik II.

Visited the Makuta Law Firm, founded by Meseret Seyoum, the first female founder of a law firm in Ethiopia.

Meseret has incorporated offices for Chinese lawyers into her suite since her firm represents Chinese companies.

[184] Mount Entoto

L-R Me, Meseret and Counsel Claude Gasito Mutorero (Rwanda, Chair PALU Energy and Natural Resources Committee)

Returning to the operations of the NBA, traditionally, candidates for the next election year begin distributing their campaign materials at the current annual meeting. Flyers, sleek posters, biographical material and so forth. There is generally also a preparatory presentation by representatives connected to the next annual meeting venue to show us what to expect when we get there.

As time went on, the NBA created new committees, sections and divisions to assist in meeting the needs of a more sophisticated legal world.

At my first NBA meeting, I was dismayed by the amount of partying that the candidates for office sponsored to try to win over voters. By the time Friday rolled around, we were all exhausted from partying at night and attending seminars during the daytime. Finally, in the mid-80s, in the administration of Dennis Archer, of which I was one of the Vice Presidents, we shortened the annual meeting from a week, to begin on Saturday and end on Thursday, with the elections now being held on Tuesdays.

Initially, I had decided that these people were not serious about the practice of law, and I was not going to waste my time with them. Thank God for Henry Williams, an older lawyer, who said that if I wanted to change the attitude of the attendees, from so much partying to concentrate more on serious business, I should not quit but become part of the policy-making body of the NBA. I took Henry's advice, and I have been working officially and informally to help broaden the horizons of our members for the past 55 years.

Among the coterie of members in the "Harlem" contingent, was Henry, O.T. Wells, Reuben Schofield, William "Bill" Chance, Donald "Covey" Covington, Cora Walker, Lawrence Bailey, among others. Later members of this contingent are Monica Dula, and Taa Grays. In June 2025, Taa became President-Elect of the New York State Bar Association.

From this group, Henry and Covey would become judges. Cora would be the driving force behind the creation of the Commercial Law

Section. One of our annual breakfasts is named after her. I worked with her, Ron Samuels from Chicago, and Don Reed who was a member of the NBA staff to establish the section.

From Brooklyn, Renee Cuyler, Priscilla Hall, Esmeralda Simmons, and Emmanuel Townes, Betty Staton, Yvonne Lewis, were among the regular members.

Over the years, our New York members would become members of the judiciary at every state level, including the New York Court of Appeals, our highest court. In the federal system, many federal district court judges throughout the United States are NBA members. Several are also members of the United States Circuit Courts of Appeal.

Because of their common interests, the Harlem Lawyers Association and the Bedford-Stuyvesant Lawyers Association (from Brooklyn) agreed to combine to form one bar association, which resulted in the creation of the Metropolitan Black Bar Association. ("MBBA.")

Other black Bar Associations in the State of New York are: The Westchester Black Bar Association, of which I was a founding member, the Rochester Black Bar Association, and the Amistad Long Island Black Bar Association.

The brilliant leadership of the NBA at the time I joined were successive Presidents, Ed Bell (Detroit), O.T. Wells (NY), James Cobb (D.C.), George Allen (FL). The NBA would elect Arnette Hubbard (Chicago) as its first female President, in 1981, although one of its founding members in 1925 was Gertrude Rush, a woman. The complete list of past presidents can be found at Past Presidents - National Bar Association.

The 12 NBA founding members were George H. Woodson, S. Joe Brown, Gertrude E. Rush, James B. Morris, Charles P. Howard, Sr., Wendell E. Green, C. Francis Stradford, Jesse N. Baker, William H. Haynes, George C. Adams, Charles H. Calloway, and L. Amasa Knox.

In 2025, the NBA celebrated its 45th Annual Midyear Conference and Gertrude Rush Awards in Des Moines, Iowa, the birthplace of the NBA.

Robert Bell (D.C.), the NBA historian, is updating our history. The present history of the NBA may be found at NBA History - National Bar Association.

I am a Life Member of the National Bar Association, where I served as Vice-President, Special Assistant to the President, Chair of its Annual Awards Committee, and as a member of the Executive Committee and the Board of Governors.

In 2011, the National Bar Association inducted me into its Hall of Fame .

In 2020, the National Bar Association (NBA) honored me with the Ronald Harmon Brown International Distinction Award.[185] In 2022, the National Bar Association conferred this award on Hon. Akinwumi Adesina, CEO of the African Development Bank, so I am in good company.

Me and Hon. Akinwumi Adesina, former CEO of the African Development Bank at NBA Convention in Memphis (2023)

[185] Ron Brown was a friend of mine, stemming from the time we both resided in Mount Vernon, New York.

I was selected for Marquis' Who's Who in American Law (1st Edition) (1977); Marquis' Who's Who in the East (1977); Marquis' Who's Who in the World (1994); Marquis' Who's Who in America (2009).

Each year The American Registry culls through millions of recognitions to identify those who have been awarded more than all the others. I was designated one of Americas Most Honored Lawyers - Top 1% 2023.

Perhaps my greatest contribution to the NBA was my work through our International Law Section (ILS) to connect the interests of our members to those of continental African lawyers. We had also established relationships with the Canadian Black Bar Association and some bar associations in the Caribbean.

Beverly Baker Kelly, Esq.

When I first became active in the International Law Section, Beverly Baker Kelly was the Chair. Beverly is an Alumna of the Berkeley School of Law, my law school.

Among the most significant achievements during her tenure, was the NBA's contribution to the International Criminal Tribunal for Rwanda (ICTR).

The National Bar Association (NBA) played a role in supporting legal efforts related to the International Criminal Tribunal for Rwanda (ICTR), as distinguished from the International Criminal Court (ICC). The ICTR was established by the United Nations in 1994 to prosecute those responsible for genocide and other serious violations of international humanitarian law during the Rwandan Genocide.

The NBA's involvement included:

Advocacy for Justice and Human Rights – The NBA, as an organization committed to civil rights and legal equity, advocated for accountability and justice for the victims of the genocide.

Legal Assistance and Capacity Building – Members of the NBA provided legal expertise to help with the ICTR's work, including training lawyers and judges in Rwanda to strengthen the country's legal system.

Supporting Defense and Prosecution Efforts – Some NBA members worked with the ICTR in various legal capacities, including assisting in the prosecution of genocide perpetrators or ensuring fair trials for the accused.

Public Awareness and Education – The NBA also helped to bring international attention to the Rwandan Genocide and the importance of international justice in addressing mass atrocities.

Beverly, who had been the NBA head of the International Law Section for eight years, was the ICTR'S Deputy Registrar for two years (2000-2001) while working closely with the NBA to provide services to the tribunal.

Specifically, she and Maurice Foster worked with Harold D. Pope, the president of the NBA from 1999 to 2000, to have West Publishing Company, a well-known legal publishing company in the United States, to provide 200 passwords to the ICTR and send one of its top associates to Arusha, Tanzania, the seat of the ICTR, to teach its professionals how to use Westlaw as a research tool. The Westlaw associate gave several lectures to the ICTR professionals and opened vistas for them to enhance their legal research skills. During this time West Law donated the largest gift ever to the NBA to carry on this same type of work in the United States.

As the Deputy Registrar, Beverly helped at least five NBA members to be hired as defense attorneys at the Tribunal. She helped develop legal theories with the Prosecution at the ICTR. She handled detainees' requests while both awaiting trial and thereafter in detention.

She played a significant role in the tribunal's administration during that time.

There were almost 120 different nationalities working at the Tribunal. Communication and languages presented challenges. Attorney Baker-Kelly spoke some of these languages which helped ease this problem.

Her time at the tribunal was fruitful and an unusual experience. She left the tribunal in order to have more time with her husband and two daughters.

Other ILS Chairs

Kendal Tyre, a partner in the law firm of Nixon Peabody, continued some of the unprecedented history of the NBA in the international arena. He concentrated his law practice in the areas of franchising and commercial law.

Over the years, Kendal's law firm underwrote the ILS luncheon and seminar, which was a part of each meeting. The luncheons were invaluable in bringing together continental and American lawyers of African descent to interact with each other and to her a stimulating presentation on some topic of international law.

Succeeding Chair Simone Williams introduced many of our members to immigration law.

Barbara A. Simmons achieved two notable firsts-execution of Memoranda of Understanding with the Pan African Lawyers Union (PALU)(2023) (whom I assisted) and the African Continental Free Trade Area Secretariat (AFCFTR)(assisted by Johanna LeBlanc)(2025). After the NBA signed the MOUs in the United States, the parties followed up with a ceremonial signing in Livingstone, Zambia and Accra, Ghana, respectively. I attended the signing in Zambia.

2025 Centennial ILS meeting in Chicago cufflinks award

Sometime ago, an African Union Ambassador to the United States, gave these cuff links to Barbara A. Simmons, who is Chair of the International Law Section of The National Bar Association. Only a limited number of these cufflinks were commissioned. Barbara decided that she would keep the cufflinks until she found a person worthy and present them at the appropriate occasion. You can imagine that I was quite surprised and shocked when Barbara presented these cufflinks to me during our International Law Section Award Reception on 28 August 2025 at the Quarles & Brady Chicago Office during the Centennial Anniversary of the founding of the National Bar Association.

The most ironic thing is that I'm traveling light, and I decided to bring only one or two dress shirts; both of them have button down cuffs so I have yet to wear the cufflinks. I will have to wait for an occasion when I would need to wear cuff links, and I can show them off at that time.

I also received one of the Centenary Presidential Awards for exemplary service to the NBA.

South Africa Bar Associations

Every year, the NBA schedules an international meeting around May/June, the first of which took place in 1991.[186]

In 1992, the NBA took a delegation of American lawyers and judges on a study tour of South Africa which lasted approximately fourteen days and included joint meetings and seminars on democratic principles and other areas of law relevant to preparing black African lawyers for leadership and participation in a new government.[187]

In April 1994, as the only bar group sanctioned by the International Elections Committee, sending nine representatives to participate in a United States delegation which served as official observers for the first all-race democratic election conducted in South Africa.[188]

The NBA held international affiliate chapter meetings in South Africa in 1993 and 1995.[189]

In 2001 NBA President Evett Simmons led the NBA Affiliates meeting in South Africa, with a focus on Human Rights.[190] Some of those who participated in the meeting were Priscilla Hall, Clyde Bailey,

---

186 National Bar Association Subdivision Handbook at 15.

187 Id. at 16

188 National Bar Association Subdivision Handbook, 16.

189 Id. at 15, 16.

190 Howard University/National Bar Association Connections in the South African Liberation Movement Paper, written by Jean Bailey, Ph.D., and Tara Hammonds, J.D., presented by Dr. Bailey at the 2025 National Bar Association Centennial International Affiliates Meeting CLE Program in Johannesburg (Sandton), South Africa, May 13, 2025.

his wife Dr. Jean Bailey, Fred Gray, Nano Matlala, Richard Thornell and Dr. Tony Mbewu.[191]

Seated: Priscilla Hall, Charlotte V. McClain-Nhlapo: Standing L-R Evett Simmons, Clyde Bailey, Nano Matlala, Unknown, Fred Gray, Dr. Tony Mbewu - South Africa Medical Research Council , Professor Richard Thornell (Howard University School of Law), (2001)

[191] When prompted with, "What are the names of the NBA members who were in the delegation that Yvette Simmons led in the 2001 the NBA Affiliates meeting in South Africa?" Co-Pilot generated this response (Microsoft, 22 Aug 2025 at 5:05PM)

Carol Gray, Fred Wife, Fred, Evett and Me at the NBA convention in Minneapolis, Prince's Museum in St. Paul. (2023)

In 2002, the International Affiliates meeting in South Africa, the National Bar Association assisted in the creation of the Pan African Lawyers Union (PALU).

At this meeting, Penuell Maduna played a prominent and strategic role as South Africa's Minister of Justice and Constitutional Development.[192]

[192] When prompted with, " What was Penuell Maduna's role at this meeting?" Co-Pilot generated this response (Microsoft, 22 Aug 2025 at 4:33 PM)

Penuell Maduna's Role at the Meeting

- Host and keynote figure: As the sitting Minister of Justice, Maduna welcomed delegates and lent official support to the formation of PALU.
- Symbol of constitutional leadership: His presence underscored South Africa's commitment to continental legal cooperation and the rule of law.
- Facilitator of transcontinental dialogue: Maduna helped bridge African legal institutions with diaspora organizations like the NBA, reinforcing shared goals around justice, governance, and human rights.

Minister Maduna was one of the signatories of the PALU founding documents.

Guiseppe Bisconti, former President of the International Bar Association (IBA) (1991–1992), was also present in a diplomatic and advisory capacity to lend international credibility and support to the formation of PALU.[193]

Others who played key roles in the formation of PALU at this meeting were:

Name	Role at the Meeting	Affiliation/Title
Mavis T. Thompson	Lead NBA delegate; supported PALU's formation	President of the NBA
Femi Falana	Founding member and advocate for continental legal unity	Prominent Nigerian human rights lawyer
Titus Mlengeya	Organizational architect of PALU	Tanzanian lawyer; later PALU Secretary General

193 When prompted with, " What was Guiseppe Bisconti's role at this meeting?" Co-Pilot generated this response (Microsoft, 22 Aug 2025 at 4:30 PM)

Representatives of the Law Society of South Africa	Institutional hosts and facilitators	Law Society of South Africa
Delegates from African Bar Associations	Founding members and signatories	Regional and national bar associations across Africa

The late Clyde Bailey was sworn in as President of the NBA in August 2003 in New Orleans. Minister Penuell Maduna attended his swearing in.

Clyde led the 2004 delegation meetings in South Africa, Botswana and Zimbabwe, along with his wife Jean Bailey, Ph.D., who teaches in the graduate education program at Howard, and co-directs the Howard University South Africa Research project. I was part of the 2004 NBA delegation. The delegation is pictured below.[194]

Part of the delegation had the pleasure of attending a meeting hosted by Kgosi Lerou of the Royal Bafokeng Nation in Phokeng, South Africa and the Queen mother. The Kgosi's deceased older brother was a graduate of Howard University.

The trip was scheduled for June 2004. I think I did not realize that June was really the middle of winter in southern Africa, but I survived. Cameron R. Hume, The American Ambassador to South Africa installed outside gas heaters to help with the chill during our reception at the American Embassy.

The American Ambassadors in South Africa and in Botswana briefed our delegation of about 40 people about the economic, political and social conditions in the country in which they served.

[194] For some reason, Clyde and Jean, his wife, do not appear in this photo.

Our visit to the Constitutional Court of South Africa, was the most memorable part of the South Africa visit for me. His Lordship Albie Sachs, pictured in the yellow blazer above, standing next to Beverly Baker Kelly, gave us an extensive tour and lecture about the conception, history, local community consultations and construction of Constitution Hill and the organization of the Constitutional Court. Maurice Foster, Deputy Executive Director is standing to the extreme right, with Kendal Tyre standing off his right shoulder.

The entrance to the courthouse displayed the name of the Constitutional Court in each of the 11 official South African languages.[195]

[195]https://www.bing.com/videos/riverview/relatedvideo?&q=What+do+the+languages+mean+at+the+entrance+to+the+South+Africa+consitutional+court&&mid=ED9203804E6F37EAAB4CED9203804E6F37EAAB4C&&mcid=861AC6CE9BB14A04B63DFC43B0F77E51&FORM=VRDGAR (Accessed 30 December 2024)

Expressions of the local cultures of South Africa were expressed throughout the courthouse in paintings, drawings, sculptures, the blue dress, and other pieces of visual artwork.

Inside the Constitutional Court of South Africa hangs Judith Mason's The Man Who Sang and the Woman Who Kept Silent, more commonly known as The Blue Dress.[196]

The blue dress told a story of the abduction, torture, gender-based degradation, and murder of Phila Ndwandwe. The blue dress was stitched together from fragments of discarded blue plastic bags. She was captured by apartheid police and tortured in an attempt to force her to provide information on the resistance movement. She did not betray her comrades.[197]

Harold Sefola was an ANC activist, who—along with two of his colleagues, Jackson Maake and Andrew Makupe—was abducted, tortured and murdered. During his interrogation, Sefola requested to sing Nkosi Sikelel' iAfrica (God Bless Africa). Maake, Makupe and Sefola were electrocuted to death. Nkosi Sikelel' iAfrica is now the national anthem of South Africa. Sefola was the man who sang.[198]

We met with members of the Black Lawyers Association of South Africa, the National Association of Democratic Lawyers, and others. The meetings were memorable in that we met with the highest-ranking Legal officials in South Africa, including Penuell Maduna, former

---

196 https://16daysblogathon.blog/2020/12/02/day-ten-south-africas-blue-dress-art-as-an-alternative-record-of-sexual-and-gender-based-violence/ (Accessed 30 December 2024)

197 https://www.bing.com/search?q=What+is+the+significance+of+the+blue+dress+that+hangs+in+the+Constitutional+Court+building+in+Johannesburg&form=WSBEDG&qs=SW&cvid=db62dfeef98e45c59fca505a64ffd9d0&pq=What+is+the+significance+of+the+blue+dress+that+hangs+in+the+Constitutional+Court+building+in+Johannesburg&cc=BW&setlang=en-US&nclid=5818987FB4D68F5BAD3F221AD7D26E69&ts=1735566656546&wsso=Moderate (Accessed 30 December 2024)

198 Intentionally left blank.

Minister of Justice and Constitutional Development, his successor Brigitte Mabandla, and the Head of the National Prosecution Authority.

Some of the features of the Constitutional Court are pictured below.

Left photo - Constitutional Court Library

Right photo – one view of exterior of Constitutional Court

Left photo - Bench of indigenous wood;
Right photo – another view of court's exterior

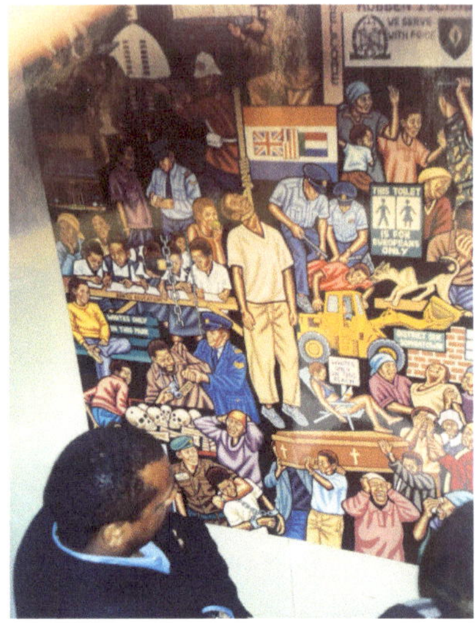

Left – artwork (unknown person);
right – Andrew Brown looking at painting of apartheid scenes

Phila Ndwandwe's blue dress

Painting of dancers

Jude Kearney, an African American lawyer, treated the delegation to a reception. Jude managed the Johannesburg office for LeBoeuf, Lamb, Greene & MacRae LLP, an American law firm. Nowadays, Jude is the Managing Partner at the Washington, D.C. offices of ASAFO & CO. (U.S.) LLP[199].

Left photo – Me, Penuell Maduna
Right Photo – Reggie Hicks, Me, Jude

In our 2004 meeting in South Africa, Henry "Muzi" Msimang, the President of the Black Lawyers Association of South Africa (BLA),

199 ASAFO bills itself as Africa's International Law Firm. https://www.asafoandco.com/

vowed to bring a delegation of South African lawyers to the next National Bar Association annual meeting.

The 2005 annual meeting was held from July 30 – August 6, 2005, at the JW Marriott Orlando and & Ritz -Carlton Hotels. Twelve or thirteen BLA South Africa lawyers attended.

Many attended our annual meetings since then and I have maintained my personal contact with several of them over the past 20 years.

I have visited the Law Offices of two of these lawyers, Muzi being one and Nano Matlala, being the other. I loved the way they organized their litigation files. I was also happy to re-acquaint myself with Mma Puleng Keetse, another of the lawyers in Muzi's office, whom I had met when the delegation came to our meeting in Chicago or Detroit. I made sure that she would make the remarks at our gala dinner on behalf of the delegation from South Africa to do my bit to make the status of South African women lawyers more visible.

Muzi took me to visit his second house situated on a lake and regaled me with many tales about his extensive wine collection. To this day I remember one label that he was extremely fond of – Rustenberg Cabernet Sauvignon, made by the Rustenberg Wine Estate which was founded in 1682.

Muzi, standing, with Mma Puleng Keetse standing next to him, Lettie Monyane seated first on the left, Maleta, my fiancée at the time, me, Wycliffe Mothulwe, and Justice Lettie Molopa at the 2005 NBA convention in Orlando, Florida.

We maintained our friendship, and I was happy to see on television that he was one of the lawyers representing the families in the police massacre of mine workers in Marikana in August 2012. The Marikana massacre was the killing of thirty-four miners by the South African Police Service (SAPS) on 16 August 2012 during a six-week wildcat strike at the Lonmin platinum mine at Marikana near Rustenburg in South Africa's Northwest province. The massacre constituted the most lethal use of force by South African security forces against civilians since the Soweto uprising in 1976 and has been compared to the 1960 Sharpeville massacre.[200]

I understand that Mma Puleng also represented some of the miners and their families.

Nano succeeded Muzi. By virtue of their bar organizations, the President of the BLA automatically became the Co-Chair of the Law Society of South Africa (LSSA).

L-R Reggie Hicks, Arlene Gordon Oliver, Mpho, Nano's wife, and Nano at the 2005 NBA convention in Orlando, Florida.

200 https://en.wikipedia.org/wiki/Marikana_massacre (Accessed 05 FEB 2024) (internal footnotes omitted)

Nano began to connect me with the common and joint history of the NBA, the BLA, and the LSSA. That was preserved on the BLA-LEC website.

Nano gave me the opportunity to explain the American judicial system to the LSSA and to serve as the keynote speaker at the LSSA Annual General Meeting Gala Dinner (2012). It was on this occasion that I met Hon. Mogeong Mogoeng the then Chief Justice of the Constitutional Court of South Africa. He and I appeared on different parts of the same program.

Nano also Introduced me to Hon. Philip Waki, retired Judge of the Kenya Court of Appeal. Who also sat as Elected President of Residual Special Court for Sierra Leone. We got to know each other from the seminar and as Nano's house guests.

I led the audience through a PowerPoint presentation of the American legal system, using slides that I obtained through the International Office of the Federal Judicial Center in the Thurgood Marshall Federal Judiciary Building.[201]

The LSSA honored me with a Ballman Ballpoint pen set, which I used only to sign certain documents.

Pritzman Busani Mabunda, Nano's successor, extended the same honor to me to speak at the 2015 BLA Gala Dinner. He gave me a black notebook as a token of his appreciation, and inscribed the same, with a note that read

> "My dear brother Leroy Wilson Junior, I Busani Mabunda, in my capacity as president of the Black Lawyers Association I am greatly humbled by your gracing the occasion of the 38th Annual General Meeting of the Black Lawyers Association (BLA) and delivering a keynote address as a member of the National Bar Association (NBA).
>
> I am equally grateful of the honor and respect which the organization accorded you as it was a duly deserved one.

---

201 PowerPoint Presentation (fjc.gov) (accessed 16 November 2023).

I will cherish this moment for the rest of my life. You should cherish this moment for the rest of your life."

He signed it "PB Mabunda President (BLA)

Date: Backdated 23 October 2015. "

I am attached to that little notebook.

At that meeting, I was accompanied by Herbert Moreira - Brown and Donald Watson, two of our NBA members. Each of them also addressed the BLA Annual General Meeting (AGM). All of us attended at our own expense. They traveled from the United States. I traveled from Botswana.

L-R Herbert Moreira-Brown, President Busani Mubanda, and Donald Watson (in South Africa)

Early in 2020, Busani and I sat together at the Apartheid Museum to witness a ceremony of about 100 African American judges who were visiting South Africa. They were members of the NBA Judicial Council. Dr. Jean Bailey, who was responsible for getting the funding for the special museum exhibition the Judges were invited to see, asked me to make a few remarks about the connection between African Americans and the black community in South Africa, including my own contributions, before and after I was a public member of the New York State Banking Board.

The South African government provided a very visible show of force to provide security and to protect those judges. Defense force, as well as police officers present were heavily armed.

I saw Busani again, in 2023, this time on my computer, as he gave remarks at the virtual celebration of the life of Prof. Shadrack Gutto, a brilliant lawyer and activist scholar. He and Nano sat together. I met both Shadrack and Judge Philip Waki at Nano's residence.

In 2024, the NBA International Trip scheduled its trip for the French Riviera & Barcelona (Optional) May 8-18, 2024 – French Riviera, May 18-24, 2024 – Barcelona.

In a delegation led by Centennial President Wiley S. Adams, the NBA returned to South Africa and Zambia May 4-19, 2025, for its NBA International Affiliates Meeting Before retiring in 2020, Wiley worked as the Chief Legal Officer of PGIM, Inc. I was part of the South Africa NBA delegation.

Centennial President Wiley S. Adams

Those who attended include ***Vanita Banks,*** NBA Past President, Committee Chair, Senior Privacy Counsel, Axiom, ***Lisa Adams,*** NBA Member, Sponsor, ***Professor Jean Bailey,*** NABBS Member,

Mvundlela Nkoana Francois, Black Lawyers Association of South Africa President, ***Daryl D. Parks,*** NBA Past President, he resides in Florida and is the managing partner at Parks Law, L.L.C., ***Nano Matlala,*** Black Lawyers Association of South Africa Past President, **Shirley Birts** lives in Chicago and is semi-retired, **Henry Coker** was appointed Public Defender of San Diego County in 2009 and retired in 2017, **Judge Donna Cooper** resides in Chicago, **Shirley M. Dawson**, resides in Chicago, and is a clinical research attorney, **Judge Denise Langford Morris** (retired), Oakland County Circuit Court, **Sharlyn Grigsby** resides in Washington, D.C., and is a retired Federal Human Resources Director, **Byrnes Guillaume** is a private law firm owner with two practices in West Palm Beach and Port Saint Lucie, FL., **Jaunita Harris** resides in Houston, Texas and serves as Assistant VP & Senior Legal Counsel to Human Resources at DIRECTV, **Norma Hutcheson** is Chair of the District of Columbia Board of Ethics and Government Accountability, **Patricia Mack** resides in New Jersey. She has been a solo Practitioner at The Law Office of Patricia Mack since 1994, **Tiffany Pinder Patierno** resides in Los Angeles, California., **Jessalyn Pinder** is Assistant City Attorney with the Los Angeles City Attorney's Office, from December 1994 to Present, **Wilma J. Pinder**, a civil litigator, retired as an Asst. City Attorney, Office of LA City, **Bernice Prewitt** lives in Burr Ridge, Illinois, **Judge Randa Trapp** retired in 2021 as the Supervising Judge of the Civil Division of the San Diego County Superior Court, **George Westry** is an Emeritus Attorney and Counselor at Law,

Among the panelists, not otherwise listed above, were:

- South Africa

  Christine Qunta, Attorney and CEO of Pholosang BEE Resolution Services (Pty) Ltd; Chairperson of the Legal Sector Charter Council, Cape Town, South Africa.

- Zambia

  Steven Hunter, Partner, Quarles and Brady, LLP, Chicago, IL

The complete program, including biographies may be obtained through the National Bar Association offices. +1 (202) 842-3900 (Washington, D.C.)

Top photo – Tshepo Shabangu and Me at the May 2025 International Affiliates Meeting in Sandton
Bottom photo - Nano Matlala, Past President of the Black Lawyers Assn of South Africa and past Co-Chair of the Law Society of South Africa, Leroy, Christine Qunta, chairperson of the Legal Sector Charter Council at the meeting.

“HISTORY OF THE BLA | HISTORY OF THE LEC |

Black lawyers association legal education centre (bla-lec) history

The BLA-LEC gives some very important history of the connections between the NBA and the BLA and LEC on its website.[202] We have also prepared an NBA-BLA history for the ILS 2025 International Meeting which was held with the BLA from 04-19 May 2015 in South Africa.

In 1982 the BLA invited a group of American Lawyers to come to South Africa, a visit funded by the Carnegie Corporation of New York. The group comprised of Justice A Leon Higginbotham (Jnr) of the U.S. Federal Court of Appeals; [United State District] Justice Thelton Henderson; Mr. Julius Chambers, a Civil Rights Lawyer of Charlotte, North Carolina, Director-Counsel of NAACP Legal Defense and Educational Fund, Inc, and his wife Viviene; and Ms. Sarah Mitchell also a Civil Rights lawyer.

The lawyers were to observe and gain an impression of the South African legal system and the potential of using the law as an instrument of social justice. In addition, they were to:

a) Observe the nature of the legal practice of black lawyers in SA

b) Hold talks with black lawyers;

c) Be informed about the special problems facing black lawyers in term s of influx control, the Group Areas Act, etc.

d) Address black law students;

e) Meet members of the white legal establishment to make them more aware of the need to train more blacks for legal practice

The group visited Pietersburg, Johannesburg, Pretoria, Durban, Ciskei, Cape Town, Soweto and Benoni. They exchanged ideas with

---

[202] A recent version of this history may be found at https://www.blalec.co.za/about/history/ (Accessed 02 Feb 2024)

members of the BLA, the Azanian's People's Organisation and the public.

They experienced the hardships of living in South Africa when they visited some townships. They went to Seshego and Lebowakgomo Townships in Pietersburg and Lenyenye Townshp in Tzaneen, where they met among others, Mamphele Ramphela, a lady medical practitioner who had been banished to Tzaneen and restricted to the township by Government decree. They visited a resettlement area in Phepeni, Tzaneen where several hundred families had been dumped after being uprooted from their traditional homes following a government proclamation that their homes were situated in an area zoned for the homeland of Gazankulu.

At the time of their visit, shanties had been put up. There were no sanitary facilities available, and no clean water supplies to the village.

A meeting was held between the students of the University of the North, the Black Academic Staff Association later known as Black Staff Association and the visitors. They also visited the Universities of Natal, Cape Town and Zululand.

En route to Cape Town, the visitors went via Bisho in the Ciskei where they were harassed by the local police. It is alleged that they were taking photographs of a court building, when they were approached by the local police and taken to a local police station and interrogated by the Ciskei Intelligence Service. They were later released after it was established that they were foreigners.

On their return to the US, several American newspapers reported on their experiences in South Africa and, said Judge Higginbotham (Jnr) "They have been unanimous in their condemnation, not merely of the adverse treatment we received, but more importantly of the daily plight of blacks in South Africa".

It was during this visit when Judge Hlgginibotham (Jnr) suggested to the BLA executive that a Legal Education Centre (LEC) be set up. It was to serve as a centre for education; research, publication, and establishment, directing and administration of law clinics.

Realising that the birth of the Centre would assist towards achieving the BLA's objectives, a skeleton staff was selected early in 1984, and the first few meetings were held at the Adviser House on Commissioner Street in Johannesburg, offices of the Chairman, Mr. Pitje,

On October 1, 1984, the BLA LEC moved to a temporary office at the Legal Resources Centre, Hook Street Legal Clinic along Bree Street. Mr. Pitje was appointed by members to be Director of the Centre.

Without receiving any compensation in return, BLA members persuaded him to leave his practice to head the Centre, which he did for three years. He said, "I did it for the love of the BLA, the profession and my desire to see the black lawyers progress".

His first staff consisted of Mr. Modise Khoza - Progromme Officer and Mr. S. Hlongwane - Research Officer.

In December 1984 premises were found on 2nd Floor, Manchester House, 68 Vonwielligh Street, Johannesburg. The staff was joined by Mr. Abbey Mothokoa who headed the Law Clinic in Johannesburg and Alexandra, Ms Faith Maqubela - administrator, Mrs. ldah Motsoeneng - secretary and Ms Marie Mochawana - messenger.

The Centre received funding from the Carnegie Corporation of New York, Ford Foundation, and Rockerfeller Foundation, among others.

In 1986 Mr. Pitje stepped down as Director of the LEC and reopened his practice on Commissioner Street in Johannesburg.

For a few months thereafter a Management committee ran the Centre. Members of this Committee were Mr.

G. S. Maluleke now judge, Mr. J.F.T. Vilakazi, Mr. M. Pitje, Mr. J.D.S.S. Moshidi, Ms. A. Cornwall, Mr. E.D. Moseneke now judge of the Constitutional Court and Mr. C.S. Mhinga. The post for Director was advertised, Mr. Justice Moloto, an attorney from Durban, was appointed.

Three other members joined the staff, being. Mrs. Mojankunyane Gumbi, who headed the Legal Defense Fund Department, Mrs. Dolly Mokgatle, Litigation Officer and Ms. Nomonde Mnqibisa who headed the Education Department.

As the BLA membership grew gradually, the LEC focused on professional enhancement. The Centre established Education and Litigation departments which have made their [mark in previous years.]

Departments within the LEC were responsible for the following:

i. To educate and enhance the competence of the black lawyers. Several schemes operated within the education department being the bursary fund scheme for university students, conducting trial advocacy seminars and mock trials at university level, a salary subsidy scheme to encourage law firms to take in black candidate attorneys.

ii. Running three law clinics in Johannesburg, Alexandra and Owa Qwa. Cases that were brought to these clinics were mainly labour and housing problems;

iii. Increasing the number and enhancing the efficacy of black lawyers through the Legal Defense Fund program me.

iv. The fund covered all cases arising out of resistance to apartheid laws in the country

v. Litigation of political cases, police assaults, student rights housing and labour.

vi. Publication of the African Law Review that encouraged lawyers to write articles on case notes, features and their activities in the law field. The Review was launched in 1987 and was intended to provide the much-needed knowledge of the law beyond the legal profession.

It was mainly through the establishment of the LEC that the Association became well known within the country and outside. Invitations poured in from countries like the United States and some African states requesting members to address lawyers and human rights groups.

One such invitation was to attend the ABA Annual Conference[203] in Washington in July 1988 on the theme "The Legal Aspects of Apartheid". The conference was co-sponsored by the Washington-based Lawyers Committee for Equal Rights Under Law and the Individual Rights and Responsibilities Committee of the American Bar Association.

Twenty-five South African and Namibian lawyers were invited. Those who represented the BLA at the conference, were Advocates Moseneke, now judge, Khoza and Skweyiya now judge and attorneys Moshidi, Pitje, Mr. Mathew Phosa, Jana and Nkadimeng who formed the largest unit of these lawyers.

BLA members delivered well researched papers on a variety of apartheid laws including forced removals, torture in detentions, inquests, bantustans, impartiality or otherwise of the South African judiciary, trade unionism and others.

Also from South Africa were two black attorneys and one white attorney from the Eastern Cape who delivered papers on the Uitenhage shootings and the Kannemeyer Commission of Inquiry.

An exiled attorney, one black and one white attorney represented Namibia. Also present were Advocates Bizos now SC; Raym and Sutt ner, a lecturer, Professor Ranchod of Durban-Westville University and David Saggot of the Johannesburg Bar. Exiled South African liberation movements, the UN Council on Namibia, Churches, the US judiciary and many other individuals and associations were represented.

Another visit worth mentioning, was when four lawyers visited the United States under the United States South African Leadership Exchange Program me (USSALEP) for comparison and training in the necessary expertise and skills relating to broad legal aid institutions,

---

203 The more recent history reports this as International Bar Association's (the IBA) Annual Conference in Washington

public interest law projects and civil rights and liberties. The scheme, conducted by USSALEP in conjunction with the trustees of the LEC and the executive of the BLA was in preparation for the establishment of the LEC.

The BLA LEC enjoys a number of successes, these being among others;

i. A bursary fund scheme for students at university level. Mock trials at black universities, where these are not part of the curriculum.

ii. A candidate attorney subsidy scheme to induce black lawyers to take in articled clerks. According to the Director, Mr. Moloto: "This has been a major success."

iii. A candidate attorney tuition refund scheme which enables students to register with Practical School in preparation for the admission examinations. The scheme required that students pay a deposit and the Centre pays the balance. The students' progress is monitored closely and should the student be successful the deposit was refunded in full.

iv. A funding scheme is run for seminars and conferences aimed at dealing with specific problem areas of law that are regularly received in practice.

The BLA was the first organization to introduce Trial Advocacy in South Africa. Trial Advocacy training is highly recommended by judges and lawyers alike.

The first members of the Board of Trustees of the BLA LEC were: Mr. G.S.S. Maluleke, now judge of the JDP (Chairman). Mr. D. Ntsebeza now advcate, Mr. J. Yekiso now judge of CPD, Prof. N. C. Manganyi, Mr. T.L. Skweyiya,

Mr.J.F.T. Vilakazi and Mr E.D. Moseneke later judge of the Constitutional Court (secretary) and the International court of Justice. Directors of the BLA - LEC.

1. Mr. Pitje: 1984 - 1986

2. Judge Moloto: 1986 - 1992
3. Adv. Mojanko Gumbi: 1992 - 1993
4. Adv. Pansy Tlakula: 1994 - 1996
5. Adv. Ishmael Semenya: 1996 - 1997
6. Mr. Sibusiso Gamede: 1997 – 2001
7. Miss. Andiswa Ndoni: 2001 - to date."

Another insightful history of the contributions of many of these remarkable people is told in Kenneth S Broun. Black Lawyers, White Courts: The Soul of South African Law. With a message from Nelson Mandela, foreword by Julius S. Chambers.[204]

After the October 2015 BLA Annual General Meeting where President Busani Mabunda presided, the next year, 2016, Katlego Mokwena, who had been present at one of the associations dinners where I spoke, asked me to come to Polokwane, South Africa to help launch the Polokwane Society of Advocates (2016) and serve as the Gala dinner speaker. I traveled to Polokwane to assist with the launch.

Katlego Mokwena

[204] Athens, Ohio: Ohio University Press, 2000. xxiv + 286 pp. $45.00 (cloth), ISBN 978-0-8214-1286-2.

Top - Me at the launch of the Polokwane Society of Advocates (2016)

Bottom - Charlotte H.C Pik Maunatlala P.A to PJ Mlambo, and me, at the launch of the Polokwane Society of Advocates (2016)

Katlego and I continued to exchange information as we stayed in touch with each other. Before COVID, he and I and an eminent Botswana architect and urban planner met to discuss a proposal for the development of a real estate project South Africa. project. Unfortunately, COVID came along and disrupted this project.

In 2023, Adv. Mokwena was appointed as an Acting Judge of the High Court of South Africa, Limpopo Division, Polokwane. He handed down his first Judgment in the case of Sebe and Mabilo v. Minister of Police on August 16, 2023 (Case # 7592/2019).

On September 30, 2023, Adv. Mokwena and Tseleng Matotola were married. I planned to attend but did not because of logistical reasons.

I have also maintained my relationships with South African lawyers Nano Matlala, Tshepo Shabangu, Henry Msimang, Puleng Keetse, Edward Lesufi, Stanley Boikanyo, Thembani Michael Chauke, and others, of South Africa, all of whom have attended NBA meetings.

In one instance, I connected Stanley Boikanyo with NBA lawyers to investigate a South African citizen's potential lawsuit against American individual and corporate defendants in an intellectual property case. These are the kinds of collaborations we should be having.

L-R Mkwanazi Mzwakhe BLA, NBA member Leroy Wilson, Jr., Tebogo T. Hlaphosa BLA, Stanley Boikanyo BLA, attending NBA Judicial Council Mid-Winter Meeting Michaelangelo Hotel Johannesburg (29 JAN 2020) Other Delegations

L-R Me, Busani Mabunda, Past BLA President, Judge Craig Strong (ret) , T. Michael Chauke, BLA, and Herbert Moreira-Brown, NBA (NBA Convention)

L-R Unk, me, Busani, Willie Gary, T. Michael Chauke, Donald Watson, T.J. Cunningham

L-R Herbert Moreira- Brown, Penelope Magona (NBA Convention)

L-R Unknown, Busani, Me, President Judge High Court of SA, Limpopo Division, Uknown (Johannesburg 2020)

Botswana Law Society

After Ambassador Joseph Huggins greeted us, his staff briefed us on what was happening in Botswana.

He also hosted dinner for us at the Maharaja Restaurant. Maurice Foster, NBA Deputy Director, gave him a Directory of NBA members.

We also attended continuing legal education seminars at the Gaborone Sun. I sat next to David Newman, a founder of Collins and Newman, later Judge of the High Court, and Ambassador to the United States. I paid him a courtesy visit while he was Ambassador.

I also met Peter Collins, although I am not sure if it was at this meeting. I later successfully represented Carla Collins, his daughter, in New York state and federal district courts in the Spamalot Model case which I write about below.

Advocate Duma Boko also presented at one of the fora. After his party won parliamentary elections in 2024, he was elected President of Botswana. The election was a historical landslide as his party, the UDC, trounced the BDP which had held power since 1966, when the country became independent. The BDP finished in fourth place with 4 seats out of 61.

Advocate Unity Dow was also present. She is a lawyer, author, human rights activist, former national and international judge, and Member of Parliament for Kgatleng West since November 2024. She formerly served as the first woman judge on the High Court of Botswana and in various Botswana government ministries.[205] After graduation, she also established the first all-women's law firm in Botswana.

U.S. Judge Arthur Burnett, Unity Dow, and Clyde Bailey at the Gaborone Sun (now Avani) for our meeting with the Botswana Law Society

In 2004, Botswana was just setting up a group of laws, but no regulations yet, to handle intellectual property issues.

I am not sure if I met Tebelelo M. Seretse at this meeting, but I did meet her later. She attended one of our meetings in 2014. However, I had met her prior to that time.

In 2011, President Ian Khama appointed her as the first woman to serve as Botswana's Ambassador to the U.S. Her term ended in 2014.

She was returning to familiar ground, as she earned her BA in Economics and Accounting from Morgan State University.

While there she stayed with the family of Clarence Mitchell, an important NAACP lobbyist, who earned the nickname the "101st Senator." I learned that she stayed with them in a conversation that I had

205 https://en.wikipedia.org/wiki/Unity_Dow (Accessed 21 January 2025)

with Michael Mitchell, his son. During our Sister Cities meeting at Sandton, SA, I telephoned her and enabled her and Michael to connect again.

Amb. Seretse also earned an MA in Economics from the University of Cincinnati, and an LL.B. from the University of Botswana

On a visit to the Notwane Club in Gaborone, Amb. Seretse's sister related to me how their mother plowed the fields, often at night, to earn the money to send them to college and university.

I now live in Botswana, but the most peculiar thing is that I know only a handful of lawyers here. I know many more in South Africa, Ethiopia, Nigeria, Democratic Republic of Congo, Cameroon, Jamaica, Kenya, Tanzania, and other countries than I do in Botswana.

I love it here. As I have stated many times, Batswana are among the most lovely, courteous people in Africa. Most of the people I have met in other countries in Africa are also very courteous. The way they respect Bagolo[206] here reminds me of my hometown of Savannah. A Mogolo is a senior or elderly person.

Finally, when one settles into the culture, the hand gestures, greetings, and body language come quite naturally. The right word, at the right time, can turn an unexpressive face into a warm rainbow of smiles.

---

206 Plural for Mogolo, seniors or elderly people.

New York State Bar Association

Although I had been a member of the New York State Bar Association (NYSBA) for many years, I did not become active until around the 1980s. Since most of the work of the association was done through committees, ad hoc task forces and similar entities, I started participating actively in those parts of the NYSBA that I was interested in. Some of those are the Trusts and Estates Section (and served on the Estate Planning Committee; Trial Lawyers Section; the General Practice Section; Torts, Insurance and Compensation Law Section, and International Law Section.)

I also served on the Commercial and Federal Litigation Section where I was one of the editors of that section's newsletter or journal, along with Lesley Rosenthal, who became the Chief Operating Officer and Corporate Secretary of The Juilliard School, after serving as EVP, General Counsel & Secretary of Lincoln Center for the Performing Arts in New York City. Lesley wrote an extremely helpful book "Good Counsel, Meeting the Needs of Nonprofits."

By the 1990s, I became more active in the NYSBA. The Special Committee on Solo and Small Firm Practitioners (1991) was formed to investigate issues that these firms were encountering. Bob Ostertag, a friend and very well-respected lawyer, chaired the committee.

> "Throughout his involvement in the NYSBA [Bob] was a dogged champion for all the solo and small firm practitioners in the many small towns in NY who often struggle to make a living, making sure they had a strong advocate in their bar association

and a seat at the table when important decisions were to be made. He was responsible for 2 publications designed to address the needs of those attorneys, as Chairman of the Editorial Board producing the New York Lawyers Deskbook, NY State Bar Ass'n 1989, and as Co-Editor, General Practice in New York (6 Volumes), West Group 1998, the latter a labor that took up his "free time" for almost 2 years."[207]

Although I was also a member of the Committee on Minorities in the Profession, I was not an active participant.

I was Chair of the Committee on Civil Rights during an interesting time (1991-2000). The issue of same sex marriage came up during that time, and the committee debated the issue of whether to support civil unions or same sex marriage. I think we came out in favor of civil unions. In any case, the debates were spirited and civil.

I served in the following capacities: Task Force on Judicial Independence (1996); Solo and Small Firm Lawyer Task Force (1991-92), where I was privileged to work with Bob Ostertag, mentioned above; the Advisory Committee on Solo and Small Firm Practice (1992-93); Special Committee on Ombudsman Plan (4/29/98); Special Committee on Fiduciary Appointments (11/19/01); Special Committee on Law Practice Continuity (2002); Member By-Laws Committee (6/1/2007); and Member of Audit Committee (2009).

Since I did not know what an audit committee did, I called my friend and colleague, Dennis Archer, to refer me to someone who could tell me. He referred me to an ABA member who had been head of the ABA's Audit Committee who gave me an understanding of how his committee had functioned. Dennis had been President of the NBA, American Bar Association (ABA), Mayor of Detroit, Supreme Court Justice of Michigan and Chairman of Dickinson Wright PLLC, a law firm in Detroit.

---

[207] Robert L. Ostertag Obituary - Poughkeepsie Journal (Accessed 20 November 2023)

I participated as an active member in the House of Delegates (2004-2009), where we set policy for the association.

Special Committee on Cameras in the Courtroom (9/7/00) It is interesting to see this debate surface with full force again in the state and federal cases of Donald Trump. I am still not sure what is the best policy. I do think that the public benefited by watching the O.J. Simpson case and the George Floyd murder case on television.

Neither of them carried the deleterious effect on the justice system that televising a Trump case would invite. Televising any one of the Trump cases would, in my opinion, require a judge to be prepared and willing to jail Trump for breach of courtroom decorum. In a jury trial, his behavior would show great disrespect for them, and he would try to use the courtroom as a circus to destroy any authority that would yield power over him.

The past is prologue.

Indeed, that is exactly what he did in the E. Jean Carroll defamation case in New York before Justice Engeron, in state court without a jury.

His case in federal court with Judge Lewis Kaplan and a jury was a different story. In each case he tried to bait the Judge; however, neither Judge bit the bait nor held him in contempt. Judge Kaplan told him aloud that he would not bite the bait and hold him in contempt. The Judge recognized that this would make him a martyr before his cult followers.

I met many wonderful people in the Association and benefitted from their experiences.

In one instance, at one of the NYSBA's annual January meeting, I was sitting next to Alexander Forger, former President of the NYSBA, who had drafted Jacqueline Onassis' will. I had read about it in Fortune magazine some months earlier.[208] I was curious about some issues. He carefully explained that sometimes you make plans for your children,

[208] Susan E. Kuhn, *LESSONS FROM THE WILL OF JACQUELINE KENNEDY ONASSIS*, Fortune, p.23 (July 11, 1994)

but they have other plans. So, he told me that after Jackie passed away, her children disclaimed certain gifts that she had left for them.

Another instance was where the American Bar Association (ABA) planned to give South Africa's Frederik Willem de Klerk a prestigious award. One of my South African colleagues contacted me with documentation from a young man that argued that de Klerk had been involved in the murder of his father.

He also provided me with a document which quoted Nelson Mandela expressing his unhappiness from having to share the Nobel Prize for Peace with de Klerk. I forwarded the information to a friend of mine who had been active in the New York State Bar Association and was continually active in the ABA. That person then conveyed the information to the chairman of the ABA committee who was vetting de Klerk for the award. After they reviewed the material and conducted their investigation, they withdrew their invitation to de Klerk.

This again shows that it is important to get to know people.

Westchester Black Bar Association

These photos show some of the members of the Westchester Black Bar Association (WBBA), and Surrogate Hon. Brandon R. Sall (left top photo, blue shirt 6th from left) (2023)

I served the Westchester Black Bar Association in many capacities.

Director; Chairman of the Board (1987); Outstanding Lawyer Award (2002); Founder's Award (2008), 50-year Community Appreciation Award (2023).

In August of 2023, during my home visit, I attended the WBBA annual picnic and BBQ. Sharon Matthie, a past President of the WBBA[209], drove me to the event, without disclosing a hint of what was about to happen there. The association gave awards to me, Thomasina Laidley-Brown, Chair of the Ossining Democratic Committee, a phenomenal woman who had been instrumental in the Westchester political arena and was responsible for helping many judges of color ascend to the bench in local town and village, city, family, county, and supreme court races; to my friend Bruce Tolbert, a retired Supreme Court Judge, who served with distinction in that role and in many others in the community.

At a time when I was about to prosecute an appeal in state court, when I knew little about appellate practice, Bruce gave me a helpful book on appellate practice and procedure, and to me. I was quite surprised because I did not know we had members of the association who were appellate lawyers.

My plaque reads:

> "Presented to Founding Member Leroy Wilson, Esq. In recognition of 50 years of your selfless dedication and commitment to the bar and to the community - August 19th, 2023."

Unfortunately, I was unable to attend our 50th Gala Dinner celebration on October 27, 2023, as I had returned to Botswana by that time. Sharon thought perhaps I could send a statement which she would read at the dinner. I think that besides Bruce Bozeman, I am the last remaining survivor of the founding group. I understand that the dinner was well attended although they had to re-schedule because of the weather.

She read the statement, with a couple of edits, to the attendees:

---

[209] Lower photo in white shirt and black pants, all the way on the right.)

"STATEMENT FROM LEROY WILSON, JR., ESQ., TO BE READ AT THE CELEBRATION OF THE 50TH ANNIVERSARY OF THE FOUNDING OF THE WESTCHESTER BLACK BAR ASSOCIATION

PRESIDENT JUDGE TIMOTHY LEWIS, MEMBERS OF THE BOARD OF DIRECTORS AND OFFICERS OF THE WESTCHESTER BLACK BAR ASSOCIATION, DISTINGUISHED LADIES AND GENTLEMEN

ALL PROTOCOL OBSERVED

I REGRET THAT I COULD NOT ATTEND THE CELEBRATION TONIGHT, AND, LEST QUESTIONS BE RAISED ABOUT MY ABSENCE ON THIS AUSPICIOUS OCASSION, I STATE SIMPLY THAT I NOW RESIDE IN BOTSWANA, A BEAUTIFUL COUNTRY IN THE SOUTHERN PART OF AFRICA.

HOWEVER, IT WAS MY GREAT PLEASURE TO HAVE BEEN PRESENT IN AUGUST OF THIS YEAR TO ENJOY THE WONDERFUL COMPANY OF MANY OF MY COLLEAGUES AT THE WBBA ANNUAL BARBECUE.

PAST PRSIDENT SHARON MATTHIE DROVE ME TO THE BARBECUE VENUE AND NEVER LET ON THAT THE ASSOCIATION WOULD BE GIVING ME A PLAQUE HONORING MY 50+ YEARS OF SERVICE. GOOD JOB SHARON!

I WAS PLEASED TO SEE THAT MY LONG-STANDING FRIEND, RETIRED JUSTICE BRUCE L. TOLBERT, ALSO RECEIVED AN AWARD.

IN THOSE 50 OR MORE YEARS AGO, ATTORNEY BRUCE BOZEMAN TOLD ME ABOUT A SMALL GROUP OF BLACK ATTORNEYS WHO WERE MEETING FROM TIME TO TIME AT THE OFFICES OF ATTORNEY ARTHUR PULLEY AT HIS OFFICE [SIC]. SINCE HIS OFFICE WAS ALSO DOWNSTAIRS IN HIS RESIDENCE ON 5TH AVENUE IN NEW ROCHELLE,

MS. BERNICE COSEY PULLEY, HIS WIFE, ALSO PREPARED MOUTH-WATERING DINNERS FOR US.

AS I REMEMBER, IN THAT INITIAL GROUP WERE ARTHUR PULLEY, H(IAWATHA) HAWTORNE HARRIS, DANIEL BODDIE, JOSEPH CALENDAR, BRUCE BOZEMAN, AND WARREN JACKSON.OVER TIME. THE LITTLE GROUP GREW TO INCLUDE EVE BUNTING SMITH, CAROLYN MINTER, MICHAEL THOMAS, LARRY SYKES, BRUCE TOLBERT, ROGER AND GAIL RICE, C. DOUGLAS DIXON, G DABIRI, VALERIE SOMMERSVILLE, LARRY SYKES, EDWARD DUDLEY, GARY COOPER, AND DR. ARTHUR T. DAVIDSON, ESQ. (TO NAME A FEW).

I WAS FORTUNATE TO BE ABLE TO INTRODUCE GODFREY L. BINAISA TO THE GROUP WHO ATTENDED MANY OF OUR MEETINGS. GODFREY HAD BEEN THE FIRST ATTORNEY GENERAL OF UGANDA AND LATER PRESIDENT. WE MAINTAINED A LIFELONG RELATIONSHIP UNTIL HIS DEATH IN 2010.I WAS THE ONLY AMERICAN TO DELIVER ONE OF THE EULOGIES AT HIS STATE FUNERAL IN KAMPALA.

AT SOME POINT, I DRAFTED THE ARTICLES OF INCORPORATION AND BYLAWS, MODELED AFTER THOSE OF THE ASSOCIATION OF THE BAR OF THE CITY OF NEW YORK, INC. WE WERE THE ASSOCIATION OF THE BAR OF WESTCHESTER COUNTY,INC. AS I REMEMBER. THE ASSOCIATION THEREAFTER CHANGED ITS NAME TO THE WESTCHESTER BLACK BAR ASSOCIATION.

LITTLE DID I REALIZE THAT FROM THAT SMALL BEGINNING, OUR ASSOCIATION WOULD GROW TO HAVE OVER (100/200) MEMBERS TODAY, SEVERAL OF WHOM HAVE ASCENDED TO THE BENCH AND ARE NOW JUDGES.

AT OUR MEETINGS, WE DID HAVE GUEST SPEAKERS FROM TIME TO TIME. FOR ME, ONE OF THE MOST INTERESTING WAS JUDGE SCOVEL RICHARDSON OF THE UNITED STATES CUSTOMS COURT AND THE UNITED STATES COURT OF INTERNATIONAL TRADE. HE WAS A NEW ROCHELLE NATIVE. HIS TOPIC WAS OUTSIDE OF THE DISCIPLINES WE NORMALLY HEARD.

ONE OF MY ROLES WAS TO IDENTIFY AND INVITE THE KEYNOTE SPEAKER FOR OUR GALAS. SOME I KNEW PERSONALLY; OTHERS I KNEW THROUGH MY 50+ YEARS ATTENDING NATIONAL BAR ASSOCIATION CONVENTIONS. OFF THE TOP OF MY HEAD, THESE INCLUDED JULIAN BOND (WHO WAS MY CLASSMATE AT MOREHOUSE), WILEY BRANTON, THE NAMESAKE OF THE NBA'S ANNUAL SYMPOSIUM, WHO WAS INSTRUMENTAL IN INTEGRATING THE PUBLIC SCHOOLS IN ARKANSAS, JUDGE A. LEON HIGGINBOTHAM , JR. (WHO WAS ARTHUR PULLEY'S SCHOOLMATE AT YALE LAW SCHOOL), JUDGE BARRINGTON D. PARKER (WHO PRESIDED OVER THE JOHN HINCKLEY CASE-HINCKLY WAS TRIED FOR THE ATTEMPTED ASSASINATION OF PRESIDENT RONALD REAGAN.) HIS SON, BARRINGTON D. PARKER, JR., IS A UNITED STATES CIRCUIT COURT JUDGE. OTHER SPEAKERS WERE CALIFORNIA ASSEMBLY SPEAKER WILLIE BROWN, AND REP. MAXINE WATERS. ALL OF THIS IS SUBJECT TO CORRECTION BY THOSE WHO HAVE A CLEARER MEMORY, AND BY THE NOTES AND MINUTES OF OUR MEETINGS OVER THE YEARS AS CONTAINED IN THE FOLDERS THAT I DELIVERED TO MS. MATTHIE.

WARREN JACKSON, WHOSE COLUMNS APPEARED IN THE GANNETT NEWSPAPERS, AND GODFREY L. BINAISA, Q.C., ESQ, FORMER ATTORNEY GENERAL AND PRESIDENT OF UGANDA, ALSO ATTENDED SOME OF OUR MEETINGS.

WHEN I WAS IN NEW YORK, I PRACTICED IN THE STATE AND FEDERAL TRIAL AND APPELLATE COURTS. DURING THE PAST 25 YEARS, MOST OF MY PRACTICE WAS CONCENTRATED IN THE SURROGATE'S COURT OF WESTCHESTER, QUEENS, NEW YORK, AND NASSAU COUNTIES.

PRESENTLY, I AM STILL EXCHANGING IDEAS AND INFORMATION WITH LAWYERS IN VARIOUS AFRICAN COUNTRIES. I HAVE GOTTEN TO KNOW MANY OF THEM FROM PARTICIPATING AS A BAR ASSOCIATION KEYNOTE SPEAKER AT THEIR ANNUAL GENERAL MEETINGS AND ASSISTING IN THE CREATION OF AT LEAST 2 OF THEM – THE EAST AFRICAN LAW SOCIETY (GOES BACK TO CIRCA 1994), AND THE POLOKWANE ASSOCIATION OF ADVOCATES (SOUTH AFRICA)(2016).

I AM NOW A PARTICIPATING MEMBER OF THE PAN AFRICAN LAWYERS UNION (PALU) AND PARTICIPATED ON ONE OF ITS PANELS IN LIVINGSTONE, ZAMBIA IN JULY. ON THAT OCCASION, I WAS PART OF A TWO-MEMBER DELEGATION FROM THE NATIONAL BAR ASSOCIATION TO ATTEND THE SIGNING OF A COOPERATION AND COLLABORATION AGREEMENT BETWEEN THE NBA AND PALU. BARBARA SIMMONS, ESQ. WAS THE OFFICIAL NBA REPRESENTATIVE. THIS AGREEMENT WAS THE RESULT OF A PROCESS THAT LASTED OVER MANY YEARS. PALU IS COMPRISED OF 54 NATIONAL AFRICAN BAR ASSOCIATIONS AND OVER 1000 INDIVIDUAL LAWYERS SPREAD AFRICA AND IN THE DIASPORA.

THANK YOU FOR YOUR KIND ATTENTION, GOD BLESS YOU, AND BON APETIT! "

In August 2025, I was pleased to receive an email introducing Christina T. Hall, Esq., as the newly elected President of the Westchester Black Bar Association. How thrilling it was to see that the organization which I helped found over 50 years ago is continuing to thrive with new leadership.

The Pan African Lawyers Union (PALU)

Since the 1950s, I have been interested in international affairs, particularly with those arising in Africa. Since the early 1970s, I have also been interested in exchanging information and methods between the National Bar Association in the United States and the various bar associations and the law societies in the continent of Africa.

To that end, I became active in the International Law Section of the National Bar Association (ILS). I was a beneficiary of the tutelage of Beverly Baker Kelly and Kendal Tyre.

In April 1995, the NBA sponsored a delegation of twelve lawyers and bar leaders from Ghana, Kenya, Tanzania and Uganda on a thirty-day study tour of the United States. These included; from Uganda : Ms. Harriet Busingye, Mr. John Matovu, Sebalu & Lule Advocates, Mr. John M.M. Mugisha, Muhanguzi, Mugisha & Co. Advocates; from Tanzania: Mrs. Mwandaidi Maajar, Maajar & Rwechungura Law Mr. Mohamed Ismail, Mr. Evarist, Hubert Mbuya; Kenya: Mrs. Lucy M. Kambuni, Law Offices of Kambuni & Githae, Mr. Paul Matheri Wamae, Munoru, Kagiri & Wamae Advocates, Mr. Peter Mubia Mwangi, Law Society of Kenya; from Ghana: Mrs. Dorcas A.F. Coker-Appiah, Mr. Patrick Ambrose Dery, Bimi, Dery & Co., Mr. Jones Victor Mawulom Dotse, Mawulorm Chambers,

One day in the mid-1990s, some of these lawyers met with Deputy Director Maurice Foster at the NBA offices to discuss creating a bar association in East Africa. The next morning I met with them in New York City to discuss some last-minute details. I understand that they went back to Africa and formed the East Africa Law Society, (EALS), now headed by David Sigano (2024). I met David in 2023 in Livingstone, Zambia at the 13th Annual Conference of PALU.

In April 1999, United Nations Secretary-General, Kofi Annan, appointed Beverly Baker-Kelly as Deputy Registrar of the International Criminal Tribunal for Rwanda (ICTR), located in Arusha, Tanzania. This position made her the highest-ranking American at the Rwanda Tribunal. The Tribunal prosecutes those allegedly responsible for the genocide committed in Rwanda.

Maurice Foster recruited NBA Executive Director John Crump to clear away some of the bureaucracy. Maurice was able to get Westlaw to furnish software and hardware through the National Bar Institute to assist the Court in carrying out its functions.

When Harold Pope became NBA President later in the year, Maurice and Harold visited the courts and toured Rwanda.[210] They topped off the visit with a formal dinner with Secretary General Annan, the President of the Courts, and A. Okali, Registrar of the International Criminal Court (ICTR) for Rwanda.

After I made my appearance at the Law Society of South Africa (LSSA) Annual General Meeting in 2012, I asked Muzi if the Law Society maintained a listing of the various law societies and bar associations throughout Africa. He then asked Barbara Whittle, the Communication Manager for the LSSA, to locate and send me the information. She did so and I began contacting all the organizations that were listed to invite them to the National Bar Association annual conferences. Unfortunately, that effort did not result in increased attendance from the continent, but I then began to see the names of some of the African lawyers who were active on the African continent.

After interacting with African lawyers as early as 1973, I arrived at the stage where I made formal contact with Donald Deya, the CEO of

210 On July 27, 2021, at a Covid-19 virtual award banquet, the NBA bestowed its Ronald Harmon Brown Award of International Distinction upon Harold Pope.

the Pan African Lawyers Union (PALU)[211] in 2023. Don had started the Secretariat of the East Africa Law Society (EALS) on 1 June 2002, and that of PALU on 1 January 2010.

Along with Barbara A. Simmons, Esq. of the NBA's International Law Section, Alfreda Robinson, Vanita Banks, George Edwards, George Walker, Simone Williams, Johanna Leblanc, Derick Hart, Darren Riley, Gloria Johnson, and Maurice Foster, we begin in earnest to create relationships between the NBA and PALU by way of a Memorandum of Understanding (PALU MOU).

In addition, Barbara Simmons and Johanna Leblanc are co-chairs of a subcommittee to create a Memorandum of Understanding between the African Continent Free Trade Area Secretariat and the National Bar Association (AFCFTA MOU). NBA President Wiley Adams and AfCFTA Secretary-General Wamkele Mene signed the MOU on April 7, 2025, in Accra, Ghana. Barbara Simmons and Johanna Leblanc attended the ceremony.

Additional active members on this subcommittee are Carl Turpin and Rebekah Ratcliff who are focusing on the ADR aspects of the MOU.

In 2023, Donald Deya, the Executive Director of PALU attended the NBA Annual Meeting in Minneapolis and participated in the meetings.

---

211 https://www.lawyersofafrica.org/ (Accessed 28 January 2025)

Left Don after lunch, right -Don speaking with NBA Chaplain Sheila Boston at the closing Gala Dinner

My Role in Naming the United States Mother Courthouse after Hon. Thurgood Marshall – The Haywood Burns Award (2004)

At about 2:45 PM on December 4, 2003, Peter Sherwin, Chair of the New York State Bar Association's Committee on Civil Rights, called to tell me that the Committee on Minorities in the Professions and the Committee on Civil Rights had jointly selected me as the recipient of the New York State Bar Association's Haywood Burns Memorial Award for 2004. The award was to be presented at a luncheon at the Association's annual meeting on January 28, 2004, at New York Marriott Marquis Hotel in New York, NY. The luncheon was scheduled for approximately 12-2 PM

After receiving the notice, I sent out invitations. Unfortunately, we had a very heavy snowfall in NYC the scheduled day and the event was postponed.to February 10th. On February 10th, 2004, the New York State Bar Association's Civil Rights Committee gave me the State Bar's Haywood Burns Memorial Award.[212]

---

212 Because it is made of glass, it was too difficult to produce a usable image of the award.

Christopher, Me, and Jason at the awards ceremony (2004)

Former Court of Appeals Associate Judge Joseph W. Bellacosa attended, along with Kim and Lorna Foote, who helped me over the years with my computer issues, Peter Sherwin, my sons Jason and Christopher, Michele Hamilton, the owner of Sara Mae Oats, Inc., who gave out cookies, and others.

Some years earlier, when I was Chair of the Civil Rights Committee (1997-2000), I was able, with the help of Gail Wright - Sirmans and others, to have the New York State Bar Association name one of its awards after an outstanding African American lawyer for work in the field of civil rights law. That lawyer was Haywood Burns.

William Haywood Burns (June 15, 1940 – April 2, 1996) was an American lawyer, author, professor, civil rights activist, the second dean of the City University of New York Law School (he served from 1987 until 1994) and a Civil Rights Movement leader.

A fuller description of his life and work is documented in To Be Of Use - W. Haywood Burns (obituary), by Michael Ratner & Judge Eleanor Stein.[213]

One of the cases in which I was tangentially involved with Haywood, was the Attica prison riot case. The Attica Prison Riot,[214] also known as the Attica Prison Rebellion, the Attica Uprising, or the Attica Prison Massacre, took place at the state prison in Attica, New York; it started on September 9, 1971, and ended on September 13 with the highest number of fatalities in the history of United States prison uprisings. Haywood Burns played a major role in the Rebellion, as lead defense counsel for the inmates, and other roles.

I got involved through Fred Hayes, Esq. Fred Hayes had been hired to represent Vernon Lefranque, the first of the inmates to be tried. However, Fred wanted to enjoin the trial from going forward because even though money had been set aside for defense counsel to conduct investigations, none of that money had been given to defense counsel, including Fred. To prepare to defend Mr. Lefranque, Fred needed this money.

He argued that he had not been given the resources to prepare a defense. He wanted me to bring a federal court civil case to request an injunction. At the time I didn't know very much about the Younger v. Harris doctrine[215] which placed certain restrictions on bringing civil actions in federal court to enjoin a criminal proceeding from going forward.

I dutifully prepared my various papers and flew off to Buffalo to have the order to show cause signed and to then serve Judge Ball, and the custodian of the funds. Judge Ball had been assigned to preside over Mr. Lefranque's case. I called Haywood and he gave me a tutorial on how the Younger v. Harris doctrine might apply.

---

213 Michael Ratner and Eleanor Stein, *To Be Of Use - W. Haywood Burns,* 106 The Yale LJ 753 (1996)

214 Vernon Lefranque, Attica - Search (bing.com) (Accessed 23 December 2023)

215 **Younger v. Harris, 401 U.S. 37 (1971)**

The weather in Buffalo was a bit chilly. Grey and overcast.

I filed the action in the United States District Court for the Western District of New York, Judge John Curtin presiding. I established a good rapport with the Judge but, after hearing, he denied my motion to enjoin the criminal proceeding. He and his clerks prepared whatever he needed to prepare for me to docket an emergency appeal from his order to the United States Court of Appeals for the Second Circuit. He had the transcript prepared and gave me the documents that I would need to bring to the clerk in the Second Circuit to hear the emergency appeal the next morning.

The Second Circuit, by a vote of 2 to 1, upheld Judge Curtin. The Circuit Court allowed me a full argument and seemed to appreciate the fact that I had been educated with respect to the Younger doctrine, and that I was prepared to argue it within the context of this case.

This meant that Fred would have to go forward with the defense.

From the smile on his face and general demeanor, Judge Ball was somewhat amused that someone would file a civil action to try to keep him from proceeding to try Mr. Lefranque. When I walked into the courthouse the entrance was fortified by a heavy steel fence contraption that one had to walk through to get to Judge Ball's chambers.

Judge Ball was very pleasant, sitting behind his desk guarded by two policemen standing on each side of him with machine guns. After serving him, I left his chambers and then went to serve the custodian of the funds and who was an official of some kind. He was in the courtroom overseeing the escort of prisoners into the courtroom that morning.

That was a very depressing sight, seeing pale white police officers bringing in these black accused persons who were sort of connected to each other by chains or handcuffs or ropes of some kind. It took me straight back to the remembering seeing captured Africans being led through an African trail or forest with white overseers.

Although Judge Curtin denied the motion, and the Second Circuit upheld his judgment, the custodian released the funds to Fred.

Returning to the main topic here; namely, the naming of the Thurgood Marshall Courthouse I tell the story behind the many hurdles we had to leap across to name the mother United States Courthouse in Manhattan after Thurgood Marshall.

As you will see from the recitals below, it was anything but straightforward. We began the effort in 1996 to have the new White Plains federal courthouse after Justice Marshall. However, we switched to trying to have the United States Courthouse at Foley Square in Manhattan named after him. That Courthouse was opened to the public in 1936 and was designed by Cass Gilbert, who also designed the United States Supreme Court building in Washington, D.C.[216]

After many organizations, including the White Plains-Greenburgh Branch of the NAACP, the Association of Black Lawyers of Westchester County, the National Bar Association, the Society of African American Law Firms, the Westchester County Bar Association, and the New York State Bar Association passed resolutions to have this courthouse renamed the Thurgood Marshall United States Courthouse, President George W. Bush signed the bill to rename the building on Monday, August 20, 2001. The dedication was not held until April 14, 2003.

The "we" included Gail Wright - Sirmans, who had suggested that I succeed her as Chair of the Civil Rights Committee, Thomas Santacrose of the NYSBA administrative office, who was superb with his excellent support, suggestions and preparation of meticulous minutes of our committee meetings, and Josh Pruzansky, who was NYSBA president when the House of Delegates adopted a resolution supporting the naming.

Kathryn McCary, who succeeded me and brilliantly continued to make the case that the courthouse should be named after Thurgood Marshall, Ron Kennedy, assisted by Tom Barletta, who handled legislative affairs for the New York State Bar Association, and gave us his inestimable guidance on how to navigate governmental issues

---

[216] Program Brochure *Dedication of the Thurgood Marshall United States Courthouse, New York City, Monday, April 14, 2003.*

Jason Steinbaum and John Cavelli, of Congr. Eliot Engel's Office worked with us every step of the way in keeping up with what was happening with the votes in Congress. Although I had contacted all the Congressional representatives in our area, Congressman Engel introduced the renaming bill in the U.S. House of Representatives the first time, in 1997.

Ironically, when I dealt with Congressman Engel's local office, the person who helped me was Rachel Miller. Some years earlier, she had worked in my office as a secretary. I also worked with Kris Balderson, one of Senator Hillary Clinton's aides, and of course, Hillary Clinton and Chuck Schumer.

In fact, early in the naming process, I mentioned the idea to Sen. Chuck Schumer at the 2000 swearing in of Ernie Davis as Mayor of Mount Vernon New York. Without hesitation, he said that he would support the idea.

1995-1996-CONCEPTION OF IDEA AND WHITE PLAINS

My idea for naming the United States mother courthouse in New York City originated with the proposal to name the new courthouse planned for White Plains after Thurgood Marshall.

One day, as I entered the temporary federal courthouse in White Plains, then located at 101 East Post Road, White Plains, New York, I saw a model of the then proposed new federal courthouse building for White Plains. I immediately thought that that courthouse could be named after Thurgood Marshall. I was aware that the federal courts judicial center building in Washington DC had been named after Thurgood Marshall and did not know if this would cause a complication.

I realized that we would need to get local and federal political support.

It seemed to me that the most logical first group to pass a resolution to this effect was the White Plains Greenburgh branch of the

NATIONAL ASSOCIATION FOR THE ADVANCEMENT OF COLORED PEOPLE (NAACP). My friend, Lola Hunter, was President of the branch at that time.

For some background, Marshall had opened a law practice in Baltimore but soon joined Charles Hamilton Houston at the NAACP in New York. Houston had been his mentor and teacher at Howard University. They worked together on the segregation case of Missouri ex rel. Gaines v. Canada; after Houston returned to Washington, Marshall took his place as special counsel of the NAACP, and he became director-counsel of the newly formed NAACP Legal Defense and Educational Fund.[217] It was during his tenure at LDF that he and others made their mark as the nation's leading civil rights lawyers. Marshall himself had argued 32 cases before the United states Supreme Court and won 29 of them.[218]

Thurgood Marshall was America's greatest civil rights lawyer.

In 1961, President John F. Kennedy appointed Marshall to the U.S. Court of Appeals for the Second Circuit, where he favored a broad interpretation of constitutional protections. Four years later, President Lyndon Baines Johnson appointed him as the United States Solicitor General.[219]

After serving as the Solicitor General of the United States, President Lyndon Johnson nominated Marshall as a Justice of the United States Supreme Court, where he served for many years.

After conceiving of the idea, I then presented the resolution substantially in the same form to the Association of Black Lawyers of Westchester County, now the Westchester Black Bar Association, the Westchester County Bar Association, the National Bar Association, the Society of African American Law Firms, the National Bar Association, and the New York State Bar Association.

---

[217] Thurgood Marshall - Wikipedia (accessed 23 November 2023)
[218] Id.
[219] Id.

All passed the resolution.

Along with a small group of supporters, I met with congresspeople Hamilton Fish Junior, Ben Gilman, Nita Lowey, Charles Rangel, and Eliot Engel.

Congressman Engel, who was facing a stiff challenge for his seat, took the resolution and ran with it.

Congressman Engel introduced a bill in the House to name the new federal courthouse in White Plains after Thurgood Marshall.

During this period, I also spoke with Thurgood Marshall Junior and learned that there was a high school in the vicinity of Washington DC who had been renamed after Thurgood Marshall. I think that the competing name for naming the school was John Jay, the first Chief Justice. Jay was also a native of Westchester County, New York.

When we first circulated the idea of naming the courthouse in White Plains after Marshall, someone from the Westchester County Bar Association suggested that perhaps the White Plains should be named after John Jay as well. But that person acquiesced in naming the White Plains courthouse after Marshall. The White Plains courthouse was ultimately named after Judge Charles Brieant, who had served as judge for the White Plains courthouse for many years. I appeared many times before Judge Brieant.

Although the House twice passed a bill to name the courthouse after Marshall, Senator Patrick Moynihan would not support the bill in the Senate. His office gave us many reasons the Senator could not support the bill, including that the Federal Judicial Center had already been named after Marshall. In the end, we overcame all of Sen. Moynihan's objections. We persevered and were able to have the mother U.S. courthouse in Manhattan named after Marshall despite Sen. Moynihan's lack of genuine support.

1996-1997
JULY 1997[220]

After many delays in trying to get courthouse in White Plains named after Justice Marshall, Cora Walker, Esq., and I discussed a change in focus, to have the mother U.S. Courthouse in Manhattan named after Justice Marshall. Cora was a pioneering black woman attorney based in Harlem, and stalwart member of the National Bar Association.

Cora Walker (Harlem) on left, and Carolyn Howard (Florida) on right during an NBA meeting

John Cavelli of Cong. Engel's office called to tell me that Rep. Engel would be introducing a bill to have the mother United States Courthouse at Foley Square in Manhattan named after Justice Marshall. He asked for a resolution in support of the bill from the New York State Bar Association (NYSBA). He had the others.

SEPTEMBER 10, 1997

The Civil Rights Committee met in the offices of Conrad Harper[221] at Simpson Thatcher & Bartlett to adopt a resolution that would wend

---

[220] See Thomas Santacroce's September 18, 1997, Letter to John Williamson

[221] Conrad was one of the first African American partners in a white Wall Street firm. Mr. Harper joined Simpson Thacher in 1971 and was elected as the Firm's

its way through the NYSBA Executive Committee and its processes for a full vote by the House of Delegates. I was Chair of the Committee at that time.

Conrad Harper was one of the first black partners on Wall Street, after having had a stellar career as a civil rights lawyer with the NAACP Legal Defense & Educational Fund. Charles Hamilton Houston was his guiding light. He told me that Whitney North Seymour had been a protector in one particularly egregious racist attack on him. The offender was removed from his position. The offender never knew the reason. Seymour was a partner at Simpson Thacher.[222]

The Civil Rights Committee unanimously adopted the resolution and faxed it to Mr. Cavelli on September 26,1997 for his review and presentation to Rep. Engel.

The committee members present at the meeting in person were Peter Bain, Diane Gatewood, Loren Gesinsky, William Miles, Stephanie McGregor, and Thomas Terrizzi. Those present via telephone were Robert Heverly, Pamela Katz, Kathyrn McCary, Kenneth Ritzenberg, and Robert Silverstein. Tom Santacrose, NYSBA Committee Staff Liaison, also attended the meeting in person.

OCTOBER 30, 1997

Mr. Cavelli faxed a copy of H.R. 2187 to me that Cong. Engel proposed to introduce to name the United States Courthouse at Foley Square after the late justice Thurgood Marshall. The cosponsors of the bill were New York Congresspersons Nadler, Rangel, Velasquez, and Maloney.

---

first African American partner in 1974. Conrad Harper Receives Lifetime Achievement Award (Accessed 08 September 2025)

[222] https://www.nytimes.com/2019/06/29/obituaries/whitney-north-seymour-jr-dead.html (Accessed 09 February 2024).

NOVEMBER 1, 1997

I appeared at the New York State Bar Association House of Delegates meeting to ask them to support the proposed resolution and bill and to present it to the body.

On behalf of its then 60,000 members, the House of Delegates passed the resolution unanimously, including a friendly amendment offered by NYSBA Past President Stephen Crane to list the address of the building as 40 Foley Square. We accepted the amendment.

NOVEMBER 25, 1997

NYSBA President Josh Pruzansky sent a letter to the Editor of the New York Times telling the public that the New York State Bar Association had passed the resolution to support the naming of The US Courthouse at 40 Foley Square after Thurgood Marshall. The building was designed by Cass Gilbert, one of America's foremost architects, but had not been named since it was erected in 1935.

DECEMBER 8, 1997

Katherine David called to tell me that Congressman Engel would be asking the appropriate subcommittee to take up the bill as soon as Congress reconvened.

NOVEMBER 1998

Many months would pass with little reported activity on this bill. However, Congressman Chuck Schumer from Brooklyn defeated Senator Al D'Amato and he became New York's junior senator. Senator Daniel Patrick Moynihan was the New York State senior senator at that time.

NOVEMBER 5, 1998

At a meeting in one of the private dining rooms at the United Nations, I reported to the Civil Rights Committee that Congressman Engel's bill had passed the House, but it did not have a sponsor in the Senate.

MARCH 23, 1999

After the new Congress convened in early 1999, Congressman Engel reintroduced the bill as H.R. 130 in the new Congress. H.R. 130 passed the house.

MARCH 24, 1999

The House passed bill H.R. 130 was then sent to the Senate Committee on the Environment and Public Works.

APRIL 1999

Thomas Rice, the new NYSBA President reappointed me as Chair of the Civil Rights Committee.

At this time, Ron Kennedy replaced Tom Santacrose as the NYS liaison to our committee. Both were excellent support to our section.

MAY 14, 1999

Ron Kennedy reported that he had contacted Senator Schumer's office to request his assistance in getting H.R. 130 passed in the Senate.

NOVEMBER 15-WEEK OF

Ron reports that he and Tom Barletta met with the congressional staff to discuss H. R. 130.

JANUARY 1, 2000

At Ernie Davis's inauguration on New Year's Day, as Mayor of Mount Vernon for his second term, I introduced myself to Congressman Engel, whose support we already had, and then I introduced myself to Sen. - elect Schumer to ask for his support of H. R. 130. Without hesitation, Senator Schumer enthusiastically said that he would support H.R.130.

JANUARY 26, 2000

I reported these contacts to the Committee at the 2000 NYSBA annual meeting, held at the Marriott Marquis in New York City.

Those present at the meeting were Neil Angel; Peter Bain; Diane Ridley Gatewood; Donald Mapp; Diane McFadden; William Miles; and Ron Kennedy.

I made a follow-up call to senator Schumer's office and spoke with Ms. Ipyana Critton.

MAY 11, 2000

The committee met at the Princeton Club of New York. About that time the composition of the Committee had changed a bit there were Ms. McFadden, Msss. Archer, Catherine McCary, Diane Gatewood, Stephanie McGregor and Mr. Peter Bain.

I reported on the excellent conversations that I had with Jason Steinbaum in Cong. Engel's D.C. office.

AUGUST 8, 2000

Senator Daniel Patrick Moynihan was New York's Senior Senator at that point, and I began to make telephone calls to his office. The person that I was supposed to speak to was Tony Bullock.

I am not sure that I spoke with him on this occasion, but the next day I did speak with Susan, Tony Bullock's assistant.

When I spoke with Susan in Senator Moynihan's office, I explained my lack of support from his office. She told me that Thurgood Marshall already had an office building named after him in Washington DC and that we could not name more than one federal building after the same person. I disputed this.

Fortunately, by this time, I had already learned (probably from Jason Steinbaum) that this is not true. There were several facilities named after Sen. Strom Thurmond (S.C.)

I reported that I called Senator Strom Thurmond's office to confirm what I had been told. They confirmed it.

In this connection, Congressman Jim Clyburn (S.C.) told me an amusing story about Strom Thurmond memorials.

This story unfolds as follows. During her tenure as President of the National Bar Association (1998-1999), Beverly McQueary Smith appointed me as Chair of her Awards Committee.

In 1999, I was chairing the awards portion of our NBA program which was held in Kiawah Islands in South Carolina.

I was seated next to Congressman Clyburn. I was telling him about the lack of support that I had been getting from Senator Moynihan's office, including them telling me that one person could not have more than one federal facility named after him. I told him that I had checked with Senator Thurmond 's office and confirmed that that was not true because several facilities had been named after Senator Thurmond.

Congressman Clyburn then told me that they had been trying to get a new federal courthouse in Columbia SC named after Judge Matthew Perry an African American. Sen. Thurmond was resisting that effort. Thurmond had already had the federal courthouse in Charleston named after him, but he wanted to have the new courthouse in Columbia named the Strom Thurmond Courthouse Annex at Columbia.

Congressman Clyburn said that after doing some research they found that Congress had never passed any legislation designating the federal courthouse in Charleston after Strom Thurmond. So, he sent a note to Sen. Thurmond telling him what he had found. Almost immediately, he received a handwritten note response to "Jim" from "Strom" telling him that he had no objection to naming the courthouse in Columbia after Judge Matthew Perry.

Sen. Moynihan's office threw another obstacle in our way. They told me that we also needed to get the support of the Chief Judge for the Second Circuit. I was fairly sure that this would not be a problem since the Chief Judge had been one of Justice Marshall's clerks.

AUGUST 12, 2000

Meantime, the Board of Directors of the National Bar Association passed a resolution unanimously to name the United States Federal Courthouse at 40 Center St. at Foley Square in New York City NY "Thurgood Marshall United States Courthouse, and that they place a suitable statue or plaque in front of the courthouse in honor of Thurgood Marshall."

As you will see, we were ultimately successful in having the courthouse named after Thurgood Marshall, but as far as I am aware there is still no statue or plaque in front of the courthouse.

AUGUST 23, 2000

Kathryn McCary succeeded me as Chair of the Civil Rights Committee and took up the fight. We were fortunate to have such an able leader to carry our issues forward.

Kathryn and I telephoned Ipyana Critton, a staff member in Senator Schumer's Washington DC office to discuss the delays. This was the beginning of the final days of negotiations. In response to a comment that Kathryn made, Ms. Critton told us that she had not seen any letters of support written to the Senator.

During the discussion she said that she would speak to her legislative director. I don't think we ever knew who this person was. She assured us that the Senator supported the bill.

After the call with Ms. Critton, Kathryn sent an e-mail to Paul Hassett, the new President of the New York State Bar Association. She recounted our conversation with Ms. Critton and asked Paul if he would send the same letter to Senator Schumer that he had sent to Senator Moynihan asking for his support.

President Hassett responded to Kathryn's e-mail as follows:

"Tom Barletta wrote to Schumer on that issue in May '99 and Ipyana called Tom later in the year to discuss it. Her memory may be subject to the same lapses as mine.

In any case the letter has now been sent to Senator Schumer with a copy to you."

Ms. Critton suggested that we write to Sen. Robert Smith (N.H.), Chairman of the Senate Environment and Public Works Committee and to Max Bacchus (Montana), the ranking minority member to get their support.

We then spoke with Tony Bullock, Sen. Moynihan's Chief of Staff. Kathryn pointedly asked him what was holding up action on the bill. He told us that Sen. Moynihan supported the bill, but the main objections came from a committee staff person; presumably, the Committee on Environment and Public Works. Sen. Moynihan was a member of that Committee.

Tony Bullock also told us that the committee staff member told him that one building in Washington DC had been named after Thurgood Marshall and that was enough. Further, there were only so many buildings that people could be named after, and that there had been some objections from judges in the Southern District of New York. He then said that the Committee likes to see that there are no objections. This is the first time we had heard of this and didn't believe some of it.

He explained that Senator Moynihan was the ranking member on the Finance Committee and could not be present at the meeting of the Senate Environment and Public Works Committee because they were scheduled for the same day. We reminded him that there were only five weeks left before there was a new Congress, which would require the re-introduction of the bill in both houses. He gave us the address to send the letter to the Senate Environment and Public Works Committee, Room 410 in the Dirksen building.

Following Tony Bullock's suggestion, Kathryn and I telephoned Chief Judge Ralph Winter's chambers to explain the project to his staff and ask for his support.

We would need to act quickly because Judge Winter was soon to take Senior Status.

However, it was fortuitous that Chief Judge Winter had been one of Judge Marshall's Clerks when he served on the United States Court of Appeals for the Second Circuit.

Meantime, Jason Steinbaum of Congressman Engel's office sent me a 4-page fax listing multiple facilities that have been named after the same person. This list did not include the Strom Thurmond facilities. I learned from my call to Se. Thurmond's office in Columbia, South Carolina (1-(803) 765-5494) at about the same time, that Thurmond had several public facilities named after him.

Jason also suggested that I send a copy of the Sen. Smith letter to him. I expanded this suggestion to also send the Smith letter to all members of the Environment and Public Works Committee.

Kathryn suggested that she would copy Senators Moynihan and Schumer on the Smith letter, as well as NYSBA President Paul Hassett.

Meantime, the Senate was about to adjourn.

AUGUST 24, 2000

Following our phone call to Chief Judge Winter's chambers, Kathryn faxed a copy of H.R. 130 passed by the House to his chambers.

Kathryn, as new chair of our committee, and I, worked together on the text of the letter that we sent to Senator Robert Smith of New Hampshire and Senator Max Baccus of Montana as Chair and Ranking Minority Member, respectively, of the Senate Committee on Environment and Public Works, asking that they work to report H.R. 130 out of committee.

Because of the critical nature of this letter, I have set it out in full below. Kathryn sent the letter on official NYSBA letterhead.

"RE: Bill Number H.R. 130

Dear Senators Smith and Baccus:

I write, on behalf of the Civil Rights Committee of the New York State Bar Association to urge you to send Bill Number H.R. 130 to the Senate floor for action. This bill would designate the United States Courthouse located at 40 Centre St. in New York City the "Thurgood Marshall United States Courthouse," an appropriate act to honor Justice Marshall, who both practiced as a lawyer and sat as a judge in that courthouse for many years.

The House of Delegates of the New York State Bar Association proposed this action three years ago; a number of other national and local organizations have passed similar resolutions. The House of Representatives passed H.R. 130 on March 23, 1999, almost a year and a half ago. The bill was referred to the Senate on March 24, 1999, and has yet to be reported out of committee for the consideration of that body as a whole. There is some urgency to act on H.R. 130 since Congress will adjourn on or about October 6, 2000, and, if the bill is not enacted in this session, it will have to go through the entire process again.

We are unable to understand the reason for the delay in acting on this surely non-controversial bill to honor a great jurist and great American. We are particularly puzzled because at least one other naming bill, first introduced in April of this year, has already been passed by both houses and signed into law. If it is not possible to report H.R. 130 out of the Committee at this time, we would be grateful for a clear explanation of the reasons for the delay.

It has been suggested to us that there may be some concern over naming another building for Justice Marshall, inasmuch as Congress named a new Federal office building for him within the last few years. We would note, however, that many political figures - including Richard Russell, George Mahon, and Strom Thurmond - have multiple federal buildings named after them. I attach a brief list found by one of our committee members in a quick search of the GSA database.[223] We would submit that Justice Marshall's place in history is at least as illustrious as that of any of those already honored by multiple designations.

Of course, I would be delighted to receive a letter from you telling me that your committee has acted favorably on HR 130 and that you have sent the bill to the Senate for its consideration and approval. In any event, please let me hear from you as soon as possible so that I can report the status of this matter to the 67,000 members of the New York State Bar Association through our President, Paul Hassett.

---

[223] This list does not include the Strom Thurmond Federal Office Building in Columbia, South Carolina, the Strom Thurmond Support Center at Fort Jackson, South Carolina, or the section of Interstate Route20 designated for Senator Thurmond.

AUGUST 24, 2000

We followed up by Kathryn sending a fax to Chief Judge Winter asking for his support. We also mailed copies of the letter to all the committee members, to Senators Moynihan and Schumer, Congressman Engel, African American bar associations around the country, and to others who were constituents of the committee members to try to get the committee to report out the bill, H.R. 130.

Meantime, we began to solicit support from people we knew to be interested.

AUGUST 25, 2000

I sent a follow-up fax to Elaine Jones, Esq. c/o Miss N. Lewis. Elaine had been the became first female director-counsel and president of the NAACP Legal Defense and Education Fund in 1993. So, I sent her a copy of H.R. 130 as well as the list of multiple buildings named after one individual and the list of the members of Senator Smith's Committee on the Environment and Public Works. I also noted that, in addition to the list, there were also two buildings or facilities named after Strom Thurmond in South Carolina.

AUGUST 29, 2000

I faxed a letter to Evett L. Simmons, Esq., the then President of the National Bar Association (NBA) asking her to send a letter of support to Senators Moynihan and Schumer and Representative Engel, and to copy the members of the Senate Environment and Public Works Committee.

Pursuant to Evett's suggestion, I also wrote a letter to Marc Douthit, Esq., President of the Florida Bar Association asking for his support. He was also a constituent of senator Robert Graham, a member of the committee. We asked that he copy Senator Graham. I cannot be sure if the letter reached him because of a possible error in his address. I sent it to 550 NW 124th Street, Miami, whereas publications list him at 550 NE 124th Street, Miami. In any case, I did not hear from him.

SEPTEMBER 7, 2000

I received a copy of Chief Judge Winter's letter, of this date, to the Honorable Robert Smith, United States Senator, Chair, Senate Committee on the Environment and Public Works. Because of the critical importance of this letter, given the tortuous history that this renaming bill had up to this point, I recite Chief Judge Winter's letter in full:

"Dear Senator Smith:

I write in enthusiastic support of H. R. 130, now pending in your Committee, that would name the United States Courthouse at 40 Centre Street, New York City, the "Thurgood Marshall United States Courthouse."

Justice Marshall was, in my view, and in the view of most Americans, an historic figure. He was well known as a champion of civil rights in the courts of law but also played a major role in causing the court of public opinion to view the cause of civil rights as a mainstream movement in the interest of all citizens. These accomplishments alone would have constituted a magnificent career for most persons, but he then went on to serve with distinction as a United States Circuit Judge, Solicitor General, and Associate Justice of the Supreme Court.

Justice Marshall's roll in our history alone suffices to justify pasage [sic] of this legislation. However, it is particularly appropriate that the 40 Centre St. courthouse be named after him. That courthouse is where my court, the United States Court of Appeals for the Second Circuit, hears cases. Justice Marshall served as a judge of that court before becoming Solicitor General and a Justice of the Supreme Court. During his service on the court of appeals, his chambers were in the 40 Centre St. building. Moreover, New York City was his home and the principal location of the NAACP Legal Defense Fund, Inc., where he practiced law for many years.

I therefore urge you to support this legislation.

Sincerely,

/S/

Ralph K. Winter

Chief Judge"

I note, *en passant*, that Judge Winter had also served as a law clerk for Judge Thurgood Marshall of the United States Court of Appeals for the Second Circuit from 1961 to 1962.

SEPTEMBER 12, 2000

Contance Slaughter – Harvey, Esq., President of the Magnolia Bar Association, Inc. in Mississippi, sent me a letter saying in part,

"Please know members of the Magnolia Bar Association whole heartily support the Thurgood Marshall Courthouse Resolution passed at the recent National Bar Association Convention. Furthermore, we intend to make certain that the good work and the positive and committed life of our beloved Thurgood Marshall is recognized and becomes a part of our legacy. We intend to make certain that the United States Courthouse at 40 Centre Street, Foley Square, New York is named after the late Justice Thurgood Marshall. We, in Mississippi, owe Justice Marshall so very much and we intend to give credence to his work in this effort.

Please know that we are contacting Senator Trent Lott (R-Miss.) and asking for his support of this well-deserved effort and honor in memory of the work and the life of the late Justice Thurgood Marshall."

The Magnolia Bar Association, Inc. is a National Bar Association affiliate chapter located in the State of Mississippi.

Attorney Harvey, on behalf of the Magnolia Bar Association, Inc., followed up by writing a letter to chairman Smith and ranking member Baccus asking that they send bill number H.R. 130 to the Senate floor for immediate action.

Her letter stated " we trust that you will understand the urgency of this matter and request that you act on this non-controversial bill to honor a great jurist and Great American. We in Mississippi are especially concerned because of the assistance Justice Marshall provided us and our parents in obtaining full citizenship. He left a legacy not only in New York but in Mississippi as well."

She also stated that "We look forward to hearing from you and your committee with the report that you have acted favorably on H.R. 130 and that you have sent the bill to the Senate for consideration and approval. We hope that we can report to our membership positive action concerning the status of HR130."

She copied Senator Trent Lott, Congressman Bennie Thompson, NBA President Evett Simmons, me and Winston Kidd Esq. (I'm assuming Winston was an officer of the Magnolia Bar Association)

SEPTEMBER 13, 2000

My friend, Lola Hunter, President of the White Plains/Greenburgh branch of the NAACP, also wrote a letter to Senators Smith and Baccus, patterned after Kathryn McCary's letter, asking them to send bill number H.R. 130 to the Senate floor for action. I was active in this branch for many years.

SEPTEMBER 28, 2000

The New York Daily news published Catherine McCary's note as follows:

"Do Him Justice

Albany: It would be a fitting act of recognition to name the U.S. Courthouse at 40 Centre St. after Justice Thurgood Marshall. He spent a great deal of time there, both as a lawyer and a judge. Sen. Chuck Schumer should show the same leadership on this matter as he did when sponsoring similar legislation to rename the Pearl St. courthouse after retiring senator Daniel Moynihan."

(The opinion piece identified Kathryn as the chairwoman of the New York State Bar Association. That would have been nice, except that she was a chair of the New York State Bar Association's Committee on Civil Rights)

OCTOBER 2000

J. Stewart Moore, President of the Amistad Suffolk County Black Bar Association sent me a note saying that he had received my letter asking for their support of H.R. 130 and that he would present it to the Amistad Board.

NOVEMBER 2, 2000

The New York Times, By Eric Schmitt,[224] reports that Senator Moynihan's office was caught up in one of several fights to name federal courthouses in New York, California, and Washington State, none of which involved the U.S. Courthouse at 40 Centre Street, Foley Square.

To me this was a rather curious omission.

The article stated that "Naming courthouses, post offices and other federal buildings is one of the most routine acts of business Congress conducts-the legislative equivalent of licking stamps. Dozens are named every year, usually by acclamation."

The New York courthouse in question was a proposed new courthouse in Long Island that Representative Rick A. Lazio, a Long Island

224 The New York Times NATIONAL, Thursday, November 2, 2000, p. A29

Republican, wanted to name after Theodore Roosevelt. At the time Mr. Lazio was running against Hillary Clinton for senator. In the end, that courthouse was not named after Theodore Roosevelt.

However, in 2008, the United States Courthouse at 225 Cadman Plaza, Brooklyn, N.Y. was renamed the Theodore Roosevelt United States Courthouse, It houses the U.S. District Court for the Eastern District of New York, with President George W. Bush signing the legislation into law

Relevant to our proposal to name the US courthouse at 40 Centre St. after Justice Thurgood Marshall, was Mr. Schmitt's observation that "Senator Moynihan should know. By coincidence, a federal courthouse in Lower Manhattan will be dedicated in his honor In December, after a bill sponsored by Senator Charles E. Schumer, a fellow New York Democrat, breezed through Congress this summer."

The article also quotes Mr. Tony Bullock extensively, who had set up obstacles as we went along trying to have the US courthouse in Manhattan named after Justice Thurgood Marshall. Bullock did the same thing in the Lazio-Clinton fight, arguing against Mr. Lazio.

NOVEMBER 2000

After Hillary Clinton is elected as the junior senator from New York, Congressman Engel's office asks her to sponsor the Marshall bill in the Senate. She immediately did so.

MARCH 13, 2001

After the new Congress convened in 2001, Congressman Engel reintroduced H.R.130 as a new H.R. 988 (H.R.988 - 107th Congress (2001-2002): To designate the United States courthouse located at 40 Centre Street in New York, New York, as the "Thurgood Marshall United States Courthouse". | Congress.gov | Library of Congress) (Accessed 07 December 2023)

MARCH 22, 2001

On this date the New York Law Journal reports that Senators Clinton and Schumer had introduced legislation on March 21st, 2001, to name the US courthouse at 40 Centre St., Foley Square after Justice Thurgood Marshall.

JUNE 19, 2001

Rachel Miller, in Congressman Engel's office, called to tell me that he had contacted Congressman Costello on the House Transportation and infrastructure subcommittee to ask him to mark up the Thurgood Marshall naming bill so that it could be sent to the floor of the House.

By coincidence, Rachel had also worked for me for short while before she went to work for Congressman Engel.

JULY 18, 2001

Khris Balderson called me from Senator Clinton's office, and I also spoke with Rachel from Congressman Engel's office. They both told me that they are working to get the bill out of the Senate Environment and Public Works Committee. Mr. Balderson was Sen. Clinton's Legislative Director. By this time, Senator Jeffords (Ind. Vermont) had become Chairman of the committee. He tended to caucus with the Democrats, beginning in 2001.

JULY 26, 2001

H.R.988 - 107th Congress (2001-2002): To designate the United States courthouse located at 40 Centre Street in New York, New York, as the "Thurgood Marshall United States Courthouse". | Congress.gov | Library of Congress[225]

[225] (Reported to House without amendment (07/26/2001 - Accessed 07 Dec 2023)

AUGUST 3, 2001

Rachel called me while I was attending the National Bar Association convention in Dallas TX to tell me that the House passed the new Thurgood Marshall courthouse naming bill the night before.

The Senate also passed the bill H.R. 988 on August 3, 2002. (Text - H.R.988 - 107th Congress (2001-2002): To designate the United States courthouse located at 40 Centre Street in New York, New York, as the "Thurgood Marshall United States Courthouse". | Congress.gov | Library of Congress)(Accessed 07 December 2023)

AUGUST 4, 2001

Two New York newspapers, the Daily News and The Post, report that the Senate that passed the legislation the day before to name the courthouse after Thurgood Marshall, with the Daily News noting that "the measure got off to a rocky start in March, after Clinton surprised Schumer with her plan to put Marshall's name on the courthouse. Schumer had considered naming it for Constance Baker Motley the first female African American federal judge." The Daily News then reported that Senator Schumer immediately backed the measure.

Senator Schumer faced a political dilemma.

Some years earlier, Senator Moynihan had sent Judge Constance Baker Motley a telegram[226] to tell her that he would sponsor legislation to name the new United States Courthouse at 500 Pearl St. after her. However, after he retired, knowing that we have been fighting to have The United States courthouse at 40 Centre Street named after Justice Marshall, and there was no certainty that he would have the proposed

[226] Wilson Email to Conrad Harper dated 25 August 2001. Personal files. (file:///D:/THUSO%20EXTRACTION/Documents/memorandum%20of%20law- state/Bar%20Associations/wilson%20reply%20To%20Conrad%20K%20Harper%20re%20Marshall%20bill.htm) (Accessed 08 December 2023). [On 12 Feb 2024, I moved all the Thuso Extraction Thurgood Marshall background documents to Memoir and Morehouse after I discovered they were misfiled.]

restored Penn Station post office named after him, and since Senator Clinton had honored Congressman Engel's request to support our efforts, and since Senator Moynihan wanted a building named after himself, Senator Schumer had little choice but to sponsor the legislation to name the courthouse building at 500 Pearl St. after Senator Moynihan. This upended his promise to Judge Motley.

Had it not been for Senator Clinton, we would not have succeeded in having the 40 Centre St. building named after Justice Thurgood Marshall.

The Jury Room in the Daniel Patrick Moynihan United States Courthouse located at 500 Pearl St. in New York City is named after Judge Constance Baker Motley, who was the first black woman to be appointed to a lifetime judgeship under Article III of the Constitution of the United States.[227]

Judge Motley learned to practice law under the tutelage of Justice Marshal when he was the Director Counsel of the NAACP Legal Defense and Educational fund.

AUGUST 10, 2001

H.R. 988 was presented to President George W. Bush. (Actions - H.R.988 - 107th Congress (2001-2002): To designate the United States courthouse located at 40 Centre Street in New York, New York, as the "Thurgood Marshall United States Courthouse". | Congress.gov | Library of Congress (Accessed 07 December 2023)

AUGUST 20, 2001

Ten days later, President Bush signed it, and H.R. 988 became Public Law No: 107-33. (All Actions) (https://www.congress.gov/bill/107th-congress/house-bill/988; accessed 07 December 2023).

[227] (nysd.uscourts.gov - accessed 07 December 2023)

AUGUST 23, 2001

The NYSBA's Ron Kennedy called me to tell me that President Bush had signed the Thurgood Marshall courthouse naming bill on August 20th while he was in Crawford, TX.

I then telephoned Khris Balderson, Senator Clinton's legislative director, and Jason Steinbaum or Rachel Miller, of Congressman Engel's office. Neither office had heard that President Bush had signed H.R. 988 naming the US courthouse at Foley 40 Centre Street after Thurgood Marshall. My recollection is the President Bush signed the bill at night, with no publicity.

AUGUST 24, 2001

I sent an email to Kathryn McCary telling her what I had just learned.

Kathryn then wrote to me exploring what the next steps will be and said that if there is an opportunity for is there any ceremony "But I have to admit, if there is any opportunity for a signing ceremony you could attend, I think that would be grand, since this truly has been your baby for so long."

In its news release the NYSBA quotes Kathryn McCary: "McCary credits the committee's immediate past chair, Leroy Wilson Jr. of White Plains for his hard work in initiating, actively pursuing and vigorously monitoring the process."[228]

---

[228] NYSBA News Release *Manhattan Courthouse Renamed in Honor of First African-American U.S. Supreme Court Justice* , August 23, 2001; New York, NY CARIB NEWS, New York City Met Area, *Honoring of The First African American Named U. S. Supreme Court Justice,* August 28, 2001; Legislative Gazette (Albany, NY), *Manhattan courthouse renamed for Marshall,* September 4, 2001; Country Folks New England Ed Palatine Bridge, NY, *Congress Moves to Rename Manhattan Courthouse in Honor of First African American Named US Supreme Court Justice,* Sep 10, 2001; Westchester County Press, *Manhattan Courthouse Renamed in Honor of First African American U.S. Supreme Court Justice, October 18,2001, page 5.*

The bill was sponsored by New York Sens. Hillary Rodham Clinton and Charles Schumer, both Democrats, in the Senate. Rep. Eliot Engel, D-Bronx, was the lead sponsor of the bill in the House.[229]

This bill was Clinton's first to pass the Senate.[230]

Meanwhile, while I was pursuing the renaming of the U.S. Courthouse, my friend, Conrad Harper, was raising funds for a portrait of Thurgood Marshall to hang at the Association of the Bar of New York on 44th Street in New York City.

After noting several parallel paths that we travelled during part of our lives, he wrote[231]

> "I shall send you the type of solicitation letter which I have been using to raise money for a portrait of Justice Marshall to hang at the Association of the Bar. Conrad"

I then sent a note[232] to Conrad which memorialized the connections among Justice Marshall, Conrad, and our mutual friend Gail Wright-Sirmans, i.e.

> "Conrad, The one and only time that I met Thurgood was at the ABCNY[233] when you were President[234]. Gail Wright-Sirmans brought me into the dining [sic] room and introduced me to him. You were sitting next to him. By the way, I drafted the final

---

229 Newsday.com *Federal courthouse renamed in honor of Thurgood Marshall, August 23, 2001,* http://www.newday.com/news/local/wire/ny-bc-ny-brf--marshall-court0823aug23.story (Accessed ____)

230 Id.

231 Harper to Wilson email dated August 24, 2001- Personal files D:\THUSO EXTRACTION\Documents\memorandum of law-state\Bar Associations (Accessed 08 December 2023.) [On 12 Feb 2024, I moved all the Thuso Extraction Thurgood Marshall background documents to Memoir and Morehouse after I discovered they were misfiled.]

232 Wilson-Harper RE New York State Bar Press Release-Thurgood Marshall Courthouse.txt. D:\THUSO EXTRACTION\Documents\memorandum of law-state\Bar Associations [On 12 Feb 2024, I moved all the Thuso Extraction Thurgood Marshall background documents to Memoir and Morehouse after I discovered they were misfiled.]

233 Association of the Bar of the City of New York.

234 1990-1992.

version of the NYSBA support for the naming bill in your firm's conference room at Simpson Thacher & Bartlett.

My next project will be to raise funds to build a statue or to place a plaque in front of the building."

AUGUST 25, 2001

In response to an inquiry that Conrad made to me, I explained Sen. Moynihan's failure to act, and the reasons I think he failed to act:

"Conrad-no, Engel is a Democrat, representing a portion of Westchester (including Mount Vernon and Yonkers). A possible rational follows. Engel is the sponsor of both original bills in the House to name the courthouse in White Plains after Marshall and when that did not work out, the bill to name 40 Centre Street after Marshall. Although the White Plains bill passed the House 2 or 3 times, Sen. Moynihan never moved it or tried to move it in the Senate. The House also passed the 40 Centre Street bill; again, Moynihan did nothing and when we met all of the various excuses that he put forward, he still did nothing. I think he lured Schumer into a trap by getting Schumer to name 500 Pearl Street after himself-after he had sent a telegram to Motley that he would sponsor legislation to name 500 Pearl after her. He then must have persuaded Schumer to ignore Marshall and try to have 40 Centre named after her. This was after I had gotten a personal commitment from Schumer in January 2000 to introduce the Marshall 40 Centre Street bill in the Senate, after it had already passed the House. Hillary beat Schumer to the punch when she introduced the 40 Centre Street bill in the Senate"[235].

[235]Leroy Wilson Jr personal files Re: Thurgood Marshall Courthouse. August 25, 2001: 00:14:46 (D:\THUSO EXTRACTION\Documents\memorandum of law-state\Bar Associations) (Accessed 08 December 2023) [On 12 Feb 2024, I moved all the Thuso Extraction Thurgood Marshall background documents to Memoir and Morehouse after I discovered they were misfiled.]

NOVEMBER 16, 2001

I sent a letter to Kathryn McCary telling her that I had just spoken to Rachel and that Rachel told me the dedication of the renamed building would probably take place in the Spring, because she was aware that President Bush was trying to clear his schedule to attend.

She also told me that signage issues and placing the plaque and statue in front of the courthouse rested with the GSA.

I copied Lola Hunter (White Plains/Greenburgh NAACP chapter), Arlene Gordon Oliver (NBA member), and Michael Rosier (NBA President).

APRIL 14, 2003

A public ceremony was held at the Courthouse on Monday, April 14, 2003, to rename the United States Courthouse at 40 Centre Street, Foley Square, New York, NY to honor Thurgood Marshall.[236] The Dedication program booklet gives an extensive history of Justice Marshall and that of the Courthouse itself.[237]

Wikipedia tells us that "The United States Courthouse originally did not have an official name. In 1999, the United States Congress proposed renaming the courthouse after the late Supreme Court of the United States, Justice Thurgood Marshall. Before being elevated to the Supreme Court, Marshall had worked at the courthouse from 1961 to 1965 as a judge of the Second Circuit Court of Appeals. The United States Congress passed a bill in 2001, renaming the building in honor of Thurgood Marshall. The legislation was signed into law on August 20, 2001, and the building was rededicated on April 15, 2003. Thurgood Marshall United States Courthouse" – Wikipedia (accessed 23 Nov. 2023)

---

236 From my copy of the Dedication program. This corrects the Wikipedia entry which stated that the dedication was held on Monday, April 15, 2003.

237 Id.

The resolution I drafted and circulated to the various bar associations, organizations, congresspeople from Westchester, Rockland, and Bronx counties[238] give a more inclusive background for Justice Marshall.

APRIL 28, 2003

Congressman Engel sent me a letter saying:

"Recently the Federal Courthouse in Foley Square, Manhattan, was renamed in honor of the late Supreme Court Justice Thurgood Marshall. I was proud to have introduced the legislation which led to the renaming.

Justice Marshal changed America through the law for the better and forever. He served in the Foley Square Courthouse and it is fitting that this great citadel of law be named after him.

I want to thank you for all that you did to help bring this renaming to fruition. It was this dedication by you and others like you that made it possible.

Sincerely,

/S/

Eliot Engel

Member of Congress"

At the renaming ceremony, even though Congressman Engel mentioned that a White Plains lawyer started the renaming of the courthouse project, he could not recall my name. I was present, but I was standing in the back of the courtroom I thought it would be a bit awkward for me to raise my hand. I did go up afterwards and introduced myself.

My son Christoper, and Roni Jacobson, my law partner, were also present.[239] My friend, California Superior Court Judge Horace

---

[238]I think I also circulated it t to Hamilton Fish, Jr of the Poughkeepsie area

[239]Jason was not present. .

Wheatley, who was visiting from California, was present. He and my late wife, Jane, attended Lowell High School in San Francisco together. His daughter Adrienne and my son Jason attended Princeton together.

They became friends, and one day after summer break Adrienne told Jason the story of a man who was at a party in Berkeley and as he was walking out saw a woman quietly reading a book in the corner. Jason's eyes widened as he realized she was telling the story of how his parents met. Adrienne went on to explain to Jason that her father and Jane went to high school together.

When I introduced myself to Thurgood Marshall Jr. at the dedication, his greeting was less than enthusiastic. He later told me that I had allegedly telephoned him at some point and cursed him out.

I did not do that. When I learned the date from him of when he received the call from someone alleging to be me, he gave me a date when I was in the Dominican Republic.[240] I was flabbergasted.

As you will read shortly, that was not the only weird thing that happened. Throughout the process, someone associated with Congresswoman Nita Lowey's office had been feeding her misinformation about me. There was an African American man by the name of Brown who was running for an office and who tried to claim credit for the work that I had done. Arthur Pulley, then President of the Association of Black Lawyers of Westchester, wrote a letter to the editor of the local newspaper refuting the claim of this imposter.

---

240 Wilson to Harper letter giving chain of email correspondence among me, Conrad, Delores Braithwaite (who must have been President of the Westchester Black Lawyers Association at the time), Thurgood Marshall, Jr. Wilson personal files D:\CORRESPONDENCE 1-11-2021\2004 – 2007 ("At long last, I am able to find some time to send you the information that I promised you some 7 months ago. I apologize for this long delay, but I have been suffocatingly busy and was also deciding whether I should just let this pass. I don't want to let it pass simply because I spent so much time with this project." With respect to the alleged telephone call to Thurgood, Jr., I wrote "On March 16, 2004, I wrote to Thurgood, Jr.: "However, in this March 16 email I also tell Marshall that I am in the Dominican Republic until March 21."

Unfortunately, Congresswoman Lowey's office never contacted me about this allegation.[241] She is now late.

JANUARY 26, 2004

Congressman Engel sent me a letter saying, "Congratulations on your receiving the New York State Bar Association Haywood Burns Memorial Award and thank you for your kind mention of my work in getting the Foley Square Courthouse named for the great Thurgood Marshall." I think he forgot that I initiated he idea for naming the Courthouse after Justice Marshall and gave it to him by way of the resolutions.

APRIL 7, 2004

Despite the foregoing history, Conrad told me that Westchester Congresswoman Nita Lowey's office contacted Mrs. Marshall and told her that I had opposed the naming of the U.S. courthouse at 40 Centre Street, Foley Square after her late husband, Thurgood Marshall. This accusation caused me a lot of pain.

As I write this account of the history of renaming the courthouse, I think this and the imposter's call to Thurgood Jr. played a significant role in causing me to write this detailed history to accurately reflect the record.

When Conrad related this story to me, on this date, I sent him the following letter, with attachments:[242]

"Dear Conrad:

---

241 This was the second time that someone had tried to sabotage a major event that I was involved in, the bogus calls to the Herald Record and local radio stations that the West Point Sickle Cell anemia benefit concert was cancelled, being the first one.

242 Wilson to Harper Letter dated April 7, 2004. Wilson personal files D:\CORRESPONDENCE 1-11-2021\2004 - 2007 (Accessed 09 December 2023)

Needless to say, I was devastated by the news that Cong. Lowey's office said that I somehow opposed the naming of the Courthouse at Foley Square after Justice Marshall. In order to quickly deal with this matter, I am enclosing the following documents from third parties, for the most part, marked at the bottom, to show that Cong. Lowey's information was erroneous.

1. Minutes of the September 10, 1997, Committee on Civil Rights meeting in your office (incidentally) where the Civil Rights Committee passed the first resolution to name the Courthouse at Foley Square after Justice Marshall. We did this after Cong. Engel told me that Sen. Moynihan's office was not cooperating in having the White Plains courthouse named after Justice Marshall. We had initially tried to have the White Plains Courthouse named after Justice Marshall. Although the House passed a bill twice (as I recall), Cong. Engel could not get any support in the Senate for his bills to name the White Plains courthouse after Justice Marshall. He then asked me to try to get the New York State Bar Association's support and the support of other organizations for his bill to have the courthouse at Foley Square named after Justice Marshall. I did so without reservations. Jason Steinbaum, Rachel Miller and John Cavelli of Cong. Engel's office know of my efforts on this project.
2. September 18, 1997, letter from Tom Santacrose to John Williamson and me about the process of having the resolution adopted that I had drafted. I drafted the resolution that served as the model for all the various organizations.
3. A digest of the relevant pages to show that on November 1, 1997, I presented the resolution to the NYSBA House of Delegates for passage.
4. A copy of the January 26, 2000, Committee on Civil Rights' minutes that discuss my further contact with Cong. Engel and Sen. Schumer regarding the naming of the Courthouse.

5. The envelope and letter that I received from Judge Winter's Chambers after my successor, Kathryn McCary, and I contacted his chambers to get his support as Chief Judge to have the Foley Square Courthouse named after Justice Marshall.
6. Cong. Engel's April 28, 2003, letter to me thanking me for my efforts to have the Courthouse at Foley Square named after Justice Marshall.
7. Cong. Engel's letter to me after learning of my receipt of the Haywood Burns Memorial Award. At the luncheon, I told the attendees about the process of naming the Courthouse came about.
8. The New York State Bar Association's press release giving me credit for my efforts to have the Courthouse at Foley Square named after Justice Marshall.

I hope that this error can be corrected swiftly. How it could have happened is beyond me. I am in pain by this mis-information, although I fully understand Ms. Marshall's reaction to it, as well as her son's. It is simply wrong.

Very truly yours,

Leroy Wilson, Jr., Esq.

President"

In 2007, my friend Linda Greene[243] stopped by my office in White Plains, New York. We had been discussing Thurgood Marshall and the

---

[243] Inaugural Dean of the Law School at the Michigan State University. Before coming to the MSU College of Law, Greene was Evjue Bascom Professor of Law at the University of Wisconsin Law School, associate vice chancellor at the University of Wisconsin and the inaugural vice president for diversity at the University of California, San Diego. Harvard Law School invited her to teach there in 1984.
Greene also served for three years as counsel to the U.S. Senate Judiciary Committee where she specialized in the confirmation of federal court judges and federal court jurisdiction and proposed constitutional amendments and civil rights legislation.

renaming of the courthouse over the telephone. I showed her the above documents and some others and told her I would be writing the story about how the renaming came about.

I returned to the story from time to time, which I finished telling above. At the time, she was Chair, American Bar Association Accreditation Site Review Team, Pace University School of Law, 2007. Pace is located in White Plains, where I had my offices.[244]

Linda is now the recently retired inaugural Dean of Michigan State University College of Law, effective at end of 2023. She has announced her intention to remain on the faculty and to finish her book on Thurgood Marshall.

Congressman Engel and me at the renaming dedication of the Thurgood Marshall Courthouse.

---

244 At the time she told me that she was writing a book about Justice Marshall. Linda co-authored a book titled I Dissent!: The Dissenting Opinions of Justice Thurgood Marshall alongside Wendy B. Scott. As of summer of 2025, it was not yet available for ordering, according to the publisher's website. CAP - "I Dissent!": The Dissenting Opinions of Justice Thurgood Marshall (9781594604683). Authors: . Carolina Academic Press (Accessed 11 September 2025)

Horace Wheatly, from Oakland, CA., me, my law partner Roni Jacobson, son Christopher at the renaming dedication of the Thurgood Marshall Courthouse.

The 1989 NAACP-JAPAN Mutual Interest Tour – Ronald Reagan, Hosea Williams and Ralph Abernathy, Admiral Robert Toney and His Brothers

In 1980, Reverends Hosea Williams and Ralph Abernathy, who had been part of Dr. Martin Luther King Jr.'s inner circle, supported Ronald Reagan over fellow Georgian Jimmy Carter. Rev. Williams had supported Jimmy Carter in the 1976 presidential race.

After Reagan won the election, he asked Reverends Williams and Abernathy what they wanted. They told him that they wanted a letter of introduction to various influential people in Japan, hoping that they would be able to convince the Japanese to make investments in Atlanta GA to improve the economic conditions of African Americans.

President Reagan agreed and gave them the letter.

President Reagan wrote:

> "As you know, our national economic revitalization is my top priority. If your proposed ventures with the Japanese become a reality, they should result in the creation of new jobs for our fellow citizens. Job creation is at the heart of my plans for our economic renewal. The private sector approach of leaders, such

as yourselves, is the only viable long-term solution to the problem of joblessness."[245]

I knew Hosea from the time I was growing up in Savannah, Georgia and had kept in touch over the years. Most people know him as one of Dr. Martin Luther King's most trusted Lieutenants. Some will remember him as leading the march with John Lewis over the Edmund Pettus Bridge in Selma, Alabama on bloody Sunday - March 7, 1965.[246] A lot remember the beating that John suffered, but until Amb. Andrew Young explained how the march leaders were chosen; it was not widely known how Hosea was chosen. Amb. Young tells us how that happened during the panel discussion on **Clark Atlanta University Presents "Andrew Young: The Dirty Work" Panel,** streamed live 14 October 2025.[247]'The documentary itself was aired on 17 October 2025 at 9:00 p.m. on MSNBC.

Most do not know that 1) he had worked as a research chemist and scientist,[248] and he was associated with the Atomic Energy Plant near Savannah, known as the Savannah River Plant, 2) nor about the serious heroic injuries that he received during WWII or 3) the merciless beating he suffered in Americus GA for drinking out of a "white" water fountain. while wearing his full military uniform, including his medals such as the Purple Heart. This happened in 1945.[249]

This water fountain incident must have been on his mind when Hosea took Tyrone Brooks, and me with him to attend a meeting in Thomasville, GA. With the elected officials (commissioners) who had

---

245 Letter from Ronald Reagan to Revs. Hosea L. Williams and Rev. Dr. Ralph D. Abernathy dated December 15, 1981. Leroy Wilson, Jr. private collection.

246 https://blackpast.org/african-american-history/bloody-sunday-selma-alabama-march-7-1965/ (Accessed 31 OCT 2025.);

247 https://www.youtube.com/watch?v=qoyWJATodys&t=3856s (Watched starting 28 October 2025)

248 Undoubtedly, it was this knowledge of science that enabled him to establish several companies.

249 Rolundus Rice has recently written a biography of Hosea Williams- Title: *Hosea Williams: A Lifetime of Defiance and Protest,* Published: 2022, University of South Carolina Press, Foreword by: Andrew Young Jr.

invited him to come to assist them with some local problem. It was late at night and we stopped to use the rest room at a filling station. The signs on the 3 doors read "white men," "white women," and "other or colored people." I forgot which ones we used, but Hosea protested to the attendant. He later protested to the elected officials. Of course, they were white.

The officials greeted him like a long lost, beloved brother. They assured him that they would take care of the problem.

In 2009, during Dr. Martin Luther King weekend, I traveled to Savannah to accept an award on behalf of my late father and to acknowledge the community's recognition of him. The two other awardees were Reverend Hosea Williams and Mr. John W. McGlockton.

Mr. McGlockton had been the President of the Citizens Democratic Club. Yvonne, his daughter, is one of my classmates. Yvonne was present at this ceremony to accept the award on behalf of her late father. The ceremony was sponsored by the Economic Opportunity Administration in Savannah, which was headed by my classmate and good friend, John Finney, its CEO.[250] John presided.

Although Hosea was well-known as one of Dr. King's top lieutenants, and his activities in Atlanta and Selma, relatively little is known about his civil rights history in the City of Savannah. The Herald, one of our local black newspapers, reported as follows:

"The Beginnigns [sic] of the Boycott: Newspaper Article

[250]Achievements recognition of Leroy Wilson Sr., Reverend Hosea Williams, and Mr. McGlockton, (Yvonne's father). January 17, 2009.

NAACP Sunday Mass Meeting
"NAACP Slaps Easter Bunny at Mass Meeting"
From Vol 14 The Herald April 2, 1960[251]

Nearly two thousand enthusiastic Negroes filled to overflowing the vast auditorium of the Greater St. James A.M.E. Church for the third mass meeting of the NAACP in support of economic freedom. The twenty-five young persons arrested and subsequently tried in City Police Court were on hand for introduction, as well as the group picketing downtown stores in protest of the lunch counter affair.

Hosea Williams, who has been acting chairman of the association's committee of legal redress drew a pledge from all present that they would withhold all Easter purchases from downtown stores, to realize full integration of all facilities offered by these stores. Williams urged that everyone recognize picket lines formed by the association at downtown stores and not enter the store for any purpose…"[252]

In connection with the letter that President Reagan had given them in 1981, Hosea formed the Afro-American/Japanese group. Hosea was Chairman and Rev. Abernathy was its Vice-Chairman. He included me in a group of people that he invited to attend the "National Departure Activity," in Atlanta on April 1, 1982. Hosea also listed me as one of the 14-member National Board of Directors

For the trip to Japan, Hosea called and asked me to create a corporation for him, and I did so, through the offices of CT Corporation. It was called Afro-American/Japanese International Economic Institute, Inc.

Hosea asked me to come to Atlanta for the sendoff. The Afro-American Japanese International House of America sponsored the trip of him and Rev. Abernathy to Japan.

---

[251] I was still in Vienna at that time. I remember that my brother Bubby and Jr., our next-door neighbor, telling me about their participation.

[252] Hosea Williams | Ralph Mark Gilbert Civil Rights Museum (rmgcivilrightsmuseum.com) (Accessed 11 October 2024.)

I went to Atlanta and the sendoff ceremony was held in Atlanta's World Trade Center. The State of Georgia gave them a sample of Georgia gold to give as a gift to the Japanese leaders. Atlanta Mayor Andrew Young also gave him an elaborate glass sculpture to present as a gift to Japan Prime Minister Zenko Suzuki.[253] Rev. Abernathy also gave Prime Minister Suzuki a bronze medallion containing the image of Dr. Martin Luther King, Jr., inscribed with the phrase "I have a Dream."[254]

This was the first time that I knew that the State of Georgia held gold deposits. Indeed, Speaker Thomas B. Murphy told us that the Dome of the Georgia Capitol was adorned with Georgia gold. That surprised several people, but when looking at the Dome one could see the gold sheet covering.

On the other hand, the elaborate glass structure presented a problem. How to take the structure all the way to Japan without breaking it. They decided that they would carry the glass sculpture in the seat with them somehow.

And then of course a misunderstanding developed as to who would be the spokesman for their team. They resolved this by saying that one of them would be the spokesman on this side of the international dateline and the other would be the spokesman on the other side of the dateline. I don't know how that worked out, but the controversy was elevated to the point that Hosea suggested that he would leave Rev. Abernathy off and name me to take his place. I told Hosea that this was not a good idea. Thankfully, he and Rev. Abernathy resolved the misunderstanding.

After they arrived, The Atlanta Journal Constitution reported on their meeting with Japan Prime Minister Zenko Suzuki on Tuesday

---

253 Davidson, Martin "Black Atlantans Seeking Japanese Interest In Joint Business Work," Atlanta Journal Constitution, 17 April 1982. (Melvin Washington private library)

254 Id.

April 13, 1982. The article outlined the objectives of the discussion Williams and Abernathy had with Suzuki:[255]

ATLANTA JOURNAL/CONSTITUTION
Saturday - April 17, 1982

Black Atlantans Seeking Japanese Interest In Joint Business Work

By Martin Davidson

TOKYO — An Afro-American trade mission, headed by two Atlanta civil rights leaders, urged Japanese Prime Minister Zenko Suzuki Friday to help promote joint business ventures between black Americans and Japanese businessmen.

"They know that we do not come begging or asking for anything," said Dr. Ralph Abernathy, former Southern Christian Leadership Conference president. "We merely want investments and coventures. I think they see black people in a different light today, and I have a very strong feeling that something is going to come of it. It will really depend on the follow-up."

Abernathy and State Rep. Hosea Williams, D-Atlanta, said at a news conference that their meeting with Suzuki was "very fruitful."

They specifically asked Suzuki to:

• Promote Japanese investments in the U.S. by offering tax incentives to [illegible] Japanese-Afro-[illegible]

• Invite President Reagan to Japan to discuss, among many other things, Afro-American-Japanese joint business ventures.

• Use his influence to help establish a Japan branch of the Afro-American International Institute.

Suzuki did not respond immediately to the requests, but he is considering them.

The mission will leave behind the seeds of an organization called the Japan Afro-American Friendship Association, headed by Melvin Washington. Washington said he will call on the various companies that Williams and Abernathy visited during their trip here, in an effort to firm up relations between Japanese businesses and Afro-Americans.

"Nothing will happen after one meeting, or even after five," said Washington, who also promotes tourism for the government of the Bahamas. "Trust takes a long time in this country. Maybe after the 55th meeting, they will begin to trust us. We are going to persist, and evaluate our relationships as they develop."

Abernathy and Williams presented a large glass art work to Suzuki as a gift from Atlanta Mayor Andrew Young. Dr. Abernathy also presented the prime minister with a bronze medallion bearing the image of the late civil rights leader Martin Luther King Jr., and inscribed with the phrase "I have a dream."

The trade group met with educators and professors of various universities in an effort to set up exchange programs with such U.S. institutions as Atlanta and Howard universities, Tuskegee Institute and other colleges with strong technological and agricultural programs.

"All we want is to provide more jobs for blacks in America," Abernathy said of the purpose of his mission to Japan. "We do not intend for white or yellow people to control our workers. We don't want control. We want to work as brothers."

Japan's Suzuki With Hosea Williams (middle) And Ralph Abernathy

L-R Prime Minister Suzuki, Rev. Wiliams, Rev. Abernathy

Hosea said this was the first time in American history that black Americans had an audience with a Japanese Prime Minister.

L-R Warren Latham, Mel Washington at the Mike, Hosea, Ralph Abernathy 1982 in Japan

[255] Id. (four pillars to support Afro American and Japanese joint ventures). Davidson, Martin "Seeing Light In Japan's Success," The Atlanta Constitution, April 8, 1982, p. (Leroy Wilson, Jr. private collection.)

They were also scheduled to meet with Shintaro Abe, then Japan's Minister of International Trade and Industry, U.S. Ambassador Mike Mansfield, and Japanese business leaders.[256]

In their meetings with foreign correspondents in Japan, they expressed a desire to create a joint venture to manufacture automobiles, to visit factories to "get a first-hand look at the current state of technology and labor relations in this industrialized Asian nation," "to send black workers for training to Japan so they could learn how to run Japanese-financed factories and farms in the Southeastern United States using Japanese know-how."[257]

In this connection, the Japanese had been successful farmers in Florida before they were forced to give up because of "fruit blight" and "competition from Cuba."[258] All but one, left the Yamato colony that the Japanese had created. His name was George Morikami. George became very wealthy. The story of Morikami is still being told today. Morikami donated some of his land in the 1970s to Palm Beach County for a park to preserve the memory of the Yamato Colony. That is Morikami Museum and Gardens.[259]

Both are exceptionally beautiful. I visited them on a trip with members of the National Bar Association during one of our meetings in Florida.

---

256 Id., Abe later wrote a book titled *The Japan That Can Say No,* to fend off American government bullying.(At one time, Regge Life, a renowned filmmaker on Japanese topics, gave me an English version of this book, so I read it)

257 Id.

258 https://clemsonwire.usatoday.com/story/news/local/boca/2024/12/22/yamato-the-story-of-a-japanese-colony-of-farmers-in-boca-raton/75337131007/ (Accessed 04 February 2025)

259 Id.

During the Second World War, the Japanese farmers in California experienced a different history:[260]

> Nobumitsu Takahashi, agricultural coordinator for the Japanese-American Citizens League, warned, as internment began in 1942, that removal of the Japanese would disrupt the California vegetable industry. Japanese truck farmers, he said, produced crops valued at 40 million dollars annually and interned Japanese "stand to lose approximately 100 million dollars in investments" because of confiscation or forced sale by the U.S. Government.
>
> The California Farm Bureau was quoted by *The News,* saying that Japanese farmers were responsible for 40 percent of all vegetables grown in the state, including nearly 100 percent of all tomatoes, celery, strawberries and peppers.

I cite these references to show that Hosea had a basis for seeking business relationships with the Japanese farming community, as well as manufacturing.

They also met with educators of various universities to set up exchange programs with such U.S. institutions such as Atlanta and Howard Universities, Tuskegee Institute, and other colleges with strong technological and agricultural programs.[261]

Among those who supported the mission were Mayor Andrew Young, Georgia Governor George Busbee, Lt. Gov. Zell Miller, and Herman Russell.[262]

It fell to Mel Washington, a young African American, then resident in Japan, to follow up in Japan. Through Hosea, Mel and I began to communicate.

---

260 http://www.sfmuseum.org/hist9/harvest.html#:~:text=The%20World%20War%20II%20evacuation%20of%20Japanese%20farmers,confiscated%20farmlands%20to%20new%20%E2%80%9Cnon-Japanese%E2%80%9D%20owners%20and%20lessees. (Accessed 04 February 2025)

261 Davidson, Martin, "Black Atlantans Seeking Japanese Interest In Joint Business Work," The Atlanta Journal/The Atlanta Constitution, April 17, 1982, p._____

262 Id.

Hosea sent me a videotape of some aspects of the visit, including robots building automobiles – first time I would be aware of this kind of robot activity.

Mel was fluent in Japanese and had lived in Japan for many years. Mel and I first met in person in 1989. We have remained in touch with each other over the years.

The NAACP–Japanese Delegation and How I Got To Go

In 1989, I received a telephone call from Mel saying that the Western Region of the NAACP was sending a delegation to Japan to discuss the derogatory statements that present and past Japanese leaders had been making about African Americans. He asked if I could assist them. I agreed; however, when Jim Martin or Matthew Thomas asked what my fee would be, I requested that they include me as part of the delegation as my fee. They did. Jim was the Western Region Director.

> "In [September] 1986, then Prime Minister Yasuhiro Nakasone said U.S. intelligence is low "because there are many blacks, Puerto Ricans and Mexicans." Two years later, Michio Watanabe, who later became foreign minister, said blacks did not repay debts. And in 1990, Justice Minister Seiroku Kajiyama compared prostitutes in a Tokyo district to "America when neighborhoods become mixed because blacks move in and whites are forced out."[263]
>
> Members of the Congressional Black Caucus and Hispanic Caucus immediately took to the floor of the House demanded an apology after Prime Minister Nakasone's remarks, among other things. Other members of the House spoke to support what they

---

[263] https://www.thefreelibrary.com/Black+business+courts+the+Japan+market%3b+penetrating+this+tough...-a015429440 (accessed 24 February 2024)

said. There were several standing ovations.[264] But the insults continued.

It turned out that I knew some people who were going to be on the delegation.

I knew Jim Martin, whom I had met earlier that summer when Adm. Bob Toney took a few people for a boat ride (pictured below). I had also known Donald Hopkins from our days at the University of California at Berkeley. Bob and Don were two of my closest friends.

L-R Virginia Poindexter, Adm. Bob Toney, Warren Widener, Me, Jim Martin, Don Hopkins before Bob took us sailing on the Admiral's yacht (the barge)

[264] These were Congressmembers Parren Mitchell, Mickey Leland, Mervyn Dymally, Cardiss Collins, Esteban Torres, Albert Bustamante and Walter Fauntroy. Other Congressmembers made strongly worded statements of support; i.e., Matsui, Rose Oakar, and Badham. https://texasarchive.org/2022_00518 (Accessed 26 Feb. 2024). See also https://texasarchive.org/2022_00583 (Accessed 26 Feb 2024)

Japan Airlines scheduled us to leave from JFK on JL flight #7 to Narita Airport in Tokyo on 07 OCT 1989 at 5:15 P.M.

We were to stay in Tokyo until 14 October, then leave for Osaka on JL 913 at 11:55 a.m. on 14 October 1989. We spent 24 hours in Osaka, then down to humid and hot Okinawa (where my brother Louis was stationed for a while when he was in the service). Finally, to Fukuoka, then back to Tokyo and return to JFK on October 15, 1989.

I, and the delegation, would meet Mel Washington at breakfast at Keio Plaza Hotel for the first time.

We also met Aurelia Erskine Brazeal, who was the Commercial Attaché in the US Embassy in Tokyo, Japan. I must admit that I was startled when a familiar person that I had seen almost 30 years earlier came walking into the room. She would go on to serve in the American foreign service and to several high positions, including ambassador to three different countries (The Federated States of Micronesia , Kenya, and Ethiopia). Aurelia is the daughter of Dean Brailsford R. Brazeal, who was the Dean of students at Morehouse College when I was a student there. I knew her sister Ernestine better.

To cater to their American and non-Japanese guests, the hotel prepared American style breakfasts for us to complement the Japanese -style breakfast. One of the things that I noticed is that the Japanese breakfast menu contained several items that we would normally eat for dinner.

On a personal note, Aurelia was the first person who taught me that one of the ways to alleviate the acidic properties of orange juice was to dilute it with water.

James Martin who, as the head of the NAACP western region office, was leading the delegation. William Pickens III was an NAACP member who also appeared to be fluent in Japanese. O. Matthew Thomas and Rhuenette Washington also joined as part of the western region delegation.

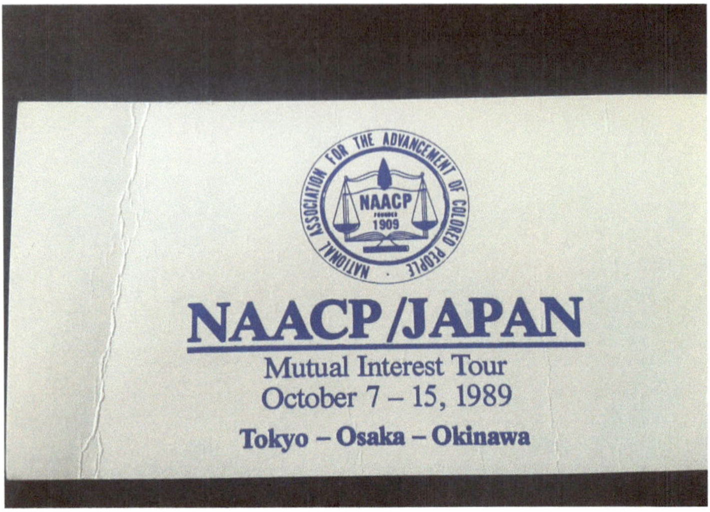

Our identity badge

Top Photo L-R Major General Harry Brooks, Second from left, Jim Martin, on right in red tie facing the camera. Others in this photo are Mitzi Johnson, Karen Johnson, Noah Griffin, and Nancy Driver.

Middle Photo L-R Bill Pickens, tall man wearing red tie and tan raincoat, Diane and Mark Christensen, California State Sen. Diane Watson. Mel Agassi is also in this photo.

Bottom Photo L-R William Penn, Rev. Archibald Buchanan, Sen. Diane Watson.

I took these photos when we were on the train platform in Tokyo waiting for the train to Osaka.

Also on the trip were Donald Hopkins, who at that time ran Congressman Ron Dellums's local district office in Oakland, California. I knew Don from the time that he was in law school at the University of California at Berkeley's "Boalt Hall " (now Berkeley Law). After he graduated from law school in around 1965, Don became the first African American Assistant Dean for the Graduate Division. In that capacity, he helped me defray my first-year law school expenses by giving me a $250 student grant.

Other members of the delegation were:

Rhunette Washington, executive on loan to the NAACP from Pacific Bell Company, who served as the project manager for the trip.

William Penn, National Director of Branch and Field Services for the NAACP, whose interest was trade and diplomacy.

William Pickens, III, former National Board Member of the NAACP, whose interest was diplomacy.

Mel Assagai, Chief of Staff for Senator Roberti, whose interest was trade and diplomacy.

Shelly Assagai Whitaker, Education Consultant, whose interest was education and culture.

Thomas Mitchell, management consultant and group leader, whose interest was culture and education.

Leon Eastmond Jr., President of A. L. Eastmond and Sons, manufacturer of steel boilers, who was interested was establishing business contacts. Unfortunately, during the trip, a labor issue arose at Leon's business back in Queens NY and he had to leave the trip.

California State Senator Diane Watson, California 28th District Chairperson and Chairperson of the California Black Caucus, whose interest was in culture and education.

Senator George Fleming, Democrat, Washington State, whose interest was in economic development,

Nancy Driver, Manager at Pacific Bell Co., whose interest was in establishing business contacts.

Karen Johnson, Manager at Xerox Corp., whose interest was business contacts.

Mark Christiansen, Southern California Gas Co., whose interest was economic development.

Mrs. Mark Christiansen, Southern California Gas Co., whose interest was economic development.

Alex Johnson, Security Pacific Bank, whose interest was economic development.

Frank Mingo. President Mingo Group Advertising, whose interest was business contacts. Although he was named, I do not remember Frank as going on the trip. I knew him from New York and our business activities in Uganda during President Binaisa's term.

Elizabeth Kimbro, Real Estate Developer, whose interest was in culture and education.

Assemblyman Morse Arberry, Las Vegas Nevada, whose interest was economic development.

Assemblyman Wendell Wiliams, Las Vegas, Nevada, whose interest was economic development.

Risa Martin, President Communi-Comp, Inc. whose interest was business contacts.

Senator Carolyn Walker, Phoenix Arizona, whose interest was in trade and diplomacy.

Major General Harry Brooks, President and CEO of Western Computer Group, Inc., whose interest was establishing business contacts.

I see him in a photo from the trip. I think th that I did not connect him to the sickle cell anemia benefit at West Point in 1972. At that time, he was a Lt. Colonel, and he had been newly appointed Army Director of Equal Opportunity Programs at the Pentagon. I was civilian counsel to the black cadets in connection with the sickle cell anemia benefit concert. I discuss our connection under the heading of "organizing the sickle cell anemia benefit at West Point – May 20, 1972."

Vivian Macdonald, Real Estate Broker, whose interest was in culture and education.

John Nance, National NAACP board Member, whose interest was economic development.

Noah Griffin, Public Relations for the City of San Francisco, whose interest was in culture and education.

Donald R. Hopkins,[265]whom I described above.

Marvell Allen, MCA & Associates, whose interest was economic development.

O. Matthew Thomas, The Concept Group, whose interest was business and economic development.

Rev. Dr. Archibald Buchanan was with us at the train station in Okinawa, but I am not sure when he joined us. He gave us valuable information at the Gala dinner that we had in Okinawa.

Some background on how some of us met. Sometime around 1966, Clarence Hampton, a schoolmate from Morehouse College in Atlanta GA, introduced me to Lonnie Poindexter, who became my roommate. One of the places we lived was in an apartment on the third floor of our apartment building in Berkeley CA.[266]

Ray Norton was an Olympian and a track star in the 100- and 220-yard dash from high school through college. He lived next door to us, but on the first floor lived Robert Toney and his wife Flora. We all became good friends. Lonnie, who had been a dental technician in the Navy, was famous for his roast leg of lamb on Sundays, stuffed with garlic.

We did have parties from time to time. Perhaps the most famous one was the time when we filled a bathtub with ice, cold drinks, and beer. We thought the party was over about 2 A.M. and were closing down because most people had left. Lo, and behold, about 3:30, Bob shows up again with some of our friends, and we resumed the party. Everyone had a fun time.

Bob had several brothers and one sister. Sam, died at a relatively early age after marrying Lily. They had one son, Laurence, who would meet my older son Jason many years later and after they were both successful young businessmen.

---

265 The lawyer of the same name as Donald Hopkins, the medical doctor.

266 Berkeley was contiguous with Oakland CA, so we were still in the same neighborhood.

As fate would have it, after Bob retired from the Navy, he met my son Jason, on his visit to Softnet in San Francisco, where Jason worked as counsel. When Larry Brilliant, CEO of Softnet introduced Jason to Bob as Jason Wilson, Bob, hearing Wilson, asked him if he was related to me. When he answered yes, the connection across decades and generations continued.

Then there was Walter Toney who was a civil engineer and the first black civil engineer that I had met. Glen Toney worked for Waste Management but did not live in the immediate vicinity at the time. Chucky was the youngest brother. All had been in the Navy except Chuck. I think Chuck was in the Air Force. Although I met Virginia, I didn't know too much about her. Sam, Bob and Walter were all officers in the Navy.

Bob was honorably discharged by the Navy at some point and decided to re-enlist. He retired for good in 1991. He would eventually rise to the position of Rear Admiral. He would oversee the San Francisco naval base at Treasure Island. I was in San Francisco during the period when there was a debate among Chairwoman Diane Feinstein and the San Francisco Board of Supervisors and the gay community as to whether the historic USS Missouri would be berthed at San Francisco, because of the "don't ask, don't tell" policy of the Navy.

The USS Missouri was a storied battleship which served as the site of the official Japanese surrender after World War II. Eventually it was decided that the Missouri would be berthed in Hawaii along with some other vessels instead of Treasure Island. It is now a floating War Memorial at the naval base in Pearl Harbor, Hawaii.

This was a huge economic loss to the Bay Area, as the project would call for some 4,000 units of housing and spin off considerable dollars in the neighborhood.

The BARGE (Adm. Bob Toney, Jim Martin, Lonnie Poindexter, Summer 1989)

When Bob oversaw the Naval Base at Treasure Island, he took a group of us on a boat ride in some of the waters near the East Bay, winding up at Alcatraz, and also a place where boats pulled up to a restaurant. Pictured above

When we arrived at Alcatraz, a couple of the guards arrived to greet us with their weapons. It was electrifying to see them snap to attention when they recognized the Admiral's flag and his cap. They then took us on a tour of Alcatraz. Last I heard, Bob's son Robby had risen to Commander. I am sure he is higher now.

Bob also took me on a tour of the flags display at Treasure Island and explained how flags were used to communicate – who knew?

Along on the boat ride were James Martin, Lonnie Poindexter, his wife Virginia, and Donald Hopkins. I am not sure who the others were. Perhaps O. Matthew Thomas was one.

Lonnie married a Virginia, different from Virginia Toney, with whom they were blessed with a son, Paul. Don married Ann Ashmore, who had attended Spelman at the time I attended Morehouse. Sadly, Lonnie, who was not on the trip to Japan, died shortly after we returned from Japan. Don and Ann divorced, and she is now married to James Hudson, one of my Morehouse classmates.

Picking up where I left off, we landed at Narita Airport in Japan after midnight. A coach collected us and carried us to the Keio Plaza Hotel, where we would be staying in Tokyo. The Keio Plaza was in Shinjuku, Tokyo, and was 47 stories high. I think 47 is the number of a certain elite group of Samurai.

We also visited Osaka, Fukuoka and Okinawa. I remember Okinawa being extremely hot and muggy. Something that Louis, my youngest brother, confirmed. We also got a chance to see the source of a Japanese complaint, which was the U.S. military base there occupied all the land up to residential areas, which squeezed people into a tight living space.

During the trip, we had an opportunity to travel on the bullet train (Shinkansen) and to ride it past Mt. Fuji. I watched Mel Washington make a coin telephone call from the moving train. That was a new experience. There were no cellphones at that time.

We met with Mr. Yukio Okamoto, Director, First North America Division, Ministry of Foreign Affairs and learned something about the Japanese position on the US-Japan mutual security treaty and the issues involved in our trade relationships.

Meeting with Japanese Officials and NAACP Branch 2323

Yukio Okamoto (Japanese: 岡本 行夫, Okamoto Yukio; 23 November 1945 – 24 April 2020) was a Japanese diplomat, diplomatic analyst, and proponent of strong economic and political Japan–United States relations. Okamoto guided Japanese and American diplomatic relations throughout the 1980s, during an era when both countries simultaneously competed for economic influence on the global stage. He served as a diplomatic advisor and analyst for several Japanese prime ministers, including Ryutaro Hashimoto from 1996 to 1998 and Junichiro Koizumi from 2003 until 2004.[267]

We also met with Mr. Kazuo Nukazawa, Managing Director, KEIDANREN Japan Federation of Economic Organizations.[268] Prior to this position, Mr. Nukazawa had been the Director of the International Economic Affairs Bureau of the Federation of Economic Organizations of Japan.

The Keidanren is one of the major Japanese business organizations. It deals with all matters concerning the business world except for labor issues. Before we visited there were 110 member organizations made

---

267 https://en.wikipedia.org/wiki/Yukio_Okamoto (Accessed 23 Feb 2024).
268 https://www.jstor.org/stable/42800078 (Accessed 23 Feb 2024)

up of minor enterprises; however, when we visited, the group was comprised mainly of major enterprises. Mr. Nukazawa had also been the Deputy Director on the Economic Cooperation Bureau and the Director of the Financial Affairs Bureau. He was the Economic Research Consultant of the US-Japan Trade Council in Washington DC from 1968 to 1971 and was a visiting research fellow of the Rockefeller Foundation from 1978 to 1979.[269]

We met with Mr. Nukazawa and his Japanese delegation at the Keidanren Kaikan International Conference Halls in the Palace Hotel. As you can see in the photos below, the Keidanren received us as important visitors. We met in either Room 902 or Room 903.

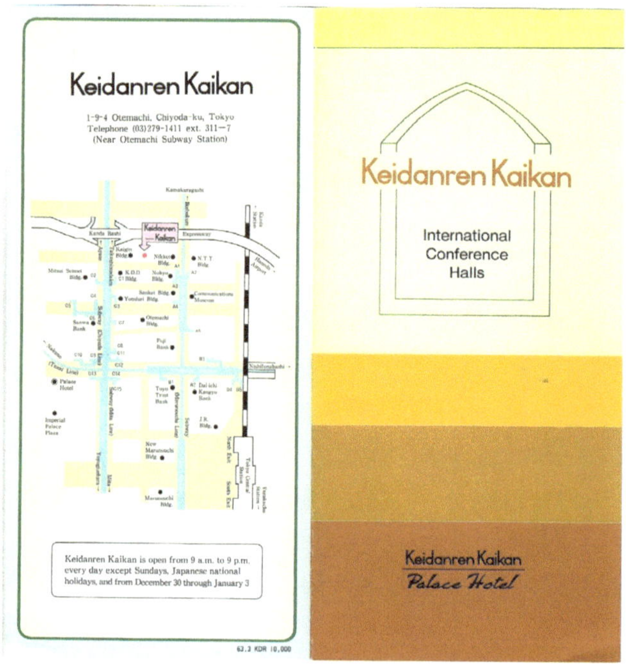

[269] Id.

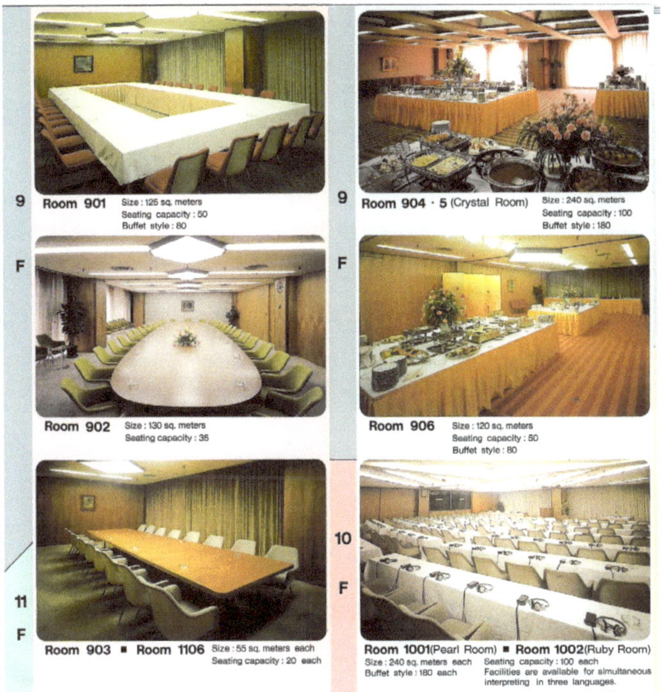

Photos of the International Conference Halls in 1989 which show these rooms and others. I am not sure where we met with Mr. Okamoto.

In our meetings with these gentlemen, there were several other people in their delegations. I recited the background of Mr. Okamoto and Mr. Nukazawa above, to show that we met with some of Japan's top policymakers which was an indication that they took our delegation seriously.

At that time, Mr Nukazawa told us that the Japanese government, or other Japanese organization had established a mechanism to fund a Congressman Mickey Leland project to the extent of 1% of each enterprise's profits or revenues. Mickey had been tragically killed in an airplane Gambela, Ethiopia, during a mission to Fugnido, Ethiopia in severe weather.

We also attended a gathering of some kind where we learned about Japanese culture and the concept of Wa (Harmony).

Dr. Archie Buchanan, D.D. was an African American religious scholar who taught Greek at Sophia University in Tokyo. He was the President and founder of the NAACP branch in Japan. He traveled with us from place to place.

On 14 October 1989, our last night in Japan, we attended a dinner at the Kaduna Officers Club in Okinawa Japan from 6:30 to 9:00 PM, sponsored by Okinawa, Japan NAACP Branch 2323.

The branch officers and committee chairpersons present were;

- Dr. Archie Buchanan, President and Founder
- Mr. Jimmy Lee, Jr., , Vice President and Freedom Fund
- Mrs. Judy G. Washington Secretary
- Mr. Raymond H. Legall, Treasurer
- Mr. Daryl Drenon, Parliamentary and Membership Committee
- Mr. Lucious Dickey, Press and Publicity
- Mrs. Addie DeCastro, Women's Auxiliary
- Mrs. Sandy Perkins, Education Committee
- Mr. Jim Harris and Mrs. Linda Harris, Youth Advisors
- Dr. William L. Cody, M.D., Assistant Chairperson of Membership Committee
- Mr. Vincent Glover, Life Membership Chairperson

Mr. Lee, acting as Master of Ceremonies, welcomed us on behalf of the NAACP Branch #2323.

We also received welcoming remarks from the Honorable Mr. Lawrence F. Farrah, Consul General of the United States of America in Japan.

The motto of branch #2323 is taken from second Timothy chapter 1 verse 7: "For God has not given us a spirit of fear, but of power and of love and of a sound mind."

Although this was the first time I became aware of this scripture, I think I have subconsciously followed it all of my life.

Mrs. Rhuenette Washington, the project manager for our trip, introduced the members of our delegation to the guests present.

Mr. Jimmy Lee Jr. introduced the life members, youth members, and executive committee members, of NAACP branch #2323 to the guests present.

Mr. Lee then introduced Dr. Buchanan, who gave us a brief history and case review of the NAACP in Japan and Okinawa.

Doctor Buchanan said that the reason that the branch was created was because there was a lot of racism within the military services and in Okinawa, and that there were gross inequities in the administration of justice in Japan. He said there had been too many black Americans in prisons in Japan and that there was a serious need to educate Japanese about African Americans.

He related the poignant story of a sister who was trying to get help for her brother who was in Tokyo. Dr. Buchanan also received several calls from service people covering many different racial issues, including employment discrimination.

My brother Louis, who had been stationed in Okinawa in 1973, told me about an incident that he experienced, although we do not know if it was racial or not. He recounted the incident to me as follows:

> They allowed us to play dice on the tiny bandstand. When I walked in the club, I noticed Staff Sargent Jake (My racist supervisor) and pals at the end of the bar, including Mr. Charlie, all with mischievous looks... I walked in the room with the small bandstand and noticed a dice game in progress. I went over, threw in a bet and eventually got to roll the dice. I eventually crapped out, and Mr. Charlie had parked next to me... Now....... Mr. Charlie, who was on The Rock [where they were stationed], for whatever reason.... temporary duty (TDY) kept forgetting his (point) and kept hunching me with his elbow.

After the third time, I just picked up my money and walked back across the street to the barracks. I went into the latrine (bathroom) to deposit some of the Orion beer that I was renting... Mr. Charlie walked up to me as I was making my deposit, and he was getting uncomfortably close... As I was zipping up, Mr. Charlie was putting on his war face, so I gave him a light right hook, hoping to knock him out; cause if I killed him, I was going to Leavenworth Prison. Mr. Charlie snapped his head around and got so uncomfortably close, I could smell his breath.... I jumped up about 8 inches off the floor and grabbed him around the neck and locked on; and I drew my knees up to create a dead weight to take him to the floor, I could tell that his immediate concern was not to hit that tile floor too hard. So, I landed him in such a way that he would be able to think rationally relative to the condition he suddenly found himself in. [Two other white men] opened the door but chose not to intervene, Well......long story short: Mr. Charlie, after conceding, came out with two black eyes, a broken nose, a considerable amount of skin rubbed off his forehead on the tile floor, and a very painful crook in his neck.

As I laid in my bunk that night, contemplating our inevitable reunion as usual at the bar, I was surprised when I walked in, he was sitting there with a half-smile.... all his support group with Jake (My supervisor) intently observing. I walked over, shook his hand, and bought him a beer. I got an ovation and didn't have any more problems with bullies.

While at Kume Jima, I took all the proficiency tests to be a Tech Sargent (5 stripes) and passed.

Jake never put me in for a promotion.... I guess cause he only had four stripes.

So, I left Okinawa with the same two stripes I had when I got there...

Doctor Buchanan introduced Mr. Martin, who delivered the dinner keynote address.

Mr. Penn, the National Director of Branch and Field Services made some remarks, as did Mr. Murayama Seibin, Director, Okinawa

Prefecture Governor's office, Mr. Choko Kuwae, the Mayor of Okinawa City, and Brigadier General R. T. Browning, CG, 313 U.S. Air Div.

Dr. Buchanan closed us out, and we flew from Tokyo to JFK the next day.

While writing this book, I came across a paper presented by Prof. Lee Gallo at the International Cultural Exchange Symposium (Tokyo, Japan, June 1989).[270] Dr. Lee Gallo taught Spanish at Morehouse College at the time and in 1988 Dr. Leroy Keith, Morehouse President, appointed her as Director of Studies Abroad.

Dr. Keith was one of my contemporary upperclassmen at Morehouse in the 1960s. He saved me from drowning in the school's swimming pool. We were supposed to swim across and back. I got off to a slightly delayed start and tried to swim across and back underwater when I gave out of breath. Dr. Keith saw my distress and jumped in and saved me. When he left Morehouse, he became the owner of Carson Hair Products in Savannah, Georgia, my hometown.

In 1997, Keith executed a buyout of Carson Products—makers of Dark & Lovely and Magic Shave—becoming its first African American chairman and CEO. Under his management, the company quadrupled in value and became a publicly traded company.[271]

Dr. Gallo's paper is titled "Morehouse College offers a new direction in Japanese African American relations."[272]

Dr. Keith told Professor Gallo that the first thing she must do is meet with Mr. Seiho Tajiri, a local "retired" Japanese businessman who had relocated to the Atlanta area.

---

270 Available from NAFSA Publication Order Desk, 1875 Connecticut Ave., N.W., Suite 1000, Washington, DC 20009-5728. Reports Descriptive (141) Speeches/Conference Papers (150).

271 Rhea, Shawn (October 1997). "Carson Gets a Makeover". *Black Enterprise*. Vol. 28, no. 3. pp. 122–128. Retrieved 30 July 2020 (Accessed from Wikipedia 08 February 2025)

272 See n. 244.

When I represented Rev. Hosea Williams circa 1982, in connection with the trip that he and Rev. Abernathy took, Hosea spoke in glowing terms about Mr. Tajiri. So now, I make all these connections.

On 12 May 1993, The Atlanta Constitution (Atlanta, Georgia) · published an article about Mr. Tajiri's efforts to foster social, cultural, and business relationships between Japanese and African Americans.[273]

Mr. Tajiri had also acted as the go-between to arrange the trip for Revs. Williams and Abernathy.

Dr. Gallo met with Mr. Tajiri. At their meeting, Mr. Tajiri encouraged her to create a plan that would involve Morehouse College with Japan.[274]

Dr. Jann Adams, the lead director of the Andrew Young Center for Global Leadership wrote, in answer to my inquiry " I can say with certainty that the program to Japan does not exist at this time and has not existed since 2012."[275]

Mel Washigton has created a beautifully excellent website that captures the history of the relationships between the Japanese and black descendants of Africa, starting with Yasuke, the first African samurai in 16th century. See website at www.jafausa.org.

---

273 May, Lee (May 1993) "Seeds of Understanding" *The Atlanta Constitution (Atlanta, Georgia),* page 15.

274 n. 211

275 Adams, J. Dr., Email to Leroy Wilson, Jr. "*Re: Question for Office of International Education.*" February 10, 2025.

Private Practice – Union Carbide and Different Types of Cases

At various times in my private practice, I was assisted enormously in my legal work by my late wife Jane, sons Jason and Christopher, and Roni Jacobson, my associate, later law partner. All brilliant lawyers.

At this point, I must single Christopher out for his participation in the investigation of how the Securities and Exchange Commission failed to notice Bernard Madoff's Ponzi scheme, which was the largest in history ($64.8 billion).

He thus became the first family member to have his photo appear in The New York Times. The photo below shows Chris and his team members seated directly behind I.G. Davis Kotz as he was testifying before Congress. (Ca. January 2009). This is the photo that appeared in the New York Times.

Photo of Chris and others sitting behind Inspector General David Kotz as Kotz gave his report on how the SEC missed the many red flags telling them something was wrong with Madoff's practices. Harry Markopolos is seated on the left, and Christopher is fourth from the left, with the bald head.

Chris was a part of an SEC Special Detail: Special Investigator, Office of the Inspector General (2009), selected by the Inspector General to investigate the SEC's failure to uncover Bernard Madoff's Ponzi scheme. He Co-led the investigation into the SEC's nine Madoff examinations, Shana Madoff's romantic relationship with a former SEC Senior Official, and the "Madoff" exception to the SEC short sale rule.

He drafted sections of the Inspector General's report on the SEC's nine examinations conducted from 1992 to 2005 and the 2006 enforcement investigation of Bernard L. Madoff Investment Securities.

Among other things, he also prepared Harry Markopolos for his part in the investigation. Markopolos was the star witness. Harry wrote a note to me in his book "Your son's service to the nation into this case was both exemplary and courageous. His work restored my faith in government."[276]

Some of those other things were;

- Conducted forensic review of over 3 million e-mails, examination work papers, and enforcement files.
- Created extensive chronology, main source work product used for testimony outlines, and exhibits.
- Prepared the Inspector General for testimony and participated in over 140 testimonies and 122 interviews.
- Managed assignments of the 12-member investigative support team (auditors, consultants, and paralegals).

For his work, he was given the 2010 Council of Inspector Generals for Integrity and Excellence Gaston L. Gianni, Jr.'s Better Government Award: SEC Investigative Team - Bernard L. Madoff Ponzi Scheme. (2010).

Meanwhile, Jason was busy establishing himself as an executive in the thoroughbred horse racing industry, leaving his mark at The Jockey Club, Equibase, TJC Media Ventures.

Prior to joining The Jockey Club, he spent three years as the assistant general counsel for SoftNet Systems, Inc./Aerzone Corporation in San Francisco and later served as an associate in the Healthcare Investment Banking group of Deutsche Bank Securities and as Vice President in the real estate, gaming and lodging group of Banc of America Securities.

Returning to Union Carbide, from September 1974 to December 1981, I worked in the Law Department section that provided services

---

[276] Harry Markopolos, *No One Would Listen- A True Financial Triller,* Wiley (2010) (New York Times Best Seller)

to the Linde Division of Union Carbide Corporation. The headquarters of Carbide was located at 270 Park Avenue in New York City.[277]

In 1981, Carbide sold its building and moved to Old Ridgebury Road, Danbury, CT in 1981, where I worked until March 1982. I resigned to open my office in White Plains, New York in April 1982. As I explained earlier, Union Carbide was my first client when I opened my office.

In 1982 Union Carbide Corporation was merged into Dow Chemical and no longer exists. Neither does the Union Carbide building that I worked in at 270 Park Avenue.

I continued to serve as Counsel to Welding Products & Equipment Department (all components, domestic and foreign); Distributor Marketing Department; Counsel for Midwest, Southwest and Western Regions for Bulk Atmospheric Gases, Gas Products Department; Cryogenics Department; Medicare Law; general corporate and commercial practice; structuring shareholder agreements and drafting and assisting in negotiating and closing acquisitions and mergers involving distributors.

---

[277] The location of this building has been recently in the news as the new headquarters of JPMorgan Chase Bank -, completed building substitute new building in the same spot at a cost of $3 billion.

Acquisitions and Mergers and Commercial Practice at Union Carbide

I drafted a large number of agreements regarding acquisitions and mergers, general corporate and commercial practice, loan agreements, shareholder agreements and option agreements.

Pennsylvania

The first transaction that I handled involved the acquisition of all the issued and outstanding stock of a Linde Welding Products distributor in a small town in Pennsylvania. This was to be an exchange of Union Carbide stock for stock of the distributor.[278] We were required to follow certain rules of accounting and of taxation, as well as law for these kinds of transactions.

The relevant accounting rule required that Union Carbide exchange its shares in the same proportion has the ownership shares were held by the shareholders of the company we were acquiring.

When we arrived at the closing, the majority stockholder decided that he did not want to go ahead with the deal because in his opinion the minority shareholder would have received a windfall. I was crestfallen after all the work I had done to prepare the relevant documents.

---

278 Most if not all the distributor entities were corporations.

I returned to Union Carbide and continued to do my other work. About a year later the majority shareholder of the distributor contacted us and said he wanted to do a cash for stock deal. We would pay him and the minority shareholder cash for their respective shares. This one-year delay caused the majority shareholder to lose about $1 million.

Because the majority shareholder did not have a family member who was interested in taking over his business, and there was an individual within the Linde Division who was amenable to operate the business, Union Carbide, as sole shareholder now, appointed this individual to run the company. I don't remember if we sold the stock to him.

One interesting sidelight here is that one of the members on my team told me that the banker who was involved wanted to take us all to lunch at one point, but he had to check with the local eating establishment to see if they had any exclusionary practices or policies where they would not serve African Americans. Mind you that this was in the 1970s. The banker was a very courteous gentleman, and he wanted to pave the way to be sure that I would not be disrespected. I think he was a director of the distributor company as well.

Nevertheless, I was happy to have my first closing under my belt.

I would continue to close transactions of various kinds in Louisiana, New Jersey, Virginia, California, Ohio, Georgia and other states. Where necessary, we hired local counsel to assist us with these transactions.

Cases Excluding Tabary and Brisbane

With some exceptions, instead of listing cases by name, I think it is better if I describe what happened in those cases that might be useful to current practitioners. The cases may not follow in chronological order.

As I pointed out above, my experience with using software in my practice began with using MultiMate. As I continued practicing, I began to use a lot of more advanced software. I list some of those as follows.

Microsoft programs (WORD, Excel, PowerPoint, CoPilot, OneDrive), Time Matters (for keeping track of time and billing), Adobe Acrobat, and several litigation software tools designed to assist attorneys with case analysis and management programs which were in the Casesoft suite of programs.

These were CaseMap – a case analysis tool that helped attorneys organize facts, issues, and evidence in a structured manner, Note Map – a legal outlining tool designed to help attorneys structure their arguments and case notes; however, I found it useful to prepare deposition questions. TextMap – a transcript management tool that enabled users to annotate and search deposition transcripts, Timemap - a timeline visualization tool that allowed users to create graphical timelines for cases.

I also used several of the interactive forms (such as New York State Bar Association's Hot Docs program in my Estate and Trusts litigation practice) and references provided to the members of the New York Bar Association, in addition to using Fastcase for legal research after using Lexis Nexis to do research for many years.

For lawyers who fear using software, it might be useful to point out that I learned how to use the software by immersing myself in learning how to use it. I learned as I went along.

Church Client (1978 +)

I cite this client to show how I used a creative alternative to bank financing to enable the church to purchase a synagogue.

The church had been conducting services in a small storefront location in Mount Vernon NY. However, the congregation was growing and needed some additional space. At the time, Claude Johnson, a young man whom I would eventually come to represent in his business, recommended me to the minister of the church to see if I could assist them in acquiring the synagogue. They would be moving from a location which accommodated about 100 people to one that would accommodate about 2500 people. The synagogue wanted to sell because is membership had declined significantly.

I agreed to represent the church and the first thing we had to do was to negotiate the transaction with the synagogue and then get financing.

At the time, the church and its members had saved approximately $40,000.00 in one of the local banks; however, that bank refused to give them a loan for $125,000 to purchase the synagogue on the ground that if the church defaulted it would look bad for the bank to have to foreclose on a church.

After some discussion, and my recommendation, the church decided to pull all its money out of their bank and to deposit it in the Community Savings and Loan Bank in Mount Vernon. Fortunately, we met a loan officer who was very sympathetic and who listened to reason. Initially he had wanted audited financial statements and the organization documents for the church and so forth.

I said to him that the church did not have certified financial statements, but we could provide him with proof that the church paid the rent on time for the administrative offices that it was operating over a period of many years and likewise they had a radio program on Sunday, and they had also paid on time over a period of many years. And there might have been something else. So, lo and behold, the bank agreed to give the church the loan secured by a mortgage. When the mortgage matured, the church paid off the mortgage.

I continued to represent the church in many matters over the following decades.

Consultant Client (1987+)

I met Lloyd Foote at a small business dinner. I had left my seat to go to the restroom and returned to find him sitting in my seat. Lloyd did not want to give up the seat, so I sat elsewhere. After some discussions that night and over time, Lloyd and I became friends. He was a very brilliant man and referred one of the clients he was providing consulting services to. Lloyd was estranged or divorced from Barbara Niles, who I mentioned did my initial secretarial services when I first opened my White Plains office.

I represented his client's small consulting company in connection with various legal matters, some of the most interesting ones involved audits by either the Commerce Department or another agency of the federal government. The terms of the money that the client received required the client to comply with various rules, including two circulars, I think they were OMB Circular A-122, now titled "Cost Principles for Non-Profit Organizations," which establishes principles for determining costs of grants, contracts, and other agreements with non-profit organizations, and OMB Circular 110 which sets standards for obtaining consistency and uniformity among Federal agencies in the administration of grants to and agreements with institutions of higher education, hospitals, and other non-profit organizations.

I am not sure if the consultant was operating as a profit or non-profit agency at the time.

The money was supposed to be used in a certain way, and expenditures were supposed to fall into specific categories. When the government did the audit of the books of this client, it alleged that certain amounts should be disallowed because they were not spent according to the way they were allocated in the budget. The net result of these findings was that the client would be on the hook to pay any money that it did not spend properly.

Usually, I would review the text of the funding documents to see what the conditions and terms were that the client would have to comply with, then I would look at the so-called yellow book which would tell me how the audit should have been conducted. Auditors of government entities and entities that receive government awards use Government Auditing Standards, commonly referred to as generally accepted government auditing standards (GAAS) or the Yellow Book, to perform their audits and produce their reports. The Yellow Book contains standards for financial audits, attestation engagements, and performance audits as well as specific requirements for individual auditors and audit organizations.[279]

The auditors would normally prepare a draft audit report and give the client an opportunity to comment on the draft. Through the process of reviewing the terms and conditions, the circulars, and the yellow book, I was successful in either reducing the amount of the draft liability or eliminating it altogether.

In my review of the various governing documents, I discovered that in one of the official regulations several sentences had been omitted. The text contained a word like ***conxyzment***. This was quite odd and prompted me to review the text of the original proposed regulation which had been printed in the Federal Register. No one else had ever pointed this out to the funding agency. It turns out that they missing language was helpful to us.

This illustrates the importance of being thorough in your work.

One of the executives of my client went on to become the CEO of a major media company. I assisted in the negotiation of his employment contract with the media company.

The Fatal Newburgh, NY Auto Accident. (1990)

This was a particularly tragic accident. A police officer had gotten off from work after working several hours and was driving on Broadway late at night when he struck a man who was crossing the street and killed him. He left his mother, three children and his unmarried girlfriend. His mother retained a well-known high-powered law firm in Newburgh at the time and when they found out I had been retained, sought to challenge the standing of the mother of the children to represent the young man's estate.

---

279 https://www.gao.gov/yellowbook (Accessed 01 Mar 2024)

As in all matters, I had done my research, and I knew that the young man's mother could not replace the mother of the children as the representative of his estate. The wrongful death action was brought on behalf of the children. To do so, we had to first ask the Surrogate's Court to appoint the children's mother as a guardian of their property. Then we applied to Surrogate's Court in that capacity to have her appointed as the personal representative of the estate of the children's father.

The only viable asset of the officer was his auto insurance policy, which he surrendered to the children.

Another great tragedy occurred in this case when we learned the news that our brilliant African American accident reconstruction expert had drowned in an accident at a location out of the country.

The Swinging Hook and Wrongful Death Case (1982)

This was a particularly painful case. A friend and Union Carbide coworker came to me after her boyfriend was killed when a swinging crane hook swing around and struck him in the head killing him instantly. She wanted to bring a wrongful death case; however, my research disclosed that she did not have standing to bring a wrongful death lawsuit because she was not married to her boyfriend; they had no children together, and we could not establish a common law marriage for them under New York law.

So, the lesson here is if you are in a relationship whether you have children or not, you should seek the assistance of an estate planner.

The Case of The Missing Safe Deposit Box (1983)

In this case, the widow found a safe deposit box key, but we were unable to find the box after a diligent search.

The lesson here is to tell your family members where they can find your assets when you pass away.

The Case Of the Bankrupt Liquor Store (1984)

In this case the client came to me when the sheriff's sale of his liquor store inventory was to take place within a few days. The only way that I knew to quickly prevent this sale was to put the liquor store into bankruptcy. I did not know much about bankruptcy law, and time was not on our side, so the question was whether a liquor store could file for bankruptcy. I couldn't find the answer, so I went to the court to ask simply if they would accept a petition if we presented it. They said yes, so we filed a bankruptcy petition on behalf of the liquor store. The effect of the filing was to automatically stop any proceedings. It therefore gave me immense pleasure to serve the sheriff just as he was about to begin the sale.

I do not remember the outcome of this matter.

The Case of Questionable Financing (1984)

One afternoon I received a telephone call from a former Morehouse classmate of mine who, with some other men, was looking to receive several millions of dollars in financing from a Middle Eastern source. However, they were being asked to put up $308,000.00 as an "earnest money deposit." They were about to come to New York from Los Angeles to meet with the man who was brokering the financing of several million dollars. I knew the man because he lived in New Rochelle.

This man had forwarded to them some documents about the way the financing would work. So, I asked him to fax the documents to me. I reviewed the documents and had a discussion with him, and I am not sure if this was on the same day or the next day but next thing I knew, the Los Angeles group had stopped over in Washington DC on their way to New York to meet with the broker, and wanted to know if I could come down to Washington to meet with them that night. I had a court appearance in NY the next morning, so I would only be able to make a round trip that night.

We agreed that I would fly down to meet them and catch an airplane to bring me back to New York that night. I met with my classmate and his group, but the only person that I could see who would be getting paid, regardless of what happened, was the man that I knew from New Rochelle. So, after a thorough discussion, they decided not to come to New York to go through with the transaction.

Again, I was only able to give my opinion after I had thoroughly analyzed what they had sent me.

The Case of the Veteran Who Could Not Rent An Apartment Because He Was Black (1985)

I received a telephone call from a man who told me that he and his wife lived in the Midwest but had been told over the telephone that apartment that they wanted to rent in White Plains , N.Y. was available. However, after driving all night, the landlord or his agent told the man, who was a veteran, and his wife, that they were sorry, but the apartment was taken. When he came to me, I quickly prepared a complaint and a motion for temporary restraining order and for a preliminary injunction to prevent the landlord from giving the apartment to anyone else.

We filed the lawsuit in federal court, which was in temporary quarters, at that time, at 101 E. Post Rd. in White Plains, less than a block from my office. The Court issued the temporary restraining order. I had also asked for accelerated discovery in my order to show cause. When we arrived at court on the return date, I made a motion to consolidate the request for a preliminary injunction with a request for a permanent injunction, based on the oral and documentary evidence we had.

The court ruled from the bench in our favor. I was startled because it is rare to get a judgment from the bench right after oral arguments and a hearing. I then learned that the court relied on a case styled Robinson v. 12 Lofts decided by the United States Court of Appeals for the Second Circuit, with which the court was intimately familiar. Our district court was bound by that decision.

What I later learned is that the reason that the trial court was so familiar with the Second Circuit case was that the facts in that case were almost identical to our case and the Second Circuit had reversed this same trial court in the Robinson case.

The Court also awarded my attorney fees, which it ordered the landlord to pay.

The Case of the Musician and the Flu (1985)

I had set up an appointment for a famous musician to come in to discuss his estate plan. Unfortunately, I should have cancelled the appointment, but I went to the office anyway. I knew he traveled a lot, so I wanted to relieve his anxiety. His wife accompanied him, and he wanted her present in the room. During the discussion, I could feel the wife becoming very uneasy and I was feeling ever so much more ill.

They left the office, and he did not contact me again.

The lesson here is not to go to work when you are sick.

The Case of the Deadbeat Celebrity (1986)

In this case, a well-known African – American political celebrity had hired a Savannah, Georgia based photographer to provide him with photos to use in his political campaign. After the photographer took the photos, which the celebrity actually used in his campaign, the celebrity refused to pay the photographer.

Over 100,000 photos, as I remember.

I am not sure if we sued the celebrity or his campaign, but I know we did recover some money on the photographer's behalf. I held his auto registration and some other documents as security for payment of my fees. I returned them.

As we have seen from the case of perhaps America's most well-known celebrity, and from my observations over the years, it is always prudent to collect a retainer fee from the celebrity at the time of engagement. And to always obtain a signed engagement or retainer letter from the client in advance. Otherwise, one runs the risk of not getting paid.

That celebrity is well-known for not paying his contractors.

The Case of the Erratic Karate Client (1988)

This case had great potential for the reduction or elimination of a property tax. I filed a complaint in federal court, probably on deprivation of property without due process.

As we proceeded, the client began telling me about the problems he had had with the Clerk of Westchester County. His conversations had been quite rational up to that point. Then he began telling me about his karate expertise and how he had had several bouts with the clerk. In his own mind, I knew that he believed what he was telling me.

I was then faced with the dilemma of representing a client who was existing in a phantom universe.

Even the judge was surprised when I filed a motion to have a guardian ad litem appointed to protect the rights of my own client.

After further discovery, the suit was either withdrawn or dismissed.

The Case of Part of the Missing Transcript Record (1988)

This was a case of race discrimination against a well-known company. During the trial, the judge asked the company's star witness if the company was beginning to look at my client as a "pest". When I read the transcript, I was faced with the problem of what to do when a transcript omitted this word, which I considered to be a significant error of bias on the part of the Judge.

I requested a conference with the judge at which both sides were present. I presented the issue as one of human error, as the court reporter failed to record this word. The judge asked if anyone had heard him say this word. A young female junior attorney for the company blurted out that she had heard it but was stopped by senior company counsel midsentence.

The judge claimed he did not recall making the statement. The reporter followed him. I was dumbfounded, but at least made this part of the record. The court decided against my client-a brilliant, hard-working African American woman. We did not have the resources to appeal.

The Meeting With Muhammad Ali (1988)

When I returned from my studies in Vienna in 1960, two African American males were all over the news – Malcolm X and Cassius Clay. I had read about them in JET magazine that my dear mother faithfully mailed to me while I was in Vienna. JET published information about black people not generally covered in the white media.

One of the most famous statements in the black community "If it was not reported in Jet, it didn't happen." So, I relied on Jet, the Black World, Ebony and weekly black newspapers to read news of black people.

Curious about this Malcom the Tenth, I went to hear him or a representative of the Nation of Islam at the mosque in Atlanta. As it turns out Muhammad (then Cassius) was sitting directly in front of me. I did not know who he was until he was asked to stand after being introduced as the 1960 light heavyweight Olympic boxing champion. At that time I was still studying or traveling in Europe as a Merrill scholar and did not know much about these two men.

Later, I would witness Malcom and Dr. Lonnie Cross (Lonnie Shabazz, later Abdulalim Abdullah Shabazz) having a very probative discussion at Yates and Milton's store on the corner of Fair Street and Chestnut Streets in Atlanta.

I took a course in advanced calculus from the brilliant Dr. Cross, who was a pure mathematician, and I graded the papers for his class.

Aside from mathematics, he taught us that wherever we find ourselves, ignore the stares of people around you and forge ahead with whatever it is you're doing. I found that to be most useful when I was the only black person in the room.

The next time I was that close to Muhammad Ali, was during a meeting in his suite at the Waldorf Astoria hotel in New York City. I had been contacted by a gentleman from Los Angeles whose name escapes me now to meet with him and Muhammad to discuss a legal issue of some kind. He was a friend of Muhammad's.

I went to the meeting and whatever the issue was, we resolved it. I'll never forget how hard Muhammad's hand was when he greeted me. Especially since my son Christopher was always teasing me about how soft my hands are. But Muhammed was interested in showing us some of his magic tricks and that's when I discovered that he enjoyed doing magic.

One of the tricks involved him levitating off the floor. I don't know how he did that because he turned his back to us. It did appear that he levitated.

Having witnessed this trick, I had a napkin in my hand, and he had done another trick where he turned a handkerchief from one color to another or took several of them out all tied together. So, I asked him if he could take the napkin and turn it into a $20 bill. At that point he drew back his famous right hand as if to hit me. I won't tell you the outcome of my request.

I enjoyed being in his company and his wife. Lonnie.

The Medical Records Case (Around 1987/88)

In this case, a tenant couple who resided in a house my client owned in the Bronx sued my client for money damages for more than a million dollars, allegedly because of some emotional damage that my client had caused the wife, and the husband derivatively.

The wife claimed she had seen a doctor for her injuries. The doctor produced a massive stack of medical records during discovery. After laying the foundation that the doctor had taken a careful medical history of his patient, I asked a simple question: "doctor please review that stack of documents and tell the jury if my client's name is mentioned anywhere in your medical records?" He answered "No." The jury ruled in favor of my client.

Of course, I had reviewed the records beforehand, as part of my preparation, so I followed the golden rule cross examination that you should never ask a question unless you know the answer. In this case the answer was dispositive.

As an aside, I felt I was doing a respectable job when the judge said he had asked his son to come in to watch how a lawyer should try case.

Again, preparing thoroughly is the key to success.

The Case of the Businessman Who Complained About Technicalities (1988)

We often hear of cases where a legal issue has been decided based on a technicality. Sometimes laypeople do not understand that there is a procedural aspect to the law, that is, how a case is supposed to be processed and decided. This procedural aspect involves certain rules that are technical.

The businessman in this case kept up with current events and from time to time he would tell me about how wrong it was for certain people to get off or have a case dismissed because of a technicality.

Well, in the 1989/1990 period, I was in the South of France visiting my client who lived in Cannes when I received a message from this client that he had been cited for DUI. I called him back, but he was so nervous I had to guide him through the paper that he had been served with, so that I could understand what it was.

He now wanted to take advantage of every technicality he could to relieve himself on the charge. He now realized that these technicalities meant something.

The Case of the Reluctant Police Officer in Assisted Suicide By Cop (1989)

This officer had come to see me about an issue that arose in his employment.

During my investigation of this case I learned two things. First, it is important to thoroughly interview a client to determine if the client has already signed away certain rights. Second, I learned of the concept of "suicide by cop" which I was not familiar with.

As to the first in this case, I learned that he had already signed a document dismissing his employer from the claim that he had come to see me about, and under the circumstances I thought it would be difficult to overcome what he'd already signed.

As to the second item, he told me that a man had threatened him with a butcher knife. He told me that he had been reluctant to shoot the man but that he realized that the man wanted to be shot to death and had attacked him with a lethal weapon. My recollection is that he shot the man but I'm not sure whether it was fatal or not. However, there was a departmental investigation which found that my client had been justified in acting to protect his own life.

The Case of the Use of the Abacus in a Commercial Setting (1987)

One day a lovely Chinese husband and wife contacted me to assistant them with a contract to buy out the interest of a third party. The husband had been a student at one of the Historically Black Colleges and Universities (HCBUs). They took out the contracts and shareholder agreement; however, it was written entirely in Chinese. So, they handled the translations, but I was in for another treat.

They did their calculations using an abacus.

An abacus (pl.: abaci or abacuses), also called a counting frame, is a hand-operated calculating tool which was used from ancient times in the ancient Near East, Europe, China, and Russia, until the adoption of the Hindu-Arabic numeral system.[280]I was familiar with it, but had never used it.

We successfully completed the transaction, and they sent me a beautiful, framed thank you note.

I continued to represent them in several other matters.

The Case of the Thoroughbred Horse Racing Groom (1992) and Buying Our House – Remembering Joseph Lewis Dozier

I was hired by one of the trainers of racehorses at the famed Belmont Racetrack to see if I could stop the immigration services from deporting the trainers' horse groom. One of the first things I did was to sign up for an equine law seminar to be held in Kentucky within a day or so of the Kentucky Derby to get some background.

I learned that there is a special relationship between the groom and the horse. Hence it was important to try to help the groom in this case stay in the country. Just before the 4th of July weekend, the immigration authorities had conducted a raid at Belmont. They detained many people who worked at the racetrack and were holding them in detention at a facility on Varick Street In New York City.

I obtained a photograph of the person on whose behalf I would be acting and went down to that facility to meet him. I met several lawyers who were representing some of the detainees. One was a young woman who had had some experience in this area. We exchanged business cards. Later, I received a telephone call from her telling me that

---

280 https://en.wikipedia.org/wiki/Abacus (Accessed 04 March 2024)

the immigration authorities were deporting some of the detainees in groups of 10 and that I should do something.

I had prepared an order to show cause which was supported by an underlying complaint that I had filed before bringing on the order to show cause.[281]

The numbers of detainees were diminishing rapidly, and it didn't help that the day that I had to act was the 4th of July, a major national U.S. holiday. I then learned something which I am passing on and that is, least in federal court, there is a duty judge in the courthouse during holidays.

So, I presented my order to show cause to the judge through the proper channels at the courthouse. Her law clerk started negotiating with the detention center to see if they would delay the deportation of my client until we had gotten a chance to resolve some legal problems that had been raised under a consent decree involving certain people who had entered the United States from Mexico. That consent decree had been entered in one of the western states before I became involved in the case but could apply to our case in New York. I learned about it through an attorney in one of the northwestern states, Washington or Oregon.

These negotiations between the detention center and the Judge's law clerk lasted for a few hours and I didn't know if the judge was going to sign the order to show cause.

However, late in the afternoon, while I was at home, I received a telephone call from the clerk asking me to come down to the courthouse, because the Judge was about to leave to celebrate the holiday and that I should come to the courthouse and collect the signed order to show cause from the U.S. Marshall.

I did so and immediately carried the order to show cause over to the detention center. One of the most unforgettable moments in my

---

[281] An Order to Show Cause is an emergency court order telling the person on whom it is served to come into court on a given day at a given time to show cause why that person should or should not do something.

practice as a lawyer happened when the desk officer at the detention center called upstairs for the commanding officer to come downstairs because I had an order to show cause to serve on him. He came downstairs.

His face was half shaven and there was shaving cream on the other half of his face, and he looked at me with some astonishment. I had told the duty officer at the entrance of the detention center that I had a federal court order that I needed to serve on the commander. That immediately stopped them from shipping my client out of the country. I was able to keep him in the country for another two years while we ironed out the problems under the consent decree.

Serving the order to show cause on the commander gave me a great feeling of the power of our courts.

I must pause here to give thanks to the late Joseph L Dozier. Joe was a consummate gentleman whom I first met in the 1970s when he and I worked at Howard Grant Hagood, and Holland at 10 Columbus Circle in New York City. At the time, this firm occupied the most prestigious location for an African American law firm in the City of New York. Even though Joe was not a lawyer, he knew more about how the courts operated than many lawyers. It was the discussions I had with Joe about the procedures to follow to keep the young man in the country.

One lesson here is it even on holidays, there is always a federal judge on duty to take care of emergencies.

Joe was helpful in many other ways. One other that I will mention was when he helped me prepare the legal papers to prevent the white owners from selling their house to others that Jane and I wanted to buy. They were refusing to sell to us. We both looked young, and we were black. We alleged that it was because of our race. They denied it, saying that their religion forbade them to discriminate. After we prepared the papers, Joe served them.

We resolved the case. We bought the house.

A second lesson is that lawyers don't know everything.

The Case of the Mutual Separation of the College President (1996)

One of my closest friends had become President of a prestigious college in one of the nation's largest cities. He made significant contributions to the math and science curriculum. Unfortunately, he also developed some health issues that might have played a role in his decision to resign. He accepted the college's findings that he did not employ best practices in accounting for some of his expenditures. We were able to negotiate a reasonable separation package for him.

Given his position and the circumstances this story was carried in a newspaper of worldwide wide circulation. My role was to keep his reputation intact as much as possible. He was exceptionally brilliant and made many innovations in curriculum development.

News reporters wanted him or me to make a statement. I advised him to refer all inquiries to me, and I would handle them. My approach was to make the target of the follow-on news as small as possible. I did so successfully. The story had a short shelf life.

These cases which have a high probability of becoming very visible and keep reporters busy with irrelevant, and as well as relevant subject matter.

They key is evaluating how big a target you want to give them to shoot at.

Case of the Survivor of the Tulsa Race Massacre (1997)

I first met Dr. Olivia Hooker at meetings of the White Plains-Greenburgh, New York chapter of the NAACP (National Association for the Advancement of Colored People).

For long time, I knew her only as a member and, a little later, as a Ph.D. clinical psychologist.

Little did I know that I would represent one of the witnesses to the most savage attack on black people in our history – the Tulsa race massacre of 1921.

Our first assignment was to draft a will for her. At the time, my younger son, Christopher, was working with me as an associate in my office. He assisted with the drafting and filing the will with the Clerk of the Surrogate's Court for safekeeping. We often followed this practice so that clients or their representatives would be able to locate the original will.

On December 1, 2005, she revised her will and it was duly filed, and the Clerk duly issued a receipt which would be needed to retrieve the will. We generally would ask the client to tell the Executrix named in the will that it is on file. Of course, this requires the client to keep track of the receipt.

We followed this practice because oftentimes people lose or misplace their wills.

She executed another will in 2011. We followed the same procedure.

By this time, we had learned that Dr. Hooker was a survivor of the Tulsa race massacre.[282]

She told me that she had escaped harm, as a 5-year-old, when her father hid her under a large dining room table.

Because the history of this massacre has so often been left out of U.S. history courses, I recite some of it here.

The Tulsa race massacre, also known as the Tulsa race riot or the Black Wall Street massacre,[283] was a two-day-long white supremacist terrorist massacre that took place between May 31 and June 1, 1921, when mobs of white residents, some of whom had been appointed as deputies and armed by city government officials, attacked black residents and destroyed homes and businesses of the Greenwood District

[282] https://en.wikipedia.org/wiki/Tulsa_race_massacre (Accessed 21 March 2024)
[283] Id. Internal footnotes omitted

in Tulsa, Oklahoma. The event is considered one of the worst incidents of racial violence in American history. The attackers burned and destroyed more than 35 square blocks of the neighborhood—at the time one of the wealthiest black communities in the United States, colloquially known as "Black Wall Street".

More than 800 people were admitted to hospitals, and as many as 6,000 black residents of Tulsa were interned in large facilities, many of them for several days. The Oklahoma Bureau of Vital Statistics officially recorded 36 dead. The 2001 Tulsa Reparations Coalition examination of events identified 39 dead, 26 black and 13 white, based on contemporary autopsy reports, death certificates, and other records. The commission gave several estimates ranging from 75 to 300 dead.

About 10,000 black people were left homeless, and the cost of the property damage amounted to more than $1.5 million in real estate and $750,000 in personal property (equivalent to $36.92 million in 2022). By the end of 1922, most of the residents' homes had been rebuilt, but the city and real estate companies refused to compensate them. Many survivors left Tulsa, while residents who chose to stay in the city, regardless of race, largely kept silent about the terror, violence, and resulting losses for decades. The massacre was largely omitted from local, state, and national histories for years.

I recite this brief history, because as just stated, this history was hidden for decades.

Recently, Tom Hanks expressed his disappointment that he had never heard of this race massacre. Neither have many other Americans.

Of course, Florida's Gov. Ron DeSantis, is trying his best to erase all the ugly racist incidents that took place in Florida and elsewhere regarding black people, Native Americans and the Japanese settlers in the Yamato Colony in Florida; for the Japanese, Yamato Colony.[284]

---

[284] We know about the Trail of Tears and the Native Americans. Less well known is the history of the displacement of the Japanese population in Florida. I learned about this as drove to visit my client in West Palm Beach, Florida. He gave me an overview of that history. I was happy to be able to visit the Murakami Museum in

Pat Weems, Dr. Hooker's long-time confidant, organized several events to celebrate Dr. Hooker in her centenary year.

One was her February 12, 2015, celebration her 100th birthday at Trinity United Methodist Church, 130 S. Lexington Avenue, White Plains, NY. which I attended. Many of Dr. Hooker's friends were there too, including Pat, Gail Wright Sirmans, and Barbara Dodds. Gail related the humorous trials and tribulations of how she and Olivia attended the first or second Barack Obama inauguration.

Another was the March 12, 2015, naming of the Coast Guard Dining Hall after her, at the Coast Guard base on Staten Island, New York. Dr. Hooker had been the first African American female to join the Coast Guard. She received many other honors, including having a coast Guard Cutter ship named after her.[285]

Dr. Hooker being interviewed at the ceremony, with me and Lena Anderson, the President of the White Plains Greenburgh Branch of the NAACP standing behind her.

Palm Beach as part of a National Bar Association local event. See, for example https://discovernikkei.org/en/journal/2020/6/22/yamato-colony/ (Book review of Yamato Colony: A Japanese Village in Southern Florida, By Arthur A. Hansen / 22 Jun 2020)(Accessed 21 March 2024)

285 https://en.wikipedia.org/wiki/Olivia_Hooker#Career (Accessed 21 March 2014)

She passed away November 21, 2018 (aged 103).

Several people spoke at her memorial service, but I just want to single out Pat Weems and Gail Wright Sirmans, Esq..Pat told us about her relationship, but Gail kept us in stitches when she related the happenings of her trip with Dr. Hooker to witness the swearing-in of President Barack Obama in freezing weather..

The Case of the Airlines Refusing to Properly Seat a Paraplegic Man And Removed Him from the Airplane After He Had Followed All Their Procedures (2002)

Tragically, this gentleman was diagnosed with prostate cancer in February 2002. He was the husband of one of my clients.

By the time they came to see me later in 2002, the cancer had metastasized to his spine, bones, and other organs. He was paralyzed from the waist down and confined to a wheelchair.

Although he and his wife had made prior arrangements to accommodate him on the return flight from Charlotte NC to La Guardia Airport in New York, in a bulkhead seat, the airlines refused to honor the arrangement, crammed him into a different seat, and forcibly removed him from the aircraft, causing considerable pain, stress and discomfort.

After continually refusing to attend to Michael and removing him from the airplane and taking him to the terminal, the airline's employees refused to get his luggage which contained his medication, other assistive medical aid, and eventually required him and his family to take a later flight by way of Atlanta.

I then began to research the potential claims against the airlines that he and his wife might have under federal and state law.

However, it was touch and go as to whether Michael would survive until we could prepare and file a complaint on his behalf.

Under Rule 27 of the Federal Rules of Civil Procedure, a potential claimant is allowed to file a petition to take depositions to perpetuate testimony because the claimant might not be available to testify in the case when it comes to trial.

Early in 2003, under Rule 27, I made an application to Hon. Charles LaMonte Brieant Jr., a United States district judge of the United States District Court for the Southern District of New York, sitting in White Plains, for an order to take Michael's deposition. From my discussion with the clerks, no one had ever applied for such an order in this court. This is notable because Judge Brient served from 1971 to 2008. He issued the order.

Because of the urgency of this matter, we also served the potential defendants with a notice to waive service so that time to answer the petition would be shortened before the expiration of the ordinary answering date.

We took Michael's deposition.

I filed the complaint around April 25, 2003. I also prepared discovery requests before and after filing the complaint.

By June 2003, the Defendants had not answered the complaint, so I filed an application for a default judgment. Judge Brient assigned Magistrate Mark Fox to oversee these preliminary matters.

Michael did not survive and passed away before September 15, 2003. We made the necessary applications to the Westchester County Surrogate's Court (Scarpino, J.), to substitute Michael's Estate to represent his interests.

By November 2003, Delta had been heavily fined for not providing adequate assistance to disabled passengers between 2000-2002.[286]

The case was settled with a cash payment to my clients, including attorney's fees and costs.

---

286 Feds fine Delta for wheelchair allegations , By RUSSELL GRANTHAM, The Atlanta Journal-Constitution: 11/14/03

I cited this case to point out how to use Rule 27 of the Federal Rules Of Civil Procedure,[287] and how important it is to know the rules and attend continuing legal education programs to learn of rules one might not ordinarily run across.

The Case of Spamalot's Unauthorized Use of Botswana Beauty's Photograph (2006)

On a given Sunday afternoon in 2005/2006, my then fiancée, Maleta Luna-Rosa Mogwe, and I, met Carla Collins for lunch at a restaurant in New York City, not far from the Shubert Theatre, to celebrate her birthday. Carla is Maleta's goddaughter.

Spamalot, the number one musical play on Broadway at the time, was playing at the Shubert Theatre. Carla is a pretty young lady, with blonde hair and blue eyes. She was in New York for some further study at the Lee Strasberg Theatre and Film Institute.

She is a British citizen but was born in Botswana and had spent part of her life there, which is Maleta's home country. I had already met both her parents. She had brought some of her portfolio photos with her, and as we chatted about them and other things, Carla mentioned that on her way to the luncheon she saw a photograph of herself above the marquee of the Shubert Theater, which was showing Spamalot, the top Broadway show at the time, and she did not know how it got there.

---

[287] There is probably a New York State counterpart, as well.

The photo of Carla blowing a kiss.(2006)

She had several modeling, acting, dancing and video credits, played the piano, saxophone, and is a singer.

I thought that this was peculiar, so, when we finished eating lunch, we all walked around to the theatre. Sure enough, there was no mistaking her likeness above the Shubert Theater several stories high and prominent as advertising for the hit show.

What happened is that in 2002, she had appeared for a photoshoot in Yzerfontein, South Africa. After the shoot was over, she jokingly blew a kiss at the photographer when he took the photo later used by Spamalot without Carla's consent.

We wrote a letter to the Shubert Theatre requesting a copy of any consent that Carla gave to use her likeness. They ignored us.

On January 20, 2006, the attorneys for Serino Coyne, Inc., Shubert's advertising agency, responded to our letter by saying that the image that appeared above the marquee on the theater was that of a different model altogether, and that it was not a likeness of Carla:

"Any resemblance that you or your client may perceive between Carla Collins and the model in the billboard is purely coincidental.

Accordingly, we consider this matter closed."

Of course, we knew their conclusion was absurd.

We initially filed a lawsuit in New York State Supreme Court in late January 2006, but a few days later, we stayed that lawsuit and filed suit in federal court under the Lanham Act and New York's civil rights privacy statute. We filed the federal lawsuit on February 8, 2006.

We knew that in June 2005, SPAMALOT had won three 2005 Tony awards. According to the official SPAMALOT website, these included Best Musical and Best Director. It also won the Drama Desk and Outer Critic Circle Awards for Best Musical.

At that time, the confirmed advance sales to attend SPAMALOT were $27,000,000.00.

With the assistance of Federal Magistrate Judge Gabriel W. Gorenstein, we settled the lawsuit about 3 months after we filed it. By that time Carla had returned to England; we contacted her from Magistrate Gorenstein's chambers by telephone during the settlement conference and were able to come to an agreement.

After we settled the case, one of the attorneys for the defendants, either Maureen McLoughlin, Esq., or Jennifer Schatzman, Esq., offered me two or more theatre tickets to see Spamalot. She did not know that even though the play had been sold out, I had already secured 2 tickets earlier from Wendy Life, my cousin, to see Spamalot. Wendy worked at a large entertainment company at the time. Maleta and I went to see the play for the first time.

The second time I went to see it, with the tickets they gave us, my law partner Roni, and her husband Ron went with us. So, I saw Spamalot twice and of course I was always on the lookout for their use of Carla's likeness in any of their merchandise or in the play.

One bonus of the second showing is that Quincy Jones was seated right in front of us. When the play was over, I shook hands with him as we were leaving, acknowledging each other, but without conversation.

In 2024, while I was visiting the Spice Restaurant in Westbrook Beach, Durban, South Africa, Lutchmee "Linda" Burger gave me a copy of Anant Singh's book, *In Black and White*. Anant tells an amusing story about him, Marlon Brando, Quincy, and another man named Leroy. Lutchmee owns the Spice Restaurant.

In the beginning of our case, our chief obstacle was being able to locate the photograph that was taken after the 2002 photo shoot in South Africa. Peter Collins, Carla's father, who is a retired Botswana High Court judge, had expressed his doubts about whether we were going to be able to find the original photograph that had been taken in Yzerfontein.

We began searching all over the place.

One Saturday night Maleta and I went to dinner in New York City. I received a telephone call from my brilliant intrepid partner, Roni Jacobson, Esq. I got up from the table and went to a private space so as not to disturb the restaurant patrons. Roni, who was a whiz with technology, asked if I was sitting down. She then told me the explosive news that she had searched the web and found the exact original photo of Carla used by Spamalot. All of us who were connected with the case were overjoyed.

Another thing that Roni did was to contact her cousin Jimmy, a photographer who took several wide-angle photos of the Shubert theatre showing Carla's likeness fixed above the marquee. We used a couple of those photos as exhibits to the complaint.

Dr. Babatunde Soleye, a podiatrist, now a teacher and photographer, assisted us by helping to define some of the discovery demands concerning photographs we needed to request.

Babatunde has been a great friend, going back to the 1980s. It was also an immense pleasure to visit with him again when he and his fiancée were visiting here in Botswana. Incredibly, in 1999/2000 he was the photographer that Maleta had retained to take photographs of Mpule Gwelagobe, the 1999 Miss Universe. Maleta trained Mpule. That was many years before I met her.

Me, Maleta and Babatunde in Gaborone ca. 2023

Initially, when we filed the complaint in state court, around January 23, 2006, the clerk collected the complaint and placed it in a media basket indicating that it might be newsworthy. The next morning as I was getting ready to take Maleta to the airport to return to Botswana, Roni had arrived at the office; she telephoned to tell me that I had received telephone calls from various news outlets about the complaint.

I told her that I would try to return calls on my way to the airport. One of the people that I spoke with was with the Associated Press (AP), a wire service, so I thought that I would return that call first and then return calls to the television stations and print media. I thought that the wire services would be carrying the story the quickest.

I spoke with Sam Maull, the AP reporter, to tell him that I was driving my fiancée back to the airport so that she could return to Botswana. He said, "tell her that I said dumela." So, I said she's sitting right here, and you can tell her yourself. Whereupon Maleta and Mr.

Maull began to carry on an extensive conversation in Setswana, one of the two official languages of Botswana. It turns out that he had been in the Peace Corps in Botswana in 1966 and had not heard or spoken the language since then.

When we got off the phone and I returned to the office we discovered that he had drafted a fabulous article that appeared in The Age, an Australian medium, and within a brief period of time we had gotten over 800,000 hits on his article

I had the pleasure of meeting Mr. Maull, when he accepted our invitation to attend my 70th birthday celebration at the Fair Deal Café in White Plains, New York, owned by my friend Koshy Chacko.

The lesson here is to use all the resources you possibly can to get the information you need to represent your client effectively.

The Case of the Estate of the Star Physician Who was Killed Because He Abused His Family (2005) And the Forged Check

This is a particularly painful case to write about.

A young man killed his father. The father was a very well-respected emergency room physician who was held in extremely high esteem by his colleagues and friends. He appeared to be a model father in a model family. Friends and colleagues knew him as a strict disciplinarian, in what he regarded as keeping with his Uganda customs. I never witnessed any such conduct while I visited Uganda in the 1970s, 1980s, or in 2002.

What was not known is that the father had severely abused his children and his wife over an extended period of time. He generally beat the 5 boys and 2 girls in the basement of his Westchester home, sometimes tying them to a pipe. All were adults or near adults by the time of his death.

What apparently triggered the son to act was the father's continued abuse of the mother.

The son pleaded to manslaughter and was sentenced to a jail term of 20 years.

He was later released after serving 15 years, because of a new Domestic Violence Survivors Act which considers the circumstances surrounding the crime.[288]

All the children were getting mental health support. One or two were in or had recently been in a treatment facility at the time of the father's death. I specifically remember one of the girls and one of the boys. Lovely human beings.

During the tragic aftermath of the death, John, one of the young adult sons, drowned himself by walking into a lake in his hometown.

We were all shaken.

Upon the recommendation of my friend Godfrey L. Binaisa, Q.C., Esq., the mother retained our firm to handle the father's estate. Roni worked extensively on this case, and some others. We visited the family and attended the services.

As the world continues to shrink, it is more important than ever that we get to know one another across borders.

One aspect of the case concerned the payment of the estate's share to the father's minor child who lived with his mother in Uganda. I had suggested to the child's guardian ad litem that we arrange to transfer that money by wire. She insisted on a check. I knew that there would be an added cost to clear the check, and that it would take some time. That did not matter to her.

We sent the check to her; then the unexpected happened. When the check was returned to our bank, I received a call from the bank saying that the check bounced because the trust account was overdrawn.

---

288 https://www.bing.com/search?q=Sentence+of+Lumumba+Kazigo&form=WNSGPH&qs=SW&cvid=f1754e03a3e84c74917db36e1fe9535c&pq=Sentence+of+Lumumba+Kazigo&cc=BW&setlang=en-US&nclid=A291A2AFFA13590C2BD72420E7416BFD&ts=1712226852833&wsso=Moderate (Accessed 04 April 2024)

When this happens, the bank usually contacts the grievance committee for investigation to see if disciplinary charges are warranted against the attorney who established the trust account.

I asked the bank to fax me a copy of the front and back of the check. When I received it, I immediately identified 22 forged items on the check, including misspellings and endorsements by Chinese banks (Chinese characters stamped on bank.) I suspected that someone within the bank had a Chinese associate, and they changed the amount to be paid.

I immediately contacted the grievance committee and asked them not to open an investigation because I could easily show that this was a forged check which would have caused the trust account to be overdrawn. They agreed and asked for a letter from the bank and a copy of the check. They were satisfied and did not open an investigation.

The Cases of the United Nations and the United States Using and Occupying the One Square Kilometer Compound Owned By a Somali National in Mogadishu without Paying Compensation (1995)

In the late fall of 1995, my friend, Godfrey L. Binaisa, QC, Esq, former Attorney General of Uganda, told me that a fellow Ugandan had contacted him to see if we could bring a case against the United Nations, and other parties to recover some kind of compensation for Mr. Abdi Hosh, a Somali national.

a) The Case Against the United Nations Alleging Wrongful Use and Occupancy of Mr. Hosh's Property in Mogadishu, Somalia

The Court recited the basic allegations as follows.

"This is an action to recover in excess of $190 million in damages relating to the alleged unauthorized and unlawful possession of the plaintiff's property in Mogadishu, Somalia during the United Nations' military and humanitarian operations there beginning in or about April 1992.

The plaintiff's property is a compound encompassing approximately one million square meters containing an office complex, a hotel, recreational facilities, restaurants, and other facilities. The compound was allegedly occupied and used as a military logistics and supply base by the United Nations and its agents, Brown Root Services Corp. ("Brown Root"), and the Doe Corporation defendants. The plaintiff alleges that the United Nations wrongfully and without proper authorization occupied approximately one-quarter of the compound for a period of about eighteen months. The plaintiff maintains that the fair rental value of the compound over that period of time is approximately $190 million, one quarter of which he alleges is allocable to the United Nations.

The plaintiff asserts claims against the Secretary General of the United Nations, Boutros Boutros-Ghali and the Under Secretary General for Administration and Management, Joseph E. Connor, (the "U.N. Defendants"), in their official and individual capacities, claiming lost rental value, (Count 1); gross negligence in failing to ensure payments to the plaintiff, (Count 2); and violations of the New York Human Rights Law, Executive Law § 296, arising out of the failure to pay the plaintiff based on his race and national origin, (Count 3). In addition to his claim for compensatory damages of $193,779,447, the plaintiff also seeks exemplary damages of $750 million and prejudgment interest at 18% per year compounded daily, and attorney's fees and costs."[289]

We dismissed Secretary Boutros-Ghali in order to cure a jurisdictional defect. The Court ruled that we could not have a foreign plaintiff and a foreign defendant in the same lawsuit.

The Court said further "The U.N. Defendants have not been served with the summons and complaint. Legal counsel for the United Nations has submitted papers, however, asserting absolute immunity of the United Nations and the U.N. Defendants and requesting the Court

[289] https://casetext.com/case/askir-v-boutros-ghali; 933 F. Suppl. 368 (SDNY 1996)

dismiss the Complaint sua sponte. At the Court's request, the United States, while not a party in this case, has submitted papers in support of the U.N. Defendants' suggestion of dismissal. The plaintiff opposes dismissal of the U.N. Defendants and seeks an order permitting the U.S. Marshal Service to serve the U.N. Defendants."[290]

In dismissing the complaint in the UN case, the Court held that the United Nations was acting in its sovereign capacity and not in a commercial capacity, explaining the differences thusly:

> "Under the restrictive, as opposed to the "absolute," theory of foreign sovereign immunity, a state is immune from the jurisdiction of foreign courts as to its sovereign or public acts (jure imperii), but not as to those that are private or commercial in character (jure gestionis) . . . . [A] state engages in commercial activity under the restrictive theory when it exercises "`only those powers that can also be exercised by private citizens,"' as distinct from those "powers peculiar to sovereigns."' Put differently, a foreign state engages in commercial activity for purposes of the restrictive theory only where it acts "in a manner of a private player within" the market.
>
> Saudi Arabia v. Nelson, 507 U.S. 349, 359-60, 113 S.Ct. 1471, 1478-79, 123 L.Ed.2d 47 (1993) (citations omitted)."

We had argued that the United Nations was acting in the commercial capacity of a landlord. The Court disagreed.

The Court reasoned:

> "A military operation, even one directed at ensuring the delivery of humanitarian relief, is not an endeavor commonly associated with private citizens — indeed, military operations are a distinctive province of sovereigns and governments. The occupation of property during such an operation to house troops, store and distribute supplies and ordinance, or manage the logistics and planning of peacekeeping and humanitarian relief efforts is part and parcel of such an operation. The United Nations mission in

[290] However, Mr. Binaisa was able to get a UN employee to serve Secretary Boutros-Ghali, so I am not sure about the accuracy of the Court's statement.

Somalia provided "a military force to enable relief agencies to deliver food and other supplies to the Somali people." (Compl. 11.)

The Court dismissed our case against the United Nations defendants.

Askir v. Boutros-Ghali, 933 F. Supp. 368, 372 (S.D.N.Y. 1996)"

b) The Case Against the United States

I had already developed the theories of recovery in this case while preparing the United Nations case Askir v. Connor and Brown & Root Services Corp., 95 Civ. 11008 (JGK), (S.D.N.Y.). (the "Southern District Case"). In that case, we filed the complaint on December 29, 1995. (Koeltl, J.)

We filed the action against the United States in the Court of Federal Claims in Washington, D.C. on January 14, 1996. The case was initially assigned to Chief Judge Loren Smith, File # 96-351 L.

By this time, Judge Koeltl had dismissed the case we filed in the Southern District of New York. As a result, Mr. Hosh fired us and substituted Philip Musolino of Washington, D.C. to represent him. That is the reason Mr. Musolino's name appears in Judge Allegra's opinion as counsel for Mr. Hosh, and not mine or Mr. Binaisa's.

The case was decided in 1999, 3 years later, after it had been reassigned to Judge Allegra. We sued on the theory that the United States had taken Mr. Hosh's property temporarily for a public use without compensation under the Fifth Amendment to the U.S. constitution.

Judge Allegra dismissed the action against the United States, on the grounds that the court lacked subject matter jurisdiction, since neither Mr. Hosh nor his property was located within the territory of the United States. Moreover, neither had any substantial connection with the United States.

Among other experiences I learned were these. First, the cases filed in that court normally involved vast sums of money. Second, to close out the continuing legal education program of Court of Federal Claims Bar Association, we were served a dinner in the beautiful Corcoran Gallery of Art. The elaborate dinner was introduced by a gold serving plate which would come to hold the dinner plate, and the dessert was topped with fine gold trimmings. Third, the importance of exercise. Several of us walked back from the Gallery to our hotel. As we walked, I handled the walk with relative ease; my companions were huffing and puffing. I think this is because I was using a 20-minute walk in my routine every morning before I went to my office.

The Case of the Estate of Anna H. Gatison and the Benefit of Good Client Relations (1987)

Ms. Anna Gatison was employed in the New York City education system, as a teacher, as I recall. Her sister was Ms. Maude Frazier, a resident of South Carolina. Ms. Gatison passed away, leaving an adult son who had a mental disability and was in the mental ward of a New York City hospital at the time of her death. His name is Raleigh Gatison.

Someone referred Ms. Frasier to me to handle her sister Anna's estate. My recollection is that the main asset of her estate was the money that she was entitled to under her pension plan. Since Ms. Gatison passed away in New York City without a will, we filed her administration papers in the Surrogate's Court in Manhattan.

In 1997, my son Attorney Christopher and I collected the assets of her estate. We established a supplemental needs trust for the benefit of Raleigh. Ms. Muriel Mayers, an indispensable paralegal, assisted us with many issues, but worked mainly on accounting issues in this and other cases. In this case, Muriel prepared the annual budgets and accounts that the Court required.

The Court appointed Ms. Frasier as the trustee. Chris sent Ms. Frasier a copy of the statute that governed her powers and duties.

Since Ms. Frasier lived in South Carolina, we also prepared the necessary legal instruments to have Raleigh relocated to South Carolina, so that Ms Frasier would be better able to look after him.

In August 2014, we filed a petition on behalf of Ms. Frasier, who was elderly, to have her daughter Karon Anderson succeed her as trustee. The Court granted the petition and appointed Karon.

In the interim, my family reunion was scheduled to take place in 2009 in Olar, South Carolina, where my father was born and spent his early childhood.

I notified Ms. Frasier that I would be coming and asked her if Maleta and I could visit her. She was happy and invited us. I, not thinking it was anything out of the ordinary, was pleasantly startled when she said that she would never forget our visit for the rest of her life. I don't think I showed it, but we tackled several legal issues together and bonded.

But that was not the only benefit.

Ms. Frasier told us we should visit the Boone Plantation in North Charleston and the Penn Center to learn some history of the region.

We had intended to visit the Boone Plantation for lunch but wound up staying the whole afternoon. They have reconstructed 10 slave cabins on a roadway. Cabin number 3 yielded a wonderful surprise – a photo and history of the Rev. Daniel Jenkins, a distant cousin. It shows his likeness and the fact that the Jenkins Orphanage was established in 1891 for African American Children, the first of its kind in Charleston.

In addition, he organized the Jenkins Orphanage Band. Rev. Jenkins hired local musicians P.M. "Hastie" Logan and Francis Eugene Mikell to tutor the boys in music. The band takes credit for originating the "Charleston" dance. The band performed in old Citadel uniforms, using donated musical instruments, They performed on the streets of Charleston, in the Inaugural parades of Presidents Theodore Roosevelt and Howard Taft, and played in Paris, Berlin, Rome, London and Vienna.

2009 Olar – Orangeburg SC Reunion – Jenkins Band

2009 Olar – Orangeburg SC Reunion reconstructed slave street

L-R 2009 Olar – Orangeburg SC Reunion — top inside slave cabin, middle tree outside Boone and bottom main house tree-lined drive leading to Boone Plantation,

Likewise, the Penn Center would turn out to yield some valuable information. Unfortunately, we arrived near to closing time but quickly toured the bookstore and museum. Maleta was beside herself when we came across a mounted photo of a man in a classroom teaching in Botswana, her home country.

I wound up buying an extensive collection of books about the civil war and reconstruction in South Carolina. As a result, I began to study African American Civil War history.

Living in Botswana

Top - partial view of Gaborone Central Business District, circa 2018

Bottom - partial view of Gaborone City looking southward, showing landmark Kgale Hill

These photos do not show the lovely residential areas, such as where I live. Maybe an AI search will give some idea.

I am often asked what it is like to live in Africa. Africa is a huge continent which can accommodate within its borders the land area of the United States, China, India and have space left over. Sometimes I must break it down to them that I live in Botswana, one of 54 African countries within the continent.

The official languages are English and Setswana. Many of the local people speak both, and sometimes one or more of the other local languages.

It is customary to greet others as you pass or approach them, even if they are total strangers. Simply say "Dumela," or "Dumelang." Similar to our greetings when I was growing up in Savannah.

For an American, the cost of living is quite affordable as the currency exchange rate is about 13 -14.00 Pula to the U.S. Dollar. This enables me to live affordably on income from a small annuity my wife Jane left me, my social security, and some savings from my law practice.

In the United States, the house I am buying in Lobatse, and the apartment I am renting in Gaborone would cost considerably more than I am paying here. I live in one of six apartments in a small complex in Gaborone that houses a pool, patio, an ample walled in garden and walk area, and a swimming pool. There are trees everywhere, and the ladies who clean the apartment are present 5 and ½ days per week.

I had the good fortune of meeting Prof. (ret.) Monageng Mokalakwe, who introduced me to his friend, Mma Masire, who leased my apartment to me. I am very happy here.

Top - Panoramic View of garden in front of my apartment, showing the patio and pool on the left, with a nicely laid out dry climate garden that I use to walk around in and a huge, lovely tree, directly in front of my apartment with a balcony.

Bottom – my apartment with balcony

Botswana faces several challenges. To name a few - Youth unemployment, including college graduates, gender-based violence, huge disparity in wealth, loss of export revenue support due to the drastic reduction in the sale of diamonds, and the lack of diversification, the lack of useful land to meet the need for affordable housing. This latter issue arises because there is some unserviced vacant land that could be developed, but they need costly infrastructure development, i.e., water and electricity. These

One striking aspect of life here is the high degree of personal hygiene and concern about public health. Long before Covid, hand sanitizers greeted one upon entry to various shops, especially supermarkets. After Covid, they are still present but not as ubiquitous.

While dining, adequate facilities are made available for people to wash their hands, including basins in the dining room as well as in the bathrooms. In the villages, similar hygiene is practiced. At mass gatherings, and in the rural village areas, funerals and weddings, for example, a young person will come around with a picture of water to wash one's hands, followed by another young person with a towel to dry them.

When Covid arrived, various public and private organs had disseminated detailed information about how people should care for themselves and others.

Likewise, going out with a spot on one's shirt is a no-no. Dressing appropriately for various events is highly desired.

This is a country of many beauty pageants because it is blessed with many beautiful women, entertainment, sporting events, vigorous politics, an independent free press (although the members of the media might challenge me on this, and to some extent they would be right), some corruption, peaceful quietness, but a vast gap in income levels.

Here in the capital of Gaborone, I find it exciting to turn into the side streets and continually discover lovely self-contained neighborhoods.

In the beginning the Botswana government was looking for a place to relocate its headquarters from Lobatse to another place in the country. Gaborone, the current capital, was completely undeveloped; the land area was full of trees and bush.

This allowed urban planners to orderly design the City of Gaborone. Recently I took a couple of visitors from Nairobi, Kenya and Kigali, Rwanda on a quick tour of Gaborone. They were impressed with the orderly organization of the city.

The people could not be more friendly and courteous. Disputes, especially loud public ones, are discouraged to promote a sense of harmony and lessening of tensions. Similar to the Japanese cultural practice of Wa (harmony).[291]

There is some kind of hierarchy in Botswana. I have seen it in operation both in the Botswana context and in the African continental context. The lengthy recitation of protocol at formal events, for example. Also, who sits where. The same may be said of other cultures, including our own, but this is the first time it struck me.

Also, once Batswana get to know you, there is a tendency to check on you to see if you are alright. Aone had not seen me come into the Pavilion for some time, so she called today to check on me, and to let me know of the Global Expo taking place at the Fairground. I am going in for lunch and to visit the expo, since a friend of mine is exhibiting. Friday is local cuisine day, so I am having Seswaa, Letlhodi, Setampa, I think?, Morogo, Lephutshe

Although Batswana have a local reputation for not reading books, there are a few thriving booksellers in the country. The same is not true for newspapers as these seem to have a large, vigorous readership.

One factor that contributes to the cohesion in society as a whole is the Kgotla system where Ministers, the President and other officials meet with local residents on a regular basis to discuss issues that affect the local communities. These meetings are well attended, even on early, cold mornings. Citizens are given an opportunity to voice their opinions. As I have witnessed in many contexts, attendees pay close

---

291 https://en.wikipedia.org/wiki/Wa_(Japanese_culture) (Accessed 31 May 2025)

attention to what is being said, without taking notes. But they remember what was said.

Also, there is a thirst for knowledge, with people showing up for workshops and at kgotla meetings in large numbers, even early in the morning, and when it is cold.

Oddly enough, although I have been traveling to Botswana since 2004, and moved here in 2016, I have not visited any of the diamond mines, even though Botswana is the world's first or second largest producer of rough diamonds. In 2024, I did visit a Debswana diamond display at an expo in Gaborone. It is amazing how they produce a sparkling piece of jewelry out of sometimes nondescript looking rocks.

In this connection, through my wife Maleta, on January 1, 2006, I met the late Lou Nchindo at a New Years luncheon at his residence in Gaborone. Lou had been Managing Director of Debswana, the joint mining, distribution and sales joint venture to sell Botswana's high-quality diamonds under the DeBeers label.

This was a continuation of the posh New Year's eve party that he gave the night before. During that party, I was voted the best male dancer – probably because they had never seen such a spectacle.

Although Lou and I had seen each other from time to time, we had never had a conversation until the luncheon.

Lou shared with me a significant historical event; namely, during President George W. Bush's visit to Botswana, when asked where he wanted to sit at the dinner, Lou said he wanted to sit next to President Bush. Bush asked Lou if there was anything he could do as President of the United States to help Botswana. Lou asked him if he could lift the embargo on the sale of DeBeers branded diamonds in the United States. These were in fact, Botswana diamonds. President Bush honored his promise to Lou and lifted the embargo.

I never had the opportunity to talk with him again.

Maleta and I were stunned a few years later when we were living in New Rochelle, New York, to learn that Lou had been found dead in a rural area of northern Botswana.

People I Met Along the Way

Jefferson A. Beaver (Late Wife Jane's Father)[292]

I want only to cover a specific part of Mr. Beaver's illustrious life, covering the story behind the creation and first days of operation of Trans Bay Savings and Loan bank.

Some of his biographies expand out in other publications. Here I just want to cover how and why he and his friends created Trans Bay Savings and Loan bank which lead to home ownership for black people in the bay area and expanded home ownership opportunities for Japanese and Chinese people living in the bay area..

On the 22nd of November 1990 I sat down with Mr. Beaver and interviewed him with respect to the reason that the bank was created.[293] He then proceeded to tell me a very fascinating story with some history that I had not heard of in terms of the relationships that the bank created and fostered among African Americans, whites, Chinese and Japanese people who lived in San Francisco.

There were a few black churches in San Francisco when he first settled in the early 1950s, but they were old, and they were having problems getting loans. He investigated to find out what the reason the banks would not lend money to churches. They told him that it didn't look good for a bank to foreclose on the church if it defaulted on its mortgage payments. However, he had graduated with a BA

---

[292] Taken from my computer files that records an interview that I did with Mr. Jefferson August Beaver, my father-in-law 22 November 1990.

[293] I edited the interview slightly to make it more readable in places.

degree in business administration from the University of California at Berkeley.[294]

So, it occurred to him that if he could collect deposits from the members of the churches that they might support a bank. This was the initial idea for establishing a financial institution. Once the institution was established, they made a lot of loans to churches and to church members. He explained to them that the bank would need deposits to lend that money out.

Their approach was different from churches that were governed by some kind of religious order as opposed to those that were independent. As one example, he said that "the Episcopal Church for example, you don't make a loan to the individual church, you make a loan to the Bishop of the diocese, and the diocese actually owns the property and you have protection and that connection."

There were other such organizations such as the Methodist Church and some Baptist churches.

In trying to organize the savings and loan company, they had many meetings with the clergy, the governing board and in some cases the members of these churches to explain that they needed those deposits and that the deposits would be insured by the federal government, up to $5000 at that time. After he explained to them what they were doing they seemed to have been satisfied and started making deposits.

In the early 1950s there were recruiters from the shipping industry, the airplane industry and other war related industries that went into the South to recruit people to come to San Francisco to work; However, there were no places for black recruits and their families to live.

During World War II, the state of California moved all the Japanese from their residences in San Francisco; however, the black people were

---

294 This was the same rationale that Barclay's Bank was using in 1978, some 25 years later, for refusal to give a mortgage to the White Plains Deliverance Evangelistic Center, Inc. However, the Community Savings Bank in Mount Vernon did give the church a mortgage loan for $125,000.00. This church paid the loan off in full.

limited to housing surrounding the Japanese area. The Japanese were taken away and placed in concentration camps without any regard to their loyalty or citizenship; the fact that they were Japanese was enough.

The white banks would only lend black people up to $3000.00 regardless of the value of the house, even though the law allowed banks to lend up to 80% of the appraised value of the house.

Primarily, African Americans occupied Japanese Americans homes and some businesses while the Japanese were interned. Both communities were adjacent to one another; i.e., Japan Town/Fillmore District San Francisco, and the Crenshaw neighborhood in Los Angeles.[295]

At the time, Mr. Beaver was a part of a group of about 10 people who were working to organize insurance companies in northern and southern California. The group up north organized a company called Carver National Life Insurance Company, while the group in the south organized a bank called Broadway Federal Savings to provide mortgages to black people who were coming in and had no place to live.

Through the friendship that a member of their group had with state senator Nolan, and that Mr. Beaver had with a local congressman, they were able to get the information they would need to prepare documents for the application for a federal bank. There were three questions that they had to answer: "First was there a need?" Second, "were there sufficient resources in the community to organize an institution to meet that need? and third, if it were proven that there is a need and there were resources to meet the need, and the government agreed to issue a charter, to the institution, in the event the government issued the charter, how would it affect similar existing institutions?" It was Mr. Beaver's job to collect the various statistics to prepare the documentation. Once it was prepared, they sent the proposal to the two friends that they knew and had them review the documents; then they

---

[295] Email dated 07 January 2024 from Melvin Washington, Founder & Executive Director, Japan Afro-American Friendship Association (JAFA).

submitted it. However, they waited quite a while and heard nothing even after the friends made inquiries to the regulator for banks.

Finally, they heard from the regulators; the regulators told them that they would have to go out and collect money and pledges to show that there was enough money to support the bank and deposit them with another bank while the authority made up its mind. It is instructive to quote what Mr. Beaver said:

> "I said OK. So, I had to go from door to door, business to business, to get people, all they had to do was put down their names and how much they pledged. And God, that was hard. We'd go to black people personally; it was hard to get them to pledge. They'd pledge $50 a $100, shoot. Which was a lot of money at that time. They only required - thinking in today's money - that requirement was exceedingly small. I think it was $150,000…it was just like pulling hens teeth… When you looked at the list and you saw a $1000, you knew that it was a white person. And we had six months to do it…
>
> And we were $40,000 short. We had about $110,000 pledged. And the time was up…. So, what we did was to - we couldn't think of any individual who could put up $40,000 but, the men in our group were all members of something. And one of the fellows had been, he was a former grand master of the Prince Hall Masonic Lodges of the state of California and Hawaii.
>
> These other fellows are members of the Methodist Church, AME church, and I think somebody was Baptist or they had exceptionally good friends that were Baptists. And so, my friend who had been the grand master of the Masonics contacted the Masonic Lodge, and they agreed to put up $20,000…
>
> And we got, particularly good friend of mine was the minister of the Third Baptist Church, he is a very good friend of all of us. So, he was a Masonic, he was a member of the Masons. And Cecil Pool[sic] was their lawyer of the church. And this church had just sold its property down in downtown San Francisco, down Hyatt Street. They got quite a bit of money selling the property. And they had cash money. So, I talked to Rev. Hagans,

talked to 2 or 3 members of the governing board and Rev Hagans said he couldn't do anything by himself, he had to have support of the board or that he asked me to talk to Cecil, talk to some of the members of the board and he'd hold a meeting and see what he could do.

Well, we talked, talked, talked. Then, we invited the board, the minister, the lawyer, and all of them, invited to dinner one night and the Fisherman's Ward [sic]. We had a private, private room. And we had a great dinner. And after that dinner, they agreed to put up $20,000.[296] They gave us all the money we needed. And on the basis of that, the government issued us the charter."

But that was not the end of the story. They needed operating capital.

Again, he tells us

"so, I used to walk up and down the street right, I didn't have a car, used to ride the trolley car, buses, walk, going around trying to get people to deposit money, which was hard. People were afraid. And the first things they would say is, man, these people aren't going to let you run no n@#$%* bank. And so, we convinced them that the money was insured. Not only were black people thinking this way, but white people were also thinking this way. And we had a tough time.

But, in order to pay our expenses, we had to have loans out there with the interest getting back that would permit us to pay our expenses and then in addition to paying expenses, you had to set aside a certain percentage of your earnings in reserve. So, we had one hell of a time."

He co-founded "Transbay Federal Savings and Loan in 1949 and Golden Gate National Bank in 1961".[297]

---

296 So, never underestimate the social and business value of having meals to work out a deal.

297 https://www.blackpast.org/african-american-history/beaver-jefferson-1908-1991/ (Accessed 08 JAN 2024)

When they first opened for business, they kept all their records by hand. Then, he decided that they needed to use an NCR bookkeeping machine. After negotiating for the machine, NCR sent a white man to show them how to operate the machine. He was demonstrating the operations to the young black employees at the front of the bank.

At about the same time, he put an ad in the local newspapers saying that his bank was paying interest at one quarter of a percent above the interest rate that other banks were paying. The article appeared on the weekend and Monday morning people were lined up to get into the bank, mostly white people. They would come into the bank; they would see these black people and then they would turn around and walk out but some of them started going over to the white NCR man because they thought he was working at the bank.

When Mr. Beaver saw this, he went to the young man and told him to tell the people who came over to him that he did not work for the bank but that he could refer them to someone in the bank that could help them.

A week later, they had received a phenomenal amount of money and at a board meeting the board wanted to know how he had accumulated so much money. He told them what had happened and that they were going to have to change their policy and hire some white people. One man said over my dead body.[298] Mr. Beaver's reaction was

> "Jesus Christ over my dead body, Jesus Christ. So, I said, oh my god, what are we going to do now? He never brought in so much money. So, I said one day, the hell with that guy. I said I'm going go ahead and employ some white guy. So, I did. I employed a couple of white girls."

He then hired a "Oriental" girl, and then a Mexican fellow. From that time forward, they began to get a lot of deposits.

---

298 Which I later identify as Mr. X, the only other Board member from San Francisco.

He tells the story a white woman who came into the bank and asked him to explain to her what the institution was all about. He told her and they had a discussion, and she said that she had her money in her bank down the street, but she wanted to put some money in his bank. So, she said that she would go and get the money and bring it back before 5:00 when Trans Bay closed. When she went to the other bank to withdraw her money the person at that bank asked her if she knew that black people operated Trans Bay, she said she did and asked them if the government insured black banks. They said yes, so she took out some money and came back to Trans Bay. Government insurance at that time covered up to $5000 in deposits.

He also had discussions with the white-operated banks, which had some customers with deposits of 10 - $12,000 or more. He got them to tell their customers that their deposits were only insured up to $5000 regardless of how much money they deposited into the bank. Those banks would tell their customers that even though they had that limitation, there was a bank over there, meaning Trans Bay, that you could deposit your money in, and it would be insured up to $5000.

In this way, customers could spread their risks, by having deposits in multiple banks, each account insured up to $5,000.00.

This behavior on the part of the white banks led him to question the premise of the black Muslims at the time that all white people were devils. He had seen in practice that this was not the case.

Mr. Beaver gives us some insight of what he sees as the differences among the various ethnic groups and racist, African Americans, Chinese, and Japanese.

Black borrowers will come into the bank and since he knew the hardships that they faced, he would lend them the money even if they had poor credit or no credit. Six months later they would start missing payments. He would call them into the bank. Invariably, the grandmother had died, and they had to go out of town to attend the funeral and so forth.

In addition, these same guys would come into the bank with white brokers. They thought that if they want to buy a house in the hills the white broker would be able to do more for them. However, they told my father-in-law that they didn't know that the white broker was going to come to him to try to get financing. My father-in-law related the following story:

> I said, well man you better wake up, damn, you could give your money to the black brokers he can do anything for you. And then I had one guy come in once. I'll never forget this. And this guy told me that he had bought this home. It was in an area where there were no blacks. And [banks] would not ordinarily make him a loan in that area but he was black, and he had bought this property, and he assumed the loan, there was an existing loan. And in the loan document and the mortgage document there was a clause to the effect that in the event there was a change of title, the bank had the authority and the right to call the loan. This guy didn't know that. And he didn't [show] me the assumption papers, he just assumed the loan. So, he was so happy to have the property in this nice neighborhood that he just wanted to make the payments on time and every time and be sure the money got there. And he didn't put the money in the mail. He went into the office. He said take the payment and they saw him. And when he got a letter a week later, they called the loan.
>
> Now, legally there wasn't a damn thing he could do. So, he started looking around, trying to find another loan. And he went to every *** **** bank in town, and they turned him down. So, finally, he ended up in my office and I said, well, I'll be damned. So, I asked him, "Well, how much did you pay for this house? I don't know, it was a damn good house, and I think at that time he paid $50,000 or something and at that time it was a hell of a good price. So, I said well, how much did you put down? I put down $25,000; he put down half of what the damn house cost. Jesus, I said you got that much money? Where did you have the money? He had it in Bank of America I said, now, Jesus, if you had that money in this bank, there would be no question about

it. I said, ain't you been back to the Bank of America, the branch where you had the money and ask them for a loan?" Yea, but they wouldn't do anything. I said, well. No, I'll be damned. So, I played with him, I played with him. I took him over the coals. Let's see, we're getting ready to foreclose. You need that in a day or two. But I played with him. I really tortured him. Sometimes I think about it. It was really brutal what I did to that man. But in the final analysis, we took him out of his predicament. And but, we had a lot of instances like that. And but, at the same time, you kept these black people, now I don't know if there are other people like that, I just don't know…

But I do know one thing, the Chinese people, they had problems, too. Until these black people started the revolution and made it possible to buy property in San Francisco, at least. I think you ought to be able to buy property anywhere you can pay for it. These Chinese are all over San Francisco. They are everywhere and we made a lot of loans to the Chinese."

In response to my question about the Chinese having problems getting money, Mr. Beaver said the following:

"oh, yes. They used to. With them, it was more or less where the property was. They could only get it in Chinatown. They could get a loan in Chinatown if they measured up with credit and assets and all that. But I made loans to Chinese all over the place. Never had a problem. Never any problem. They paid debts, they made their payments just like clock. Never any problems with a Chinese loan. Never any problem. But, the one thing about them, the Chinese, they recognize the fact that blacks have made it possible for them to purchase property because prior to the 1960s and 1970s they were confined to Chinatown that was it."

He then relates the story of how a Chinese man went into one of the white banks and the officer had turned him down for a loan. As the man was walking out of the bank the officer called him back and said well, I might as well give you the loan because if I don't you will go over to this bank down the street, meaning Trans Bay.

Mr. Beaver made a lot of speeches all over the place and related a lot of these experiences to the audience so that they could understand how important it was to have this black bank.

I then asked him how he was able to raise his personal initial capital. There were 5 of them, 3 from the East Bay, and 2 from San Francisco. Atty. George Vaughn, Imus ____, and Slim, a restaurant cook, from the East Bay, and he and Mckinley Thomas, M.D., from San Francisco. The first decision they needed to make was where to have the office. He and McKinley wanted it in San Francisco; the East Bay fellows wanted it in Oakland. He and McKinley determined that George Vaughn and Imus were concerned with status so they proposed that Imus would be the Chairman of the board, George would be the President, the office would be in San Francisco, but all their decisions would have to be made on a unanimous basis. They agreed.

At the time Mr. Beaver was a member of another corporation called United Security Investment Corporation which was organized to provide housing for all the migrants who had come to work in the shipyard and other industries. They made loans to them based on their salaries. They also made loans somehow connected to automobiles. They had to have a special license to do this.

He was the youngest in the group. George told him he should put in as much money as everyone else, so he would be equal. They all had money; he did not. So, he went to his mother, explained his situation and what he wanted to do. She gave him the $5,000.00 he requested.

It was not enough. So, the bank could only hire two people - a young woman and him. They only had money to pay her salary. He continued to work and then called his friend Chet McAfee early one Sunday morning while he was at work. Chet was a member of the Board of Supervisors. Mr. Beaver knew that Chet was also a good friend of the head of the juvenile court. My father-in-law told him that my mother-in-law, Fanny Beaver, had passed the examination for probation officer, and asked Chet to call his friend to see if he could employ her. He did, she was hired.

Meantime, he worked for the full year without a salary.

Two things motivated him. He did not want to lose his mother's money, and he knew that there was a need for his bank.

Fred Gray

Fred was Rev. Dr. Martin Luther King's first lawyer. He was involved in the civil rights movement in Alabama. He represented the Montgomery Bus boycott and the local branch of the NAACP. Both were in their twenties.

In Bus Ride to Justice: The Life and Works of Fred Gray (1994) tells his story,

Fred Gray grew up in Montgomery, Alabama, but he had to leave the state to finish his education because blacks were not allowed to attend Alabama law schools. He returned to his hometown in 1954 and became one of two black lawyers in the city. He was, he writes, "determined to destroy everything segregated that I could find." He did not have to wait long. When his friend Rosa Parks was arrested in 1955 for violating the segregated seating ordinance on a Montgomery bus, 26-year-old Martin Luther King, Jr., was chosen to lead the Montgomery Bus Boycott, and 24-year-old Fred Gray became his and the movement's lawyer. Gray's legal victory in the federal courts ended the boycott 381 days later. Over the four decades since then, Gray has won scores of civil rights cases in education, voting rights, transportation, health, and other areas. He represented the Freedom Riders, the Selma-to-Montgomery marchers, the victims of the Tuskegee Syphilis Study, and many more. Bus Ride to Justice is the exciting story of a courageous life in the courtrooms of America and in the pulpits of churches where Fred Gray began as a child preacher and continues today, and of a strong human being filled with love and admiration for his fellow man.[299]

Growing up in Savannah, Georgia during the era of segregation and Jim Crow, I read everything I could about civil rights.

Fred Gray, of Tuskegee Alabama, is one of America's greatest constitutional and civil rights lawyers. I have lived long enough to witness his career, including wins and losses but over the past 70 years, long before I met him in person. I even had the opportunity to successfully represent him in a small matter in White Plains NY. It was always a great joy to be in his presence. He has been honored in many ways, including being elected as President of the National Bar Association, of which I have been a member since 1970.

On July 7, 2022, President Joe Biden bestowed the Medal of Freedom on Fred D. Gray, Sr., then 91 years old and still practicing law. This medal is our highest civilian service award.

However, I now recite a personal note of what happened in 2023 at Harry Reid Airport in Las Vegas.

Along with 1,000 – 1, 500 African American members of the National Bar Association, (NBA) I attended the 99th annual meeting of the NBA at Caesars Place.

At 6:51 a.m. on July 19, 2024, when I was to check out of Caesars Palace, I received a text from my son Jason in New York telling me that several airlines had been grounded worldwide because of a coding error in Crowdsource software. As the airlines were trying to upgrade their software, all systems went down, including airline systems. I turned on the TV for local news and saw a huge crowd waiting at Harry Reid. I received a notification from Delta later.

On July 23rd, I was finally able to get a flight out of Las Vegas NV back to New York after the catastrophic worldwide grounding of

---

299 https://www.amazon.com/Bus-Ride-Justice-Life-Works/dp/1588381137 (Accessed 24 FEB 2024)

Delta, American and United Airlines flights. My flight was on a Delta plane. The airports have gotten so big that I now always reserve a wheelchair to get me to the gate and to save the strain on my lower back. As we approached the wheelchair assistance area I saw and sat next to Fred and his wife Carol in the Assisted Passengers area. We had a chance to reminisce for a few minutes before the wheelchair assistant wheeled us off to our respective destinations.

As I was being wheeled into the elevator - they wheel you backwards into the elevator, so that you're facing passengers in the terminal through the doorway. I involuntarily blurted out to my fellow passengers "that man that you see sitting there is very great he is one of America's most distinguished constitutional and civil rights lawyers," to which I received approval applause responses. I did so, so that these people would know that they had been in the presence of greatness.

Mma Puleng Keetse, Amanda Magagula, Linda Damane, Mandy, Linda Lutchmee Burger, and Collin Govender

This is a story of how two of my friends separated by a period of 20 years after I met them, banded together to arrange one of the most pleasurable vacation trips of my life.

I met Mma Puleng Keetse around 2005 at a National Bar Association meeting in the United States. I met Amanda Magagula at a Pan African Lawyers Union meeting in July 2023 in Livingstone, Zambia. Both are South African.

In August 2024, I had a compulsive and overwhelming desire to see the ocean, watch the waves and listen to the sound of the water as it hit the shores.

Since I now reside in Botswana, I thought that it would be impractical to try to go to the Caribbean. The question now was which of the African beaches I should visit.

I had been speaking to Amanda about a legal issue that she had and referred her to Mma Puleng. Mma Puleng's offices are in Johannesburg and Amanda lived in Johannesburg.

I knew that Amanda had spent some time in Durban as a part of a missionary initiative that she was working on. When I mentioned my desire to see the ocean, she told me that Mma Puleng owned some property in Durban overlooking the ocean, and that she would inquire about its availability.

They agreed on arrangements, and I was all prepared to visit Mma Puleng's property. However, severe flooding subsequently damaged Mma Puleng's property so I could not stay there. Amanda being ever so resourceful, then located a condominium in the 32 flat Bali Hai building next door to Mma Puleng's property. She arranged with Linda Damane (Linda D), owner of the Norizana condominium, for me to stay there at a very reasonable price; she also arranged with Linda (Lutchmee) Burger (Linda B), the owner of Spice restaurant on the ground floor of the Bai Hai building for me to get food to eat, even when the restaurant was closed.

Spice Restaurant at bottom of Bali Hai Flats

Amanda, Me and Kim, my PA, having dessert at Table50two Restaurant in Gaborone

Kim's excellent personality trait is that she is very even-tempered, people-oriented, and resourceful.

Breakfast at Linda B. (Lutchmee's) Spice Restaurant overlooking the Indian Ocean at Westbrook Beach, Durban.

Linda D's flat had 3 bedrooms and a magnificent view of the Indian Ocean from the fifth floor.

Later, Linda D would arrange for me to hire Mandy, her niece, to take me shopping for food so that she or I could cook my own food. Mandy also collected my laundry to clean.

She would later come to Johannesburg to help me after my double cataract surgery. Mandy watched over me like a mother hen.

Mbangatha Nonzame Carrina (Mandy)

I don't think anyone, including myself, has ever made a more perfect set of arrangements. The location of the premises overlooking the Indian Ocean from the 5h floor showed continuing changing magnificent and spectacular ocean views. The breezes, some might say they were winds, reminded me so much of San Francisco, the Caribbean, and of Cape Town.

Overall, I love the place. I spent the first two or three days relaxing and trying to cope with my jet lag after visiting the U.S.

By the 4th day, Linda Band I had become good friends. She arranged with her friend, Collin Samuel Govender, to drive us and her son on a journey into Zululand.

Linda B. was very much interested in seeing the world-famous Drakensberg Boys Choir. Although I wanted to see the Choir, I was dying to see the Drakensberg Mountains that I had seen videos of during the promotion of 2010 World cup. Neither was a disappointment.

Following are some photos of the Drakensbergs that I took from the beautiful Castle Champagne Hotel in Cathkin Park, Winterton Website in parenthesis (Champagne Castle Hotel - Drakensberg Experience):

To prepare for the meeting of the G20 in South Africa in 2025, President Ramaphosa described South Africa as being the most beautiful country in the world. Based on what I had seen over the past 21 years in South Africa, he had reason to make this statement, although the United States and Botswana are no slouches.

Aside from the breathtaking beauty as we traveled along the road, we visited a place called Prince's Grant, which by now been turned into a golf residential estate, with a beautiful golf course, vacation second homes, and rental properties. Situated next to the Indian Ocean, the location reminded me of what Pebble Beach in California must look like. home - Prince's Grant (princesgrant.co.za).

Me at our stopover for breakfast at Prince's Grant

Linda B. at our stopover for breakfast at Prince's Grant

Collin at our stopover for breakfast at Prince's Grant

We ordered breakfast, and while mine was being prepared, Collin arranged for Vincent, one of the course golf cart drivers, to take me on a tour of the premises. How they built all these facilities on undulating hills with perfect, intricate landscaping, I will never know. I think I remember that Vincent told me they started building the place in the 1990s.

Kwa Siza Bantu Mission

After breakfast in this exquisite place, we set out for the Kwa Siza Bantu Mission.

Mission Sanctuary

Over a period, the vision of Rev. Steger, as a 26-year-old man, had grown into an especially important socio-economic organization in Kwa Zulu Natal (a combination of the areas where the Zulus and Indians lived, created after the adoption of the democratic constitution of South Africa.)

This place blew our collective minds, including that of James, Linda B's 12-year-old son. James would later show us that he had been paying attention when we were trying to remember how long David, our exceptional tour guide, had been working at the Mission. James supported the recollection that David had been with the mission for over 30 years.

> "KwaSizabantu is a non-denominational Christian mission station that reaches out to people of all racial and cultural groups bringing a message of repentance and hope and providing spiritual guidance, educational support and counselling."
>
> https://www.ksb.org.za/#:~:text=KwaSizabantu%20is%20a%20non-denominational%20Christian%20mission%20station%20that,and%20providing%20spiritual%20guidance%2C%20educational%20support%20and%20counselling. (Accessed August 18, 2024)

As far as I could tell, the staff was comprised of two sets of people – missionaries and counselors. Many of the counselors needed the services of the Mission themselves at some point in their past. David is one of the missionaries.

Although there are organizations that have a similar mission, I was Impressed by the work the mission had done to improve the lives of people in its area.

Tellingly, during the riots of 2021, the premises of Kwa Siza Bantu were not disturbed. The unrest was severe. The situation in KwaZulu-Natal remains tense, with renewed fears of unrest echoing the devastating **July 2021 riots** that left over 300 people dead and caused an estimated R50 billion in economic damage.[300]

Undoubtedly, the Mission had been spared due, in large part, to the fact that the Mission helped a lot of the local people and also provided them with jobs in the hospitality field, agriculture, using advanced techniques to grow bell peppers (which the Mission somehow could never

300 https://www.enca.com/news/july-unrest-anniversary-four-years-looting-chaos-and-bloodshed; https://www.msn.com/en-za/news/other/four-years-after-the-july-riots-sa-s-crime-intelligence-remains-broken/ar-AA1IeuAq (Accessed 20 July 20, 2025)

meet the great demand), avocados, bottled water, and other useful items.

Archibald M. N. Mogwe (Ex-Wife Maleta's Father)

I include the story of Archibald Mogwe here because we know so little about African personalities. I took this part of the book from a government write-up about his life that had been prepared by the government of Botswana, which Maleta and I edited.

In a telephone conversation I had with him a few years ago, when I was calling him from Botswana about another matter, Ambassador Andrew Young told me that there was one person who he would never forget – Archibald Mogwe. I then told him that Mr. Mogwe was my father-in-law and that he was due to arrive momentarily. In a few minutes he did arrive, and I put him on the phone so that the two of them could re-connect.

In every country, there is a tendency for individuals to emerge with the power, the will and the intellectual prowess/impetus to change their nations for the betterment of the welfare of their fellow citizens. In Botswana there is an individual whose contribution to the development of this country is legendary and second to none. That individual is none other than Mr Archibald Mogwe who not only witnessed what happened in Botswana during her formative years, but he selflessly participated in its growth both locally and internationally. Mr Mogwe recalls that when he was the Permanent Secretary to the President in the 1970's under the founding President of the Nation, Sir Seretse Khama, he used to calculate the development and recurrent budget of this country on the back of a box of matches – this narrative is an illustration of how poor the country was then.

It is, therefore, fitting to tell the story of this iconic figure for posterity. His account of the history of this country is moving and absorbing. There are few individuals still alive in Botswana, who are a depository of such in depth, richness and invaluable knowledge. His profile is an important historical account, full of startling insights, candour and a sweeping sense of from where Botswana has come as a nation state. Mr. Mogwe is not only an embodiment of Botswana history but also the long tested national principles of Democracy, Development, Botho and Self Reliance, on which the survival of Botswana has been anchored since 1966.

Mr Archibald Mooketsa Nehemiah Mogwe, is a former Botswana politician and a consummate diplomat par excellence. Having served as Botswana's Foreign Minister from 1974 to 1985, and the Minister of Mineral Resources and Water Affairs from 1985 to 1994 as well as the Botswana Ambassador to the United States of America from 1995 to 1999, Mr Mogwe has undoubtedly played an immense role in the socio-economic development of this country during both its pre- and post-independence eras.

EARLY LIFE

Mr. Archibald Mooketsa Mogwe was born at Macheng o-o-Moswaana, near Kanye on 29th August 1921. In 1928 he began his primary school education at Tigerkloof in South Africa, where his father, Morutwana Mogwe was studying Theology. However, his primary education journey was interrupted several times in his early years, due to 'the phenomenon of the Setswana cattle culture that denied a lot of children an opportunity to go to school.' In 1929, following his return to Kanye from Tigerkloof, Mr Mogwe had a year of Primary school education in Goo Moswaane before moving to Molepolole.

In 1930, after his father was ordained as a minister in the London Missionary Society, his father moved his family to Molepolole. Mr Mogwe was enrolled at No. 1 Bakwena School where he began his Sub-Standard B. He stayed in Molepolole with his parents for a little over two years during which time he recalls during that time, the banishment of Kgosi Sebele II to Gantsi, the ascendance of Kgosi Kgari Sechele to the Bakwena royal position and his marriage to Mohumagadi Gagoumakwe Magogwe. After passing his standard 2 in

1933, Mr Mogwe moved to Macheng to stay with his paternal Grandmother and uncles, where he continued with his primary school education up to standard 5. It was a challenging year.

"Life was so difficult and at times we slept without food. A two-litre drum of water was rationed among four families, and it was meant to last for three days, sheep and goat had water once in two weeks, so they supplemented their water intake with certain indigenous trees."

Mr. Mogwe recalls how, in 1934, they had rejoiced when the rains finally came after a drought in 1933, however, little did they know that their celebration would be short-lived. The red locust eggs which had been long buried, hatched, and it was a disaster as people lost all their crops. For the young Mogwe and other youngsters they decided to make the best out of that situation - they made locusts their meal.

In 1935 Rre[301] Mogwe says they celebrated the Silver Jubilee of King George V and 'We were given bronze medals bearing the King's effigy although no arrangements had been made at our school to celebrate the occasion'.

Although he did well at school despite his young age and the fact that he had to herd cattle and find time to study, looking back to those days Mr Mogwe says he could have done much better than he did, however life was difficult because of the underdeveloped status of Botswana then.

Reflecting on those early years of his life Mr Mogwe says;

> "Whenever I reflect on my poor performance in my early school years, I can only blame the phenomenon of the Setswana cattle culture that denied a lot of children an opportunity to go to school. Many people were denied schooling in order to look after cattle. Others went to school in their late teens after herding cattle"

---

301 Mr.

The acute shortage of water forced the young Mogwe to tend more to his father's livestock in order for it not to stray while searching for water, and this meant him missing schoolwork.

In 1936 Mr. Mogwe moved to Kanye to do his standard six since the primary school in Macheng only taught up to standard five. Unlike Macheng, Kanye had more developments in that there was water and there were a few shops. To the 15-year-old Mogwe these developments were a flicker of hope that he would concentrate more on his studying than livestock. However, his glimmer of hope would fade as he was assigned to herd his new guardian's cattle. However, despite all these happenings, Mr. Mogwe persevered.

Like his father and grandfather, in January 1937 Mr. Mogwe was enrolled at Tigerkloof. It was there that he shaped his future of being an educationist, political stalwart but most importantly, an ambassador for Botswana.

The Native Institution, as Tigerkloof was called then was a microcosm of the Southern African global village. With students from High Commissioned territories of Bechuanaland, Basutuland, Swaziland, Northern and Southern Rhodesia, Nyasaland, South West African and the Union of South Africa; this was where African diplomatic relations started.

Rre Mogwe's father then forced him to return to Kanye to teach. During his tenure in Kanye, where he taught for 18 months, he secured a position as a boarding master at the Mooderpoort School in the Orange Free State. He taught there for 10 years.

After Moodepoort, he returned to Tigerkloof to teach Setswana, English, and Geography, among other subjects.

Meanwhile, Maruti[302] Mogwe, his father, complained to a high-ranking Bechuanaland official that Rre Mogwe, his son, had graduated with a degree and Bechuanaland was not employing his own citizens. This

---

302 Maruti means priest or Rev.

led to an invitation from Dr. ______, a Bechuanaland official in Mafikeng[303] for Rre Mogwe to meet with him.

The Mafikeng official then arranged for Rre Mogwe to ride a train to Capetown to meet with other Bechuanaland officials. Rre Mogwe recalls fondly that the train made an unscheduled stop in Tigerkloof on its way to Capetown to pick him up as its special passenger.

He met with the Bechuanaland officials in Capetown where they offered him a position of Inspector of Schools for Bechuanaland.

He returned home where he started his career in the then Bechuanaland Protectorate civil service as Inspector of Schools, based in Mochudi. He was completely unaware that fate would put him on a path of major responsibilities in this country.

MR. MOGWE'S FAMILY

Mr. Mogwe met Ms Lena Mosele Senakgomo, a Lesotho national in Mooderpoort, in the Orange Free State, South Africa. They were married seven years later. He loves classical music and what attracted him to his wife was her voice on the radio. According to his daughter Ms. Alice Mogwe:

> "What brought my father and my mother together was classical music. He fell in love with her voice before he even met her whilst he listened to her voice on the radio. He made sure that he joined her musical group. As they say the rest is history."

Mr. Mogwe and Mma Maleta were blessed with three children namely; Maleta Luna- Rosa, who became my wife in 2006, Hugh Letlhogonolo Moabi, and Alice Bahumi Tholoana Zita-Mary. Tragically, Hugh, his only son, died on Christmas Eve, 2012.

---

303 Bechuanaland was being administered from the offices in Mafikeng.

Mr. Mogwe has always loved education and as such he encouraged his children to take education seriously from their youthful years. Therefore, it is not surprising that he was one of the founding members of Maruapula Secondary School in 1972 and he was its Council Chairperson for twenty-three years.

Alice explained that people are not aware of the fact that Maruapula was built on the spirit of self-reliance, one of the key principles on which Botswana was built. In this context students at Maruapula engaged in compulsory social service. She says the values that she learnt at home also formed the value system of Maruapula where she attended Secondary School.

Whilst her father loved classical music which he used to buy for them in the form of tapes from overseas, her mother was a devout Christian and a member of the Botswana Council of Churches which also teaches the spirit of volunteerism. Mr Mogwe and Mme Mogwe were members of Mr. David Slater's choir at Maruapula Secondary School for a long time.

He also loved traditional choirs and he used to take his children to Molepolole and Mochudi to view the performance of different choirs.

Since I have lived here in Botswana, I have witnessed some of the choir competitions, like what we have in the United States.

Mr. Mogwe was also a founding member of Notwane Football Club before Independence. He was also President of the Club for many years and was fondly addressed and greeted as "Prez." He says that the Club grew out of discussions in Mafikeng.

"I remember clearing the bush with other children at the Notwane Grounds to make way for the football pitch and that was a normal thing to do those days without any form of payment" recalls Alice. Maleta also told me about clearing away the bushes.

In this same spirit of self-reliance, Batswana sold cattle, grain, eggs and other products to raise funds to build the University of Botswana. At any given time, there are 15-18,000 students enrolled.[304]

Rre Mogwe remembers seeing his wife, Mme Mma Maleta and wives selling ginger beer, scones, clothing and other items to help raise money for the Club.

Those were the days in the 1970's when Notwane Club was well known for entertainment by prominent local artists. It was a major hang out spot in Gaborone.

Mr. Mogwe is a strict and fair-minded person. Ms. Alice Mogwe remembers the time when her father had taken her and his team for a football game in Mafikeng. On their way back home, they stopped at a store where some players stole food items, and he did not know about the incident until she told him while he was driving.

She says, "Upon hearing this, Mr. Mogwe made a U-turn and forced the footballers to return what they had taken unlawfully from the store." He also made them pay for any items that they had consumed. Mr. Mogwe was a football player for the better part of his life and at the time of his death on 25 February 2021, he still had his leather football boots which he acquired many years ago. They have been passed on to his grandson.

Mr. Mogwe is also a very generous person whose love for other people is well known. In the 1970's he hid Mr. Joachim Chissano, the Former President of Mozambique, in his home, during the Liberation war in that country.

I had a chance to meet Mr. Chissano during an American Embassy celebration of Rre Mogwe's 90th birthday at the American Ambassador's residence.

---

[304] CoPilot, Accessed 22 September 2025

His first wife Mme Mma Maleta sadly passed on in April 1992. He married his second wife Professor Serara Khupe in 1997 in Washington DC whilst he was working as Botswana Ambassador to the United States of America.

CAREER IN CIVIL SERVICE AND POLITICS

In 1964 he worked in the Imperial Reserve in Mafikeng, which was then the seat of the Bechuanaland Government, as the Principal Officer in the shadow Ministry of Local Government. His position in Mafikeng required him to establish the Ministry of Local Government when the seat of Government was moved from Mafikeng in South Africa, to the newly established Gaborone in 1965.

In 2014, Maleta and I took him to visit the impressive Imperial Reserve on a trip to South Africa. Below is a photo of him reading a plaque annexed to one of the buildings which describes the activities of the reserve during the time he was the Principal Officer, a photo of the Imperial Reserve and a photo of him looking into one of the buildings at the Imperial Reserve where he worked before independence

When he left Mafikeng Mr. Mogwe worked in Serowe, where he helped to facilitate the first elections in Botswana, serving as an elections officer in Letlhakane.

While in Serowe, Rre Mogwe remembers how the Establishment Secretary invited him to his office in July 1965 to inform him that he had been selected for a Foreign Service study course at the University of Oxford in the United Kingdom which was to start in September

1965. Unbeknown to the world and himself at the time, Maleta told me that this was the beginning of Mr. Mogwe's exposure to the world of diplomacy.

It was while studying at Oxford that he was summoned to London to attend the Bechuanaland Independence Talks where he was assigned protocol responsibilities.

At the Marlborough Hall he joined the Commissioner of the Bechuanaland Protectorate Sir Norman-Walker who was the head of delegation, accompanied by Sir Seretse Khama and Sir Ketumile Masire of the then Bechuanaland Democratic Party and Mr. Motsamai Mpho of the then Bechuanaland People's Party.

Sir Seretse Khama had been independent Botswana's first President, succeeded by Sir Ketumile Masire. I did meet Sir Masire, shared the post – funeral repast and discussion with him at his table following the death of his wife, Gaone, and attended his funeral.

Mr. Mogwe said 'Little did I realise the historic significance of the occasion and my involvement in it. Little did I know that I would appear and be counted among those men who endeavoured and succeeded in transforming the Bechuanaland Protectorate to Botswana as we know it today.'

After he had finished his studies as an international relations student at Oxford, Rre Mogwe had to learn firsthand by visiting British embassies in other countries and so he was sent to Vienna, Austria. To wind up his assignment in Vienna he had to go to the Prime Minister's office in The Gambia. The overall objective of the visit was to prepare him to set up the department of external affairs in the office of the Prime Minister in Gambia whilst preparations for Botswana's independence were in full stream.

Incidentally, I was an African American student studying at the University of Vienna/Institute of European Studies, as well. I had been awarded a Morehouse Merrill Fellowship, although many years later, in 1959-60.

Although the concept of independence was still very unclear to him, he was happy to have been given the opportunity to be there. It was also during his study at Oxford that he was bestowed the honour of the Member of the Most Excellent Order of the British Empire (MBE) by the Queen. His elevation to being one of the two Batswana who were promoted to senior 'super scale' civil service positions came while he was still a student at Oxford.

In June 1966, Britain accepted proposals for a democratic self-Government in Botswana and upon his return from Oxford University, Mr. Mogwe assumed his role as the First Motswana Permanent Secretary to the President, serving under the First President Sir Seretse Khama.

In 1974, President Seretse Khama appointed Rre Mogwe as Botswana's first Minister of External Affairs, a position he occupied until 1985.

POLITICS

In the 1974, he was also elected a Member of Parliament for Kanye. Maleta, my wife, was his campaign manager.

To mark the occasion of the election of Kanye's first BDP Member of Parliament in history, the Bangwakeetse organized a motor caravan, picking up supporters along the route from Kanye to Gaborone, via Lobatse, to escort Rre Mogwe to the front door of Parliament.

When re-election results came in, Mr. Mogwe lost, but due to his commitment and dedication to his work he was appointed a Special Member of Parliament.

"[In 1974], he was appointed Minister of Foreign Affairs, marking a pivotal moment in Botswana's regional diplomacy during the era of decolonization and liberation struggles in southern Africa.

His election was historically significant—not just for Kanye, but for Botswana's evolving political landscape—as he transitioned from top civil servant to elected representative, bringing institutional memory and diplomatic acumen into the legislature."[305]

During his tenure as the Minister of Foreign Affairs, Mr. Mogwe played a crucial role as a peace broker between the Zimbabwe African National Union (ZANU) and the Zimbabwe African People's Union (ZAPU) in Zimbabwe.

It was due to his relentless efforts that on 8th December 1974 the two parties signed a declaration and agreed to suspend military activities as well as negotiate and rally behind Bishop Muzorewa. This, according to Mr. Mogwe, was a giant step forward and it needed to be supported by the Front-Line States (FLS) and by other states surrounding Rhodesia. The FLS was a loose coalition of African countries committed to ending apartheid and white minority rule in South Africa, South West Africa and Rhodesia.

Following the declaration, leaders of the FLS, being Kenneth Kaunda, Mwalimo Nyerere and Seretse Khama sent Mr. Mogwe and Mr. Joseph Legwaila to brief Lesotho, Swaziland, Malawi, Mozambique, Mauritius and Madagascar on the developments in Rhodesia. They had succeeded in persuading Ian Smith to release Joshua Nkomo, Ndabaningc Sithole and Robert Mugabe from Prison.

In 2012, in Mangaung, Free State, South Africa, I met Kenneth Kaunda, during the 100th anniversary of the African National Congress during the Gala Dinner. Revs. Andrew Young and Jessie Jackson were among the American dignitaries at the celebration and the dinner. I reintroduced myself to both. I met Joseph Legwaila of Botswana somewhat earlier.

The first port of call for the FLS delegation was in Lesotho where they briefed Prime Minister Leabua Jonathan, before proceeding to Swaziland where they briefed Prime Minister Dlamini. They left

---

[305] CoPilot, accessed 22 Sept 2025

Swaziland for Lourenço Marques (now Maputo) and met Joaquim Chissano who was the Interim Minister since Samora Machel was still involved in the Liberation War.

In a speech he delivered at the United Nations in New York after that assignment, Mr. Mogwe had this to say:

"For almost one year now determined and sustained efforts have been made to break the impasse and stalemate in Rhodesia through the Lusaka talks aimed at creating a peaceful atmosphere for a meaningful dialogue between the Zimbabwe nationalists and the Smith regime to achieve majority rule and independence for the country. With every moon that has waxed and waned since then, prospects for an early solution to the problem have swelled and ebbed like lunar tides, as I address this Assembly, the Rhodesia talks have entered one of their deepest troughs. This was not expected, for the Smith Regime, with the reins of power in its hands, has consistently resisted any move to normalise conditions in Rhodesia to enable the African National Council and all its members to conduct negotiations in the best atmosphere possible."[306]

Mr. Mogwe expressed the hope that, even in the face of such adversity, that the changed circumstances in Southern Africa such as the collapse of the Portuguese empire, the withdrawal of South African forces from Rhodesia and the determined resolve of the people of Zimbabwe, would compel Ian Smith to face up to the realities of the times and that majority rule will come to Zimbabwe in his lifetime.

Through him as the Minister of Foreign affairs and others in the region, majority rule did come to Zimbabwe during Ian Smith's lifetime.

---

[306] Date: 1975, Session: 30th UN General Assembly, Speaker: Archibald M. Mogwe, representing Botswana, Document Symbol: A/PV.2372, Agenda: General Debate (Item A/10251 & Add.1); General Assembly, 30th session: 2372nd plenary meeting, Thursday, 2 October 1975, New York, at page 385. (Accessed 22 September 2025).

On the other hand, the Republic of South Africa's apartheid regime was busy building nuclear weapons. It was reported that South Africa constructed six uranium gun fission weapons (similar in nature to the Little Boy weapon dropped on Hiroshima), of which they had wanted to test in the Kgalagadi desert. However, after calls from neighbouring countries, Botswana in particular, for the world to intervene, South Africa listened.

In a speech he gave at the United Nations in 1977 Mr. Mogwe had this to say about the situation:

"This assembly might wonder why a small, underdeveloped country such as Botswana trespasses on the preserve of the mighty, instead of concerning itself with agriculture and the raising of beef cattle. The reason is that we in Southern Africa are brought into the orbit of a nuclear threat from South Africa. Botswana wishes to solemnly draw the attention of those who have made it possible for South Africa to acquire nuclear capability by providing it with nuclear material and technology to the perils that this new development poses for Africa and to hold them criminally responsible for whatever disastrous consequences might flow from their action."[307]

No full test of the devices has ever been confirmed, as heavy pressure from the United States, the then Soviet Union and France helped force South Africa to cancel an underground detonation in 1977.

It was also during his term as the Minister of Foreign Affairs that he formulated the idea of creating the Southern African Development Coordination Conference (SADCC), which he discussed with President Seretse Khama. The Southern African Development Coordination Conference was the precursor to the Southern African Development Community (SADC).

---

[307] Mogwe, Archibald M., Botswana, A/32/251 9 General debate. UN. GENERAL ASSEMBLY (32ND SESS.: 1977)--GENERAL DEBATE, 1977-10-12, A/32/PV.30 at page 590, para. 171. (Accessed 22 September 2025).

Because I was familiar with the creation of SADCC and SADC from the time of their formation, in the late 1980s, when I was a member of the New York State Banking Board, I caused a meeting to be convened among the Banking Board, the New York State Division of Human Rights, and representatives from the front line states (FLS) attending the United Nations General Assembly (UNGA) to discuss the possibilities of our New York banks investing in the SADC countries.

It was at the meeting, in the World Trade Centre, that I met Presidents Mogae and Nujoma in their capacities at that time.

As far as I know, nothing came of the meeting. In 2004, when the National Bar Association met in Botswana, we were given an audience with then President Mogae and I reminded him of the meeting we had in the late 1980s.

On April 1st, 1980, a memorandum of understanding on common economic development was signed in Lusaka, Zambia and was formalised as the Lusaka Declaration. Botswana along with eight other states signed the declaration.

The Co-ordination Conference was a result of consultations in the late seventies. In May 1979 representatives of the Frontline States met in Gaborone and resolved that ministers of all member states should meet to discuss common economic development. This meeting materialised two months later in Arusha, Tanzania where the formation of SADC was decided. Since 1982, the headquarters of SADC were in Gaborone, Botswana.

In 1981 when Kenyan President Moi assumed the reins of the Organisation for African Unity (OAU) chairmanship at the annual Summit referred to as Nairobi I, he asserted himself as a prominent leader who wanted to reconcile warring factions in Chad.

Mr. Moi hosted the Nairobi II and III conferences and dispatched a delegation to officially represent him in a meeting with Chadian officials in March 1982. The delegation mandated for a peace keeping mission in Chad was made up of Mr. Mogwe as well as Kenya's then

Foreign Minister Dr Peter Onu and the Chairman of the OAU Council of Ministers Dr Robert Ouko.

In 1983 negotiations on the content of Lomé III were officially opened in Luxembourg. The talks were mainly designed to provide a new framework of cooperation between the then European Economic Community (EEC) and developing African Caribbean and Pacific (ACP) countries, in particular the former British, Dutch, Belgian and French colonies. It had two main aspects. It provided for most ACP agricultural and mineral exports to enter the EEC free of duty. Preferential access based on a quota system was agreed for products, such as sugar and beef.

When the negotiations started, Mr. Mogwe, who was then the President of the (ACP) Council of Ministers is said to have in his opening speech, drawn attention to the direct relationship between discussing human rights as ACP countries in the context of the Lomé convention and the human rights policy practice of the European Community with regard to South Africa.

He was appointed the Minister of Mineral Resources and Water Affairs from 1985 to 1994, during which time he was signatory to the formal launch of the Sua Project. While at the Ministry Mr. Mogwe also signed a Memorandum of Understanding on the 400KV interconnector transmission line between South Africa and Zimbabwe through Botswana.

Private water connections rose from Nine thousand five hundred to Twenty thousand in major villages. Furthermore, the National Water Master Plan was formulated to address the growing demand of water by the increasing Population and Industry. The Limpopo Water Utilisation Study which was commenced in 1986/87 and saw the commissioning of a Joint Upper Limpopo Basin Study which looked into how the river could be developed to the benefit of Botswana, South Africa, Zimbabwe and Mozambique.

During his time at the Ministry, the country's Gross Domestic Product grew by 65% between 1985 and 1991. The mining sector, particularly diamond industry contributed significantly to the economic growth of Botswana Exploration activities by the private sector also increased. The number of prospecting licences in Botswana also increased tremendously.

In 2024, the Botswana economy suffered tremendously, because of a severe slump in the sale of its diamonds, the sale of synthetically produced diamonds and the failure to otherwise diversify the economy sufficiently to take up the slack. The manufactured diamonds were sold at more affordable prices to the consumer.[308]

DIPLOMAT

In 1995 he was appointed Botswana's Ambassador to United States of America where he also covered Brazil, Mexico and Canada and he was instrumental in the purchase of the Botswana Chancery in Washington DC. It was during his time as an Ambassador that the United States, President Bill Clinton paid an official visit to Botswana, and he had to prepare and facilitate the trip. Those who worked with him as an Ambassador describe him as a prolific writer who used to dictate speeches to his secretary. "He was such a resourceful Ambassador who knew foreign policy very well" said one of those officers who worked closely with him.

Mr. Mogwe maintained photos of the Clintons visit in his residence at the Pitsane Farms area, near the South Africa border .In 2001, Mr. Mogwe led a delegation from Sir Ketumile Masire's Office of the Facilitator of the Inter-Congolese Dialogue that toured the 11 provinces of the Democratic Republic of Congo, supervising the selection of

[308] The current and future outlook for Botswana is grim without diversification. Lab-Grown Diamonds Threaten Botswana's Diamond-Dependent Economy (Accessed 22 September 2025)

representatives from political and civil-society sectors who were to participate in the inter-Congolese dialogue.

In recognition of his extraordinary and selfless service to this country, he was awarded the Silver Jubilee Prime Award in 2016.

Mr. Mogwe was integrally involved in the restoration of Tigerkloof School since 1991, a school he attended in the 1940s. In 2015, the school named its boys hostel "The Mogwe Hostel" honouring him as one of the Botswana icons who attended the school and later grew to prominence in Botswana's political landscape and helped create the modern-day Botswana.

He told me he wanted to simply be remembered as a "man of the bush."[309]

He enjoyed his life in the bush and his lifelong love for his cattle. His residence on his farm in his later years, was a testament to his comfort place.

The farmhouse with Ms. Serara S Mogwe, second wife of Rre Archibald Mogwe, standing in front.

[309] See also Chewing The Fat with Rre Mogwe on His 97th birthday – Botswana Gazette (Accessed 22 September 2025)

Farmhouse kitchen

When I first visited the farm about 2005, he was growing a variety of beautifully-colored roses in the sitting area in the back of the farmhouse.

APPENDIX

MOTION FOR A RESOLUTION OF PARLIAMENT TO PAY TRIBUTE TO THE LATE H E GODFREY LUKONGWA BINAISA QC, FORMER RESIDENT OF THE RESUPLIC OF UGANDA

(Under Rule 194 of the Rules of Procedure of the Parliament of Uganda)

MOVED BY: Professor Apolo R Nsibambi

The Rt Hon Prime Minister of Uganda and Leader of Government Business in Parliament

WHEREAS the Parliament of Uganda received with grief and sad news of the death of H E Godfrey Lukongwa Binaisa, a former President of the Republic of Uganda, which occurred on 5 August 2010 at his home in Makindye;

NOTING that the late Godfrey Lukongwa Binaisa was a President of Uganda from June 20, 1979 to May 13, 1980 and served Uganda in many other capacities as: Uganda's first Attorney General in 1962; Vice President of the Uganda Patriotic Movement in 1980; Chairman of the Uganda National Congress Party in 1956; started the United Front Umbrella of all African Political Parties in 1958; became the first African Queen's Counsel (QC) in East Africa; was a member of the internal [sic] Committee of Jurists in 1966;

MINDFUL that the late Godfrey sought to unite all Ugandans during the turbulent times of 1980 using his ideology of the "Umbrella";

NOW THEREFORE, this Parliament resolves as follows:

1. That it collectively conveys its deep condolences to the bereaved family, friends and the people of Uganda on the loss of this former Head of State;
2. That it takes cognizance of the distinguished services rendered by the former Head of State.

MOVED BY: The Rt Hon Professor Apolo Nsibambi

Prime Minister and Leader of Government Business in Parliament

SECONDED: Hon Professor Morris Ogenga Latigo

Leader of the Opposition in Parliament

SECONDED: Hon Mary Karoro Okurut

MP, Woman Representative of Bushenyi District

JUSTIFICATION

H. E. the late Godfrey Lukongwa Binaisa the 5th President of the Republic of Uganda born on May 30th, 1920, in Mityana by the late Rev Canon Anania Juuko and the late Mrs. Naome Binaisa, enjoyed a religious upbringing. He attended King's College Budo and Makerere College. He joined Makerere University to study medicine but did not complete the course. He went to Ankole and Kigezi and got occupied into mining in Kigezi for seven years. In 1949, he obtained a scholarship to study Geology and Mining in the United Kingdom.

In 1952-53, he joined London King's College to study law and later became a Member of the Bar at Lincoln Inn. In 1963, he became the first African Queen's Counsel (QC) in East Africa, a major legal recognition to Uganda's first Ugandan Attorney General.

He became the 5th President of Uganda on June 20, 1979, when he replaced Professor Yusuf Kironde Lule who had led the Country for 68 days.

Binaisa faced the following challenges:

First, he replaced Professor Lule who was very popular especially in Buganda who was removed because he disallowed the National Consultative Council (NCC), the then Legislative body in Uganda, to vet his proposed Ministers. The removal of President Lule sparked off riots especially in Buganda demanding for his restoration under the slogan of *"No Lule no work"*. Binaisa restrained the military from shooting into the irate crowds. He pointed out, *"Here are a people who have had no freedom for eight years. Let them let off steam."*

The late Binaisa faced a second challenge of handling different military groups under the Uganda National Liberation Front. These different groups were trying to clandestinely recruit people into their forces. He informed me later that he had sought to remove Brigadier Oyite Ojok, the Chief of Staff, because Oyite Ojok had failed to control these military factions and he was himself heavily recruiting people into his military faction. He had assigned Oyite Ojok to go to Algeria as Ambassador. Many of his Colleagues advised Binaisa against his proposed action but he refused to take the advice, and the army removed him from the Presidency in May 1980. If Tanzania had supported Binaisa's decision, it would have averted the military *coup d'etat.*

The late Binaisa faced yet a third challenge of handling these various military factions in a state which was controlled by a foreign military force of the Tanzania Army, popularly known as the "Wakombozi". This is the force that had helped Uganda in removing Idi Amin. After the coup that removed Binaisa from power, the Tanzanian Army held him incommunicado in a bid to protect him from being harmed.

The fourth challenge the late Binaisa faced was to unite the different political groups which had been disbanded in 1969. After overthrowing Idi Amin in 1979, all the former political parties and new ones were trying to reorganize and take advantage of the volatile situation. This is when the late Binaisa resurrected his ideology of the "Umbrella" as a unifying political denominator.

Binaisa faced yet a fifth challenge of being accepted, especially in Buganda. Some Ugandans wrongfully viewed Binaisa as a political instrument that was being used to bring back Milton Obote. Binaisa, therefore, had the task of showing that he had come back to make good what had gone wrong.

Binaisa's sixth challenge was that he presided over a devastated economy characterized by shortage of essential commodities such as sugar and salt.

Despite all these problems, Binaisa was a good listener and was accessible to many people. He managed to work with the National Executive Committee (NEC) of the Uganda National Liberation Front (UNLF) and the National Consultative Council. He was a consensus builder.

The late Binaisa was an exemplary hardworking man. When he fled into exile in 1973, he practiced law in Britain and America. This is a very important attribute that Political Leaders should emulate. It solves the problem of redundancy and dependency for survival. Binaisa retained his dignity.

When the political dust settled, President Museveni encouraged Binaisa to return home. He was given the facilities of a former Head of State. The facilitation is covered under The Presidential Emoluments Act, No 21, 1998. It covers the following:

i. A monthly allowance of Shs 2.4 million per month;
ii. Medical allowance of Shs 300,000/= per month;
iii. Utilities (water and electricity) Shs 500,000/=per month; and
iv. A contribution of two Domestic Servants of Shs 130,690/= each;
v. A chauffer driven vehicle with Shs 1.8 million for fuel per month;
vi. Four (4) Security guards and an escort vehicle for guards;
vii. Shs 3.5 million per month for accommodation; a furniture allowance of Shs 20 million every five years; and

viii. A Secretary to assist him/her carryout personal correspondence and a computer.

The Presidential Emoluments Act No 21 1998 will be superseded by the Emoluments and Benefits of the President, Vice President and Prime Minister Bill when it is assented to by H. E. the President.

The NRM Government has established a good culture whereby former Heads of State are encouraged to return and are given protection and other facilities.

In Uganda, the late Binaisa kept his legal aura. When he returned from exile, he associated himself with M/S Impala Legal Advocates and Consultants which benefited from his wealth of experience and wisdom in legal matters.

Binaisa volunteered in teaching in a Primary School at Mutundwe and the pupils and Teachers were animated by his articulation, his accessibility and his humour. Binaisa had a close relationship with his God. He was a regular attendant for Sunday Service at Namirembe Cathedral even when he was frail and his presence was well recognized at Namirembe Cathedral.

All his life, the late Binaisa was a man of the people. He was eager to attend to people's concerns, including visiting the sick and attending burials. He was humble, non-sectarian, humorous and patriotic who attempted to unite the whole of Uganda.

Three boys and four girls survive him.

May the Almighty God sustain the bereaved.

The Rt Hon Speaker and

Hon Members of Parliament, I beg to move the Motion.

10 August 2010

Reflections: The People, Places, and Moments

Index

B

C

D

E

F

G

H

I

J

K

L

M

N

O

P

Q

R

T

U

V

W

Y

www.ingramcontent.com/pod-product-compliance
Ingram Content Group UK Ltd.
Pitfield, Milton Keynes, MK11 3LW, UK
UKHW060007051026
15591UKWH00001B/85
9798993824901